BORDERING
ON TROUBLE

BORDERING ON TROUBLE

RESOURCES AND POLITICS IN LATIN AMERICA

EDITED BY
ANDREW MAGUIRE
AND
JANET WELSH BROWN

ADLER&ADLER

Published by Adler & Adler, Publishers, Inc.
4550 Montgomery Avenue
Bethesda, Maryland 20814

Library of Congress Cataloging-in-Publication Data

Bordering on trouble.

  Bibliography: p.
  Includes index.
  1. Latin America—Economic policy. 2. Environmental
policy—Latin America. 3. Latin America—Economic
conditions—1945-   . 4. Latin America—Politics and
government—1948-   . 5. Latin America—Population.
6. Conservation of natural resources—Latin America.
I. Maguire, Andrew. II. Brown, Janet Welsh.
HC125.B594 1986   338.98   86-7941
ISBN 0-917561-20-1
ISBN 0-917561-25-2 (Pbk)

WORLD RESOURCES INSTITUTE
A CENTER FOR POLICY RESEARCH

First Edition
Printed in the United States of America

CONTENTS

FOREWORD

THE THREAT of global suicide from thermonuclear war is widely appreciated. It is also widely agreed that arms control is essential to reduce this threat. Far less dramatic but perhaps more likely to invite civilization's undoing is the devastation—much of it irreversible—that will result from continued neglect of physical and human resources. Because this threat is more difficult to discern, it is less often featured in headlines. Yet, this danger is no less real, and no less deserving of urgent attention.

Few acknowledge, or even understand, how resource mismanagement may contribute to economic stagnation, social and political unrest, or international tensions. George F. Kennan does. He writes in *Foreign Affairs* that the world's environmental as well as its nuclear crisis must receive priority if we are to succeed in "averting these two overriding dangers," both of which are "urgent," "relatively new," and for which "past experience affords little guidance." Even fewer see clearly the connections between human, economic, and political collapse elsewhere and

U.S. economic and security interests. Charles William Maynes, editor of *Foreign Policy,* does. He says the 1980s could see "a new age of disorder" in which economic deterioration and political turmoil beyond our borders "pose grave dangers to the United States" and may affect the "global balance of power."

World Resources Institute initiated the U.S. Stake in Global Resource Issues Project in 1983 with two related concerns:

- a concern with the destructive effects of poor resource and environmental management on economic development and the alleviation of poverty in developing countries; and,

- a concern with a new generation of globally important environmental and resource problems that threaten the environmental and economic interests of the United States and many other countries.

WRI's goal is to strengthen America's interest in these concerns by showing how they relate to recognized U.S. economic, diplomatic, and security objectives and to promote U.S. actions that address these concerns.

We decided to begin explorations close to home, in Latin America, where the United States has important interests stretching back over more than a century and projecting well into the future. To be sure, what the United States does or does not do there has enormous impact. And it is obvious that the United States has, within an overall pattern of neglect, a tendency to become exercised about and often directly involved in political crises in Latin America.

Still, not many North Americans could extemporize for more than a few minutes on Latin America's history, resources, or problems. Perhaps one reason El Salvador has been so often compared to Vietnam is that both nations seemed small, remote, and inconsequential until violence erupted and caught us by surprise. Yet, El Salvador's capital is some 500 miles closer to Washington, D.C., than Los Angeles is! Our tendency to gloss over the subtleties—sometimes the essentials—of today's turmoil in Latin America runs deep, encouraging us to believe that we understand more than we do. Seeking facile parallels to Vietnam, or to the Middle East, we unwittingly blind ourselves to historical U.S. influence in the region. We continue a 150-year U.S. tradition of treating sovereign, culturally diverse nations as though they had as much in common as the Dakotas or the Carolinas. Most of all, we have failed to look at the root causes of the trouble so much of Latin America now faces.

This is a "case book" of a sort never before attempted. In it, Andrew Maguire and Janet Welsh Brown and their colleagues probe the relationships among resource management, economic health, and orderly political change in Latin American countries. From fragile ecosystems and political institutions in the Caribbean, to development dilemmas in the vast Amazon, to urban and rural frontiers in nearly every Latin nation where burgeoning populations strain against the limits of natural and man-made environments—the issues taken up here illustrate the importance and implications of resource management. In turn, they underscore the shared U.S. and Latin American interest in sound relationships between people and the land that supports them.

The authors of the essays in this volume seek to move beyond the current debate over U.S.–Latin American relations, which seems so mired in old ground. At what point should the U.S. again resort to the use of military force? How probable are more Cubas? What is the role of U.S. private capital in the region? Important questions all, but maybe not the most important. Somehow, the United States must now look more deeply than has any administration in this century at Latin America's turmoil and what the United States has done or might do to aggravate or, preferably, alleviate it.

Latin America's forests are being leveled. Its soils—some worked to exhaustion and some underutilized—are eroding. The potential contributions of its waters, including the shining Caribbean and the aortal Amazon and its life-giving arteries, to balanced and healthy economic development are being jeopardized. High population growth rates overwhelm the modest accomplishments of Latin America's own "Green Revolution." Unprecedented megalopolises threaten to topple out of control and skewed patterns of land distribution—plus, now, the debt crisis—defeat steady, balanced, sustainable development in city and countryside alike.

Small wonder that many Latin American institutions are in trouble. Some, long catering to the interests of the elite, have adopted a crisis mentality or lost the ability to plan for the future. Still others, among them some new and struggling environmental and resource agencies, lack the power to influence the ministries of finance, agriculture, trade, industry, transportation, and rural development with which they must work. And in many countries periodic states of seige interrupt and undermine hope for reform.

How does the United States fit into this portrait of near collapse amid stupendous natural wealth? In truth, we have been both friend and foe to Latin America. We need now to understand Latin America's interests, and our own, far better than we have in the past. My hope is that this book will help.

James Gustave Speth
President
World Resources Institute

ACKNOWLEDGMENTS

A WORK that involves a number of expert authors with a variety of perspectives working separately offers rich possibilities. It also poses special problems. The editors want first to thank all of the authors of these chapters. Busy as they all are, they invariably have been patient and helpful in meeting deadlines and in responding to comments from the editors.

As part of WRI's U.S. Stake in Global Resource Issues Project, this book has benefitted from the overall direction of an advisory panel composed of Ruth Adams, Kenneth J. Arrow, Harrison S. Brown, Douglas M. Costle, Donald F. McHenry, Edward L. Morse, Henry Rowen, Howard D. Samuel, Richard H. Ullman, and chaired by Daniel Yergin. Erik Eckholm, S. Bruce Smart, Jr., and Alexander B. Trowbridge also served on the panel during the first round of work on the U.S. Global Stake Project. Two members of WRI's Board, Paulo Nogueira-Neto and Marc J. Dourojeanni, have offered their criticism and advice and reviewed selected chapters.

Other chapter reviews were generously contributed by Cynthia de Alcantara, Jennifer Bremer, Shelton H. Davis, Richard E. Feinberg, David Flood, Elizabeth Hansen, James Hester, Terri Karl, Jeffrey Leonard, Abraham F. Lowenthal, Norman Myers, Riordan Roett, and Mark Schneider. Robert F. Wasserstrom, then a senior associate at WRI, gave invaluable advice on the book's initial conception and structuring, the selection of essay topics and authors, and draft chapters. Robert Repetto, WRI Senior Economist, commented perceptively on a number of draft chapters, including the introduction and conclusion. Inside WRI, comments on individual chapters were also received from Distinguished Fellows Peter S. Thacher and Montague Yudelman, Senior Associates F. William Burley and Mohamed T. El-Ashry, and former project staff member Susan Schiffman. The list of others we have consulted is too lengthy to detail here, but we thank you all. The responsibility for what appears in these essays, of course, remains that of the authors and editors.

The complicated editorial work for this volume demanded, and received, the finest efforts of Moira Ambrose, Marc Reisner, and Kathleen Courrier, WRI's Publications Director. Wenda Wright and Craig Thomas provided timely and accurate manuscripts at each stage along the way. Craig Thomas and Karen LeAnn McKay checked many a fact and footnote.

Finally, to Gus Speth, WRI's President, who conceived the U.S. Global Stake Project and made it a key element of WRI's agenda, and to Jessica T. Mathews, Vice President and Director of Research, whose thoughtfulness, encouragement, and support have been constant throughout, we express our appreciation.

A.M.
J.W.B.

CHAPTER 1

Introduction

ANDREW MAGUIRE
AND JANET WELSH BROWN

Ambassador and statesman George F. Kennan recently targeted "two unprecedented and supreme dangers": the possibility of any major war among the great industrialized powers, and "the devastating effect of modern industrialization and overpopulation on the world's natural environment." The "massive abuse of natural habitat" that Kennan heralded with alarm in the Winter 1985–1986 issue of *Foreign Affairs* is at the heart of this book.

Degradation of Latin America's natural resource base is threatening Latin welfare and hemispheric political security. In the name of development, and all too often to line the pockets of a few, forests and fertile soils are destroyed and the seas and fresh water supplies contaminated—on a scale that will make it impossible to support Latin America's growing numbers.

If, like most Americans, you think your life and your country aren't much affected by what goes on in Latin America, consider for a moment what *could* happen:

BOGOTÁ, Colombia (March 4, 1989)—Colombia's democratically elected government was overthrown just after midnight by a military junta led by Colonel Umberto Garcia, a kingpin in this country's multibillion dollar cocaine industry.

Leaders of the junta include representatives of a coalition of millionaire cocaine growers and exporters frustrated by recent government efforts, assisted by the United States, to curtail their activities, according to informed sources. Garcia himself reportedly has close ties also to U.S. crime figures involved in international drug smuggling.

Speculation is widespread that the new government plans to cut off all subsidies and aid to the country's traditional coffee bean and cane farmers and to encourage them to cultivate the coca plant for cocaine production, diplomatic and business sources say. Agrarian reforms initiated two years ago after decades of rural violence are expected to be set aside as landowners scramble to consolidate larger holdings.

"With the huge U.S. demand for drugs as a magnet, Colombia wants to corner the market," said one well-placed source who declined to be quoted.

"They're not going to be blatant about it, but what you'll hear is a lot of talk about government support for the most productive and exportable crops—and that means cocaine," said an official of an international export company.

SÃO PAULO, Brazil (November 2, 1995)—The world's second largest city, gripped by fear, degenerated into chaos and anarchy today as its more than 25 million residents sought to escape the mysterious and deadly plague named for this city.

Neither the World Health Organization (WHO) nor scientists at the Centers for Disease Control in Atlanta have been able to isolate the disease agent, suspected to be a virus, nor the mechanism by which it spreads with such astonishing speed. Deaths are estimated at nearly 750,000 in the last two weeks alone.

São Paulo's contaminated water supply is a prime suspect. Regular delivery of potable water ceased with the strike of municipal workers seven weeks ago. The Army's attempt to organize deliveries faltered after attacks by strikers. Two weeks ago fear of the new killer disease brought all city services and commerce to a final halt.

In Geneva, the Executive Council of WHO scheduled an emergency meeting after the diagnosis and sudden deaths of the first two persons discovered to have São Paulo Plague outside Brazil. A customs official in Miami and a baggage handler at Rome's Leonardo da Vinci Airport died yesterday, sending shocks of alarm world-wide. The international body may ask for a cut-off of all air travel and shipping in or out of Brazil, according to diplomatic sources.

Today all roads out of the Southern Hemisphere's largest and once most prosperous urban center are clogged with evacuees, including hundreds of thousands fleeing on foot. Foreigners and wealthy Brazilians have packed every airport in a scramble to board the few international flights.

Introduction

Vast stretches of the city center are eerily quiet, populated only by uncollected bodies. In addition to the plague itself, hundreds are killed daily in the stampede to leave the city.

This great city's decline began six years ago when the administration's inability to provide basic services—transportation, sanitation, communications—became apparent. Industrial development schemes, planned on the expectation of cheap electricity from the giant Itaipu dam, were cancelled. Nearly $200 billion in foreign debt was renounced by the government. After banks closed and established industries began to withdraw, the numbers of unemployed soared to the seven million figure typical in recent years.

WASHINGTON, D.C. (July 14, 1998)—Following the House of Representatives' vote yesterday, the Senate today approved the construction of a "Berlin Wall" along the entire 1,900-mile U.S.–Mexican border.

If signed into law by the President, as expected, the wall will be constructed by the Army Corps of Engineers to stop all illegal immigration from Mexico and other Latin American countries.

The wall, which will be longer than the Great Wall of China, will be a 30-foot concrete barrier topped with barbed wire, flood lights, sirens, guard walks, and towers.

Mexico's President, Carlos Hernán Ramírez, issued an ultimatum more harshly critical of the United States than any since the two nations were at war more than a century ago. "If this wall is built," he said in a statement issued by his office in Mexico City, "the sovereign nation of Mexico will have no choice but to break diplomatic relations with the United States."

In Washington, Pentagon sources said the president was considering options in addition to "the Wall," including occupation of Mexico's northern states, or of the capital itself.

Pressure for decisive action against Latin aliens has been building for years along the U.S. side of the Mexican border, where many migrants initially settled. Since mid-1994, protests and violent incidents have highlighted competition for jobs and for limited education, health, and social services in the major U.S. cities where immigrants reside.

A 1996 Presidential order halted all immigration into the U.S. by non-English-speaking Latin Americans and commanded National Guard units to intercept aliens along the U.S.–Mexican border and in waters off California, Texas, and Florida. The order has had little effect on the tide of illegal Latin aliens entering the United States, now estimated at more than two million annually.

3

Critics of the wall are derisive. "What will they do next," asked Vermont Senator Evelyn McAdoo, "build it across the Gulf?"

Lesser crises are already history. In 1985 earthquakes in Colombia and Puerto Rico brought farmers' fields slamming down the mountainsides, burying thousands of rural families in mud and debris. Staggering national debts, the worst in the world at $360 billion, are a dead weight on Latin American economies. In the Dominican Republic and Jamaica, strikes and riots over food and gasoline prices punctuate the 1980s. In Brazil squatters are gunned down by the hired killers of landowners. In Mexico a tenuous stability is maintained as leaders struggle to deal with an accumulating series of crises ranging from natural disasters to falling oil prices.

In truth, millions of Latin America's people have reached states of desperation unparalleled even in Latin America's turbulent history. Expanding populations throng to the world's most gargantuan cities, nightmarish in their congestion and squalor. In the countryside, neglect and exploitation have wreaked havoc and degradation on land and people alike. Many Latin citizens go hungry, even in countries that export agricultural products. Forest cover has all but disappeared in some countries. Tens of millions of Latin Americans are landless or jobless or unable to support families on mere fragments of land. Another 100 million people will be job-seeking by 2000. Political violence has claimed the lives of tens or hundreds of thousands from Guatemala to Argentina. Increasing millions stream north: destination the United States.

What has gone wrong? How will today's events in Latin American countries affect the United States and our future as well as theirs? What can we do together before we are at the point where we can do nothing?

Sometimes, North Americans imagine that what is required to "shape up" the hemisphere and solve its problems is for the "less developed countries" and their leaders to grow up and do as we do. But this belief defies fact, experience, and reason. Instead, the United States must now recognize that its national interests require that we learn from each other, that we become more knowledgeable and more sophisticated in pursuing mutual interests in the hemisphere. It is also important that we understand

4

that natural disasters may be precipitated or exacerbated by human activities and that on close inspection we find that the United States is often directly or indirectly involved.

At the outset, North Americans must acknowledge that we are as much a part of these problems as we must be part of the solutions. U.S. oil tankers wash out their tanks in the Caribbean's cobalt-blue waters. CIA-hired technicians position mines in Nicaragua's harbors. In Honduras, U.S. military construction teams build highways and airfields through virgin forests or in populated areas with regard only to "security considerations." The U.S. Drug Enforcement Administration promotes the use of toxic herbicides to control the growth of marijuana and the coca plant. The State Department encourages support for Latin American regimes whose brutality and contempt for balanced development feeds the steady stream of illegal immigrants to the north. Huge investments supported by the United States and multilateral lending institutions in which we play a prominent role are made in industrial, power, and agricultural projects that often seem to fall short of stated objectives and bear negative costs. The consequences of all these practices—and their costs— will be borne most heavily and painfully by Latin Americans, but U.S. citizens will feel them too.

Thus, it is important that North Americans recognize how much we share with Latins the mistakes, the neglect, an ostrich-like refusal to face basic resource and population problems, and also the many good intentions that lie at the base of Latin social and political turmoil. The truth is that environmental deterioration has already been allowed to go too far in many countries, populations have been allowed to grow too fast, and the need for corrective action is urgent. *Bordering on Trouble* examines the links between political and resource problems in Latin America and lays out poorly understood connections between U.S. and Latin American interests.

North Americans have a significant economic stake in Latin America. Important U.S. trade relationships and investments are in this hemisphere. A third of our developing country markets are in Latin America. Since World War I, U.S. companies have been the biggest foreign investors in Latin America. U.S. banks hold the lion's share of Latin America's huge external debt.

Between the United States and Latin America, economic interdependence is real but not equal. Whereas the United States depends upon Latin American countries, collectively, for a large portion of our trade and investment, each of the Latin countries, individually, is much more dependent upon the United States for its imports, markets, and capital. A hefty percentage of Latin imports, loans, technology, education, and foreign assistance comes from the United States.

Just as important, U.S. national security interests require that we now do more than prop up "friendly" governments whose power may rest on deep social inequity, poverty, and patterns of resource degradation. Several of the analysts who contributed to *Bordering on Trouble* underscore an indelible lesson of the last generation: economic growth without equity cannot be sustained and cannot reduce poverty. An overly narrow ideological definition of our national security, they say, still leads us to throw our weight behind unpopular governments— despite the consequences for both democracy and sustainable economic growth.

In this century, the United States has carried a big stick in Latin America, and has frequently used it. Military might has been called up to counter movements or ideologies perceived to be "un-American" or against particular U.S. business interests. But U.S. politicians and the media tend to downplay our role in the political turmoil in Latin countries and to gloss over the social and economic causes of confrontation. Latins, on the other hand, may understandably resent U.S. power and riches, but they are aghast at how we use them and at the perverse and pervasive effects of our blundering, our condescension, and our ignorance. The rich humanistic traditions they treasure in their own cultures seem lacking in the north. Their common perception is that the U.S. role has been exploitive, self-centered, and destructive.

Even as all of us broaden our definitions of national interests, U.S. policymakers must recognize the intimate connections between healthy sustainable development and wise management of the natural resource base, which is the "capital" for that development. Just as sound economic, social, and political development can be derailed by political failings, it can also be just as rudely

6

disrupted by failures in resource management and by rapid or ill-distributed population growth. Environmental problems can and do cause economic hardship and social unrest that harms Latin and North American alike. That is the message of this book.

This is a book for North Americans by North Americans. It is designed to broaden our own understanding of U.S. and shared U.S.-hemispheric interests. Armed with hindsight, the editors and authors—quite deliberately selected from the United States and with credentials in national security, U.S. economic interests, and hemispheric political relationships—examine Latin American resource, environmental, and population problems that touch the United States. They discuss institutional arrangements and policy initiatives for dealing with these problems. They probe the relationships among resources management, economic health, and peaceful political change. These chapters document U.S. complicity, U.S. assistance, and U.S. national interests. *Bordering on Trouble* reveals that Latins and North Americans together share responsibility for spectacular growth, severe environmental degradation, and enormous debts.

Bordering on Trouble also describes the rich variety of the region that all of us, authors included, too glibly call "Latin America." Here the editors and authors include Mexico, Central and South America, and the Caribbean islands when we say "Latin America" (see Map of Region, page 420). And we include the English-, French-, and Portuguese-speaking peoples of Central America, South America, and the islands when we refer to "Latins."

The variations among the region's thirty-three nations defeat easy generalizations. These countries range in size from 8,521,100 square kilometers (Brazil) to 210 (St. Kitts and Nevis), in population from 135,564,000 to 82,000. Per capita income swings widely from $6,850 in Trinidad and Tobago to $300 in Haiti. Some countries are generously endowed with natural resources; others have to scrape a living from inhospitable lands. Some are governed by open, civilian democracies; in many others, the military, directly or indirectly, controls all policy. In their relations with the United States, they represent wide degrees of independence. Size, wealth, and distance from the United States generally encourage independence, but not one Latin country takes U.S. power and influence anything but seriously.

What *Bordering on Trouble* does not do is treat all of the countries in Latin America or all of the resource issues. Nor does it deal with all the social forces that influence the development choices outlined by the authors. It neglects minority populations such as the 50 percent of most oppressed Guatemalans who are Indians, and Brazil's 40 percent black underclass that is left out of decision-making. Although inequity is raised again and again, Paraguay's deep class divisions and the oppression of the poor by the rich are not. The revolution and war in Nicaragua—where the only thing that is not changing is the United States' misguided hope for a military solution—are left to other analysts, although the fighting distracts attention, diverts resources from the land and services from people, and excuses government's limitation of civil liberties. Nor is the full role of Latin women in economic life and resource management given attention. Then too, much of Cuba's experience is left out. As important as these issues are, Latin America's experience is simply too complex to wedge between the covers of one book.

Although each of the following chapters concentrates on a specific problem or country, *four* themes run throughout *Bordering on Trouble. First,* is a sense of the longstanding nature of U.S. involvement in resource exploitation in Latin America. In some generations and countries, such as postwar Guatemala and Honduras, American corporations have been prime movers. In others, as in nineteenth-century Chile, private U.S. banks underwrote mineral development. In many instances, the U.S. government, either directly or through corporations or multinational banks, has played the major role, as in the case of Venezuelan oil. American educational institutions have trained Latin engineers and administrators. American foundations have funded research. American missionaries have brought new faiths and customs to many a village in the interior.

This historical U.S. involvement in Latin resource development accounts for the *second* recurring theme: the extent of U.S. connections with Latin America, and the ambivalence that this long intimacy engenders. The dominance of the United States in these relationships shows up in the Latin admiration for North American power, goods, values, technology, and development models. Although there are lessons in this book for U.S. relations with Africa and Asia as well, our relations with Latin American countries are closer, deeper, and more numerous—and often more hurtful because they are so one-sided.

U.S. involvement in Latin American resources has on the whole been profitable for U.S. interests, and many North American enterprises have benefitted Latin Americans. To be sure, almost all of our undertakings, at least in the postwar generation, were intended to be beneficial. But the *third* theme that binds these chapters is the consistency of certain mistakes made by the United States in Latin America.

Every president from Truman to Reagan has been a major actor on the Latin American stage. With bipartisan consistency, all administrations have added to the errors chronicled here. Their collective heavy-handedness has contributed to resource depletion, population maldistribution, social turmoil, capital flight, and the demise of more than one struggling democracy. Failing to grasp the big picture, the United States has protected U.S. industry at home against imports of shoes or textiles, or used the marines in Central America to bail out a U.S. corporation whose behavior was far from exemplary. The United States has often defended peculiarly defined national security interests, paying more attention to the ideology and rhetoric of a Latin regime than to its internal processes and its commitment to democracy, human rights, and civilian control—cornerstones of the U.S. system we would wish Latins to emulate! The seeming conflict between what we perceive as U.S. security needs and our development hopes for Latin America, our uneasiness with rapid social change and self-styled revolutionary leaders, our inability to confront the profound social problems of population growth, land tenure, and deepening inequity have led the United States to support repressive regimes, to increase the power of their militaries, and to invade small countries.

The *fourth* and most important theme is that our relations with Latin America have been preoccupied with narrowly defined, short-term economic and security concerns, while the really menacing, system-threatening problems of resource degradation, environmental pollution, and rapid population growth are treated casually at best. The pressure of poor people on the

land and of inappropriate practices on the big estates leads to deforestation, soil erosion, and damage to dams, waterways, and
coastal areas at rates that can no longer be ignored. These practices are eroding the resource base that must support future
generations.

Each Latin country currently faces severe economic problems
and bears enormous debts. Each has seen necessary development
slow so much that poverty and hardship increase. These problems
are endemic and epidemic. They promise civil strife and threaten
legal and economic institutions, financial structures, and the viability of states—even the international system itself. At root, these are
the problems—not competitive imports or the rhetoric of
revolutionaries—that most threaten Latin America and long-term
U.S. economic and security interests in the hemisphere. These are
urgent problems of enormous scale that must be addressed by Latin
leaders and by U.S. policy on Latin America.

By doggedly placing America's drive for regional security
above Latin America's need for dynamic social change, the United States has promoted some of the worst trends and practices in
Latin America and encouraged some of its least fit and most authoritarian rulers—General Videla's government in Argentina,
the current Pinochet government in Chile, Haiti's Duvaliers, the
Somozas in Nicaragua, and even the death squads in Guatemala
and El Salvador. Small wonder we are the target of much Latin
frustration and anger!

Still, it would be arrogant of us to assume that the United
States has always managed to impose its wishes against the will of
Latin leaders. Indeed, Latin American leaders have determined
their national directions and have established the policies that so
often lead to resource degradation and poverty. Today, laying
blame is not nearly as important as making headway against the
knotty problems exposed in *Bordering on Trouble*.

In the United States and in Latin America alike, understanding of the interconnections between economic development and
care for the resource base is now deepening and spreading. Given
this relatively recent recognition that mismanaging resources exacerbates poverty, can we now find ways of working with Latin
countries to stem degradation, decrease poverty, and enhance
stable sustainable growth? Can we systematically integrate resource and population concerns into U.S. foreign policy? Can we

practice environmental diplomacy? Can the Latin American nations feed their people, achieve land reform, create new jobs, curb population growth, expand markets, and pay their debts? Can we, in short, become better friends?

Fortunately, the same policies that will protect the natural environment will also feed people, keep them healthy, and make sustainable economic growth possible. Through historical and political analysis, and the simple art of putting two and two together, the contributors to this book have found some keys to a more promising future for the hemisphere. We join them and many Latin Americans in believing that a new ecology and a new politics of cooperation also are possible.

CHAPTER 2

Mexico City's Limits

DAVID DeVOSS

―――――――――――――――*Editors' Preface*―――――――――――――――

Bordering on Trouble opens, appropriately, with a chapter on Mexico. Mexico has all the promise and problems found in other Latin countries, although both sometimes seem larger than life. It also belongs first because of all the Latin nations it is the most important to the United States. Mexico seldom gets the frequent headlines given to the more incendiary and controversial incidents in nearby Central America, but its size, its long-shared border, its uneasy history of relations with the United States, its importance in trade, investment, and labor, and its potential for trouble deserve more attention in the United States.

David DeVoss writes about Mexico City, but this chapter is about the countryside as well. The city's great attractions—great modern industries and markets, its promise and hope, its services and educational opportunities—also reflect what is missing from the countryside. Mexico's decision to develop modern industry, concentrated in urban areas, is a decision many other Latin countries have made. Mexican institutional arrangements, government corporations dubbed *parastatels,* created to organize growth and modernization are not discussed here, but experience some of the successes and problems of similar institutions in Venezuela (see Chapter 5).

The population pressure building in Mexico City is exacerbated by government policies that favor the rural-urban migration, but it also reflects population growth in the countryside. With a total land area of only 21 percent of the United

States, Mexico's population is 34 percent of the U.S. population, and Mexico is both younger and increasing at a faster rate. The countryside has its own set of social and environmental problems—soil erosion, inadequate water supplies and sanitation services, fewer health and educational services, high unemployment, excessive use of pesticides—and a higher birth rate than Mexico City. If unchecked, these conditions can be expected to continue to feed both internal migration to the urban areas and external migration, mostly to the United States.

U.S. connections with Mexico are many. Our banks and industries have invested heavily in Mexico. Mexican workers, both in Mexico and as immigrants in the United States, provide many of the products and services bought by U.S. consumers. We eat Mexico's winter vegetables and burn Mexican oil. Our common border is troubled by illegal traffic in people and drugs.

The United States has enormous influence over Mexico in many ways, but we do not control its destiny in ways that we do smaller, less strong countries in the hemisphere. As a Mexican writer in exile wrote in the *Washington Post* a few years ago, Mexico is not just an oil well, but a country whose true measure *norte americanos* have yet to take.

EVERY so often Mexico City's chief urban planner, architect Fernando Padres, leaves his office early and drives to the crest of the nearby mountains. "From up there you can hear the incessant rumble of the city," he beams with pride. "It is a fantastic, dynamic place; a city that never sleeps."

But on September 19 and 20 of last year two massive earthquakes, the largest of which measured 8.1 on the Richter scale, brought the Western Hemisphere's largest city to a halt. Destroyed within the span of forty-eight hours were 400 buildings, among them seven tourist hotels, 10 percent of the city's schools, and five hospitals. Another 700 buildings are now uninhabitable.

Human suffering was more severe. Within hours of the second quake the casualty toll surpassed the government's initial estimate of 400 dead and 7,000 injured. By mid-October the government listed 4,600 dead while the city's newspapers placed the figure at 8,000. Over 40,000 Mexicans were injured, 10,000 of them seriously. An additional 31,000 were left homeless.

The initial stories of heroism by human "moles" still tunneling through the rubble two weeks after the quakes, were eventually replaced, however, by the disaster's gritty reality. Still buried under tons of concrete were more than 5,000 corpses.

More than 25 percent of the capital's water supply was unusable. "The enormous and complex consequences of the earthquake cannot be confronted by the government alone," announced Mexican President Miguel de la Madrid. "The activities taken during the emergency showed our capacity for mobilization and vitality and our spirit of solidarity. In the reconstruction, we must maintain this momentum."[1]

Unfortunately, Mexico will require more than stoic determination to surmount its present crisis. Even before the twin tremors, Mexico was on the brink of financial collapse. Because of its inability to reduce an inflation rate running at 55 percent, the International Monetary Fund (IMF) had refused a desperately needed $450 million loan. The financial impasse left Mexico with a $97 billion foreign debt, the second largest in the developing world after Brazil. In 1985 alone this foreign debt consumed about $10 billion in interest and $4 billion in principal. Within a week of the disaster the IMF relented and approved the $450 million loan, but for U.S. banks holding $25.8 billion in outstanding loans to Mexico, the loan was more a political gesture than an economic solution.

For Citicorp, the biggest lender with $2.9 billion outstanding, and Bank of America with $2.7 billion in dubious loans, Mexico's future seemed grim. For once Mexico agreed. "It would not be an exaggeration to say that the economic panorama has changed completely since the earthquake," said Jaime Serra Puche, director of the Economic Studies Center at the Colegio de México. "We are on the razor's edge."[2]

In many ways, Mexico's capital remains North America's most dignified metropolis. Majestic boulevards lined with modern office towers, elegant fountains, and manicured gardens radiate from traffic circles guarded by statues of Aztec kings. Scores of art galleries and nearly two dozen museums serve a culture-conscious city. Eleven daily newspapers and six television stations compete for attention. On any given weekend, the city's 18 million residents can choose among a dozen plays, three film festivals, several photo exhibitions, and two bull rings.

Indeed, Mexico City is unique among Latin capitals. Although the Institutional Revolutionary Party (PRI) has been in power since 1929, political debate is relatively free and open. Exiles from Trotsky to the Shah of Iran have found refuge here. "For someone who comes from a Cartesian city like Buenos Aires, Mexico is a bit disconcerting at first because of its variety," says Argentine writer Jorge Luis Bernetti. "The diversity of landscapes and urban events is enormous."

But Mexico City, for all its surface sophistication, is beset by problems common to most developing countries. Its police are notoriously corrupt, telephones routinely break down, and certain commodities are often in short supply. A jumble of civic and religious holidays, invariably stretched into four-day weekends, keeps productivity low, and the lack of an effective political opposition ensures a sluggish, inefficient bureaucracy.

Although it suffers from soaring crime, an unemployment rate of 12 percent, and the underemployment of many who do have jobs, Mexico City, even after the earthquakes, remains a beacon for impoverished *campesinos* (peasants), 1,000 of whom arrive each day in search of work. The crush produces a slum population in excess of 5 million, depletes the surrounding *ejidos* (public land used for farming legally reserved for agriculture), overtaxes the resource base intended for a city half the size, and creates a wandering population of mendicants who converge at the major intersections to sell gum, thrashing iguanas, and crudely made hand puppets.

Most city officials minimize the long-term consequences of geometric population expansion that by the year 2000 should give Mexico City a population of 31 million. "In a big city you have big problems," reasons Padres, who from the top of the mountains can seldom see more than the shimmering outline of

16

his growling hive, because much of the time (about 225 days each year) temperature inversions make a soup of the polluted atmosphere.

But opposition political leaders, such as Pablo Emilio Madero, who presides over the National Action Party (PAN) and is a great nephew of Mexican revolutionary hero Francisco Madero, insist that drastic reform is essential. "No one here seems to notice the danger implicit in all this disorder," he says. "Things that would be considered crazy elsewhere are seen as normal here. If everyone simply tolerates the problems there is little hope the government will ever do anything about them."

THE AZTEC CAPITAL

Four hundred and fifty years ago, when London was a village, Europe a collection of incestuous duchies, and much of North America still belonged to the bison, the largest city in the world was the Aztec capital, Tenochtitlán. Extending from the arid highlands south of the Sonora desert to the steamy jungles of Yucatan, the Aztec empire of Cemanáhuac, meaning "the one world," consisted of thirty provinces with over 25 million people. But the spiritual center of the kingdom was the Valley of Mexico,[3] a mile-high depression thirty-five miles long and fifty miles wide that was lined by mountains, puddled by three vast lakes, and guarded by the volcanoes of Popocatépetl (the incense-burning mountain) and Ixtaccíhuatl (the white woman).

Linked to the outside by three broad causeways, Tenochtitlán was a swarming metropolis with elaborate limestone palaces, Venetian-style canals, botanical gardens, and colorful markets. The heart of the city was a huge marble plaza surrounded by a menagerie, music conservatory, and various gem-studded temples. Dominating all in the plaza's center was a massive pyramid dedicated to Huitzilopóchtli, the Aztec god of war, and consecrated with the blood of 20,000 slaves whose beating hearts were slashed from their bodies during a four-day celebration in 1487. The top of the pyramid and the serpent-banistered staircase that they climbed to their deaths still glistened with a reddish hue even after thirty years. A rack of skulls and a luminescent "Sun Stone" carved from sparkling porphyry lent grandeur to the

Great Pyramid. But the biggest building on the plaza was the palace where 3,000 cooks, jesters, and concubines labored to satisfy the Aztec God King Montezuma II.

For its time, the regal Aztec capital was a model metropolis. An efficient sewage and garbage system kept the city clean, along with 1,000 men who swept the streets each morning. Nobles cloaked in animal skins or feathered caps sauntered along the boulevards, wearing helmets modeled after the heads of jaguars or eagles. Barges and canoes laden with produce entered the city through one of four water gates. Over it all fluttered brightly colored pennants made from the tail feathers of jungle birds.[4]

But in the second decade of the sixteenth century, a series of omens unsettled *Cemanáhuac.* In 1517, Indians along the Gulf Coast reported seeing "towers or small mountains floating on the waves of the sea."[5] Later that year, a comet appeared "like a flaming ear of corn dripping blood from the sky." The worst shock, however, came two years later, in early 1519, when messengers from the island of Cozumel brought Montezuma paintings of bearded white men with crosses. Had Montezuma attacked, the 550 Spaniards could easily have been defeated. But believing Hernán Cortés to be the feathered serpent god Quetzalcóatl, the Aztec leader thought it wiser to send gold. A fatal mistake. As Cortés later admitted in a memoir, "I came to get gold, not till the soil like a peasant."

On November 8, 1519, Cortés, his 400 soldiers and their 6,000 allies from the Acolhua, Totonaca, and Texcalteca Indian tribes finally crossed Lake Texcoco and entered the world's largest city. Although they anticipated great wealth, they were unprepared for a city that seemed to float on the massive lake. With 80,000 residents, Tenochtitlán was more than double the size of the Spanish port of Sevilla, the largest town the *conquistadores* had ever seen.[6] "The city has many plazas, the biggest being twice the size of that found in Salamanca," Cortés later wrote Spanish monarch Charles V. "Leading off the plazas are markets where they sell gold and silver, jewelry, herbs, soft leather, and honey. There is even a quantity of small, castrated dogs they use for eating. The stalls are abundantly stocked, fastidiously clean and visited by 60,000 souls each morning who come to buy or sell."[7]

The awe which the Aztecs and the Spanish initially accorded each other quickly dissipated. Indian prostitutes gave the *conquistadores* syphilis; the Spanish retaliated by importing smallpox. Montezuma was placed under house arrest and ordered to open his treasury. Eight months later, the Aztecs finally rebelled and expelled the Spanish, killing nearly 800 in what history now calls the Noche Triste (sad night). Cortés returned a year later with a small fleet of gunboats and thousands of Indian allies. Weakened by smallpox, the Aztecs could not mount an offensive and during an eighty-five-day siege Cortés demolished the city he had declared "magnificent" only two years before. Spanish friars who later sifted the debris found an anonymous poem that captured the full measure of the Aztec loss:

> Worms are swarming in the streets and plazas.
> And the walls are spattered with gore.
> The water has turned red, as if it were dyed,
> And when we drink of it,
> It has the taste of brine.[8]

Tenochtitlán was leveled by Cortés, and by the end of the sixteenth century, 85 percent of the 25 million people he discovered in Meso-America had died from smallpox. But out of that destruction a new city was born. "It was neither a victory nor a defeat," reads a plaque at the Plaza of the Three Cultures, which commemorates the Aztecs' last stand. "It was the painful birth of the *mestizo* (mixed-race) people of today's Mexico."

Mexico City, like the Mexican people, is a perplexing blend of cultures. Some of the limestone quarried to build Tenochtitlán now serves as the foundation for the Municipal Cathedral. Across the street from the teeming Pino Suarez subway station are the remains of the Templo Mayor, the main temple of Tenochtitlán unearthed seven years ago by workmen digging a new subway line. The central portion of the capital seems pure Spanish. Buildings have iron balconies and intricate cupolas. Most government ministries enjoy interior courtyards with blooming jacaranda and tiled fountains. But Mexico is not a Spanish city. Indeed, there is not a single monument to Hernán Cortés in any one of the capital's 600 square miles. The only place he is depicted is in a Diego Rivera mural inside the National Palace, and there he is shown as a demonic, hunchbacked killer.

The elegant city Cortés found and later destroyed is now almost impossible to define, let alone describe. Officially, the capital, or Distrito Federal, is composed of sixteen *delegaciones,* some of them with a floating population of up to 3 million, but where the city actually begins or ends is in doubt. Certainly, Mexico City is no longer limited geographically to the federal district. Eleven municipalities in the neighboring state of Mexico are considered part of the capital, as is one town in the state of Hidalgo. "Mexico City's alarming growth and gigantic size are out of all known proportion," Mexican President Miguel de la Madrid admitted in 1983. "Its demography distorts the profile not only of the city but also of the entire country."[9]

For centuries the population of Mexico was limited by disease and man-made disasters. It took 200 years for the smallpox-devastated population of 3 million in 1700 to grow to 20 million. Then came the Mexican Revolution and another 5 million died. But the capital's population growth has never faltered. Mexico City's turn-of-the-century population of 350,000 grew to 1 million by 1930. It took only a decade for the 1960 population of 5 million to jump to 8 million, and by 1980 14 million called Mexico City home.[10] With 17 million residents, give or take a million or two, today's Mexico City has about as many people as Australia or Canada or all of Central America. By the year 2000, if it reaches the projected population of 31 million, it will be the world's largest city.

THE POLLUTION CRISIS

Uncontrolled growth has spawned a dizzying array of related problems. After Bangkok and Tokyo, Mexico City has the worst traffic in the world. Over 3 million cars are now driven in the city. By 1988, there will be 4 million; then, theoretically, the capital could reach gridlock. Over 40 percent of all the vehicles in Mexico ply the capital's streets. Thirty percent of the cars need a tune-up, and 46 percent of the city's diesel buses need major repairs. But Mexico City motorists are accustomed to their belching fleet of vehicles, and signs alongside the steep highway from Puebla into Mexico warn motorists to "Yield to cars without brakes."

Matilde Espino Rubino, a researcher at the National Polytechnic Institute's School of Engineering and Architecture, is assertively outspoken in declaring Mexico City "the most heavily contaminated city on the planet." The pollution comes in myriad forms. The average noise level in the federal district is 90 decibels, roughly equivalent to standing near a jackhammer. It reaches 140 decibels on the highway north to the Teotihuacán pyramids. Manuel Mujica Roa, head of diagnostics at the National Institute of Human Communication, says that as a result, 50 percent of the federal district's 11 million residents have hearing problems.

The presence of one out of every five Mexicans in a relatively small valley makes adequate garbage disposal impossible. Mexico City produces 14,000 tons of garbage every day, but can dispose of only 8,000. The city solves its problem by dumping 2,000 to 3,000 tons in landfills and depositing the rest in the open. Besides providing a temporary home to an estimated 115 million rats, the dumps serve as a source of income for armies of scavengers who sift through the refuse in search of recyclable objects.[11] If these *pepenadores* are at the bottom of the social ladder, Pablo Tellez Falcón, the forty-six-year old chief of the Santa Fe dump, is at the top of the bottom. The 2,500 pickers under his command rummage through 2,600 tons of trash each day, performing an essential but unappreciated public service. "Even the families here who earn enough money to leave continue to stay. It's sociological. You get conditioned to living here."

But nobody ever gets conditioned to the feces. Because of subsidence caused by pumping ground water, sewage pipes occasionally break, spilling into the storm drains that parallel the fresh water mains. The 3 million slum dwellers without access to any sanitary facilities simply deposit nightsoil into ravines and vacant lots. During the dry season from March until the end of June, deadly clouds of powdered filth swirl through the *barrios* (neighborhoods). Nearly 30,000 children die each year in Mexico City from respiratory or gastrointestinal disease. During the month of May, it is possible to catch hepatitis just by breathing in certain sections of the city.[12]

Mexico City is slowly dying of air pollution. Its density is equivalent to smoking forty cigarettes a day. In 1937, the average visibility was nine miles; today, it is less than two. At 7,500 feet above sea level, the city has 30 percent less oxygen than cities at sea level and the altitude aggravates auto pollution. Autos in Mexico City produce twice the carbon monoxide and 80 percent higher hydrocarbon emissions than they do at sea level.

In a sense, Mexico City is a victim of its own geography. The valley floor, surrounded by mountains that soar to 10,000 feet, traps gases and prevents the flow of cleansing air. Because the air temperature immediately above the city is 10 degrees centigrade higher than that of the surrounding areas, the polluted warm air should rise as though from a chimney. But as it rises, it cools and gets trapped by a layer of cooler, stationary air above so that it spreads out and permanently blankets the city. Most of Mexico City's 131,000 factories are in the northwest corridor, where the prevailing winds come from, and many are heavy polluters— petrochemical industries and paper mills that contribute to Latin America's only known problem of acid rain. Each day, nearly 11,000 tons of solid particle matter are belched into the air. At the U.S. embassy on the prestigious Paseo de la Reforma, the daily average of suspended particulate matter is 192 micrograms per cubic meter. This compares with the acceptable U.S. maximum level of 75 micrograms per cubic meter.

"If the EPA standards were applied to this country," says one U.S. embassy official, "Mexico would surpass the highest tolerable levels for sulphur dioxide, cadmium, lead, zinc, copper and particulate matter."

Pollution is especially bad in the capital's northwestern quadrant, where the porridge-like atmosphere also contains *salmonella, staphylococcus,* and *streptococcus* bacteria. Birds are seldom seen in communities like Barrientos and Texquesquinahuac, where particulate matter is over twice the maximum level established by the U.S. National Ambient Air Quality Standards. "When I first came here three years ago I had such a sore throat that I couldn't even speak," remembers elementary school teacher Rocio Navarro Losano. Although her students are listless and often sick, she considers her school lucky since the incidence of tuberculosis in Barrientos is only a third of that in surrounding areas.

Mexico is taking tentative steps to reduce air contamination. Recently, the government petroleum company PEMEX agreed to educe the sulphur in diesel fuel sold in Mexico City by 0.8 percent (from 1.2 to 0.4 percent). A new industrial pollution law passed by the Mexican Senate in late 1983 establishes the first maximum factory emission levels. Last June, after years of procrastination, Ecology Minister Guillermo Carillo Arena finally ordered all cement and cellulose paper companies to relocate in the states of Mexico and Tlaxcala within a year. But ecologists note that the law is rarely enforced, and the mandated relocation is unlikely to be implemented in the wake of the prolonged economic crisis caused by the capital's reconstruction. "No industries have been sanctioned yet because of high unemployment and the fact that many are operating at 40 percent capacity," admits one government official. "The new law should be strictly enforced, but with a $97 billion national debt the government has other priorities."

Many experts feel that Mexico, having ignored pollution clean-up during the oil boom of the mid- and late-seventies, will never again have the resources to tackle such a huge problem. "Mexico lost the opportunity to improve the environment when the cash was there," laments Dr. Irma Rosa Perez of the Autonomous National University of Mexico's (UNAM) Atmospheric Science Department.

PEOPLE, PEOPLE, PEOPLE

Despite its many problems, Mexico's capital continues to grow at a mesmerizing rate; each year, the net population increases by 700,000. Despite warnings and official government policy, the trend is likely to continue. "Mexico City has never been known for its comfort," says U.S. Ambassador John Gavin. "After Cortés conquered the city even he decided to move to Cuernavaca. But it has remained and will continue to be the repository of national power. Some people think that it's like what I've heard they used to say in vaudeville: 'After New York, it's all Peoria.'"

Demographic changes caused by population growth and internal migration are not unique to Mexico. The population of all Latin America is growing very rapidly and should double by the end of this century. For government leaders, however, an even greater worry is the pace of urbanization. According to a recent United Nations Educational, Scientific, and Cultural Organization (UNESCO) study, about 85 percent of Latin America's population increase over the past two decades was absorbed by its metropolitan areas. Should current projections hold, the Latin America of today—which is still 50 percent rural—will enter the twenty-first century more urbanized than Western Europe or North America.

An unprecedented rural exodus is depleting villages and swelling cities all over the world. But Manuel Ordorica, president of the Mexican Demographic Association, calls his city a "case without precedent." Ordorica's associates even have coined the term "macroephaly," meaning big-headed, to describe the city that now houses nearly 24 percent of the nation's population. Some economists, Gustavo Garza among them, believe that the perpetual urbanization of Mexico City could cripple, if not forestall, the entire country's development. "Mexico City, demographically speaking, already is larger than half of the countries on our planet," he warns. "The combined areas of Mexico City and Toluca [in the State of Mexico] already constitute the largest metropolis in Latin America. If this [growth] process is not stopped, complex and unforeseen economic, political, and social consequences will occur by the end of this century. In the past it was not possible to anticipate that Mexico City would become one of the largest and most troubled cities in the world. But today it's clear that the growth of this megalopian conglomerate must be stopped."[13]

INTERNAL MIGRATION

Although 56 percent of Mexico City's annual population growth results from internal migration, Mexican officials have made reducing the birth rate their main priority. Reluctance to impose financial penalties similar to those used in Singapore and the People's Republic of China has kept the capital's growth at an unacceptable 4.6 percent. But forceful measures are now being considered because density is high—between 6,000 and 6,600 people per square kilometer in the federal district—and little parkland is left. Moreover, while the central city's saturated residential areas have stopped growing, the greater metropolitan area continues to expand by 10 percent a year.

The United Nations population office finds optimism in the city's dropping birth rate, which fell to 32.6 births per 1,000 in 1979 from 39.2 per 1,000 in 1970—a consequence of raised educational standards, a growing acceptance of family planning, and a

$26 million grant from the United Nations for birth control programs. But these gains were offset entirely by a declining mortality rate, which fell from 9.5 per 1,000 in 1970 to 4.9 per 1,000 in 1979.

In "Principle Demographic Problems of Mexico City in the Next 17 Years," the National Population Council (CONAPO) calculates that a population of 36 million would double the demand for jobs, a tall order for a country already saddled with 40 percent underemployment. Additional pressure on housing, water, and transportation also would be acute, and meeting new demand would mean vastly expanding the infrastructure. "We live in the penthouse and all the essential services are on the first floor," observes U.S. ambassador Gavin. "Water, gas and electricity have to be brought in at great cost."

According to Gavin, the frightening consequences of uncontrolled urbanization range from illegal immigration to political instability: "Demographers tell us that this country has 77 million people right now. By the year 2000 the population will be 130 million, and by 2050 it should reach 180 million. There is a desperate need to create jobs. Over 900,000 Mexicans come into the job market every year. Soon it will be a million, and by the end of this decade it could reach 2 million. Mexico City is considered by many migrants to be the city of opportunity—their last chance. If large numbers ever go hungry, Mexico could have serious problems, and problems for this country could mean a nightmare for the U.S."

The population program for the Mexico City municipal area for the years 1983 to 2000 aims to reduce area birth rates to 2 and 2.6 percent, respectively, by 1988 and overall to 1.5 percent by 2000. If the plan works, Mexico City's population might be held at 23.4 million, but to date, family planning programs have had mixed results. Urban-based campaigns such as "Have Fewer to Give Them More" and "The Small Family Lives Better" have worked with middle-class Mexicans, but the rural poor and campesinos recently arrived in the capital continue to view large families as a long-term investment that is worth the immediate financial burden.

Uncontrolled urbanization and Malthusian population growth result, in part, from the postwar economic development model implemented by President Miguel Alemán (1946–1952) and developed by his successor, Adolfo Ruiz Cortínes (1952–1958). Based on import substitution, the plan hoped to establish capital-intensive industries by attracting outside investment and encouraging domestic reinvestment by low tax rates. Between 1940 and 1970, the average annual growth rate was more than 6 percent. Agriculture's contribution to total production diminished from 21 to 11 percent, while industry's contribution increased from 25 to 34 percent. Two-thirds of the labor force was employed in agriculture in 1940. By 1970, the figure dropped to a bit over one-third.

Campesinos by the thousands poured into the Valley of Mexico, where most of the industry was located, and the human tide quickly changed the size, composition, and shape of the capital. Between 1940 and 1950, 73 percent of Mexico City's population growth was the result of migration, 44 percent the following decade, and 46 percent between 1960 and 1970. In these years, more than 4 million people moved from their homes to live permanently in Mexico City.

Internal migration continues to affect the city's demographics profoundly. In subsequent research, the Autonomous National University of Mexico (UNAM) found that 52 percent of the city's natural growth in the 1960s resulted from children born to migrants who arrived a decade earlier. Indeed, as of 1970, the migrants and their offspring comprised nearly 70 percent of Mexico City's population.

The problem of the capital "acquires a national dimension because it makes us question the political and economic values which form the basis of Mexican society," says Ángel Mercado, a professor at the recently created Department of Urban Affairs at the Metropolitan University. Mercado stresses that more than half of Mexico's industrial infrastructure is located within a day's run of the Aztec capital. "For decades industry had the support of the government in the form of tax exemptions and preferential rates," he says. "Conditions were created so people were forced to leave the countryside, though historically, migration to the cities is inevitable."

LURED TO THE CITY

Drawn to higher salaries north of the Rio Grande, greater opportunities in the capital, and, more recently, the promise of steady work in the Gulf oil fields, Mexico's rural population is more mobile than ever before. Unlike the stereotyped migrant of the U.S. depression, Mexico's urban-bound *campesinos* tend to be the brightest and most aggressive in their villages—people willing to forsake security for the greater challenges of the cities.[14] Most migrants are young with some education and some experience in agricultural employment. But this search for greater opportunity invariably spells disaster to government planners, who must further impoverish their agricultural base by shifting increasingly scarce resources to urban areas.

In Mexico, several migration patterns are in force at once. Many youths leave home, but go only as far as the nearest medium-sized town. This movement causes negligible disruption because they are, in a sense, only taking the place of their more adventurous peers who are heading to the city. More significant is circular migration, which leads *campesinos* in search of temporary employment into the cities and the United States. Rural families without title to their ancestral *ejido* and small landowners whose plots cannot support large families traditionally have viewed circular migration as an income supplement to help sustain subsistence agriculture.[15] But a growing number of Mexican sociologists are coming to regard circular migration as a curse, a cannibalism, that destroys the traditional family structure, impedes agricultural development, and perpetuates a rootless class of unskilled workers destined to spend their productive years at the bottom of the wage scale.

Why does a *campesino* choose to become a *paracaidista*—a slang term for squatter, literally, a paratrooper?[16] According to Wayne A. Cornelius, director of the United States-Mexican Studies Program at the University of California in San Diego, *campesinos* are pulled off their land by greater opportunity. For thousands, leaving home is the only logical thing to do. Even the lowest salary in the federal district averages a good 25 percent higher than the median salary paid in rural Mexico.[17] Cornelius also found, in an exhaustive survey of six Mexico City settlements favored by migrants, that despite underemployment nearly half the *campesinos* coming to the capital found employment within a week, while an additional 30 percent were working within a month.

José Toribio, a young Mixteca Indian from Oaxaca, was driven from his home by hunger. "I came to find work for them to eat," he explains in broken Spanish, gesticulating with his fingers in front of his mouth while glancing sideways at his family. José sits in a Mexico City café, pouring pasta soup into his three-year-old son Pablo. His wife, Logina, eats slowly while breast feeding one-year-old Benito under a tattered, acrylic shawl. "I'm looking for work as a brick layer," he says before confiding that street begging produced more money than he ever earned in Oaxaca. Even though this day laborer has to shelter his family in vacant doorways each night, he doubts that he ever will return to Juajuapa de León in Oaxaca. For José, money means dignity, and even though both are in short supply, more of both is to be found in Mexico City.

Impoverished *campesinos* are not only lured off the land by greater urban opportunities; they are also pushed off by economic forces. Greater investment in Mexican industry over the years slowly has reduced the level of reinvestment in Mexican agriculture. From 1947 to 1952, when 22 percent of the authorized public sector investments went into better irrigation and transportation, the average annual growth in agricultural output was an impressive 7.6 percent. But during the following decade, investment in agriculture fell to 10.6 percent and the annual growth in crop yields dropped to 3.8 percent. At least $250 million worth of resources were transferred out of the economy's agricultural sector between 1940 and 1961. The investment that continued went to the large commercial growers whose winter vegetable crops earned hard currency for the Mexican government. The political alliance between big farmers and the government provided political stability, but failed to reduce the number of landless peasants, who currently number 3 million—the same number that existed immediately following the Mexican Revolution.

Those peasants still waiting for *ejido* plots are unlikely to receive anything. Since 1913, the Mexican government has created 28,000 *ejidos* amounting to 227 million acres. Recently, the secretary of Agrarian Reform, Luis Martínez Villicaña, admitted that there simply was no more good land to give away. Some North American agronomists believe that inefficiencies within the Agrarian Reform Ministry itself force peasants into the city, especially when large estates are confiscated and allowed to lie fallow pending government redistribution; this pattern reduces the number of employees and further limits the dwindling number of agricultural sector jobs.

The Cornelius study predicts a continued flow into Mexico City of people like José Toribio. Rapid population growth, the mechanization of commercial agriculture, and the scarcity of new arable land have limited rural employment opportunities severely. As a consequence, the number of landless agricultural workers rose 74 percent between 1940 and 1960, and the salaries for those who could find work decreased commensurately. While the United States decreased its aid, employment opportunities in the social services became more concentrated in the urban centers. In these areas, the minimum wage is considerably higher than in the countryside, so the advantages for those who reside in the cities are not dissipated by the higher cost of living.[18]

COLONIA PENSIL: A TYPICAL DESTINATION

Most migrants eventually end up in places like Colonia Pensil, a nest of bleak cells only a few miles from the capital's luxurious Lomas residential district. Eighty families are packed around a central patio in tiny rooms that average 12 square meters. Doors to each room are spaced at two-foot intervals. The cells have no running water or toilets—but then the rooms rent for only $12 a month. The men of Colonia Pensil work when they can as construction laborers or truck drivers; their wives sell candy or apples on the street. The single water tap at the entrance to the compound stands near a shrine of the Virgin Mary, an alter bedecked with orange flowers. Most of the migrants here came from Oaxaca, Veracruz, or San Luis Potosí, but all eat an identical diet of beans and tortillas, supplemented twice a week with a bit of meat or an egg.

In slums like Colonia Pensil, resignation is common. People do not have enough energy for anger or even despair. Time hangs as heavy as the damp wash around the main patio. The owner, who lives next door, is more concerned with her 250 begonia plants than her 400 tenants; yet no one seems overly bothered by the absence of potable water and electricity. "Life is much better here than in Oaxaca," says Mauricio Salazar, who works on a

Pepsi Cola assembly line. "Maybe fishing I could have made enough to live on, but one seeks to improve."

Most people at Pensil have difficulty recognizing their poverty, because poverty is all they have ever known. But Agustina Molina, who lives with her husband and four children in the Tetelpan Ravine, says her economic prospects are dimmer than before. "Everyone in my *barrio* is complaining, and with good reason since we're all eating worse than before." Agustina earns $2.90 a day as a maid. Her husband brings home $105 each week from the medical supply company where he works as a chauffeur. Agustina spends $17 weekly shopping for the family. She doesn't consider her family poor because the Molinas can afford breakfast eggs. But only by lining up at six in the morning in front of the government basic commodities store can she afford milk.

By the end of his six-year term in 1982, even outgoing President José López Portillo was forced to admit that the growth of Mexico City verged on chaotic. "We have made possible the absurd feat of climbing on top of one another by millions in one of the most costly pileups in the history of the world."

Having filled the ravines with shanty towns, newcomers to the capital are now gobbling up the last vestiges of *ejido* lands that were distributed to *campesinos* following the Mexican Revolution with the provision that title would remain with the state and that the lands forever be used only for agriculture. As the capital grew over the past decades, *ejido* inhabitants on the periphery realized they could earn more from selling their small plots than from working them. The government allows these illegal sales because it can't provide housing anywhere else. "The problems arise when the people begin to demand water and other city services," say Alejandro Saurez and René Coulomb, architects who counsel squatter organizations wanting to build homes for their members. "The first thing the government does is to tell the people they are illegal and therefore entitled to nothing. Then, following a suitable period of negotiation, it relents and brings in utilities in return for the community's promised loyalty to the PRI."

Echoing Suarez and Coulomb, opposition politicians insist that the ruling Institutional Revolutionary Party (PRI), rather than preventing illegal urban sprawl, actually promotes it in return for political support. "The illegality of the city's growth is

30

the basis of the Mexican political system," says Jorge Lagorreta of the Unified Socialist Mexican Party (PSUM).

Political patronage, especially in swelling urban areas, is a time-honored tradition throughout the Americas. Political machines in New York, Chicago, and Kansas City successfully co-opted millions of newly arrived immigrants in the early 1900s. But in the United States, political machines had to contend with powerful government lobbies, an unfettered press, vigorous opposition parties, and widespread intolerance of blatant, or at least outrageous, corruption. In Mexico, none of this applies. To receive even minimal city services, a citizens' association must support the PRI, and to desert the party is to enter a powerless void where even small, hard-won gains can be taken away.

Such political tradeoffs have kept the PRI in power for half a century. But they have also helped trigger an environmental time bomb whose impact reaches far beyond the basin of old Lake Texcoco. For the development of the remaining *ejido* lands produces problems that, in their own way, seem as serious and intractable as the megalopolis' population growth.

ENVIRONMENTAL RISKS

Aside from threadbare Chapultepec Park and the Desierto de Leones astride the northwest highway to Toluca, green space in the metropolitan region has all but disappeared. The city has lost 73 percent of its woodland over the past quarter-century. The forests that don't succumb to urban sprawl soon succumb to the demand for firewood. As a result, the natural aquifers hold less water and it is harder to cleanse the air naturally. The forest loss has also diminished the water supply to a frightening degree. Four and a half centuries ago, the "Imperial City of Mexico" was the Venice of the Americas. Today, Lake Texcoco is a muddy expanse of dusty slums. To provide more water, the municipal government is building canals that will carry 19 cubic meters a second from reservoirs 75 miles west of the capital.[19] The projected goal is to bring 55 cubic meters of water a second into the city by the end of the century, but demographers estimate that the capital will need 71 cubic meters a second if present trends continue, and that is just to supply the population's barest needs. Mexico City mayor Ramón Aguirre insists that 95 percent of the city had access to running water before the earthquake, but for millions of residents that means one spigot shared by an entire block.

For the present, most of the city's water comes from 1,366 wells that produce 1.2 billion gallons of water a day.[20] Today, 45 percent of the water is lost through leaks in the city's 7,500 miles of unrepaired water mains. The shortfall is met by pumping even greater amounts from the ground, but engineers concede that this practice must stop. Some areas of the capital subsided twenty feet as groundwater tables fell, and several historical monuments are toppling, including the original Virgin of Guadalupe Shrine and the ornate Palace of Fine Arts, which has sunk eight feet since its completion in 1934.

The population crush has produced an inevitable crisis in transportation. Because the average speed of an in-town trip through congested Mexico City is twenty kilometers an hour, most Mexicans use public transport. Over 4 million people ride the bright orange metro cars every day. The actual cost of an average ride is seventeen pesos, but tickets cost one peso—less than a penny. The resulting disparity produces a government subsidy that amounts to $366,000 a day. (In October 1985 the Mexican exchange rate was 470 pesos to one U.S. dollar.)

THE HOUSING CRUNCH

Clearly, the most serious long-term consequence of Mexico City's earthquake is in the area of housing. Even before the quake left 31,000 homeless, a May 1984 study by the Mexican Social Security Institute concluded that nearly 72 percent of Mexico City's population lacked proper housing.[21] The collapse of large apartment complexes in the *colonias* (settlements) of Tlatelolco, Cuauhtemoc, Carranza, and Roma sparked anger, not only over the slow pace of reconstruction, but also raised suspicions over inefficient and corrupt building inspectors.

Of the 400 office buildings and housing complexes officially listed as destroyed by the quakes, more than a quarter either were owned or managed by the government. The deadly pattern of inattention to building specifications underscored, according to one group of Mexican intellectuals, the corruption inherent in Mexico's political system. None of the capital's 450 historic buildings suffered serious damage, observed Homero Aridjis, a respected writer and former Mexican diplomat. "The old ones were built to last," he said. "Many of the new ones were built only for profit, without concern for the people who were going to live and work in them."[22]

HEALTH CARE MALADIES

Considering the obstacles, the municipal government's efforts to fend off apocalypse are sometimes impressive. Its most notable achievement has been in health care. Over 210 community health centers have opened in *barrios* around the city. When combined with seven special clinics and four general hospitals, the Health Ministry's public health program reaches all but 3 million of the capital's 17 million citizens. "This doesn't mean these people never receive health care," says Dr. Narro Robles, director general of public health services for the federal district. "The Mexican state takes responsibility for the medical attention of everyone." Robles' statistics indicate that more Mexicans are receiving treatment every year, despite an annual population influx equivalent to San Francisco.

Some critics, however, maintain that health services are deteriorating despite a $68.5 million budget and an effort to streamline drug sales and guarantee the availability of critical medicines. "Fifty percent of the Mexico City population has no access to medical treatment," claims Social Democrat President (PSD) Luis Sánchez Aguilar. The situation will get even worse over the next ten years, predicts Sánchez Aguilar on the basis of joint studies by the PSD's economic statistics committee and the Mexican Development Institute. "According to these studies, the number of unattended people in the capital could reach 65 percent in 1995," he says.

Sánchez Aguilar says Mexican health services are paralyzed by centralization, and he fears a national health system could exacerbate the situation. "On the positive side an integrated service will optimize long-term strategies, but knowing our bureaucracy, I would say that the administration of hospitals and health services will be slow, ponderous, and inefficient. Even if the universities can fill the increased demand, the huge size of the city would make the services inoperable."

Dr. Ojeda Rodolfo, a young physician who works at a private Spanish hospital, agrees. "These general hospitals are supposedly open to everyone, but go and see the lines. People start arriving at three in the morning to get a place." Competition for a bed is even tougher, says Rodolfo. "Some desperate mothers-to-be have had their babies delivered at the Red Cross."

In the dusty *barrio* of Chimalhuacan, many people seeking specific care head for the Hospitalito de Jesús, which advertises itself with a boldly painted wall sign that reads "Births—3,000 pesos." Inside, thirty-year-old Dr. Horacio Alatorre García attends patients in a small dusty office. The wall is crowded with diplomas, but no health ministry certificate is displayed. "All we need is authorization from the town hall and tax people," he says, staring coolly through his glasses. The hospital charges about 300 pesos per consultation compared to 55 pesos at the health center, but Alatorre says his patients get thorough examinations that last up to one hour. Whatever the true status of the Hospitalito de Jesús, many unemployed doctors are obliged to create makeshift clinics if they want to practice. Medical faculties at Mexican universities are saturated, and few young graduates find jobs in the state health services. "The rest of us are floating around with nowhere to work," Alatorre explains. "This is why we set up clinics, even if they do have shortcomings."

Forced to assess its priorities in a time of limited resources, the Mexican government has put health care at the top, and, for all the defects in the system, the effort appears to be paying off. Between 1970 and 1980, infant mortality in the city fell from 74.7 per 1,000 to 38.7, while pregnancy-related deaths declined from 1.3 per 1,000 to 0.6 per 1,000. Meanwhile, life expectancy grew from 62.4 years in 1970 to 69.1 years by the end of the decade, only five or six years shy of the U.S. figure.

THE REIGN OF THE PRI

Mexico City's woeful magnificence is all a result of a half century of absolute rule by the Institutional Revolutionary Party (PRI). Imprecise as to policy and short on charisma, Mexico's official government party more closely resembles a nationwide political action committee composed of diverse interest groups than a political organization unified by ideology. Still, it has managed to give Mexico fifty years of pluralistic democracy—a Latin American record—and an economy surpassed only by Brazil's.

The PRI was established in 1929 by General Plutarco Elias Calles, shortly after President Alvaro Obregón was assassinated. The previous decade had seen the 1920 coup that culminated in the death of President Venustiano Carranza, an attempted coup in 1924, and internecine military struggles when three major generals were killed in 1928. Creating a state party to guide the revolution, Calles and his successors had hoped to depose the heavily armed *caudillos* (local leaders, often ranchers), begin land reform, retrieve the ownership of Mexico's natural resources from foreign monopolies, and create economic incentives that eventually would lead Mexico into the ranks of the world's industrialized nations.

Calles and the ten PRI presidents who followed him accomplished all but the last of these goals, although the price of success has been a ponderous, centralized government in which loyalty is prized above all else, including initiative. The PRI maintains its hold on national politics partly by adeptly bringing its critics into the system instead of alienating or imprisoning them. A law also prohibits officeholders from occupying the same position during two consecutive presidential terms, which allows upward movement and, without much loss of face, the purging of incompetents. Unfortunately, however, stability does not mean continuity. The PRI has produced a mountain of studies identifying problems, but no continuing policy to solve them.

Mexico City itself was designated a federal district in 1928. This makes it a political entity similar to the U.S. District of Columbia before its citizens won the right to elect a representative. President Alvaro Obregón formulated the plan, with the obvious intent to ensure that the city would never fall under the control of the Institutional Revolutionary Party's opposition. As part of the arrangement, the mayor would no longer be elected, but appointed by the president. In turn, the mayor appoints the heads of the *delegaciones,* which are semiautonomous communities within the city. The main criterion for appointment as submayor, of course, is a long record of loyal service to the PRI. As intended, this sytem does limit political dissent. But the price of political continuity has been the development of contiguous townships

35

instead of one cohesive city—Latin Los Angeles, only much more splintered.

Further complicating matters, there is no city council, just an advisory body powerless to enact ordinances. The mayor and his departmental secretaries run the city, although the president himself has ultimate authority because he appoints and removes mayors. In Mexico, presidential appointments have more to do with personal friendships than with job qualifications. Mayor Ramón Aguirre is an accountant by training and a close personal friend of incumbent President Miguel de la Madrid. The previous mayor, Carlos Hank Gonzales, was a crony and protégé of past President José López Portillo. Along with his mentor-in-exile, Gonzales now is being accused by the Mexican press of unsavory business deals while in office. One accusation is that he pushed through a $15 million municipal purchase of trash disposal trucks from a truck dealership he "happened" to own. Another rumor has it that the former mayor and several of his close friends profit from the purchase and resale of land obtained by city authority. "This must be the largest settlement on earth where government officials are not accountable to the people they govern," says National Action Party (PAN) President Pablo Emilio Madero.[23] "For there to be any solution to the problems people will have to be able to hold their mayor accountable. The system we have now is the Fidel Castro syndrome. People are governed by authorities they have no voice in choosing."

Because the capital's political system brooks no organized opposition, the bureaucrats in charge can deny that problems even exist. That Mexico's tap water is thoroughly contaminated by parasitic amoebae is obvious within six hours of drinking an unboiled glass of the unsavory liquid. Yet, last March, Everardo Villalobos, head of quality control for the Mexican Social Security Institute (IMSS), declared the city's water to be "the cleanest in the world."[24] (As to why people get sick from it anyway, Villalobos claims that purified water is full of microbes because of the high contamination index of its preparation process.) Similarly, after a subway accident in April 1984 left 70 people injured and 5,000 trapped underground for forty minutes, the government press secretary, Humberto Romero, acknowledged only seven injuries and dismissed the eyewitness reports of Mexican journalists. "Their only mistake," said *Excelsior* columnist

Manuel Buendía of his colleagues, "was forgetting the tenth law, which is that the government inflates its successes by 10 and diminishes its failures by a similar amount." Buendía's open and always sarcastic attacks on powerful personalities and institutions made him Mexico's most widely read journalist. They may also have contributed to his assassination in May 1984.

Four years ago, Mexico City officials attempted to increase citizen participation in local government by creating "block committees," each with an appointed leader to act as a link between the neighborhoods and officials in the various *delegaciones*. But few, if any, committees were actually formed. In real life, citizen complaints are transmitted through those formal associations that exist, stories in the press, and personal contacts. Indeed, the system by which friends help friends circumvent proper channels entirely is essential to conquering the elephantine bureaucracy.

CORRUPTION: "A LA MEXICANA"

Amazingly, the horrendous problems of Mexico City, which could easily undermine the jerryrigged social balance and produce a state of utter anarchy, don't. Inefficiency is taken in stride, almost to the point that it is considered naive to expect anything to work. The lack of regimentation is dismissed with a cheery "a la Mexicana"—"it's the Mexican way." "There is no desire to have established rules and no institutional mechanisms that determine what procedures should be," sighs Colegio de México professor Boris Graizbord. "One of the reasons why corruption exists is because there is no clarity as to what the rules are."

Mexico City's world reputation for corruption is, unfortunately, deserved. Mexican teamsters recently complained that they have to pay an average of $60 in bribes to city police for the privilege of transporting food from the State of Mexico into the city. (The cost, of course, ultimately falls on the consumer.) The official customs storage complex at the Mexico City airport, a succession of ramshackle warehouses, stretches across several acres. Television sets, computers, luggage, and thousands of less valuable items seized by customs agents sit in cluttered rows. When the traveler comes to retrieve his merchandise, an ancient and holy Mexican ritual of bribery is played out. It doesn't matter whether the items confiscated are truly contraband or simply deemed so by caprice of the customs agent; the goods leave only after the proper officials receive a "gratification." Even after the principal official has been gratified, smaller payments to various warehousemen are in order. One forthright clerk who types forms that release goods to the proper owners has a plastic cup on his desk labeled "Tips." A bill of sufficient size ensures that the form is completed immediately; small change consigns the exit permit to the bottom of the paperwork pile.

Few even enter or leave the storage complex without peso offerings; it usually costs about $3 each direction. "It's the same for all of us who do business here," complains one young truck driver. "The people in charge are rats with two feet." If one has any money left, one can stop by the visa office and get a six-month extension for $28—if one is in a hurry. Those willing to wait several days for clearance can usually bargain the fee down to $5.

Graft is ubiquitous. Traffic police take a few dollars for not writing a ticket or a few pesos to let cars advance at a red light during rush hour. Public officials in the right positions take much heftier quaffs from the public trough to augment their small salaries.

Why doesn't the press make more of it? Because, unfortunately, the press is sometimes part of it, too. Under former President José López Portillo, reporters commonly received large baskets at Christmas filled with several hundred dollars worth of imported wine, sausage, paté, and other delicacies. It is also common for Mexico City journalists to travel with government officials on out-of-town trips at government expense.

Although in one sense the "favor" system keeps the machinery of government turning, it contributes significantly to the capital's urban chaos and worsening environmental plight. For a price, squatters can ravage a forest, and polluting industries may continue to pollute.

As a candidate, Mexican President Miguel de la Madrid promised to root out corruption. "Our problems are so grave that only with a moral renovation will we be able to solve them," he insisted in his inaugural speech. To a surprising degree, he has made good on his pledge. Former PEMEX director Jorge Díaz Serrano is in jail, and the government is currently fighting to extradite ex-police chief Durazo. Mexico City residents saw more tangible results of moral renovation when they were able to renew vehicle registrations without having to pay the $25 bribe always demanded in the past.

The most notable failing, however, is in the field of political reform where, despite de la Madrid's promises to the contrary, the PRI continues to tamper with elections.

In July 1985 elections for 400 congressional seats, seven state governorships, and hundreds of other state and local offices were conducted "with strict adherence to legality," according to de la Madrid. For the first time in decades pundits noticed, and reported, a significant shift toward PAN in several states bordering the U.S. But when the votes were counted in the crucial state of Sonora, the PRI emerged victorious with 100 percent support.

In the community of Pueblo Yaqui where the PAN gubernatorial candidate, Adalberto Rosas, was born, the final totals gave five of the six precincts to the PRI by margins of 400 to 0, 320 to 0, 400 to 140, 128 to 55, and 90 to 53. "This means they [PRI] are not going to respect anything," Rosas concluded. "If they are saying I lost boxes in my own hometown by such enormous margins, there is no way they are going to respect the vote anywhere in Sonora."[25]

THE PRI: AN IRON HAND

Total domination by a nationalistic state party may have been wise following the Mexican Revolution but it is controversial in the 1980s. Disagreements over the revolution's direction created the potential Balkanization of a country that had already lost almost half its territory to the United States. Peasant armies owed more allegiance to field commanders like Pancho Villa and Emiliano Zapata than they did to a nation-state. The country's natural resources and industries were controlled by foreign interests willing to protect their investments by buying local politicians. The PRI successfully regained control of Mexico's patrimony, but at the expense of creating a system that only functions under consensus. This is common in developing nations, most of which, unlike Mexico, have failed to curtail the power of their military. But Mexico is now a semi-industrialized nation led by a one-party government that involves itself obsessively in minute decisions. Resentment over voting fraud in last summer's elections—anger that resulted in the burning of the city hall in the Sonora border town of Agua Prieta just one day before Mexico's 8.1 earthquake—could make more difficult the country's recovery and development.

Elements of every problem confronting Mexico City— pollution, overpopulation, graft, underemployment, lack of housing, and worse—can be seen to some degree in most world capitals. But Mexico, like many developing nations, lacks the tested mechanisms such as a free press, socially minded foundations, strong opposition parties, and honest citizens' lobbies to correct its manifold miseries. In its quest for continued hegemony, the PRI has ransomed itself to public greed, no matter how petty or outlandish, and Mexico City pays the price. In return for political support, land speculators are allowed to carve up the *ejidos, campesino* migrants can squat by the hundreds of thousands on vacant lots, and a false, parasitic economy based on government subsidy is maintained. So the bloated urban population grows and grows while the countryside, which must ultimately support it, becomes impoverished and dies of neglect and abuse.

The false economy from which Mexico City residents benefit is maintained by more than 900 government-owned companies called *parastatels.* Originally designed to protect Mexico's strategic resources and shield consumers from unscrupulous entrepreneurs, the parastate network now ranges from tortilla factories to Petroleos Mexicanos (PEMEX), the national oil monopoly. Although the *parastatels* consume 60 percent of the federal budget, few turn a profit or offer substantially lower prices. Conasupo, the state distribution arm for basic commodities, sells products at subsidized prices in 13,500 retail stores. In 1984, it spent $2 million just subsidizing tortillas. Statistics show that only one of every three pesos Conasupo spent in the first three months of 1984 came from company earnings. The other two came from the government. As a result, Conasupo during the same period reported a loss of $747 million, six times what it lost over the same period in 1983.

Ironically, the PRI's control of the capital has come to depend on the same chaos and skewed economics that are crippling the city. Local leaders of the slum towns where migrating newcomers land are not isolated actors who exercise power in a closed sphere, but instruments of political power, and their contacts with the state and with the PRI give them legitimacy. As a result, Mexican squatter camps have been organized for some time, allowing residents to obtain basic rights and services for the land they occupy. But it also assures their active participation in a PRI-controlled system dependent on their vote and support. These two aspects are complementary. Local chiefs are nothing but messengers in this process—instruments of control that the PRI uses to organize *colonos* (squatters).

The relationship between the PRI and Mexico's internal migrants, then, is symbiotic. "The hegemony of the PRI receives unquestioned support from the mass proleteriat because the network of local committees is the most efficient channel by which to obtain popular rights," notes University of Madrid sociology professor Dr. Manuel Castells. "Moreover, they realize that any attempt to open an alternate channel will be met with strong repression."

But the danger is that slum dwellers are easier to organize than to control. The PRI can allow migrants to remain on their untitled property; it can even provide water and bulldoze a road to the nearest bus stop. But it cannot assure upward mobility. Small wonder, then, that after being allowed to remain in the slums at Ixtacalco the 4,000 families of the "October 2 Encampment" began listening to radical students instead of PRI functionaries. As the community grew, charged confrontations with the police increased. Finally, in January of 1976, when the *campesinos* tried to form the Federación de Colonias Proletarias, the police razed the slum. Since the destruction of the "2 de octubre," the government has battled radical squatters in Chihuahua, Torreon, and Monterrey.

SOLUTIONS

Most demographers believe that a federal policy combining decentralization and rural development would help solve the immediate problem of urbanization, if not the long-term problem of rampant growth in a largely arid nation. However, little has been accomplished so far. For Mexico's 77 million people, their capital remains the center of the world. The city is home to more than one-fifth of the population and more than half of the

national industrial plants. The three largest industrial developments are here, along with 90 percent of Mexico's 1,500,000
bureaucrats. About seven of every ten banking transactions
occur in the capital. The city is a magnet: each day, 1,000 or more
campesinos are drawn there, adding to a chaos that already bog-
gles a New Yorker's or a São Paolan's mind.

The government, for its part, at least acknowledges that decentralization is the answer. In 1983, it announced a new "central
regional plan" that rivaled past pledges to disperse centralized
power. The plan was accompanied by special legislation and a
budget targeted to rural areas. But nothing tangible has resulted.
"There have been about five decentralization programs in the
past twenty years and all of them failed because there was no political determination to carry them out," says Luis Sánchez
Aguilar, president of the left-of-center Social Democrat Party.

The government has also offered tax incentives to companies
willing to relocate, although convincing new industries not to establish headquarters in Mexico City seems a more workable
policy. With the current decline in Mexican industry, Carlos
Mireles, president of the National Manufacturing Industry
Chamber (CANACINTRA), argues that decentralization makes economic sense, but not until price controls are lifted and the
government itself starts relocating.

There has been much talk and little movement. In June 1984,
President de la Madrid ordered all quasi-government industries
to formulate relocation plans by the end of the year. Some of the
biggest polluters responded that relocation was financially impossible. The Secretariat of Urban Development and Ecology
(SEDUE), which in July 1984 announced a program to move all polluting industries out of the valley, backed down, insisting it
would force the 1,100 leading polluters to clean up instead. "Massive unemployment is a more serious consequence than the
contamination of the environment," announced SEDUE's Marcelo
Javelly Girard. And, he added wistfully, "As the government's
measures continue to be implemented, we can say that the next
generation is going to encounter a capital city without contamination—say, within 25 years."[26]

Can anything divert Mexico City from what promises more
and more to be a smash-up on the limits to growth? And, if not,
why? One fundamental reason may be that the imperial city of

the Aztecs, and later of New Spain, is beyond criticism in the minds of most of its officials, if not the citizenry itself. "The creation of Mexico City is born out of myth," says the writer Octavio Paz. "There is an obscure sense of destiny here, a feeling that this city represents the history and destiny of the country." Also, some say that Mexicans are peculiarly willing to let grandiloquence take the place of deeds: words in Mexico are invoked as magical incantations; political speeches and demagoguery are forms of popular entertainment. So even if official speeches have been full of "decentralization" for years, they have inspired little action. There is no shortage of plans, but few are implemented, and all are shelved every six years when a new president is inaugurated.

Mexico's inability to plan for the long term is historically entrenched. The Aztecs cleansed and renewed their society every fifty-two years by breaking all dishes, putting out every fire, and retreating to the mountain tops to pray that the sun would again rise, allowing the New Fire ceremony to kindle another fifty-two-year "century." Today, less ritualistically, the PRI essentially does the same every six years. Thus, López Portillo's "Mexican Food System" (SAM) becomes the "National Program of Food" (PRONAL) under Miguel de la Madrid. "Every six years this cynical population goes through the pretense of change in which the names of officials change but the system remains the same," says one western diplomat. "In the symbolic sense the pots are broken. People change jobs no matter how well they were performing, and the ritual of renewal is repeated."

The official rededication to the future occurs every September 1, when the president delivers a marathon state-of-the-union report. Decentralization again appeared on the 1984 agenda. "The process of urbanization has been concentrated in just a few cities, as is clearly indicated by the fact that 26 percent of Mexico's total population lives in the metropolitan areas of Mexico City, Guadalajara and Monterrey," said de la Madrid. "In contrast, the rural population consists of 22 million people who are scattered in 123,000 villages of fewer than 2,500 inhabitants. . . . Programs are being drawn up within the National Urban System for 59 medium-sized cities on which we will systematically focus decentralization efforts."

Just as it would be wrong to be utterly cynical about such promises, it would be foolish to expect too much. Not even Manuel Camacho, undersecretary of regional development for the Programming and Budget Ministry, places much faith in the government's ability to curb urbanization. "There is a social dynamic already in existence here, and all the country's structure is built on that. All we can do is affect trends, but we can't neglect the essential needs of a great part of the city's population, which does not have services."

Given the earthquake's destruction in Mexico City and the complete collapse of the Commerce and Communication and Transportation ministries, decentralization makes more sense than ever, but many urban planners doubt that Mexico's centralized political system can ever decentralize the economy. "I see no real interest on the part of the government to stop investment in Mexico City," says architect Javier Hernandez. "All political and economic decisions are made in Mexico City. We must realize that the problem is not numerical, but rather the fact that there is a corrupt and inefficient structure at the basis of everything."

Over the past decade, control of the Mexican economy by the centralized, Mexico City-based government has, in fact, greatly increased. When Luis Echeverría became president in the early seventies, the government controlled about 25 percent of the economy. Today, a network of nationalized banks and *parastatel* trading companies dominates 70 percent of the economy. Now that they successfully have restructured Mexico's foreign debt repayment and increased the country's foreign exchange reserves from $1.8 billion at the end of 1982 to $6 billion today, many of the government's Cambridge-educated economic planners encourage a statist (as opposed to Marxist) reconstruction of stalled industries. But they may find themselves frustrated, because Mexico still faces the traditional developing-world dilemma of whether to invest in industry or agriculture. It can't afford to do both, and the decision Mexico makes will affect its development for the rest of the century and beyond.

U.S.-MEXICAN INTERDEPENDENCE

The United States is Mexico's largest market and most important trading partner, and so it will remain for the foreseeable

44

future. Sixty-five percent of Mexico's imports come from the United States, which last year imported $18 billion worth of Mexican products. American corporations have more than $3.2 billion directly invested in Mexican manufacturing alone. These and other mutual interests last year produced more than $30 billion worth of bilateral trade in 1984. Obviously, and even if the huge traffic in illegal drugs is ignored, Mexico's economy is tightly bonded to the U.S. economy.

Yet, both Mexican and U.S. officials downplay the two countries' economic interdependence. U.S. officials living in Mexico express sympathy about the country's dilemma, but intimate that U.S. investors are unlikely to start many new joint ventures with Mexico—largely because they won't be welcome. "Politically, they're our ally, but no Mexican government can risk being seen as dependent on the U.S.," confides one U.S. Embassy attaché. "Armed invasions by the French and ourselves, plus the fact that England stole their oil industry, color all decisions made here. As for U.S. investment, well, Mexico says it wants high-tech industries, but U.S. investors learn after a few weeks here that it's easier to work with Korea, Singapore, or Taiwan."

Actually, much evidence to the contrary can be found, especially along the border where 700 factories have been established since 1965 under the Border Industrialization Program. The U.S.-owned plants, called *maquiladoras* in reference to the fee once collected by millers for processing farmers' grain, use Mexican labor pools composed largely of women who deftly assemble parts manufactured and shipped from the United States. The arrangement is a financial boon for U.S. industrialists, whose products, when re-exported to the United States, are taxed only on the value added in Mexico. According to the National Bank of Mexico, *maquiladoras* in 1984 produced products valued at $1.2 billion when later resold, although only a small proportion of the revenue goes to Mexican workers. Women employed in the 107 transnationally operated plants in Ciudad Juárez complain that domestic servants in El Paso earn more money, and so they do. The average worker in a border *maquiladora* receives only $1.10 per hour, compared to $1.62 in Singapore and $1.50 in Hong Kong. Low pay makes for competitively priced clothes and electronics back in the United States, but it also creates social instability along the border: the American Chamber of Commerce in Mexico City estimates that job turnover is 35 percent a month in Nogales and 10 percent in Ciudad Juárez and Tijuana.[27]

The answer to Mexico's urban crisis, as suggested before, does not lie in higher industrial wages. Most officials now believe that the better approach is to keep peasants on the farm—a difficult task requiring a major revival of Mexican agriculture. About two-thirds of Mexico's present unemployment is found in agriculture. Because out-migration is high and the commodity prices paid by private wholesalers and the government's National Staple Products Company (Canasupo) are artificially high, the amount of agricultural land has increased only marginally over the past 20 years, and both the tonnage and quality of Mexico's agricultural output have declined. The country once known as "the land of the Green Revolution" is now self-sufficient only in beans and wheat; and it is a net importer of corn, rice, and sorghum. Indeed, Conasupo runs second only to the state oil company, PEMEX, as the main public sector importer of foreign goods. The government insists that it invests generously in agriculture, and it does, statistically speaking. But most loans go to the large, mechanized farms in the north and along the Pacific Coast, which are owned by large companies connected to major national and multinational concerns.

Mexico's mechanized and irrigated agro-industries have made some impressive strides. They now produce 50 percent of the country's food exports and nearly 30 percent of its domestic consumption.[28] They supply the United States with 25 percent of its food imports, including most of its imported winter vegetables. But while the large growers prosper, most campesinos—subsistence farmers on ejidos in central Mexico—remain on the margin of the agricultural economy.

About 300,000 people enter the agricultural job market each year, so even if the present level of migration to the United States is maintained, agricultural unemployment could top 10 million by the end of the century. Some studies indicate that the future for agriculture is as grim as that for Mexico City. "The agricultural land has been left to its own devices, which has resulted in soil depletion, abandonment due to lack of credits in some regions and overpopulation in many others. While the rural population continues to increase at a fast rate, that employed in the agricultural sector is apparently beginning to diminish, a fact which will probably enlarge the surplus population. . .and increase the migratory potential from them in the near future."[29]

Actually, economic prospects for Mexican farmers are not entirely bleak. Agribusinessmen in the Pacific Coast states of Sinaloa and Colima who have ignored Conasupo and deal directly with U.S. buyers enjoy greater revenues than comparable farmers in neighboring states. But the *ejido* farmers must usually deal with Conasupo, which does not pay realistic prices for commodities. Most *campesinos* doubt that it ever will because subsidizing urban residents' food is a higher priority. "During the seventeenth and eighteenth centuries the treasures of Asia, unloaded at Acapulco and taken to Veracruz for shipment onward to Spain, would be taxed 20 percent by the imperial city of Mexico," says a historian. "The city still collects its *quinto* (fifth), but today it is the Mexican *campesino* who subsidizes the capital's comforts."

U.S. INTERESTS

Mexico's political stability and economic prosperity should vitally concern the government and people of the United States. But half a century of stable rule by the Institutional Revolutionary Party has caused many Americans to take their southern neighbor for granted. Moreover, too often Washington's view of Mexico is a stereotype plagued by condescension, racial bias, and near-total ignorance of a culture more complex than ours. These barriers to understanding, according to Mexican writer Octavio Paz, have produced two contiguous, yet estranged, societies.

> In general Americans have not looked for Mexico in Mexico; they have looked for their obsessions, enthusiasms, phobias, hopes, interests—and these are what they have found. In short, the history of our relationship is the history of mutual and stubborn deceit, usually involuntary though not always so.

The need for greater attention and a more clearly defined policy toward Mexico is all the more urgent given the rapid comingling of the two nations' populations. Chicanos already represent a significant minority throughout the Southwestern

United States. In New Mexico, the Spanish surnamed population is almost a majority. Half the kindergarten pupils in Los Angeles have Spanish last names. Conversely, the Autonomous University of Guadalajara has more U.S. medical students than does any school in the United States.

But how many Americans understand how Mexicans really feel about us? Manifest Destiny, as all American high school students learn, was a noble quest to civilize a savage continent. Mexicans continue to view it as an anglo land grab in which half of Mexico became one-third of the continental United States. The Alamo? In North America, the battle is recounted in books such as *Thirteen Days to Glory.* Mexico, which had banned further immigration into its northern province of Tejas in 1830, proudly remembers the 1836 clash in which Santa Ana's exhausted army of illiterate Indian conscripts finally bested 1,800 illegal aliens—only six of whom had been in Texas for more than six years.

More to the point today is the matter of illegal aliens, whose presence in the United States continues to block better relations between our two nations. Many North Americans view Mexicans' salmon-like determination to enter the United States and mount its economic ladder as a consequence of a corrupt government's inept handling of its economy. According to this view, only by sealing the border—by closing the valve through which Mexico vents its population pressure and political dissent—will the entrenched powers in Mexico City be forced to reform. To be sure, Mexico's emphasis on capital-intensive heavy industry over labor-intensive manufacturing and agriculture has contributed to Mexican unemployment. But it is not—repeat, is not—the only reason for the massive illegal emigration to the United States. Mexican labor is drawn north in equal measure by the U.S. demand for cheap labor. Sealing the border may provide a short respite from the Mexicans' influx, but given Mexico's proud nationalism and historic resistance to pressure from Washington, it probably would have little influence on Mexico's development or economic policies.

U.S. officials have repeatedly expressed their concern that Mexico's social, environmental, and economic problems might eventually spill over the border. As early as 1978, former CIA Director William Colby predicted that Mexico's uncontrolled population growth could make it a greater long-term threat than the Soviet Union. In February 1984, the PRI was severely criticized by General Paul Gorman, chief of the U.S. Southern Command in Panama, who described the country as a "one-party state" that has "the most corrupt government and society in Central [*sic*] America." In March 1985 Mexico's government again came under attack, this time by Secretary of State George Schultz, who responded to the kidnapping and eventual murder of an American narcotics agent in language usually reserved for Libya and the Soviet bloc. "Our level of tolerance has been exceeded," Schultz fumed after federal policy allowed the suspected slayer to escape.

POLICY INITIATIVES

Unfortunately, none of these tirades addresses the real problems—resource management and development. Ironically, many Mexican intellectuals and newspaper columnists agree with Washington that their political and economic system desperately needs reform. Mexico's tax rate, one of the world's lowest, should, for example, be increased. At present, ordinary workers and middle-class professionals pay as much tax as all private entrepreneurs combined. Reform is needed in the Ministry of Agrarian Reform and the government-controlled National Peasant Confederation, too. Legal complications and the lack of farm credit have kept an estimated 50 percent of the lands legally redistributed to *campesinos* from producing efficiently. This openly expressed need for reform was recognized by President Miguel de la Madrid in his annual address in September 1984. "We Mexicans are making an enormous effort to overcome the difficulties that confront us," he said. "We are proving that we are a vigorous, mature people that tackle adversity with talent and decision."

De la Madrid's concern goes beyond mere rhetoric. In February 1985, he slashed $465 million from the federal budget, announced a partial hiring freeze, and put 236 state-owned companies up for sale. Five months later he took the politically controversial step of devaluing the peso by 37.5 percent and lowering the price of Mexico's popular Maya-grade crude to $23.50 a barrel.

Mexico can't solve the problems that currently endanger its future stability without help from the United States. Yet, for the moment Washington has no clear policy. Satisfying Mexico's economic interests and American security needs will not be easy, but there are a number of actions that could be taken immediately.

A Special Envoy-Ombudsman. Coming from a centralized political system to an ultra-pluralistic one such as ours, Mexicans soon learn that U.S. policy, at least toward Mexico, is seldom definitive. Immigration policy is implemented by the Immigration and Naturalization Service, but can be changed at any time by Congress. Trade policies set by the Department of Commerce can be amended in response to pressure from U.S. interest groups. In theory, gas and oil matters are resolved by the Department of Energy, but often PEMEX finds itself negotiating with the Departments of Justice and Interior. To clear a path through this maze, Washington should name a permanent special envoy to Mexico and Central America with executive authority to resolve questions of interest between the Congress and Cabinet secretaries. As a first act of business, the special envoy could ask that some of the benefits of Caribbean Basin trade incentives be extended to Mexico. Using the same logic as that behind the trade incentives to the Caribbean Basin in 1981— that Mexican stability is crucial to U.S. security—the United States would promote internal stability in Mexico by encouraging economic prosperity.

Building Positively on Economic Linkages. However, we seldom take even these opportunities for economic cooperation which present themselves. After immense oil reserves were discovered in the Gulf, a "crude for food" exchange was proposed by political scientists hopeful of bringing Mexico and the United States closer together. No agreement was ever reached. Mexican nationalists argued that self-sufficiency in food production was essential to national sovereignty; American strategic thinkers countered that the United States should not depend on any foreign power for energy. Then, in 1977, when López Portillo signed an agreement with a consortium of U.S. companies to sell Mexican gas at $2.60 per thousand cubic feet, Energy Secretary James Schlesinger nixed the deal, although not before keeping Mexico's foreign minister and the head of PEMEX waiting for forty-five minutes and then greeting them with his feet on his desk—a profound insult in Latin societies.

At bottom is the need for both Washington and Mexico City to recognize that cooperation is essential. More specifically, the United States should—in return for a guaranteed supply of oil and agricultural products—abolish seasonal tariffs, guarantee its long-term purchase of crude, and allow Mexican textile and leather goods to compete with similar American products. This would help the Mexican economy by giving Mexico's producers a constant U.S. market.

Immigration. No lasting accommodation between the United States and Mexico can be reached until the two countries come to grips with illegal immigration. Neither government has worked out common grounds for negotiation. Washington refers to the estimated 650,000 Mexicans in the United States (and the additional 1.2 million who try to cross the border each year) as "illegal aliens" while Mexico views them as "undocumented workers" responding to economic opportunities in states illegally stolen from Mexico.

In 1977, the Carter administration offered an immigration plan with four basic goals: (1) amnesty and resident status for illegals who arrived before 1970; (2) permission for illegals arriving between 1970 and 1977 to remain for an additional five years if they properly identified themselves; (3) increased border surveillance; and (4) stiff penalties for U.S. employers who hire undocumented Mexicans. In 1984, the Simpson-Mazzoli bill, which advanced many of these ideas, passed the Senate only to fall victim to election-year politics.

Although Americans like to think of immigration as Mexico's responsibility, it is a problem whose explosive nature probably demands that the United States take a first conciliatory step. Legalizing the presence of aliens already in the United States and penalizing employers who hire those entering after a specified date would eliminate the fear and insecurity that currently plague illegal aliens and decrease the U.S. demand for Mexican workers. Without sanctions, employers have no incentive to hire a legal worker at minimum wage if they can hire a Mexican worker for less. Such measures would also eliminate the hypocrisy of the current system. If, despite cutbacks in government social services, unemployed American workers still refuse to accept the lower-paid and largely agricultural jobs previously held by illegal aliens, then labor and civil rights leaders should reconsider their reflexive opposition to a revised Mexican farm-worker program.

Labor-Intensive Industry. Former president of the World Bank, Robert McNamara recommended that lending agencies establish credit policies that would promote labor-intensive industries in the developing world. Although few lending agencies or governments have taken his advice so far, now is the time. As a first step toward reducing Mexican unemployment and resulting urban and U.S.-bound migration, Washington should instruct all its agencies active in Mexico to tailor their aid programs to promote maximum employment—even if "efficiency" suffers.

Road building and irrigation projects should be funded in Guanajuato, Chihuahua, Michoacán, Zacatecas, and Jalisco—homes to most illegal aliens entering the United States. Instead of sending more helicopters and herbicides to Mexico, the Drug Enforcement Agency could provide less expensive trucks that could take unemployed peasants to cut and burn marijuana fields.

Population Control. Birth control is an extremely sensitive issue in Catholic Mexico, which prefers to speak of "family planning." Difficult as it is to deal with, it is a key underlying factor affecting both immigration pressures, the success of future development efforts, even prospects for more fundamental social, economic, and political reform—not to mention the ability of Mexico City, and Mexico, to be managed at all in future decades. Whatever the term used, the United States and Mexico should together implement under U.S. auspices a program to reduce Mexico's birth rate. Earlier efforts, fairly successful in the larger urban areas, have yet to make an impact on the rural areas, where families average 5.7 children.

Any U.S. policy initiatives, of course, depend upon Mexican cooperation to succeed. The rate at which Mexico initiates reform will probably be too slow for Washington's taste. But only continued patience, together with imaginative efforts to deal intelligently with common problems of great importance to both Mexico and the U.S., will make the "special relationship" to which both countries often refer a reality.

NOTES

1. *Los Angeles Times,* October 12, 1985, 14.

2. *Los Angeles Times,* September 17, 1985, 1.

3. Ignacio Bernal, "Mexico-Tenochtitlán," in Arnold Toynbee (ed.) *Cities of Destiny* (New York: 1968) 204; Miguel Leon-Portilla, *The Broken Spears: The Aztec Account of the Conquest of Mexico* (Boston: Beacon Press, 1972) xix.

4. Michael C. Meyer and William L. Sherman, *The Course of Mexican History* (Oxford: Oxford University Press, 1983) 87.

5. Philip Russell, *Mexico in Transition* (Austin, Texas: Colorado River Press, 1977) 1.

6. Meyer and Sherman, *The Course of Mexican History,* 87.

7. Hernán Cortés, *Cartas de relación* (Mexico: Editorial Porrua, 1984. Originally published in Sevilla, 1522.) 63.

8. Russell, *Mexico in Transition,* 4.

9. *New York Times,* May 15, 1983.

10. Unikel, "La dinámica del crecimiento de la ciudad de México," *Comercio Exterior,* 1971, vol. 21, no. 6:507–516.

11. Many statistics used come from internal memos, unpublished working papers, or interviews in which anonymity was requested.

12. *Manchester Guardian,* January 29, 1984.

13. Gustavo Garza, "Estructura productiva e industrialización de la Ciudad de Méexico," *Habitación,* July–August, 1982:7.

14. Browning, "Migrant Selectivity and the Growth of Large Cities in Developing Societies," in National Academy of Sciences, *Rapid Population Growth* (Baltimore: The Johns Hopkins University Press, 1971) 273–314.

15. *Ejidos* are former private estates redistributed to rural dwellers to serve as government-subsidized, community-held pastures, woodlands, and farms. Small plots of land are also allocated on a semipermanent basis to families for personal gardens. From Organization of American States, Department of Regional Development, Secretariat for Economic and Social Affairs, *Integrated Regional Development Planning: Guidelines and Case Studies from OAS Experience* (Washington, D.C.: 1984) 205.

16. Used to describe people who suddenly appear to occupy vacant land on the urban periphery.

17. Wayne A. Cornelius, *Los immigrantes pobres en la Ciudad de México y la política* (México: Fondo de Cultura Económica, 1980) 31.

18. Cornelius, *Los immigrantes,* 28.

19. *Los Angeles Times,* December 8, 1983.

20. Departamento del Distrito Federal, Secretária de Obras y Servícios, Dirección General de Construcción y Operación Hidraulica, 1981.

21. Schteingart, Coloquio internacional sobre formulas de financiamiento a la vivienda de bajo costo, July 1982.

22. *New York Times,* September 25, 1985, 3.

23. Chavira, R., personal interview.

24. *Mexico City News,* March 26, 1984.

25. *Los Angeles Times,* July 8, 1985, 1.

26. *Mexico City News,* August 16, 1984.

27. Rodolfo Acuña, *Occupied America: A History of Chicanos* (New York: Harper & Row, 1980) 16.

28. *New York Times,* February 27, 1984.

29. Muñoz, Oliveira, and Stern, *Mexico City: Industrialization, Migration and the Labor Force, 1930–1970* (United Nations Educational, Scientific, and Cultural Organization, 1983) 51.

CHAPTER 3

Grounds of Conflict in Central America

JAMES NATIONS AND
H. JEFFREY LEONARD

—————————————Editors' Preface—————————————

Most American citizens would be surprised to learn that U.S. troops have intervened in Central America more than twenty times in the twentieth century. President Reagan's use of force, whether directly as in Grenada or indirectly as in the supply of weapons and military training to Hondurans, El Salvadorans, and the Nicaraguan *contras,* is a time-honored, though not honorable, U.S. tradition. Most American citizens understand even less well that Central America's turmoil is deeply rooted in the pressure of poor people on the land. Most are unaware of the role of North Americans' appetite for beef or the often myopic lending and aid policies of the U.S. government and multinational and private banks.

In the name of macro-economic growth, profitability for U.S. corporations, and security for U.S. interests, the United States has pursued policies for a generation in Central America that have in various ways fostered landlessness, squatters in national forests, and "improvements" of land by deforesting it. U.S policy fails even now, as is apparent in this chapter's discussion of the Kissinger Commission's recommendations, to factor into our considerations the key Central American issues, population pressure/migration and protection of the resource base. Instead of lasting solutions for the region, the United States has pursued a model of unsustainable economic development and supported largely untenable, unpopular regimes.

James Nations and Jeffrey Leonard write compellingly here about the five tense neighboring states that regularly make our headlines: Guatemala, El Salvador, Honduras, Nicaragua, and Costa Rica. (They refer in passing also to tiny Belize and Panama.) These five countries together are approximately 25 percent the size of Mexico, and less than 5 percent the size of the United States. Together they have populations one-third that of Mexico, and one-tenth that of the United States. Their per capita GNPs range from $1,120 in Guatemala to $670 in Honduras, compared with $14,110 in the United States. Even the most stable and comfortable of these countries is poor and stressed. Each of them, regardless of how "friendly" with the United States, is seriously dependent upon it. They are dependent not just for markets, loans, arms, and police training, but for their very existence. Their leaders, friendly, unfriendly, and hopeful, make regular pilgrimages to Congress and the State Department and regular appeals through the U.S. media. Some of the most important decisions about their futures are made in Washington, D.C., by people who have never set foot in their lands.

In one sense it is difficult to generalize about these five countries. In some respects they are quite different from one another. Costa Rica has a democratically elected government, a development policy that emphasizes the rural areas and heeds environmental outcomes, and no regular military forces. Nicaragua had its revolution in 1979 when the repressive Somoza family was driven from the country. Their idle, vast, underused landholdings have been distributed to poor farmers to work as cooperatives. A crash literacy campaign taught most Nicaraguans the rudiments of written language. Attention has been given to the forests and to the development of renewable energy sources for rural areas. Education and elementary health services now reach some of the remote areas. But these efforts are only barely underway, and hopes for better have faded in the face of the war.

In other respects, however, Costa Rica and Nicaragua are not so different from their neighbors. Each government desperately ñeeds the foreign exchange from commercial agriculture; that dependency hasn't changed. Farmers suffer from lack of credit, adequate prices, technical assistance, fertilizers, and tools, as in other Latin societies. Most important is the persistence in all five countries of resource and population problems, of poverty that stems from the same historical experience and the same degradation of the land. These are the problems that U.S. and Central American policies must address.

A
T THE heart of Central America's hope for political, economic, and social progress lie the issues of land and renewable natural resources—forests, soil, and water. These resources are the backbone of the region's national economies, accounting for more than half of all economic production, half of all employment, and most exports. And their proper management is the keystone to social and economic development. Moreover, almost 60 percent of the region's 24 million people live in rural areas where they depend directly upon renewable natural resources for their livelihood.

Yet, paradoxically, Central America's forests, soils, and water are being severely degraded and destroyed. Population pressures and financial crises are prompting governments to overexploit natural resources to satisfy immediate economic needs, increase employment, and skirt such difficult political decisions as land redistribution. As a result, the region's renewable natural resources are being depleted far faster than they can be replenished. By "mining" natural resources, Central America's economies and governments are temporarily making do, but the long-term consequences will be severe: declines in income and per capita food production; financial losses; and the sacrifice of future economic opportunities. Deforestation, soil erosion, and sedimentation of lakes and harbors is already reaching crisis proportions in several Central American countries.

Although these patterns are clearly visible, international development policy is failing to halt the degradation. Some development policies are even accelerating the destruction. Multilateral and bilateral development organizations have focused on improving agricultural productivity, increasing industrial development, and improving physical infrastructure in rural areas (in addition to slowing population growth). But they have done little to sustain the natural resource base over the long term. As a result, the region's ambitious development programs rest on rapidly eroding foundations.

If resource management doesn't improve markedly during the next few decades, Nicaragua, Costa Rica, Guatemala, Honduras, El Salvador, Belize, and Panama will face even greater difficulties in coping with their already formidable problems: growing unemployment; large-scale emigration; inability to feed burgeoning populations; expanded civil disturbances; and increasing potential for economic stagnation. Furthermore, no quick fix will work. Social and economic progress in the region depends upon making sustainable use of renewable natural resources.

A HISTORY OF RESOURCE EXPLOITATION

Patterns of land and natural resource abuse in Central America are deeply rooted in the region's past. Indeed, the exploitation of land, labor, and resources has always been the key to economic and social advancement in Central America. After exhausting the region's limited supply of gold and slaves, the sixteenth-century Spanish invaders dedicated themselves to controlling large agricultural populations and to exporting raw or natural products to the Old World. One of the results of this early colonial pattern, says historian Murdo MacLeod, was monoculture— "the logical result of a determined drive by the dominant class to obtain rapid wealth from unprocessed natural resources."[1]

Colonial Central America cycled through successive economic booms and busts dependent on single crops or extractive industries. Through the centuries, Spanish overlords rode economic waves based on balsam, sarsaparilla, cacao, cattle, indigo, and sugarcane. As MacLeod notes, the disappearance of one boom "would then set off a frantic but determined hunt for another dynamic export crop."

Each of the region's export crops required many laborers, and Indian families were traded, transported, and controlled like another cash crop through colonial labor systems. In fact, control of labor was considered more important than control of land in colonial Central America, for then, as today, Central America's rural laborers formed the backbone of the state's economy. As anthropologist Robert Wasserstrom has noted, they provided "inexpensive labor at moments of intense demand, after which they were left to their own devices" to produce food for themselves and their invaders.[2]

Before Spaniards seized control of Central America, the region's indigenous families had perfected traditional agricultural systems based on maize, beans, squash, and root crops. In the precolonial world, agriculture was balanced by tree-crop cultivation, hunting, and fishing. Most of these efficient local food production systems were short-circuited by the Spanish conquest. As the Spaniards tightened their control, they pressed Indian families into either full-time or periodic labor to benefit the emerging colonial economy, turning Indians into part-time farmers and allowing most of Central America's indigenous farming techniques to fade into memory. Indian claims to communally held lands also disappeared as Spaniards seized forests and farms that Indians had controlled for millennia.

Central America's move from Spanish domination to independence during the early nineteenth century had only a minor impact on the region's patterns of land use and resource exploitation. Agricultural systems continued to focus on single crops for export. Coffee, first planted in the early 1800s, soon dominated both land and labor in much of Central America. Latin American historian Eduardo Galeano notes that "Great tracts of idle land—belonging to no one, or to the Church, or to the state—passed into private hands, and Indian communities were frenetically plundered."[3] Between 1832 and the 1870s, Costa Rica's coffee exports multiplied four hundred times. As historian Walter LaFeber has indicated, "the effect of the coffee economy on the peasants was especially devastating: before 1820 a large majority had small farm plots, but by the 1860s about half were merely wage laborers."[4]

By the early 1870s, bananas had joined the parade of Central American export crops, beginning a trend that would establish the United States as the region's premier trading partner. As U.S. banana companies bought land, built railroads, and bribed officials during the late nineteenth and early twentieth centuries, they broke Europe's hold on the Central American economies and helped bring the region into the North American economic sphere. The monoculture system became, if anything, even more dominant. By the 1930s, the Central American nations were more dependent than ever on one or two export crops.[5]

The effect of this chain of events on natural resources and rural farm families was devastating. As coffee and banana production expanded into forested areas, a small group of wealthy families and U.S.-based corporations consolidated their control of the region's farmland. Rural communities were disrupted, their communal lands wrested away through force and suspect legal manipulations. Basic food stuffs such as beans, maize, and fruit were increasingly hard to come by. In the end, says LaFeber, "peasants and Indians became little more than a hungry, wandering labor force to be used at will by the oligarchy."[6]

By the beginning of World War II, the Central American nations had become inextricably tied to the United States, both economically and politically. The United States provided the region with a foreign market for its cash crops and with much of the food the nations were concurrently forced to import. The United States also supplied loans and military equipment to oligarchic governments, which kept the system operating. During the three decades that followed World War II, nationalist revolutionary movements manned by disaffected politicians and disgruntled rural families periodically threatened the status quo. But these movements consistently were quashed, frequently with the help of U.S. finances and troops. Central America's ruling families retained control of land and natural resources, and the peasantry grew poorer.

The late 1960s and early 1970s saw a regional investment boom in cotton and beef cattle that led to new predations on Central America's rural farmers and natural resources. With the United States clamoring for frozen beef and Japan for cotton, landowners shifted farmland, banana plantations, and standing forest to pastureland and cotton fields. The region's cotton production, centered in the Pacific coastal lowlands, jumped from fewer than one hundred bales in 1953 to more than a million by 1964. Cotton soon emerged as the leading export of Nicaragua and was second only to coffee in El Salvador and Guatemala.[7]

As cotton production expanded in the Nicaraguan provinces of Chinandega and León, enterprising families linked to the Somoza dictatorship registered ownership of lands that peasant families had farmed, without title, for decades. Farmers who resisted were evicted forcibly by Somoza's National Guard.[8] The rest saw no alternative but to migrate into the nation's lowland tropical forest to clear the land and return to producing food. Some burned the forest and planted pasture to raise their own beef cattle for export. As a result, the amount of Nicaraguan territory in pasture jumped from 17,100 square kilometers to 28,200 square kilometers between 1961 and 1978, most of it at the expense of the Caribbean Coast rainforest. Generous international credit for cattle production, new road construction, and new port facilities helped push the export beef cattle industry through the thick Caribbean rainforest at a rate of one kilometer per year.[9] According to a government survey:

> Cattlemen from more developed regions of the country acquire the "improvements" effected by pioneer colonists and introduce a system of extensive cattle production identical to that practiced in their region of origin. On selling their improved lands, the pioneer colonists move further into the forest, continuing the process of spontaneous expansion of the agricultural frontier.[10]

In one eleven-year period, the number of cattle in Nicaragua's rainforest provinces quadrupled to 82,500 head; by 1973, Nicaragua had earned the dubious distinction of being the only Central American nation in which cattle outnumbered people.[11] More than half its annual beef production was shipped to the United States where Anastasio Somoza himself owned interest in six Miami beef-importing companies that netted him $30 million per year.[12]

Through similar trends in Costa Rica, Honduras, Guatemala, and El Salvador, exports of de-boned frozen beef emerged as the region's most dynamic trade commodity during the 1960s and 1970s, with a 400 percent increase between 1961 and 1974 alone.[13] Many Central American landowners combined cattle and cotton operations on their pasturelands, but newly cleared forest soils were the preferred site for cultivating either crop. As a result, the dry tropical forests of Central America's Pacific coast and the humid forests of the Caribbean lowlands increasingly fell prey to export crop production and to the axes of rural families forced from their land as *haciendas* (ranches) expanded.

In Honduras, according to LaFeber, cattlemen fenced whatever land they desired, then expelled any farmers found inside. "The peasants," says LaFeber, "were trapped on four sides: their own lands disappeared, the U.S.-owned fruit companies controlled much of the remaining soil, few jobs existed in the towns, and the Salvadorans—squeezed out of their own country—streamed into Honduras to compete for the little decent land that remained."[14]

By the late 1960s, one in every eight Salvadorans had migrated into Honduras in search of work, land, and food. When Honduras began expelling these immigrants in mid-1969, the situation exploded into the week-long Soccer War, in which several thousand were killed and 100,000 left homeless.[15] Americans would be surprised to learn that their appetite for meat and the U.S. government's lending policies were the root causes of this bloody war.

Elsewhere in Central America, environmental and political crises in both rural and urban areas helped increase unemployment, decrease per capita food production, and spread social unrest. In 1979, the situation boiled in Nicaragua, when Sandinista insurgents overthrew Anastasio Somoza in a struggle that shook U.S. policy throughout Latin America and galvanized revolutionary movements in El Salvador and Guatemala. In El Salvador, the U.S.-backed Salvadoran Army fought determined urban and peasant guerrillas and initiated reforms to win the support of rural families who provided food, supplies, and recruits for the guerrillas. Meanwhile, government officials and U.S. advisors discussed reforms in a land-tenure system that had placed most of the nation's farmland in the hands of a tiny elite, while a growing mass of *campesinos* grew beans and corn on eroding hillsides and waited for day labor harvesting coffee or cutting sugarcane.

As Central America's insurgencies increased in strength and number, the United States responded by expanding military aid and sending more advisors. U.S. attempts to counter insurrection multiplied during the early 1980s, and military aid to the region mushroomed to $300 million between 1981 and 1983.[16] To defuse the underlying conflicts, the National Bipartisan Commission on Central America, headed by Henry Kissinger, in 1984 called for a five-year, $8 billion economic development program for the region. The commission urged increased military aid to Honduras, El Salvador, and Guatemala and to the Honduran-based *contras* attempting to reverse the Sandinista revolution.

The "Kissinger Commission" pointed out that, "The crisis in Central America cannot be considered in solely economic or political or social or security terms. The requirements for the development of Central America are a seamless web." Wisely, it proposed agricultural development to counter the social and ecological problems that spurred Central America's revolutionary movements. The commission concluded that these efforts should focus on "historically neglected" local food producers, noting the enormous potential for improving the welfare of large numbers of people, while simultaneously increasing and diversifying agricultural production and dampening dependence on food imports.[17] The commission's report specifically called for increased credit to small farmers, better rural land-titling procedures, agrarian reform programs, expansion of rural roads and electrification, and clarification of the legal status of public lands to check deforestation and degradation of the environment. Unfortunately, the report earmarked no funds for these crucial efforts, as it did for military assistance and general economic development.

Because most previous U.S. development programs for Central America have focused solely on macro-economic objectives, the commission's report broke new ground by at least discussing agricultural needs. But the commission failed to emphasize the link between the increasing damage to Central America's renewable resource base and the region's political and social dynamic. This "seamless web" that the commission mentioned must be anchored somewhere or it won't hold, and in a developing region such as Central America the natural resource base is the mainstay. By failing even to recognize the frightening erosion of this resource base—let alone proposing to do much about it—the commission's recommendations fell substantially short of a serious agenda for progress and stability.

LAND TENURE AND AGRICULTURE

Central America's natural resource degradation is founded on complex problems that are easy to identify, but not to remedy. These problems stem from agricultural trends: an ever-expanding need for additional agricultural land caused by expanding international markets for commercial crops, inequitable land distribution, and rapid population growth; a predilection for raising production by cultivating new land instead of by improving yields; and an emphasis by Central American governments, international development agencies, and multilateral development banks on export crops at the expense of domestic food production. Because these trends deplete Central America's forests, soils, and water resources, only some fairly radical changes offer much hope for genuine, sustained social and economic progress in the region.

Central America's natural resource problems arise partly from the region's two-tiered agricultural economy. As during the long centuries of colonial domination, a small fraction of the population controls the region's best agricultural lands. These flat, fertile farmlands primarily produce export crops—bananas, sugar, cotton, and beef cattle—and production is frequently inefficient because large sections of land remain uncultivated. Meanwhile, the burgeoning peasant population is relegated to small plots on hillsides and forested lands, where intensive deforestation, intensive crop cultivation, and overgrazing perpetuate the cycle of ecological harm. As such, the region fits the larger pattern of inequitable land ownership that characterizes much of Latin America.

The United Nations Food and Agriculture Organization (FAO) reported in 1975 that a mere 7 percent of Latin America's landowners possessed 93 percent of the region's arable land.[18] Within Central America, land tenure statistics differ dramatically from country to country, but in all countries much of the land is controlled by a small sector of the population. In Guatemala, 80 percent of the agricultural land is controlled by 2 percent of the landowners, while 83 percent of rural farmers live on plots too small to maintain a family.[19] As elsewhere in Central America, the poorest Guatemalan families support themselves by migrating to the Pacific coastal plain each year to harvest coffee, pick cotton, and cut sugarcane, the three major Guatemalan export crops.

In El Salvador, the number of landless peasants increased from 11 percent to 40 percent of the rural population between 1961 and 1975, reflecting both rapid population growth and the nation's increasing emphasis on the production of coffee, cotton, and sugarcane—export crops that occupy more than one-third of El Salvador's arable land.[20] As in other Central American regions, El Salvador's landless rural families continue to eke out a living as wage laborers on the nation's large plantations, few of which were touched by recent land reforms. Until a land reform program was initiated in 1980, 2 percent of El Salvador's population owned almost all of the nation's fertile land and 57 percent of total national territory.[21]

Even in Costa Rica, the nation generally regarded as having the most equitable socioeconomic structure in Central America, 54 percent of the land is divided into large farms of 200 hectares or more controlled by only 3 percent of the nation's landowners. These lands produce the export crops—coffee, bananas, beef, and sugar—that account for almost three-quarters of the nation's foreign sales.[22]

Honduras, according to a U.S. AID Country Environmental Profile published in 1982, "is characterized by a grossly unequal distribution of agriculturally productive land." Five percent of Honduran landholdings account for 60 percent of the nation's cultivated land. More than two-thirds of the Honduran population, according to the AID report, is comprised of "*campesinos* [who] are barely capable of a subsistence existence."[23] And even though most Hondurans work in agriculture, Honduras grows less food per capita than any other Latin American nation.[24]

Similarly, AID reports that the best but least cultivated agricultural lands in Panamá "are in the hands of a few powerful owners."[25] There, however, the problem of concentrated land ownership is diluted because two-thirds of the nation's farmers squat on national forest land, especially in the rapidly developing southeastern province of Darien. Following a government-approved settlement program, landless farm families are pushing the agricultural frontier farther into the rainforest rather than attempting to make ends meet on small plots surrounded by large landholders.[26]

Large landholdings, most of them owned by corporations, also characterize Belize, where they comprise approximately 60 percent of the nation's productive agricultural land. Most of these large holdings produce such export crops as sugarcane, citrus, and fruit, but some lands owned by absentee landlords are maintained strictly for speculation or rented in part to small-scale farmers.[27]

Only in Nicaragua does the Central American pattern of concentrated land ownership no longer apply. Before the 1979 revolution, the Somoza family alone owned 23 percent of the nation's agricultural land. Since the revolution, the Sandinista government has expropriated more than 1 million hectares—almost half Nicaragua's arable land—from the Somozas and other absentee landlords.[28] Fully 62 percent of the nation's land still remains in private hands, but in recent years basic food production was 20 to 25 percent higher than it was under the Somoza regime because farming has become more labor-intensive.[29]

Central America's underlying problem, inadequate land for small farmers, is compounded because neither ownership nor continued access to land is secure in most countries. Small farmers can't obtain clear title to the land they work, so why should they infuse capital or labor into land that may be expropriated any day? Small wonder that productivity throughout the region s so low. Forest destruction, meanwhile, is aggravated because the most effective way to demonstrate de facto ownership is to "improve" the land by stripping it of trees. As a result, areas that should be left in forest to contain erosion and to protect watersheds and reservoirs are cleared to establish ownership claims. Indeed, along the humid Caribbean coast, clearing forest is the primary strategy for claiming land.

Thus, unequal land tenure, insecure land titling, and population growth force landless peasants to colonize and clear lowland broad-leaved forests, primarily in the frontier regions on the Caribbean side of the isthmus. Most of these lands are ill-suited for agriculture. In some cases, Central American governments have even promoted tropical forest colonization, because it can temporarily defuse pressure for land reform. The governments of

Guatemala, Honduras, Nicaragua, Costa Rica, and Panama have all developed ambitious land-development schemes in remote tropical lowland areas to reduce pressure created by population growth and unequal access to land.[30]

This dynamic has reached its extreme in Costa Rica, where the push to colonize the forest frontier has apparently run its course. As geographer John P. Augelli has pointed out,

> Settlement has spread to both oceans and to Costa Rica's borders with Nicaragua and Panama. At present, all land is either privately owned or has been set aside for national parks, forest reserves, and other public uses. As a result, for the first time in more than four centuries of post-Columbian history, Costa Ricans have no easy access to new land, and the resulting "land hunger" is cause for conern.[31]

Augelli adds that "the end of the frontier coincided with an intensification of *latifundismo* [large farms], with greater importation of foreign capital and technology, and with the expansion of external markets—all of which tended to hasten the displacement of small holders. The chief culprit was the growth and modernization of the country's cattle economy, coupled with some expansion in sugar and rice production."[32]

EXPORT CROPS AND LABOR

Central America's large landowners cannot be faulted for seeking to maximize their profits, and government's promotion of cash crops makes sense, in the short term, because these farmers provide most of the region's export revenues. Various combinations of coffee, sugar, cotton, bananas, and beef account for roughly two-thirds of all export earnings in El Salvador, Honduras, and Guatemala.[33] But this imbalanced emphasis on agricultural exports encourages neglect of domestic food production and the long-term health of natural resources.

This imbalance is exacerbated by the incredible inefficiency of certain parts of the export-oriented agricultural sector—itself the consequence of allowing a small group to own most of the land. As noted, production on many large Central American estates is inefficient because considerable acreage remains uncultivated. According to agricultural economist Kempe R. Hope, "estates usually cultivate one crop on the most suitable sections of their total holding so that, while output per acre of cultivated lands might be high, output per acre of land owned is typically much lower."[34] Moreover, export crop producers tend to raise the crops that will earn the highest profits rather than the crops that are best suited to their land.

To make matters worse, at least half of all Central American landowners with more than fifty hectares own land primarily as a hedge against inflation.[35] They can leave acreage fallow and purposely limit investments in their productive lands because most have other sources of income (usually in the cities). Their land-use strategies, then, may have little to do with maximizing agricultural production on the best lands, which is of fundamental importance for the economic development of the region. If such uncultivated lands were left in forest, the decision not to cultivate might be wise. But all too often the owners clear and burn vegetation simply to prove to title-claim authorities that the land is being "used." Then, the burnt tracts become unimproved pastures for beef cattle.[36]

During the 1970s, for example, almost half the land on El Salvador's large farms was used as pasture, and another third lay fallow.[37] Meanwhile, with so little land to go around in that crowded nation, small holders were forced to cultivate their undersized, marginal plots as intensively as possible. A 1974 U.N. Food and Agriculture Organization study showed that Salvadoran farmers who owned 10 acres or less cultivated almost three-fourths of their land, whereas farmers with more than 86 acres cultivated only 14 percent.[38] In much of Central America the best lands are the most underutilized while marginal lands are stripped of tree cover to make way for crops and fuelwood production.

To supplement the miserable income from their small landholdings, Central America's rural poor often seek seasonal employment picking cotton or cutting sugarcane on large estates. By relying on landless or near-landless rural families for labor during harvest and planting seasons, large-scale producers keep labor costs down and save on the overhead costs associated with permanent workers.[39] Although both employers and employees have something to gain from such an arrangement, the employers fare best. As rural development specialist Cheryl Lassen has written, "if somehow subsistence farmers had enough land and were not compelled to go to the *fincas* [plantations], there would be a labor shortage and the agro-export system would be in danger. The whole agricultural economy—plantations and the *minifundia* [small farms] sector—works as a single system. . . [dependent upon] large concentrations of land and a large labor force at subsistence levels to harvest the surplus of the land cheaply."[40]

The prevailing system also ties the whole farm economy to capricious international demand. When demand for export crops expands, demand for labor also expands, and food production declines in the subsistence sector. The increase of Central America's banana production during the 1960s, for example, "caused the virtual disappearance of small farm agriculture" in the Costa Rican Atlantic lowlands, according to agricultural economists Peter Dorner and Rodolfo Quiros. While the acreage of land in bananas expanded by 31 percent over six years, corn production declined by an estimated 87 percent. According to Dorner and Quiros, small-scale agriculture collapsed when the emphasis switched to export crops because a typical family on a small farm "could increase its earnings substantially by working in a banana plantation rather than cultivating its own land."[41]

A similar dynamic characterized Nicaragua during the 1960s. There, cotton rapidly became the nation's leading export due to huge sales to Japan.[42] Farmers who rented or farmed small parcels without title were divested of their farms to make room for large-scale cotton production. In the end, small farmers were displaced and production in traditional grain-producing areas fell sharply, transforming Nicaragua from a net exporter of basic grains to a net importer. Such patterns are commonplace. "Expansion of the export sector," Dorner and Quiros concluded, "has frequently been accompanied by deficits in food crops which have created inflationary pressures and subsequently led to increased food imports."[43]

Unfortunately, subsistence food production does not bounce back when the export sector shrinks. Instead, dealers who sell abroad reduce food purchases from small-scale independent producers, and large landowners switch to more profitable export crops. Diversifying in this way, Central American banana producers have gotten into African oil palm, pineapples, and beef cattle.[44] When international cotton prices fell during the mid-1960s, large-scale producers in El Salvador shifted many sections

69

of land out of cotton into unimproved pasture. Although corn production also expanded on former cotton land during the same period, allowing El Salvador to meet almost all its own needs for this basic grain, a renewed availability of land worked by small farmers was not the reason. Rather, the big landowners held on to the land and turned to mechanized grain production and other technology that subsistence farmers couldn't afford. If anything, the small farmers' plight worsened.

In general, new technologies and chemicals are modernizing Central America's commercial export agriculture. But most of the region's food is still grown on family plots with traditional farming methods.[45] As a result, in Central America, unlike most of the rest of Latin America, agricultural production for international markets has been growing faster than production for internal markets. The region's harvest of commodities for the world market grew at an average of 4.6 percent a year from 1950 to 1975, while production for internal consumption advanced annually at only 3.4 percent. This dichotomy has become more pronounced during recent decades because governments have provided incentives and assistance for commodities produced for export, but have maintained price controls on basic foodstuffs.

Admittedly, export-oriented agriculture generates needed foreign exchange; but continued subsidization of this sector at very high levels comes at the expense of domestic food production, year-round employment opportunities, and attention to improved renewable natural resources management. Ultimately, it is the low level of productivity in subsistence food production that keeps wages so low in commercial agriculture. Accordingly, the region's most important economic development objective should be increasing production in subsistence agriculture. Even so, the export sector continues to receive the lion's share of financial and technical support from both national governments and international assistance agencies.

INTERNATIONAL DEVELOPMENT ASSISTANCE: THE BEEF-CATTLE INDUSTRY

Since World War II, multilateral development banks and bilateral development agencies have injected more than $7.5 billion in loans into Central America—with mixed success.[46] Agricultural development receives most of these funds, a total of more than $1 billion between 1980 and 1984 alone for agro-industry and producer marketing, irrigation systems, crop improvement, and livestock production and research. Although the World Bank is the world's largest single lender for agricultural development, in Central America the Inter-American Development Bank has provided most funds for agricultural development projects.[47]

According to the lender agencies and governments themselves, international funding for agricultural development in Central America helps increase and diversify crop production and raises per capita food consumption. But other observers counter that the prevailing development programs have destroyed subsistence food production, undermined the natural resource base, and sucked all agricultural lands into the commercial sector.[48] Instead of fostering self-reliance, these critics charge, "international financing has fostered greater *dependence* by encouraging increased imports, mainly from the United States."[49]

The most highly criticized international aid program in Central America has been that to expand the region's livestock industry. Since 1963, the World Bank has lent funds for cattle ranching to every Central American nation except El Salvador and has provided more credit for livestock, chiefly beef, than for any other agricultural activity. The Inter-American Development Bank also recognizes beef cattle production as "highly suited" to the region, noting that such production could help earn much-needed foreign exchange.[50]

Despite some claims to the contrary by lender agencies (who are increasingly sensitive to the criticism they have received), the World Bank and Inter-American Development Bank continue to fund projects to increase the region's beef exports. During 1984, for example, the International Bank for Reconstruction and Development of the World Bank Group put up $9 million toward a $25.5 million project designed to increase beef exports and decrease milk imports in Panama.[51] Similarly, in 1983 the World Bank approved the Third Agricultural Credit Project to Honduras to "reduce dependence on coffee and banana exports" and increase revenues "from exports of beef and tobacco."[52] During the past two years, other livestock loans have gone from AID to Belize, and from the Inter-American Development Bank to Belize, Honduras, and Panama.[53]

Criticism of the development banks' emphasis on cattle production has centered on two related developments: the use of large expanses of Central America's arable land for beef cattle, and the destruction of broad-leaved forests as beef production spreads into the Caribbean lowlands. During the past three decades, livestock production has absorbed an astonishing two-thirds of Central America's agriculturally productive land.[54] Lured by the lucrative U.S. market for imported beef (much of which ends up as hamburger meat sold by fast food franchises), Central American governments began to stimulate the beef-cattle industry during the early 1960s by providing cattlemen with low interest loans and cheap land. At the same time, the multilateral development banks and international development organizations provided generous loans for road construction, new meat-packing plants, and pest eradication.

In the industry's early years, Central America's cattle were raised along the region's Pacific coast. Because most coastal forests had already been cleared for food crops and export commodities such as sugarcane and cotton, the cattle industry's environmental impacts were not that severe. Eventually, though, the burgeoning beef market enticed cattlemen to the sparsely inhabited rainforests of the Caribbean slope, where a longer rainy season allows year-round growth of pasture grasses.[55] Now, ranchers are rapidly transforming rainforest into grassland.

The creation of pastureland for beef cattle has been the single most important cause of rainforest destruction in Central America since 1960. In Costa Rica, where 71 percent of all new farmland created between 1950 and 1973 was immediately devoted to pasture, ecologist Joseph Tosi has noted, rapid deforestation stems not from the expansion of farmland, but mainly from forest cleared for export cattle production. Moreover, says Tosi, because pastures require little hand labor "forest clearing for cattle production carries no benefit to poor *campesinos,* and does not help increase the production of grains and other food products in the country."[56]

Raising beef on cleared rainforest land is often doomed both ecologically and economically. Overgrazing, exacerbated by torrential rains, can turn pasturelands into weed-infested wastelands. Ranchers may be able to raise one head of cattle per hectare during the first years of production, but within five to ten years they may have to dedicate five to seven hectares of land to each cow.[57] After ten years of production, or even fewer, the cattlemen must move on in search of new forest lands if they hope to turn a profit. Existing pasturelands are still grazed under these circumstances but yields plummet as erosion, nutrient leaching, and insects take their toll.

Although the U.S. market for imported beef helped set Central America's cattle industry—and forest destruction—into motion, the United States is now gradually reducing its imports of the region's beef. Central American beef exports peaked in 1979 at 163,000 metric tons and have fallen since, chiefly in reaction to the Nicaraguan revolution. Many Nicaraguan cattlemen liquidated their herds as the Sandinistas gained the upper hand in the insurrection, and others drove their cattle across the border for slaughter in Costa Rica and Honduras. As a result, Central America's beef exports fell from 41 percent of the region's total beef production in 1979 to 23 percent in 1984.[58] Increasingly, Central Americans themselves are consuming the region's beef. The average Central American farmer continues to eat less beef in a year than a North American house cat, but many of the region's urban, middle-class families now consider *bifstec* a vital part of their diet. In Central American restaurants, a *plato típico* used to be rice, beans, and a vegetable; now it is rice, beans, and a steak.

The crux of the beef-cattle dilemma is inefficiency—not the wisdom of converting rainforests into hamburgers or steaks. Although it does earn foreign exchange, Central America's beef cattle industry is widely regarded as wasteful. Productivity, whether measured by yield per unit of land or real rate of return on investment, is low throughout the region. In Belize, for example, investments in commercial cattle production during the late 1970s and early 1980s yielded only 3 to 4 percent—well below the average return on investment in other agricultural pursuits.[59] Similarly, one FAO consultant concluded that cattle production in the northern forests of Honduras "is carried on more for social prestige than as a profit-oriented enterprise." Although most ranchers aspire to make a profit, the consultant noted, the poor condition of pastures, poor animal health, high operating costs, and low prices combine to wipe out any profits the rancher might gain. Many ranchers could not survive economically if they did not have other sources of income.

Ironically, without further absorbing arable lands or destroying forests, beef-cattle production throughout tropical America could be greatly *increased*. By some accounts, beef-cattle production could be raised four to five times and total meat production increased tenfold if pasturage were intensified and better animal-husbandry techniques adopted.[60] Similarly, some observers argue that Central America's food-production deficits will never be erased simply by converting more land and that the trick is using land now devoted to pasture more efficiently. A recent government study in Costa Rica concluded that the only way to increase that country's crop area is to reduce pasturage.[61] Nonetheless, in Costa Rica and throughout Central America, economic incentives, sociocultural inducements, and political realities continue to encourage cattle ranching over food production in many areas that could be producing food for the region's rapidly expanding population.

POPULATION GROWTH

Although Central America's increases in total agricultural land and total agricultural production could be considered positive developments, any optimism must be tempered because such increases have come at the expense of resource stability and without a corresponding increase in per capita food production. Absolute food production did increase in Central America between 1960 and 1980, but that growth was higher during the first of these two decades than during the second. Moreover, between 1960 and 1980, per capita food production in general grew by only 10 percent, and in Honduras and Nicaragua it actually declined.[62]

Two factors explain why Central America's agricultural land increased dramatically but per capita food consumption didn't. The more subtle factor is the dedication of the region's agricultural land to export agriculture, especially beef cattle. The other is painfully obvious: Central America simply has many more mouths to feed than ever before.

During recent decades, Central America's population as a whole has grown as fast as that of Africa. The populations of Nicaragua, Honduras, and Guatemala—60 percent of Central America's people—are expanding by about 3.5 percent per year. Growth rates are slightly lower in Belize (2.4 percent), Panamá (2.0 percent), and Costa Rica (2.7 percent), but Central America's total population will nonetheless double within 24 years.[63]

Although a growing proportion of the population may end up in the region's cities, where natural population increase and rural-to-urban migration add to existing problems of inadequate housing and underemployment, the absolute numbers of people who remain tied to the land will continue to grow rapidly for the foreseeable future. Most of Central America's population growth now occurs in rural areas, where 58 percent of the region's people reside. In mid-1984, more than 14 million women, men, and children were living in rural Central America, most of them forced to exploit natural resources for a living. As the region's rural population increases, demands on these resources will expand accordingly.

Population increase and natural resource destruction do not necessarily proceed hand in hand. But, usually, when populations expand rapidly in resource-dependent nations, serious environmental disruption results. This already has proved true in El Salvador and Costa Rica, where agriculture has consumed most of the unclaimed forest land and rapid population growth has fragmented family farms. As established farmland is divided among a family's children or among new farm families, plot size shrinks. In turn, increased demand leads to over-exploitation and shortened fallow cycles, which compound fertility declines and soil erosion. The sad truth is that throughout most of Central America, rural population growth condemns farm families to perpetual poverty and dooms natural resources to continuing degradation.

Ominously, Central America's populations are growing most rapidly in low-lying tropical forest regions, where soils are generally poor and where most of the region's remaining forests are located. Rates of population increase in these tropical forest regions are high partly because rural women tend to have more children than urban women. However, another factor is population shifts: tropical forest regions throughout Central America are being rapidly colonized by landless families from more populated agricultural areas and (especially in Costa Rica, Honduras, and Belize) by refugees from political strife in other parts of the region.

Given the region's current population growth rate, Central America's pattern of natural resource degradation will continue indefinitely. Even with rapid drops in birth rates, drops that five of the seven Central American nations have yet to achieve, the region's population will continue to expand well into the twenty-first century. As increasing numbers of Central American women reach childbearing age during the next few decades, even essential steps to reduce long-term population growth rates won't alleviate critical natural resource problems in the near future. The millions who will soon be clearing the forests, exhausting the soils, polluting the rivers, and altering coastal habitats in Central America are already with us.

Population increase alone is not responsible for resource degradation in Central America. To claim that population growth *causes* resource degradation is to oversimplify. As environmental writer Erik Eckholm has noted, "The uncontrolled spread of people over the landscape is obviously fueled by population growth, but skewed landownership, too, contributes to the problem."[64] Combined, population growth, inequitable land distribution, export crops, and land titling deficiencies prompt increasing numbers of rural families to migrate to cities or to colonize such environmentally sensitive areas as hillsides and tropical forests. If the pressure is severe enough, eminently renewable resources—most notably soil, water, and forests, can quickly become nonrenewable.

ECONOMIC, ENVIRONMENTAL, AND SOCIAL CONSEQUENCES

In Central America, socioeconomic trends have produced dramatic physical changes in the landscape. Vast areas still forested in the early 1970s have been cleared of vegetation; steep hillsides have been cultivated; and established agricultural lands overworked. In turn, stress on the region's natural resource base has created bewildering economic, environmental, and social problems.

Natural resources development has been inefficient: higher economic returns have been generated mainly by increasing resource consumption, not yield. Then too, resource exploitation has outpaced the ability of land, water, and forests to recover. Worst of all, the gradual degradation has undermined the social and economic welfare of the rural poor. Because these people can't improve their lives except by exploiting the renewable natural resources around them, it becomes harder and harder to break out of the vicious cycle.

The worst of the region's environmental problems are already producing significant economic—not just ecological— repercussions. Rapid deforestation is leading to degradation of soils, watershed destruction throughout much of highland Central America, and the creation of large wastelands in lowland rainforest areas. Soil erosion from deforested watersheds and poorly managed farmland is cutting back power production in virtually every hydroelectric project in the region and threatening to silt up reservoirs long before their time. Coastal harbors, lagoons, coral reefs, and critical mangrove breeding grounds are buckling under huge sediment loads washed down from deforested watersheds, requiring dredging, and destroying valuable marine resources. Critical coastal mangrove forests are being cleared for charcoal, lumber, and pastureland, with serious effects on commercial fishing and shrimping industries. As the region's renewable natural resources disappear, Central America's economies are increasingly precarious.

Throughout America, the amount of land given over to agriculture has expanded faster than in any other major region of the world.[65] But Central America differs markedly from the rest of Latin America on one crucial point: its agricultural growth is fueled almost exclusively by expanding the amount of land under cultivation and in pasture, whereas other Latin American nations have increased agricultural production largely through more intensive use of existing farmlands and pasture.

Between the mid-1960s and mid-1970s, the Latin American countries with the highest agricultural growth rates (above 2.5 percent annually) began increasing *yields* instead of the amount of cultivated land. Brazil and Colombia, for example, achieved high agricultural growth largely by intensifying production, even though both nations have large expanses of undeveloped land. By contrast, the seven Central American nations took the opposite approach, and their agricultural growth rates were lower. Clearly, the "frontier" approach to agricultural development has inherent limitations.

DEFORESTATION

Deforestation is at the heart of Central America's natural resource dilemma. In 1960, more than 60 percent of Central America was forested and 25 percent was dedicated to cultivation and livestock. Twenty years later, forested land had declined to only 40 percent of the region's territory, while the amount of cultivated land had grown to 35 percent (two-thirds of which was planted in pasture for livestock).[66] By now, nearly two-thirds of Central America's original forests have been eradicated.

The rate of deforestation has increased every decade since 1950 and shows no sign of slowing.[67] Nicaragua lost more than 1,000 square kilometers of its broad-leaved and coniferous forest each year during the 1970s and 1980s. In Honduras and Guatemala, human activities are destroying at least 900 square kilometers of forest each year, while Panama annually loses 650 square kilometers and Costa Rica, 500 square kilometers. Only Belize, with its small population and low agricultural activity, has been spared such rapid deforestation; but it, too, loses 90 square kilometers of forest each year.[68] In El Salvador, forests are mostly a memory. The tropical forests that once blanketed more than 90 percent of that nation have been cleared for export crops, subsistence farms, pastures, and charcoal production, leaving only a single 20 square kilometers plot of cloud forest relatively undisturbed.[69]

In part, because the forests of the region's Pacific highlands were long ago cleared for agriculture, recent deforestation is worst in the lowland tropical moist forests, half of which have now been cleared and burned. In these forests, deforestation usually follows a three-stage pattern. First, roads are built, either for transportation or by logging companies and exploration teams seeking to extract commercial timber, minerals, or oil. Then,

landless farm families from outside the region or the country fil-
ter down these newly opened corridors in search of agricultural
land. They clear the forest to plant subsistence crops—maize,
manioc, and rice—and such cash crops as coffee, chiles, and bananas. After one to three years of harvests, however, weeds,
insects, and declining soil fertility tend to reduce the farmers' already low productivity, prompting them to clear additional
forest land. But instead of allowing their depleted plots to revert
to forest, they frequently devote the land to pasture for grazing
beef cattle. Or they sell the plots to cattlemen who consolidate
small clearings into beef ranches.

In such a fashion, road construction, slash-and-burn agriculture, and cattle ranching are replacing Central America's
lowland tropical forests at the rate of almost 4,000 square kilometers per year.[70] Combined with the continuing degradation of
highland deciduous and coniferous forests, this massive conversion of Central American forest land to croplands and grasslands
is the most dramatic, human-induced environmental transformation in the region's history.

Because forests contribute to the Central American economies directly through economic returns, and indirectly by
protecting ecosystems, deforestation threatens Central America's environment and economies in two ways. Although it may
produce income in the short run, converting forests to
pastureland or agricultural lands undermines the potential long-
term economic benefits that forests provide. Forestry and
forest-based economic activities have been neglected in the development of most Central American nations, and the region's
commercial forestry potential has been underutilized. Managed,
sustained-yield forestry has yet to be established anywhere in
Central America, and vast quantities of valuable timber are
felled and burned in place during every dry season. By some estimates, up to three-fourths of the hardened timber felled each
year in Central America is burned in place rather than harvested.[71] Commercial timber harvesting is economically important
only in Honduras, where primarily pine is logged; but each year
hardwood with an estimated commercial value of $320 million is
burned or left to rot after cutting in Honduras.[72] In addition,
large areas of mature Honduran pine forest worth $17,000 per
hectare have been cleared and burned to produce corn and beans

worth $1,000 per hectare over the three years such lands can sustain crops.[73] According to the U.S. Agency for International Development, at current rates of depletion Honduras' forest cover will be "virtually eliminated" within two generations, leaving "the one-third of rural Hondurans who live in or at the edge of the forests with no effective means for sustaining themselves through the life support system they presently have."[74] Forest destruction also obliterates potential income from such renewable forest resources as *chicle* gun and *xate* palm, both of which Central America exports.

Unfortunately, the region's forests are being eliminated to secure access to land of questionable value for any other purpose. Almost ironically, the soils that support lush lowland moist forests are thin and poor. Ninety percent of the nutrients in lowland rainforest are in the vegetation itself. Instead of absorbing nutrients from the soil, lowland tropical forests live off their own debris, rapidly recycling nutrients that fall to the forest floor. Truly one of nature's most successful ruses, a lowland tropical forest—like a beggar in an elegant suit—wears virtually everything it owns. Although a thick mantle of volcanic ash makes the Pacific slope's soils some of the most fertile on earth, a far larger percentage of the region's soils cannot sustain permanent agriculture. These shallow, rocky, acidic, poorly drained soils are far better suited for sustained-yield forestry or tree crops.[75]

Deforestation also destroys the indirect benefits that standing forests provide. Undisturbed, a tropical forest acts like a giant sponge, breaking the force of torrential tropical rains and allowing water to percolate slowly into the thin tropical soils. Gradually, the forest releases this captured water to the benefit of downstream agriculture. When tropical forests are cleared, however, precipitation rushes off sloped land and causes downstream flooding and soil erosion. In Honduras, deforestation and inappropriate upstream land use cost agriculture and infrastructure an estimated $3.5 million in flood damages annually in the Sula Valley alone. Flooding causes another $4.5 million worth of annual agricultural damage in the Aguan River valley, and in 1974 many of the 12,000 Hondurans who perished during Hurricane Fifi drowned.[76]

Deforestation has both local and far-reaching effects. It robs the soil of nutrients and makes it easy for topsoil to wash away.

Then, when millions of tons of exported silt accumulate in river beds, downstream flooding increases, the reservoirs behind hydroelectric dams clog, and coastal harbors, mangroves, and coral reefs are swamped. At Costa Rica's twenty-year-old Cashi hydroelectric dam, revenue losses caused by sedimentation have already reached $133 to $274 million. Similar losses have been noted at El Salvador's Cinco de noviembre project, and Guatemala's expensive new Pueblo Viejo-Quixal project is expected to have similar problems.[77] According to Frank Wadsworth, former director of the U.S. Institute of Tropical Forestry, deforestation of the watershed surrounding the Panamá Canal has added up to twenty-five feet of silt to at least one of the lakes that feed the Canal's locks. (Siltation rates in this lake doubled between 1969 and 1979). Noting that "only forests can restore and stabilize the capacity of the Canal," Wadsworth predicts that with deforestation the canal may by 1999, when Panamá will fully control it, become "a worthless ditch, a colossal monument to resource mismanagement."[78]

In the Amazon Basin, a single hectare of forested land loses only one kilogram of topsoil per year, while the same area cleared of forest may lose up to *34 tons* per year.[79] This is an extreme case, but serious erosion is occurring throughout upland Guatemala and Honduras and, increasingly, in these nations' newly colonized tropical lowlands.[80] In El Salvador, 100 percent of the land is said to suffer soil erosion. According to AID, land degradation is reaching crisis proportions in every Central American country except Belize.

Tropical forest destruction can also induce local and regional climatic changes that take a toll on agricultural productivity. Locally, deforestation causes more extreme fluctuations in surface temperature, making cultivated areas hotter by day and colder by night. More seriously, forest clearing can also reduce regional precipitation. In Panamá and Brazil, almost half the rain that falls on a lowland tropical forest is water recycled by the forest itself through evapo-transpiration. Forest vegetation breathes out water vapor equivalent to thousands of gallons per hectare per day. When the forest is cleared, this vast recycling system is destroyed and regional rainfall may decline by as much as one-third of an inch every year, markedly altering regional climate.[81]

MANGROVE DEPLETION AND FISHERIES

Central America's fishing industry, another renewable resource, is also falling victim to thoughtless resource exploitation. One grave problem is overfishing, particularly in nearby coastal waters. Fishing increased dramatically during the 1960s and 1970s in each Central American nation except Guatemala, although fish catches have stagnated or declined since then. Particularly critical is the decline in juvenile shrimp available in many parts of the region, because both commercial shrimp ponds and open water shrimp boats depend upon these for adult shrimp. Even more damaging than overexploitation is the continuing destruction and degradation of such crucial habitats as coastal estuaries, mangroves, marshes, and grass beds. Misuse of Central America's mangroves in particular threatens both current fish harvests and the further development of the region's fishing industry.

A mixture of sixty species of trees and shrubs, mangrove forests grow between the high and low tide levels along protected tropical coasts, in the littoral zone where fresh and ocean water mix. They form the border between oceans and tropical forests, reducing coastal erosion by stabilizing the edge between land and water and creating new land by gradually colonizing the sea. Central America's coastlines support almost 9,000 square kilometers of mangrove forests, comprised mostly of three species of mangrove tree. Panama alone accounts for more than 50 percent of this resource.[82]

Central Americans fell mangroves for fuelwood and charcoal, for construction materials and fence posts, and for the mangrove's bark (a prime source of tannin). Combined with the expansion of urban areas and pastureland—especially in Panama—these activities are rapidly decreasing mangroves in Guatemala, El Salvador, Honduras, Costa Rica, and Panama. Along the coast of El Salvador, clear-cutting for fuelwood and charcoal has transformed productive mangrove forests into dry, unproductive wastelands; much the same applies in Guatemala. In some areas, the insidious effects of siltation of pesticide residues only compound the threats to mangroves.

Mangrove depletion is especially lamentable because mangroves harbor high-protein food. During their postlarval and juvenile stages, marine shrimp, for example, depend highly on mangrove estuaries. Even more important, mangrove forests provide vital nutrients to the shallow bays, inlets, and channels where many of Central America's main commercial and subsistence fish species live. Some researchers believe that mangroves are linked to the life cycle of 90 percent of all tropical fish species.[83]

As Central America's mangroves shrink, so will the fish catch. Already, the eastward expansion of Panama City into the Juan Díaz mangrove forest is threatening a local fishing and shrimping industry valued at more than $1 million per year.[84] Throughout the region, the fishing industry's success or failure depends on the protection and survival of coastal mangrove forests.

THE HUMAN SIDE OF RESOURCE DEGRADATION

Resource degradation in Central America also hurts the region's rural populations. Many rural families in Central America already live in desperate poverty—at least one-half of those in Honduras, one-third in El Salvador, and one-quarter in Guatemala.[85] The further impoverishment of the region's natural ecosystems cannot help but further impoverish these nations' rural communities.

Along with inequalities in the size of agricultural holdings and with land-tenure patterns that leave large numbers of families landless, natural resource degradation pushes rural families into national forests, cities, and other countries. In those Central American nations where a forest frontier still exists, many rural families migrate into the lowland forest, perpetuating the ongoing pattern of resource depletion. Where little new land is available, migrating farm families often settle in the burgeoning shantytowns that ring Central America's cities. This influx of rural citizens has swamped the regional governments' and private investors' considerable efforts to provide adequate housing and employment. Lacking enough potable water and any access to sewage and water treatment facilities, these dense communities of underemployed urban squatters pose—and face—environmental and political problems of their own.

83

Equally disruptive is the movement of rural families from one Central American nation to another. During the past decade, tens of thousands of Central Americans have been displaced by political turmoil, natural disasters, and economic and environmental crises. Some of these refugees flee into neighboring countries: Guatemalans into Mexico and Belize; Salvadorans into Belize and Honduras; and Nicaraguans into Honduras and Costa Rica. But the United States has become the final destination of many. Each year, thousands of Central Americans migrate, legally and illegally, to the United States searching for better conditions. As Central America's natural resource problems increase, so will this tide of immigration.

Finally, Central America's natural resource problems may combine with other problems to prompt rural families to support groups rebelling against the region's political, economic, and environmental conditions. As Earthscan researchers Lloyd Timberlake and Jon Tinker have pointed out, the strength of Central America's guerrillas is based largely on the support they receive from otherwise apolitical peasants, "whose inability to feed their families from a deteriorating agricultural base encourages them to insurrection."[86]

THE SEARCH FOR SOLUTIONS

It would be naive to conclude that the current economic and political turmoil in Latin America is directly caused by natural resource degradation. The violence and economic stagnation that mar Central America's struggle for democracy and economic progress have their roots in political beliefs and economic maneuverings that are complicated by racial frictions and outside interference. Yet, the ongoing mismanagement of natural resources does exacerbate the economic atrophy and violence and, at least in El Salvador, has helped foment political violence. As a 1982 AID report on El Salvador noted, "The fundamental causes of the present conflict are as much environmental as political, stemming from problems of resource distribution in an overcrowded land."[87] It hardly seems surprising that conflicts would emerge in a region where most productive farm land is controlled by a small percentage of the population; where export crop production that benefits the wealthy few is increasing while per capita food production is declining; where natural ecosystems are being severely degraded; and where population stands to double in twenty-four years.

Defusing Central America's crises will require changes in all spheres of Central America's life—political, economic, and social. Yet, if current patterns of natural resource abuse are not simultaneously altered, potential improvements in other spheres will be stillborn. In the words of natural resource specialist Gerardo Budowski, "Action to correct the grave imbalances between human populations, resources, and environment must go hand in hand with struggles against the injustices of social and economic systems."[88]

Because the economic well-being of most Central Americans depends upon the products they glean from the region's natural resource systems, maintaining and improving these systems emerges as the region's single most important priority. In the past, development assistance efforts have focused on increasing economic production by opening additional lands and encouraging faster exploitation of natural resources. Now the emphasis must shift to increasing production by intensifying food production and employment on lands well-suited for agriculture, providing jobs for the remaining landless in a growing and balanced economy, and slowing population growth. Simultaneously, the Central American nations *must* protect watersheds and productive forests, and preserve representative areas of endangered ecosystems in national parks, biosphere reserves, and other conservation units—as Costa Rica, to its credit, has already done.

Because agriculture is so critical to economic production, export earnings, and employment in Central America, intensifying production is at the top of the agenda. The most important first step would be to end gross subsidization that encourages extensive, low-productivity cattle ranching in areas better suited to crop production or forestry. Because extensive livestock grazing exacts such a severe environmental toll and returns so few social and economic benefits, governments and international development agencies should no longer underwrite it. Development organizations should redirect funding away from beef-cattle production toward sustained-yield production of agricultural crops and noncattle livestock.

Where the livestock sector is to be supported, the goal should be intensified beef production on land already cleared through grazing, forage feeding and combined farming, forestry, and pasture systems. At the same time, Central American meat consumption could be increased by emphasizing the small-scale production of such animals as pigs, chickens, rabbits, goats, and fish, which are much more metabolically efficient than cattle. (A cow must eat around eight pounds of food to gain a pound. The figure for chickens is between two and three pounds; for fish, under a pound and a half.) Added emphasis on these "lesser" domestic species can help supply protein-rich food, provide rural employment, and improve environmental management.

The greatest emphasis, however, should be on improving crop-production systems. As Pierre Crosson of Resources for the Future has indicated, "The approach most likely to reduce pressure on the land in developing countries is research to develop new, yield-increasing technologies . . . [that permit] production [to be concentrated] on fewer and less erosive acres."[89]

The challenge to the scientific community and to development agencies is to help create sustained-yield agricultural systems that improve rural life in Central America by increasing food-crop and export-crop production on land already cleared. Accordingly, rural families must receive the technical and financial support they need to produce these products without continually having to clear forests and otherwise impoverish their natural resource base.

Fortunately, some of the techniques demanded by such goals are already proven. Tropical *chinampas* (plots built on soil containing organic debris, usually dredged from lakes or swamps), hillside terracing, and agroforestry, for instance, are all both ecologically and economically sound when farmers receive the political and technical support they require. The secondary benefits of increasing the productivity of Central America's small-scale farmers with such techniques will reverberate throughout the region. Wages for labor in commercial agriculture will have to rise commensurately as the productivity of subsistence farmers increases. Increased rural incomes may, in turn, help staunch the flow of migrants into cities and abroad and encourage slower population growth. Finally, with greater potential benefits at stake, the region's small-scale farmers will have greater incentives to invest in careful land-management and conservation practices.

Politics aside, ecologically sound, sustained-yield tropical agriculture has its problems. One is how to strike the right balance onary ? food-crop and cash-crop production. Ultimately, governments have to weigh the need to produce food for domestic consumption with the need to produce foreign exchange by exporting agricultural products. In the past, export crops consistently have received top billing, but demographic conditions alone call for a re-evaluation. The best hope for both small farmers and governments in Central America seems to be a combination of food production for subsistence and tree-based cash crops to produce income in an ecologically sound manner. Convincing small farmers to adopt these new methods is easier than many observers believe. Farmers will adopt new agricultural systems when they are convinced, by successes they can see, that these systems will increase production and profit.

Other problems with agricultural intensification are providing adequate credit to small-scale producers and finding (or creating) markets for their crops. In many cases, market transportation systems must be improved or developed. Fortunately, none of these formidable problems is insurmountable if national and international agencies give sufficient political and economic support. Social complications—not technical problems—consistently have been the major obstacles to developing sustainable agroecosystems. As agricultural ecologist Stephen R. Gliessman puts it, "We can demonstrate the soundness of a variety of agroecosystems, but we keep running up against political constraints." The long-term task, Gliessman says, is to demonstrate repeatedly "that [sustained-yield agricultural] systems work, that they are ecologically sound, and that they are competitive." In the meantime, he concludes, we have to train a cadre of agroecologists who will be ready to step in when disasters now brewing erupt.[90]

Most of the political barriers to transforming Central American agriculture involve access to land. To develop sustained-yield cropping systems, the region's families simply must have land to farm—ideally, the most productive land. But landowners are not easily convinced to surrender profitable holdings to conserve natural resources and improve the lives of small-scale farmers. Nonetheless, as resource analyst Erik Eckholm notes, "For both political and economic reasons, societies cannot afford to maintain land tenure systems that are at once inequitable and inefficient."[91] The Central American governments and international development agencies will eventually find that they must conduct land reform programs—no matter how politically difficult. The only alternative is a flood tide of migration to the forest frontier or into already overflowing cities. As Eckholm says:

> It is a delusion to think that the basic needs of the world's poorest people will be met without renewed attention to politically sensitive land tenure questions. It is an even greater delusion to think that the dispossessed of the earth will watch their numbers grow and their plights worsen without protesting.[92]

Of course, land reform and agricultural intensification will go nowhere without land titling. Without clear title to the land they farm, families have no incentive to invest the time and money required to develop productive, sustained-yield systems. Here, too, proponents of change are at loggerheads with established landowners and some government officials. The temptation is for governments to redistribute and provide title to land in uncontested or nonproductive areas—the basis of some land reform movements in Central America.

In 1961, for example, Costa Rica's Instituto de Tierras y Colonización was established to redistribute land to landless *campesinos.* The expectation was that much of the land for redistribution would come from virgin forest areas still in the public domain. By 1983, the program had distributed about 800,000 hectares to 22,000 farm families. But the program's director noted that the more land his office distributed, the more would-be farmers expected and demanded. More unsettling, says geographer John P. Augelli, is the poor quality of the "new" land and the isolation of the colonists. With little capital, third-rate social services, and large powerful landholders deadset against land reform, most colonists faced debt and despair.[93]

Land reform in Honduras has not fared any better. According to AID, "the land distributed . . . has been described as predominantly marginal land, characterized by steep grades and susceptibility to erosion." Moreover, the same report notes, "the rate of new land settlements per year is just about equal to the annual increase in the rural population." Overall, the Honduran land reform has had little net effect on the extent of *minifundia* or landlessness.[94]

El Salvador's land tenure situation did improve somewhat between 1980 and 1984 when U.S. officials helped Salvadoran agencies redistribute 3,317 square kilometers of land to the benefit of more than 440,000 rural men, women, and children. But, the crucial second and third phases of redistribution never occurred, and AID reported in 1984 that much of the land redistributed was too rocky, swampy, or steep to farm or develop. On the good land redistributed, agricultural production dropped by 10.4 percent per year due to violence, credit limitations, poor financial administration, and marketing problems.[95] According to MIT anthropologist Martin Diskin, loopholes and the small amount of land redistributed "make it plain that no significant restructuring of rural El Salvador is possible with this plan and that profound rural misery will not end."[96]

Fortunately, other attempts to restructure life in rural El Salvador are more promising. During late 1984, the nation launched an ambitious development project aimed at benefitting small- and medium-scale farmers through soil conservation, reforestation, irrigation, drainage works, and purchase of farm machinery—a project funded by a $40.5 million Inter-American Development Bank loan. How well this initiative succeeds in troubled El Salvador remains to be seen.

The obvious solution to the region's land-distribution problem is to continue to allocate productive agricultural lands to land-poor families and to follow up with adequate investment, agricultural research, and agricultural extension work. As environmental researchers Edward Wolf and Lester Brown point out, "Land redistribution without guidance and energetic agricultural assistance erodes the wealth it intends to create."[97] If the status quo in today's Central America does not change, the whole hemisphere will have to accept the demographic, economic, and resource-related consequences.

Even in the face of this admonition, however, proponents of change must remember that land reform alone will not extinguish poverty. Distributing farmland more equitably can increase employment and self-sustaining economic progress only if it is accompanied by family planning. International agencies that promote land reform and land titling must also realize that land redistribution is a stopgap measure as long as population growth continues unchecked.

So far attempts to control population growth directly have been fraught with problems, especially in largely Catholic nations where agriculture is the primary means of employment. Farm families, especially tenants, produce large numbers of children as a survival mechanism, and as long as a family's primary means of increasing agricultural labor is by increasing the number of children, fecundity will continue to increase.

To be sure, population growth will slow only if economic conditions and education are bettered. As World Bank analysts have noted, "Fertility is consistently and inversely related to household income and to education."[98] In the end, a combination of general socioeconomic development and voluntary family planning programs is the most promising course of action for the Central American nations.

Diversifying production and employment that don't stem from natural resources is another alternative for Central America. If the tens of thousands of rural families now flooding Central America's urban areas could be put to work in productive, lucrative jobs, this migration could help both the region's people and its renewable natural resources. But, as demographer Robert Fox points out, Central America will have to create more than 311,000 jobs each year between now and the turn of the century to keep up with population increases in the region's urban areas.[99] No one knows where these jobs will come from and as things now stand, it is doubtful that enough jobs will be created to employ existing urban populations. Clearly, development assistance organizations and national governments must help stimulate sharp increases in rural off-farm employment opportunities in coming years.

Programs to provide rural off-farm jobs can actually complement agricultural production increases and encourage farmers and industries to use and better manage natural resources. Direct assistance programs and indirect incentives to help small entrepreneurs develop rural nonagricultural enterprises complement agricultural development because they provide valuable agricultural goods and services—farm implements, seeds, transportation, and so forth. Frequently, they also draw upon local agriculture for raw materials—among them, food processing, textiles, handicrafts.

Some of the most effective rural employment and public works programs give people the chance to earn a daily living by improving or restoring the land's long-term productive potential. Building and repairing terraces and small-scale irrigation systems, reclaiming lands, reforesting denuded watersheds, and other such activities create jobs and protect resources. Indeed, a recent AID manual on rural employment noted that conservation and reforestation projects are among those with the greatest potential for creating jobs and long-term economic benefits.[100] Such programs also would serve Central America by conserving watersheds that feed the reservoirs essential for irrigation, hydroelectricity and municipal water supplies.

Protecting the region's cornucopia of flora and fauna is equally important to Central America—economically as well as ecologically. Much as the discovery of diosgenin in the Mexican barbasco vine (*Dioscrorea composita*) led to the development of oral contraceptives and became the basis for a prosperous industry in Mexico, additional beneficial species also await discovery in the tropical forests of Central America. Tourism, a potentially important industry, is also difficult to promote in a country whose lush forests and wildlife are all gone.

Of course, conservation of the region's endangered ecosystems can't be at the expense of human needs in Central America. Local populations must be compensated for the loss of the immediate benefits of forest clearing. It may also be wise to give Central American debtor nations discounts and credits against international debts if they agree to protect their remaining natural resources—a world heritage—in exchange.[101] It's also essential that local populations share more in the creation, operation, and profits of protected watersheds. As Mexican ecologist Arturo Gomez-Pompa has written, "It is totally wrong to earmark an area as a 'nature reserve: keep out,' and have it policed, while multitudes of starving peasants in the vicinity are looking for a suitable spot to plant next season's crop. This colonialist approach to conservation is doomed to failure."[102]

Overall, Central America's renewable natural resources are embattled but not doomed. Progress is visible on numerous fronts: declines in some nations' population growth rates; successful experiments in agricultural intensification; and more and larger parks and forest reserves. With redoubled efforts and support of both local and international agencies, the region's natural resources could be put back on an even keel. Yet, only when Central America's governing elites and the decision-makers in international development agencies realize that further steps in this direction are in their own best interests will the needed "amalgam of environmental protection and economic development" that World Resources Institute board member Robert O. Blake has called for materialize.[103] Concern for Central America's people and U.S. self-interest converge happily in efforts to restabilize the resource base in Central America, but hesitation may cost the hemisphere much of its heritage and its economic future.

NOTES

1. Murdo MacLeod, Jr., *Spanish Central America: A Socioeconomic History 1520–1720* (Berkeley: University of California Press, 1973) 46–47, 49.

2. Robert Wasserstrom, *Class and Society in Central Chiapas* (Berkeley: University of California Press, 1983) 209.

3. Eduardo Galeano, *Open Veins of Latin America: Five Centuries of the Pillage of a Continent* (New York: Monthly Review Press, 1973) 119.

4. Walter LaFeber, *Inevitable Revolutions: The United States in Central America* (New York: W.W. Norton & Company, 1984) 54.

5. See Thomas McCann, *An American Company: The Tragedy of United Fruit* (New York: Crown Publishers, 1976) and Thomas L. Karnes, *Tropical Enterprise: The Standard Fruit and Steamship Company in Latin America* (Baton Rouge: Louisiana State University Press, 1978).

6. LaFeber, *Inevitable Revolutions,* 70.

7. James J. Parsons, "Cotton and Cattle in the Pacific Lowlands of Central America," *Journal of Interamerican Studies,* vol. 7, no. 2: 149–160.

8. Roger Burbach and Patricia Flynn, *Agribusiness in the Americas* (New York: Monthly Review Press, 1980) 144.

9. Julio Cesar Molina, "Nicaragua: La Revolución agraria en marcha," *Agro-Noticias* (Lima, Peru, 1980), no. 14.

10. Dirección de Planificación Nacional (DPN), República de Nicaragua, *Potencial de desarrollo agropecuario y rehabilitación de tierras en la Costa Atlántica-Nicaragua* (Tecnoplan, S.A., Managua and Tahal Consulting Engineers, Ltd., Tel Aviv, for the DPN, 1978), vol. II:B–55.

11. Centro de Investigación y Estudios de la Reforma Agraria (CIERA), *La Mosquitia en la revolución,* Colección Blas Real Espinales (Managua: CIERA, 1981) 98.

12. "Somoza's Legacy of Greed," *Time,* vol. 114, August 6, 1979: 37.

13. See Robert C. West, "Recent Developments in Cattle Raising and the Beef Export Trade in the Middle American Region," *Proceedings of the 42nd International Congress of Americanists,* 1976, vol. I, 391–402; James J. Parsons, "Forest to Pasture: Development or Destruction?" *Revista de biología tropical,* 1976, no. 24 (Suppl. 1): 124; and Douglas R. Shane, *Hoofprints on the Forest: The Beef Cattle Industry in Tropical Latin America* (Washington, D.C.: United States Department of State, 1980).

14. LaFeber, *Inevitable Revolutions,* 182.

15. See William H. Durham, *Scarcity and Survival in Central America: Ecological Origins of the Soccer War* (Stanford: Stanford University Press, 1979); Thomas P. Anderson, *The War of the Dispossessed: Honduras and El Salvador, 1969* (Lincoln: University of Nebraska Press, 1981); and LaFeber, *Inevitable Revolutions,* 175.

16. *Congressional Quarterly,* December 31, 1983: 2, 775, cited in Jeffrey H. Leonard, *Natural Resources and Economic Development in Central America: A Regional Environmental Profile,* draft prepared for the International Institute for Environment and Development and the Regional Office for Central America, U.S. AID, 364.

17. Henry Kissinger et al., cited in Leonard, *A Regional Environmental Profile,* 40–41, 57.

18. Erik Eckholm, *The Dispossessed of the Earth: Land Reform and Sustainable Development* (Washington, D.C.: Worldwatch Paper 30, 1979) 11.

19. World Bank, *Guatemala: Economic and Social Position and Prospects* (Washington, D.C.: The World Bank, 1978) 12, 19.

20. Cynthia Arnson, *El Salvador: A Revolution Confronts the United States* (Washington, D.C.: Institute for Policy Studies, 1982) 7; and Tom Barry, Beth Wood, and Deb Preusch, *Dollars and Dictators: A Guide to Central America* (New York: Grove Press, Inc., 1983) 190.

21. Cynthia Arnson, "Background Information on the Security Forces in El Salvador and U.S. Military Assistance," *Resource* (Washington, D.C.: Institute for Policy Studies, March, 1980) 2; and LaFeber, *Inevitable Revolutions,* 10, 252.

22. U.S. Agency for International Development (U.S. AID), Costa Rica, *Costa Rica Country Environmental Profile: A Field Study* (San José, Costa Rica: U.S. AID, 1982) 6, 65.

23. U.S. AID-Honduras, *Honduras Country Environmental Profile* (McLean, Virginia: U.S.AID, 1982) 37.

24. "Latin American Farming: The Peasants' Lot is Not a Happy One," *The Economist* (London, 1982), vol. 282, no. 7219: 67–68.

25. U.S.AID-Panama, *Perfil ambiental del país de Panamá* (Washington, D.C.: U.S.AID, 1980) 12.

26. Stanley P. Heckadon and Alberto McKay (eds.), *Colonización y destruccíon de bosques en Panama* (Panamá: Asociación Panameña de Antropología, 1982).

27. U.S. AID-Belize, *Belize Country Environmental Profile: A Field Study* (Belize City, Belize: U.S. AID, 1984) 171.

28. Molina, 1980, "La Revolución agraria"; "Nicaragua," *Cultural Survival Quarterly,* 1980, vol. 4, no. 4:8–9; and "Consejo debate ley agraria," *La Prensa,* July 22, 1981: 1, 14, Managua, Nicaragua.

29. "Latin American Farming: The Peasants' Lot is Not a Happy One," 68.

30. Eckholm, *The Dispossessed of the Earth,* 29; Leonard, *A Regional Environmental Profile,* 102, 169.

31. John P. Augelli, "Costa Rica: Transition to Land Hunger and Potential Instability," in Katherine M. Kvale (ed.), *1984 Yearbook, Conference of Latin American Geographers,* 48.

32. Augelli, "Costa Rica," 52.

33. Leonard, *A Regional Environmental Profile,* 131.

34. Kempe R. Hope, "Agriculture and Economic Development in the Caribbean," *Food Policy,* 1981, no. 6:253–265.

35. Leonard, *A Regional Environmental Profile,* 138.

36. Mac Chapin, Comments on the Social and Environmental Consequences of the El Llano-Carti Road, Republic of Panama. In-house Report to U.S. Agency for International Development (Washington, D.C.: Latin American Desk, U.S. AID, October, 1980) 10; Philip M. Fearnside, "Deforestation in the Brazilian Amazon: How Fast Is It Occurring?" *Interciencia,* vol. 7, no. 2: 86.

37. Durham, *Scarcity and Survival,* 51.

38. United Nations Food and Agriculture Organization, *Agricultural Development and Employment Performance: A Comparative Analysis,* Agricultural Planning Studies No. 18 (Rome, 1974), 124.

39. Peter Dorner and Rodolfo Quiros, "Institutional Dualism in the Central America's Agricultural Development," *Journal of Latin American Studies,* 1973, vol. 5, no. 2: 222.

40. Cheryl A. Lassen, *Landlessness and Rural Poverty in Latin America: Conditions, Trends and Policies Affecting Income and Employment* (Ithaca, New York: Rural Development Committee, Center for International Studies, Cornell University, 1980) 148.

41. Dorner and Quiros, "International Dualism," 227, 228.

42. James J. Parsons, "Cotton and Cattle in the Pacific Lowlands of Central America," *Journal of Interamerican Studies*, 1965, vol. 7, no. 2: 153.

43. Dorner and Quiros, "International Dualism," 228, 229.

44. T. L. Martinson, "Rise of the Central American Beef Plantation 1960–1970," *The Geographical Survey*, 1974, no. 3: 1–13.

45. Edelberto, Torres-Rivas, "Central America Today: A Study in Regional Dependency," in Martin Diskin (ed.), *Trouble in our Backyard* (New York: Random House, Inc., 1984) 18.

46. Barry et al., *Dollars and Dictators*, 46.

47. Cheryl Payer, "The World Bank and the Small Farmers," *Journal of Peace Research*, 1979, vol. 16, no. 4: 294; Leonard, *A Regional Environmental Profile*, 390, 400.

48. Payer, "The World Bank and the Small Farmers," 298.

49. Barry et al., *Dollars and Dictators*, 11–12—emphasis supplied.

50. Michael E. Curtin, *IDB's Environmental Policy and Procedures* (Washington, D.C.: Inter-American Development Bank, mimeo, August 1983) 7.

51. World Bank, *The World Bank Annual Report 1984*, (Washington, D.C.: 1984) 122.

52. World Bank, Staff Appraisal Report, Honduras, Third Agricultural Credit Project, April 25, 1983. Projects Department, Latin America and the Caribbean Regional Office Report No. 4298-HO, 25.

53. Leonard, *A Regional Environmental Profile*, 412ff.

54. Parsons, "Forest to Pasture," 124.

55. Elbert E. Miller, "The Raising and Marketing of Beef in Central America and Panama," *Journal of Tropical Geography* (Singapore), 1975, no. 41: 68.

56. Joseph Tosi, *Los Recursos forestales de Costa Rica* (San José, Costa Rica: Centro Cietífico Tropical, 1972) 8.

57. Carlos Duahye, "Bajo rendimiento de ganado por hectárea," *Uno Más Uno* (Mexico City), February 20, 1979; Turner Price and Lana Hall, *Agricultural Development in the Mexican Tropics: Alternatives for the Selva Lacandona Region of Chiapas* (Ithaca, New York: Department of Agricultural Economics, Cornell University, 1983).

58. United States Department of Agriculture, *Livestock and Poultry Situation*, Foreign Agriculture Service Circular FL& P-2 84 (Washington, D.C., October 1984).

59. Winrock, cited in Leonard, *A Regional Environmental Profile*, 27.

60. Parsons, "Forest to Pasture," 128.

61. Secretaría Ejecutiva de Planificación, Sectoral Agropecuaria, *Diagnóstico del sector agropecuario de Costa Rica* (San José, Costa Rica: May 1982).

62. Leonard, *A Regional Environmental Profile.*

63. Charles H. Teller, "The Demography of Malnutrition in Latin America," *Intercom: The International Population News Magazine* (Population Reference Bureau, Inc., 1981), vol. 9, no. 8: 8.

64. Eckholm, *The Dispossessed of the Earth,* 29.

65. Inter-American Development Bank, 1983, cited in Leonard, *A Regional Environmental Profile,* 32.

66. Leonard, *A Regional Environmental Profile,* 153.

67. John Paul Lanly et al., *Los Recursos forestales de la América Tropical* (Rome, United Nations Organization for Food and Agriculture, 1981).

68. Lanly et al., *Los Recursos forestales;* James D. Nations and Daniel I. Komer, "Central America's Tropical Rainforests: Positive Steps for Survival," *Ambio,* 1983, vol. 12, no. 5: 232–238.

69. Howard E. Daugherty, The Conflict Between Accelerating Economic Demands and Regional Ecologic Stability in Coastal El Salvador. (Department of Geography and Institute of Ecology, University of Georgia, 1982).

70. Parsons, "Forest to Pasture;" Lanly et al., *Los Recursos forestales;* Nations and Komer, "Central America's Tropical Rainforests."

71. Leonard, *A Regional Environmental Profile,* 143.

72. Leonard, *A Regional Environmental Profile,* 212.

73. United States Department of Agriculture, Agency for International Development, *Forestry Activities and Deforestation Problems in Developing Countries,* U.S. Department of Agriculture, Forest Service, Office of Science and Technology, Development Support Bureau, Agency for International Development, PASA No. AG/TAB-1080-10-78, (Washington, D.C., 1980) 56–57.

74. United States Department of Agriculture, Agency for International Development, *Forestry Activities,* 55.

75. Leonard, *A Regional Environmental Profile,* 42–50.

76. U.S. AID-Honduras, *Honduras Country Environmental Profile,* 94.

77. Leonard, *A Regional Environmental Profile,* 239–242.

78. Frank Wadsworth, "Deforestation—Death to the Panama Canal," in U.S. Department of State and U.S. Agency for International Development, *Proceedings of the U.S. Strategy Conference on Tropical Deforestation* (Washington, D.C., 1978) 22–25.

79. Robert J. A. Goodland and H. S. Irwin, *Amazon Jungle: Green Hell to Red Desert? An Ecological Discussion of the Environmental Impact of the Highway Construction Program in the Amazon Basin* (New York:

Elsevier Science Publishing Co., Inc., 1975), reprinted from *Landscape Planning,* 1975, vol. 1, no. 2–3: 123–245.

80. Marc J. Dourojeanni, *Renewable Natural Resources of Latin America and the Caribbean: Situation and Trends* (Washington, D.C.: World Wildlife Fund-U.S., 1982) 91.

81. E. Salati, J. Marques, and L. C. B. Molion, "Origem e distribucão das chuvas na Amazônia," *Interciencia,* 1978, no. 3: 200–205; Warren Hoge, "Development is Eating Up the World's Rain Forests," *The New York Times,* August 31, 1980; and Suzanne W. Barrett, "Conservation in Amazônia," *Biological Conservation,* no. 18: 209–235.

82. International Union for Conservation of Nature and Natural Resources, *Global Status of Mangrove Ecosystems,* Commission of Ecology Papers, no. 3, Gland, Switzerland, 1983.

83. Lawrence S. Hamilton and Samuel C. Snedaker (eds.), *Handbook for Mangrove Area Management* (Honolulu: Environment and Policy Institute, East-West Center, 1984) 25, 26; Random Dubois, "Tropical Coastal Areas: Production vs. Exploitation," *Parks,* 1983, vol. 8, no. 1: 5.

84. Luis D'Croz and Bogdan Kwiecinski, "Contribución de losa manglares a las pesquerías de la Bahía de Panamá," *Revista de biologia tropical,* 1980, vol. 28, no. 1: 13–29.

85. Leonard, *A Regional Environmental Profile,* 144.

86. Lloyd Timberlake and Jon Tinker, "Soil and Trouble: Environment and War," *Not Man Apart,* 1985, vol. 15, no. 1: 12.

87. United States Agency for International Development, *Perfil ambiental de El Salvador,* draft version, 1984.

88. Gerardo Budowski, "Should Ecology Conform to Politics?" *Bulletin of the IUCN* (International Union for Conservation of Nature and Natural Resources) New Series, 1974, vol. 5, no. 12: 45.

89. Pierre Crosson, "Agricultural Land: Will There Be Enough?" *Environment,* 1984, vol. 26, no. 7: 16ff.

90. Stephen R. Gliessman, (ed.), *Agroecosistemas con énfasis en el estudio de tecnología agricola tradicional* (Cárdenas, Tabasco, Mexico: Colegio Superior de Agricultura Tropical, 1978).

91. Eckholm, *The Dispossessed of the Earth,* 41.

92. Eckholm, *The Dispossessed of the Earth,* 5.

93. Augelli, "Costa Rica," 56.

94. U.S. AID-Honduras, *Honduras Country Environmental Profile,* 42, 63.

95. U.S. AID-El Salvador, *Perfil ambiental,* 116, 173.

96. Martin Diskin, "Land Reform in El Salvador: An Evaluation," *Culture and Agriculture,* 1981, no. 13.

97. Edward C. Wolf and Lester R. Brown, "Seeds of Hope in a Dying Land," *Audubon,* 1985, vol. 87, no. 2: 106.

98. Nancy Birdsall (ed.), *World Development Report 1984* (New York: Oxford University Press, 1984) 170.

99. Robert W. Fox, *The Downhill Slope's Slope: Toward 2110 and Population Stabilization,* paper prepared for the Conference on Population for Non-Governmental Organizations held at the United Nations' Fund for Population Activities, March 10, 1982.

100. John Woodward Thomas and Richard M. Hook, *Creating Rural Employment: A Manual for Organizing Rural Works Programs* (from the Harvard Institute for Rural Development, written for U.S. AID, 1977).

101. Thomas E. Lovejoy III, "Aid Debtor Nations' Ecology," *The New York Times,* October 4, 1984, reprinted in *Focus* (Washington, D.C.: World Wildlife Fund-U.S., 1984), vol. 6, no. 6: 8; Jeffrey A. McNeely and Kenton R. Miller (eds.), *National Parks, Conservation, and Development: The Role of Protected Areas in Sustaining Society,* proceedings of the World Congress on National Parks, Bali, Indonesia 11–12, October 1982 (Washington, D.C.: Smithsonian Institution Press, 1984); and Jason Clay (ed.), "Parks and People," *Cultural Survival Quarterly,* 1985, vol. 9, no. 1.

102. Thomas Holzinger, "Preserving the Ecology in Tropical Areas," *R & D Mexico,* (Mexico, D.F.: CONACYT, 1982), vol. 2, no. 11: 29.

103. Robert O. Blake, "Moist Forests of the Tropics," *Journal '84* (Washington, D.C.: World Resources Institute, 1984) 47–48.

Figure 4.1

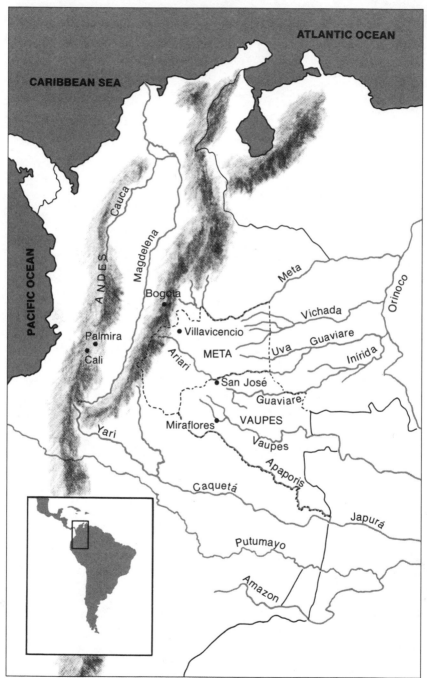

CHAPTER 4

Let Them Eat Rice?

ELIZABETH de G.R. HANSEN

—————————————*Editors' Preface*—————————————

The United States has been intimately involved for more than a generation in Colombia's economic development efforts. Every administration since Harry Truman's has had a hand in the events Elizabeth Hansen writes of in this chapter. U.S. private foundations and universities have been involved along with our aid programs, corporations, and banks. With the exception of the U.S. Public Law 480 program, which clearly was administered in President Johnson's day in the interests of U.S. wheat farmers, U.S. involvement in Colombia has been well intentioned and even magnanimous. We saw U.S. and Colombian interests in parallel—Colombia's economic growth was thought to be in our national interests, and the profitability of U.S. industries in Colombian interests.

Colombia's growth statistics over the past twenty years look good. With advice, encouragement, and pressure from the United States, Colombia's capitalized commercial agriculture has been greatly strengthened. New production techniques have caused rice to replace other food crops. It is now the major staple, the food of the poor.

On one level this is successful development, but with the advantages of hindsight, some of the negative consequences are more clear. Displacement of small farmers and rural unemployment leads, as in Mexico, to steady migration into the cities. Patterns of landownership are severely skewed as small landholdings are taken over by a small number of absentee landowners, most of them urban, who use the land inefficiently. Stripped of their land, poor farmers move on to clear the trees and bare the forest soils. Nutrition declines among the poor. The rural and urban poor, and the resource base, pay the price of national development.

These patterns are not unlike those found in Central America, Brazil, Peru, Ecuador, and Bolivia. As in many other Latin countries, violence in the Colombian countryside has been both the basis of continuing turmoil and the result.

Hansen's argument—that land tenure and rural unemployment are the true sources of poverty, environmental degradation, and political instability—is reiterated in other chapters in this book. She also makes clear how difficult it is, in both practical and political terms, to achieve land reform. More equitable land distribution is perhaps the single most widely needed reform in all of Latin America, and certainly the most difficult to achieve. Current rhetoric in the aid world about "support for the small farmer" is evidence that the United States has come full circle in the advice we give to others: just a generation ago, the watchwords were commercial agriculture and urban industrialization. This time the advice may be right, but it will not be easy to accomplish.

In addition to the financial interests of U.S. corporations and banks, the United States has three other legitimate continuing concerns in Colombia's achievement of sustainable equitable growth. There is Colombia's geography; it lies across the South American gateway to the Panama Canal. Second, is the possibility of further immigrants fleeing ecological degradation, poverty, and strife. For North Americans who think of our illegal immigrants as coming only across the borders from Mexico or by dangerously overloaded boats from Haiti, it may be important to note that Colombia has sent half a million immigrants to the United States since 1959.

And, third, 75 percent of the cocaine grown and processed in Colombia is exported to the United States. The profits to be made at every level on the sale of this drug are the primary driving force behind this major Colombian business. But the failure of Colombian traditional agriculture to sustain rural life must also be held responsible for the growing trade in cocaine, a trade whose health and criminal effects are clearly not in U.S. interests.

F ood production and the sustainable use of natural resources rank among the developing world's most pressing problems. By 1990, world demand for food will eclipse supplies by an estimated 120 to 145 million metric tons—three times the shortfall of 1975. Ten percent of this shortage will occur in Latin America, where uneven or stagnating agricultural growth rates are coupled with widespread rural poverty.[1] Inevitably, such conditions trigger migration to already crowded cities and unoccupied lands.

Recognizing that poverty, overcrowded living conditions, and agricultural stagnation may limit economic growth, the United States has in recent years greatly assisted agricultural development. Through its support of the Consultative Group on International Agricultural Research (CGIAR) the United States has encouraged a consortium of international agricultural research centers. CGIAR, established in 1971, promotes food security in developing countries through research on food crops for domestic consumption. Today, the United States and institutions receiving U.S. support supply another 50 percent of CGIAR's budget.[2]

The CGIAR has produced some of the most significant agricultural research in recent years. The high-yielding varieties (HYVs) of rice developed at the International Rice Research Institute in the Philippines and Centro Internacional de Agricultra Tropical (CIAT) in Colombia, and the high-yielding wheat developed at Centro Internacional de Mejoramiento de Maiz y Trigo in Mexico have been runaway economic successes and globally valuable research. Returns on investment in rice research through 1975 were up to 80 percent at the International Rice Research Institute and CIAT. New rice varieties yield about 40 percent more than traditional varieties, and increases for wheat were even greater. Introduced in the mid-1960s, HYVs were sown twelve years later in over one-third of the developing world's rice and wheat lands.[3]

According to the World Bank, most beneficiaries of HYVs are low-income consumers. Because production increases often lower prices, low-income consumers, who tend to spend proportionately more on food than do other consumers, can get more for their money. But the adoption of HYVs in Asia and Latin America has actually increased poverty by concentrating land, water, machinery, technology, and money resources among the wealthy. Thus, the World Bank concludes that while agricultural research "has been a powerful means to realize objectives of economic growth, particularly in better-endowed agricultural areas . . . it is a relatively blunt instrument when used in pursuit of distributional goals among agricultural producers."[4]

Emphasizing agricultural research and technology rather than development models, the World Bank's assessment is too pessimistic and simple. Agricultural research and technology per se is less important than the decision to use agricultural technology to further economic growth (based on industrial expansion). Social and ecological concerns must be considered too. Of course, agricultural technology can create wealth and social and ecological stability. But wealth and stability for whom? And for how long?

For Latin America, these are fundamental development issues. Here, the current growth model places production efficiency and wealth above social and ecological needs. Cheap staples allow industrial wages to remain low, but low food prices ensure neither a better diet nor food security. Instead, cheap food transfers wealth from the countryside to the city. This transfer, together with foreign food imports, provides a disincentive to produce. Ultimately, it threatens food security. Natural resources, land and people, are also threatened because people leave settled land for overcrowded cities, or they attempt new lives on distant frontier farms in the Amazon Basin. Since at least 1980, more than half the tropical forest destruction in Latin America has resulted from such migrations.[5]

The recent history of rice in Colombia demonstrates many of these trends. There, as in the rest of tropical Latin America, rice is the major green revolution crop. Between 1960 and 1980, Latin America's rice production increased by almost 85 percent. Indeed, by 1974, HYVs developed at CIAT in Colombia had increased Latin America's production by over 14 percent, more than the approximately 5 percent increase estimated for Asia in 1972–1973. Colombia's modern rice industry emerged largely from American and CGIAR investments in agricultural research and U.S. support for strengthening commercial agriculture at the expense of peasant farming.[6]

Dwarf varieties of rice introduced in Colombia in the early 1970s led to a 10 to 15 percent price decline. Because rice is now the main staple, low-income consumers reaped the benefits from investments in rice research. Indeed, although Colombia's lowest-income group receives only about 4 percent of national household income, it realized roughly 28 percent of rice research's economic benefits.[7] However, this gain is outweighed by Colombia's inequitable land distribution, inefficient land use, low rural wages, and low labor requirements. Since World War II, the gap between peasant farmers and the commercial farming sector (favored with the best lands, abundant credit, and agricultural research) has widened. But agricultural growth rates have stagnated or declined while agricultural imports and the potential for food insecurity have increased. Moreover, as the urban poor eat more rice, their overall diets deteriorate. The economic benefits the poor receive are more than outweighed by other more important losses and by the gains the wealthy enjoy.

The crux of Colombia's agrarian crisis is the historical refusal of the country's landowning elite to tolerate effective land reform. Colombia's elite repeatedly has substituted colonization schemes and technical solutions to increase production for agrarian reform. Colonization in the Eastern Andean frontier has destroyed tropical forests and increased rice production, but has not changed old patterns of land and wealth distribution. In Meta (see fig. 4.1), a frontier on Colombia's Eastern Plains (Llanos Orientales), new rice technologies and colonization made the region a major rice producer. But the best lands are often taken out of food production and unemployment pushes people further into the forest to work on coca fields. Without concern for equity and land reform, neither colonization nor agricultural technology will produce long-term benefits for Colombia's land or people. Indeed, their legacies are bloated cities, high emigration rates, intensified guerrilla activity, and other social tensions that threaten U.S. interests.

Predictably, Colombia's tunnel-visioned pursuit of growth and refusal to address social issues led to serious mismanagement of resources; nonetheless, Colombia's experience with rice is not an argument against rice growing, foreign assistance, or agricultural research. Instead, it provides insights into the roots of agricultural stagnation, political unrest, ecological degradation, and the relations among them.

Colombia is not the only Latin American country to send its landless poor to pioneer tropical frontiers. The cycle of frontier integration—land cleared by pioneer farmers and then incorporated into large and extensive farms or ranches—is found in Brazil, Peru, Ecuador, and Bolivia, as well as in Central America.[8] New rice varieties that can be grown in many tropical ecosystems, including the Amazon Basin's alluvial soils, threaten to accelerate a process that needlessly destroys human and natural resources. This vicious cycle can be broken through an attack on unjust land tenure and unemployment—the true sources of poverty, environmental degradation, and political instability. The current production-oriented approach to agriculture needs to be supplemented with research on farming systems that offer greater food security and sounder resource management.

THE LEGACY OF COLOMBIA'S AGRARIAN STRUCTURE

Colombia entered the postwar era with unresolved agrarian conflicts that erupted in eighteen long years of rural turmoil known as La Violencia (1948–1966). Unfortunately, U.S.-supported agrarian reform during the 1960s failed, and the country's agriculture became divided between commercial agriculture and small-farm production. Today, rice is the *only* major food crop grown in Colombia's modern commercial sector.

After Brazil and Mexico, Colombia has received more U.S. development aid than any other Latin American country. Between the end of World War II and 1973, Colombia received $2.5 billion in foreign assistance and development loans. Colombia poured these funds into internal security, the armed forces, and the expansion of hydroelectric works, paved highways, irrigation, and rural and urban development. During the 1970s,

Colombia's GNP grew by 4 to 9 percent a year, and by 1975 industrial growth, and export earnings from coffee and other agricultural exports, enabled the country to reject further U.S. assistance in favor of credit from private banks and international institutions.[9]

But, economic growth further slowed the distribution of Colombian wealth. In 1960, 5 percent of the population received 36 percent of the income; by 1970, the wealthiest 5 percent received 40 percent. Since then, labor's share of the national income has dropped farther because inflation has outpaced wages.[10]

In Colombia, industrialization and urbanization proceeded hand-in-hand. While just under 40 percent of the 1950 population lived in cities, some 65 percent were urbanites by 1981. Industry could not absorb all those fleeing rural violence and unemployment; thus, the economically active population industry rose only moderately, from 13 percent in 1950 to 15 percent in 1973. Although economically unproductive jobs in commerce and personal service absorbed large numbers of workers (22 percent in 1951; 35 percent in 1973), urban unemployment remained at over 14 percent. A recent study of Cali, one of Colombia's wealthiest cities, showed that 44 percent of the working population lived below subsistence level.[11]

Many out-of-work Colombians fled the country. By the mid-1970s, an estimated 250,000 Colombians or more had legally emigrated to Venezuela, the United States, Ecuador, and Panama. Estimates for illegal departures range from 3 to 6 percent of Colombia's total population. In 1979, an estimated 250,000 to 400,000 Colombians illegally resided in the United States alone.[12]

Those who stayed in Colombia produced marijuana and, later, cocaine. They joined a drug trade that in 1979 earned Colombia an estimated $3 billion a year, more than the combined income of all other exports, including coffee. Perhaps three-quarters of all these drugs are consumed in the United States, where they take an enormous toll on public health. In Colombia, the drug trade has intensified corruption and violence. Drug money permeates all levels of society and government—from bankers, politicians, and the military, to farm workers and housewives—and some of it is used to arm guerrillas in the southeastern jungles of Caqueta and Meta.[13]

Poverty, emigration, the drug trade, and political instability are rooted in unjust land tenure. While most of the population congregates in cities, the country's best agricultural lands are used to raise cattle, and fully half of the rural population lives on the Andean mountainsides. There is no shortage of land: Colombia has 113 million hectares, of which one-quarter is used for farming or ranching. Over half this land is in low-input—and low-output—cattle ranches, and only one-seventh of the land is in crops. The rest lies fallow or serves other uses. Of the cultivated land, only 1 percent is mechanized. Because cattle graze on the flat, central valley where farming can be mechanized, only about one-tenth of the land suitable for mechanized crop production is worked by machines.[14]

Colombian land use did not improve with the development of commercial agriculture. In fact, land given to cattle (instead of people) increased from 48 percent in 1950 to 56 percent in 1973, despite no increase in ranching productivity. Ranching provides little employment—only about 14 jobs per 1,000 hectares—and the population is too poor to create a broad internal market for meat. (Per capita meat production actually declined between 1957 and 1977, from 24 kilograms to 20 kilograms.) Instead, meat is exported at unfavorable terms. Colombia does not invest enough in ranching to compete with Australia, Argentina, or the Central American countries. In addition, Colombia's cattle suffer persistent hoof-and-mouth disease.[15]

Because Colombia's land holdings have become increasingly concentrated, cattle currently graze on lands that should be occupied by people. Almost three-quarters of Colombia's farms are smaller than ten hectares—too small to support a family. While such *minifundia* cover only 7 percent of the land in use, 0.7 percent of the farms are over 500 hectares and cover 41 percent of all land used. Colombia's smallest farms (less than 3 hectares) are concentrated on the erosion-prone hillsides of the western and southern highlands. (The Cauca watershed, for example, lost 40 tons of soil per hectare over a ten-month period, losses of a magnitude that will undermine agriculture within just a few years.) Of the 11,700 hectares opened in the Eastern Andes between 1951 and 1973, only 16 percent were used for crops. Ranches absorbed 54 percent of the land, and the remaining 31 percent are unused.

Almost half of this frontier land was swallowed by parcels larger than 500 hectares.[16]

This land-tenure system rests on historical settlement patterns and recent agrarian policies. Since the conquest, Latin Americans have suffered under conquerors' attempts to attach laborers to the land without losing its ownership. During successive and short-lived boom-and-bust cycles, food production has taken a back seat to the export of gold, tobacco, quinine, indigo, coffee, and other commodities. Food crops were not grown for export: they supplied the landed estates or the mines, dotted laborers' subsistence plots, or were grown by pioneering peasants (*colonos*).[17]

Indirectly, *colonos* have expanded Colombia's *latifundia* (large farms). Repeatedly, they migrated from large farms in the central valleys to clear forests and hillsides on state-owned lands. But few *colonos* received title to the farms they created. Far more often, the *latifundistas* claimed prior ownership, either evicting the *colonos* or forcing them to pay for their self-made farms on pain of dispossession.

To mitigate the perils of pioneering, Peasant Leagues had formed by the 1900s to help return the land to those who worked it. But neither of Colombia's two agrarian reforms during this century (1936 and 1961) made tenure more democratic. In each case, the poor received colonization schemes while the rich enjoyed increased investment and productivity.

La Violencia stemmed in part from the failure of the first land reform. In the 1930s, unemployed urban workers joined tenants and *colonos* in a struggle for land.[18] While conservative landholders demanded a massive emigration of the now surplus population to Colombia's eastern frontiers along the Amazon Basin and the Llanos Orientales of Meta, the liberal administration of Alfonso López Pumarejo legislated clearer titling procedures and increased productivity of *latifundia*. But tenants were evicted before their claims could be heard. In fact, the law helped create today's *minifundia* because tenants or pioneers bought small parcels of land from landowners or the state. And, to meet the productivity criteria of the new law and still further decrease their need for labor, many landowners put cattle on unused land.[19]

The assassination of the liberal reformer Jorge Eliecer Gaitan by conservatives in 1943 caused full-scale rebellion and class warfare. The conservative government's efforts to restore order only escalated the violence, as did regional rivalries between conservatives and liberals. The rural death toll during La Violencia was about 200,000. To escape with their lives, over 2 million small farmers, tenants, and others fled the countryside. Almost 400,000 small farms were abandoned between 1951 and 1964, and the proportion of rural residents declined from 61 to 47 percent.[20]

La Violencia also colored Colombia's development pattern, affecting the country's growth policies and agriculture/industry relationship. Import substitution and industrialization grew rapidly during the 1950s because development funds were channeled to urban capital-intensive enterprises. The institutional framework that modernized Colombia's *latifundia* and solidified the dual agrarian structure also began in the 1950s. With international assistance, the Ministry of Agriculture was established in 1947, and a Department of Agricultural Research was added in 1955. International loans provided the funding for constructing irrigation districts and importing farm machinery.

While small farms were being abandoned, liberal credit from the Agrarian Bank (Caja Agraria) and marketing subsidies boosted productivity on Colombia's large farms. Farmers were encouraged to produce coffee and sugar for export, new "industrial input" crops such as cotton and sesame, and cheap rice for the growing urban population.[21] But before these policies' impact could be assessed, the countryside had to be pacified and the agrarian question settled. Indeed, the ensuing counterinsurgency program and 1960s land reform owed much to American support and strengthening of Colombia's military forces.[22]

Signed in late 1961, Colombia's agrarian reform was internationally scrutinized by, among others, the U.S. Senate and the Canadian International Development Agency. But while Land Reform Law 235 made Colombia a showcase for the Alliance for Progress, the changes actually further concentrated land holding. As in 1936, political opposition ran high and financing proved inadequate. Moreover, as the military regained control of the countryside, the elite again pushed for frontier colonies and improved production technologies—instead of land redistribution. These landowners also opposed the U.N. Food and Agriculture

Organization's 1962 proposal to compensate wealthy expropriated landowners with land in Meta and the Llanos rather than with cash. Instead, the landowners succeeded in 1960, when a colony for peasant pioneers and guerrillas was established in the Ariari Basin in Meta.[23]

After 1964, the Johnson administration and other international backers of Colombia's agricultural development began supporting "the technical features of land reform under the Alliance for Progress, rather than the expropriation features written into the Charter of Punta del Este." The United States promised more assistance, but emphasized "colonization rather than parcelization, in an attempt to increase private investment in the agricultural sector by bettering the investment climate."[24]

These policy shifts appeared in the work of the Colombian Land Reform Agency (the Instituto Colombiano de Reforma Agraria, or INCORA). Originally, the agency had redistributed land in areas hard-hit by guerrilla and peasant rebellion during La Violencia. But INCORA ultimately became an agent of colonization. While 11 percent of the land cultivated in 1970 was incorporated into production on frontiers, INCORA purchased or expropriated only 0.25 percent of all cultivated land for redistribution. Moreover, INCORA had granted title to only 9 percent of all farms, and only 3 percent of all farms received INCORA credit. Because it cost an estimated $5,400 to establish a rural family on redistributed land in the central regions in 1963, compared to $8,000 to settle the same family in a frontier colonization project with only minimal amenities and services, the program was economical only for Colombia's elite.[25]

This limited land reform was abandoned in 1973. In the Currie Report of 1971, the World Bank had recommended further rationalization of agriculture by strengthening the commercial sector, eliminating the peasantry, and absorbing the rural poor into the urban labor force.[26] These recommendations coincided with the interests of Colombia's elite. Law No. 4 of 1973 weakened requirements for economic land use, the basis for expropriating *latifundia* since 1936. In addition, the Sharecropping Law of 1975 reversed earlier legislation that allowed tenants to acquire land once they had cultivated it peacefully for a time. This law essentially institutionalized the use of tenant or pioneer labor to establish *latifundia* and calmed landowners' fears of expropriation by abolishing tenants' usufructurary rights altogether.[27]

Even as this law took hold, the National Association of the Peasantry was repressed. From 1971 to 1974, the government-formed association had given more land to peasants and organized more peasants into cooperative farms than INCORA had in fourteen years (1961–1975). But once land reform was abandoned, the association lost its funding and the military was dispatched to force peasants off invaded lands and suppress renewed guerrilla activity.[28]

Law No. 5 of 1973 further institutionalized Colombia's dual agrarian structure. Under one provision, the Agropecuarian Finance Fund (Fondo Financiero Agropecuario, or FFAP) was created to support ranching and commercial and export crops with credit and technology. But with the emphasis on industrialization, overall public investment in agriculture declined from 21 percent of total spending (1965) to 11 percent (1973) during the 1960s and early 1970s.[29] Still, while the proportion of institutional credit given to agriculture declined from 27 percent in 1970 to 19 percent in 1975, support for commercial agriculture grew.[30] In Colombia, crops are classified according to whether they are "commercial" (sesame, cotton, rice, barley, sorghum, and sugar, grown on mechanized farms), "traditional" (beans, plantain, cassava, and brown sugarcane, grown on small peasant farms), or "mixed" (corn, potatoes, tobacco, and wheat, grown on both large, mechanized and small, unmechanized farms). Farmers of "commercial" crops were assured continued access to the best land, and consistently were favored with agricultural credit. Between 1967 and 1973, the "traditional" and "mixed" crops that cover 70 percent of all cropland received 12 percent of agricultural credit, whereas commercial crops received 88 percent. Similarly, between 0.1 and 1 percent of the area planted with "traditional" crops was financed, compared to between 34 and 59 percent of the area in "commercial" crops.[31]

After the Agropecuarian Finance Fund was created, the farmers who grew traditional food crops on small plots received even less credit. While the fund's share of total agricultural credit disbursals increased from 23 percent in 1973 to 43 percent in 1974, small farmers had to do business with the older Agrarian Bank, which charged higher interest rates. Even there, the proportion of small and medium farms receiving credit fell from 53 percent to 43 percent between 1974 and 1978.[32]

Figure 4.2 Colombia, Land Distribution, 1960–1970.									
Farm Category	Farm size (Hectares)	Number Farms (Thousand)		Distribution of Farms (%)			Distribution of Area (%)		
		1960	1970	1960	1970	Change	1960	1970	Change
Subfamily	0–5	757	700	62.6	59.5	−7.5	4.5	3.7	−7.5
Family	5–10	169	160	13.9	13.6	−5.6	4.3	3.5	−6.6
Commercial									
Medium	10–50	201	218	16.6	18.5	8.4	15.4	15.0	10.5
Large	50–200	63	74	5.2	6.3	19.3	20.8	21.8	18.9
Latifundia	200+	21	25	1.7	2.1	20.1	55.0	56.0	15.3
Total		1211	1177	100.0	100.0		100.0	100.0	

Source: de Janvry, A. *The Agrarian Question* . . . 135, from DANE, *La Agricultura en Colombia,* 1950–1970, (Bogotá, 1971).

Meanwhile, with international support, an Integrated Rural Development Program was established in 1975 to increase the productivity of small farms by financing new production technologies, especially the use of fertilizers and pesticides. However, this program essentially excluded close to half of Colombia's farms—those smaller than three hectares—on grounds that credit for such technologies was wasted on small, undersized, and eroded farms. In some areas, even the credit disbursed to farms under twenty hectares didn't cover the costs of producing new, untraditional crops (such as tomatoes) or the traditional brown sugarcane or potatoes. In the worst cases, unfavorable terms of credit, interest rates, and interest penalties actually contributed to abandonment of small farms and decreased food production.[33]

Between 1960 and 1970, the number and size of family and subfamily farms declined while all other farms grew larger and more numerous (see fig. 4.2). The number of *latifundia* increased by 20 percent while their area expanded by 15 percent, and commercial farms grew by roughly 19 percent in both number and size. Clearly, since World War II, Colombia's land-tenure system has grown increasingly inequitable and inefficient.

TROUBLED MARKETS

Commercial crops' value increased by 191 percent between 1955 and 1971 in Colombia while the value of peasant-grown food crops increased only 2 percent.[34] But, the growth in the country's agricultural imports from 111 million tons in the 1950s to 1,023 million tons in 1980 suggests that the commercial agricultural sector cannot ensure national self sufficiency and food security.[35]

Fluctuating international commodity prices and the costs of agricultural imports frustrate the production of both food and industrial crops. Pesticide prices, for example, increased sixfold between 1964 and 1974. Fertilizer imports between 1971 and 1974 increased more than 200 percent a year while international fertilizer prices rose 600 percent. These increases devastated rice and potato farmers, who together use almost half of Colombia's fertilizers.[36]

As Colombian production costs increased, agricultural prices abroad dropped and the growth rates of sesame, barley, sorghum, and many other commercial crops foundered in the face of imports. Cotton farmers faced calamity in 1978 when low international prices led the domestic textile industry to buy cotton abroad. Between 1977 and 1980, the number of hectares in cotton decreased from 400,000 to 102,000 and the number of cotton farmers decreased from 17,069 to 8,730. As a result, thousands of farm workers and industrial textile workers lost their jobs.[37] Out of the whole beleaguered commercial sector, only rice production increased between 1978 and 1982.[38]

Except for rice, food crop production fell most severely. Wheat imports, through U.S. Public Law 480, devastated wheat farmers. Small wonder: in PL-480 contracts signed in 1965, 1966 and 1967, Colombia agreed to import additional wheat at commercial prices, not to export Colombian wheat, corn, rice, or barley, and not to use PL-480 proceeds to finance internal wheat production. As a result, wheat farming declined from 176,000 hectares in the mid-1950s to 31,500 hectares by the late 1970s. Imported wheat accounted for 34 percent of Colombian wheat consumption between 1950 and 1954, but by 1975–1979 imported wheat supplied 90 percent. Production of corn, beans, chickens, and milk also declined following imports from the United States, many of these subsidized by PL-480.[39]

Rice, however, was not on Colombia's growing list of imports. Indeed, until 1974, Colombia's rice growers were protected by a 45–55 percent tariff against imports.[40] With the erosion of the country's food-producing base and the growing dependence on agricultural imports, rice became a major staple. In the 1970s, the introduction of high-yield rice varieties greatly increased production, which lowered consumer prices and upped consumption. Yet, that new technologies allowed Colombians to eat more rice is only part of the story. The rest turns on how Colombia grows that rice.

THE HIGH COSTS OF CHEAP FOOD IN COLOMBIA

Rice growing is a Colombian legacy. But rice production expanded only after import-substitution policies were adopted in the 1940s. Before that, rice was planted by the laborers and tenants of large estates for their own use, or as a subsistence crop by *colonos* establishing new farms on the frontier. By the 1920s, farmers supplying the internal urban market established irrigation-grown rice as a lucrative commodity. But rice was rarely extended to plots larger than 2 to 5 hectares because it required so much labor to harvest by hand. By the 1950s, most rice was still produced under upland (rain-fed) conditions.[41]

With international aid in the 1940s, most of it American, came large-scale irrigation and mechanization, the keys to expanding commercial irrigated rice farming. The Colombian government used an Export-Import Bank loan to construct irrigation districts in Tolima and Huila, the country's central valleys. Machinery imports financed with a World Bank loan stimulated the mechanization of not only rice, but all commercial crops. Rice growers also benefitted from international support for agricultural research. In 1955, the Colombian government, with Rockefeller Foundation backing, formed an agricultural research department within the Ministry of Agriculture, and two years later established a rice research program. With

Figure 4.3 Growth Rates of Rice Production in Columbia, 1950–1982.

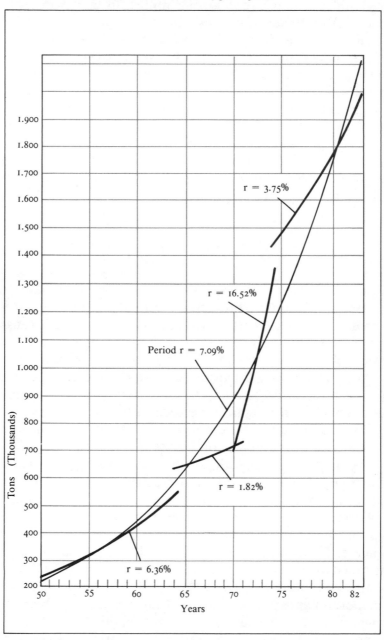

continued foundation support, these were incorporated in 1962 into the Colombian Agricultural Research Institute (Instituto Colombiano Agropecuario, or ICA). Finally, in 1968, the Rockefeller, Ford, and Kellogg foundations established the Centro Internacional de Agricultura Tropical (CIAT) in Palmira and selected rice as one of four commodities for crop research.[42]

Mechanization, irrigation, and, later, high-yield varieties vastly increased rice production. Between 1950 and 1982, the area planted in rice grew from 133,000 hectares to 474,000 hectares while average yields increased from 1.8 tons per hectare in 1950 to 2.7 tons in 1969. With the introduction of high-yield varieties, production further increased from 3.5 tons per hectare in 1970 to over 4 tons per hectare in 1982. Total production rose from 241,000 tons to more than 2 million tons between 1950 and 1982 (see fig. 4.3).[43]

Spectacular yield increases after 1968 stemmed from the continued collaboration among the Agricultural Research Institute, the Rice Grower's Federation, and CIAT to produce high-yielding seed varieties and technology training programs. Seed varieties introduced after 1970 were adopted rapidly, partly because the Colombian government linked credit for production to their use.[44]

In 1977, CIAT announced that rice research investments had paid returns of 60–80 percent and that, because rice prices had declined, technological change had especially helped the poor. CIAT also concluded that low rice prices were keeping industrial wages down.[45] Overall, however, the social costs of providing cheap rice were high. The small farms that had produced half of the country's rice under upland conditions were displaced within the decade as prices fell in the wake of irrigation, mechanization, and HYVs. The total number of farms producing rice declined from 97,000 in 1959 to 39,000 by 1970, and changes in the upland farms were especially dramatic (see fig. 4.4). Although higher yields per hectare reduced production costs by 80 percent per hectare, only farmers with secure credit and expanses of land could realize rice farming profits in the face of falling prices.[46] Changing plot sizes illustrate the trend: before the 1950s, irrigated rice was grown only on 5-hectare plots; by 1981, 13 percent of all rice plots on almost 45 percent of the area covered at least 100 hectares.[47]

Figure 4.4 Changes in the Number of Farms Between
1959 and 1970 Where Rice Is the Principal Crop
by Three Categories of Farm Size.

Size group (Hectares)	Upland sector No. of Farms	Area (%)	Irrigated sector No. of Farms	Area (%)	Percentage of total farms in irrigated sector 1959 (%)	1970 (%)
Small (0–5)	− 7,738	−55	−609	−40	4	12
Medium (5–50)	−11,885	−59	−795	−23	5	24
Large (50 +)	− 5,876	−52	+561	+19	6	40
Total	−25,499	−56	−843	−11	15	26

Source: Scobie and Posada, *The Impact of High Yielding Rice Varieties*, 36.

Besides concentrating production in the capitalized commercial sector, cheap rice also saved labor. Unmechanized upland rice required 49-person days per hectare. Irrigated production took only 28. When, after 1978, high-yielding rain-fed varieties were introduced, labor needs declined even more, because mechanized upland production demanded just 15-person days per hectare. When the number of hectares first increased, employment rates rose over 100 percent. But by 1975, after HYVs were introduced, the labor requirements declined from 27 million-person days in 1965 to 19 million-person days in 1975. Moreover, between 1977 and 1982, overall irrigation costs declined by 18 percent, because in mechanized upland production fewer laborers were needed to prepare and maintain the levees and to oversee water supplies.[48]

In Tolima, where the new technologies were first introduced during La Violencia, the landless labor force grew and the farm sector shrank, forcing small farmers to turn to part-time wage work to make ends meet. In the 1950s, Tolima's traditional products, cattle and tobacco, were replaced by cotton, sorghum, sesame, and rice. The shift increased profits but, along with rural violence, displaced sharecroppers and tenants on large estates. On the remaining small farms, men worked for part-time agricultural wages half the year, and women worked for three months seasonally at chopping weeds, picking cotton, and the like.

Where holdings were below 3 hectares, families sent their children, especially daughters, to work in the city. Industry, however, absorbed only 1.5 percent of the labor force in the early 1970s, down from 3.2 percent in the 1950s. Meanwhile, agriculture's share of total employment fell from 56 percent in 1950, to 49 percent in 1960, and 40 percent in 1970.[49]

As small producers quit farming and agricultural unemployment rose, urban diets suffered, especially among the poor. Because rice was expensive relative to wages in the 1950s, rice consumption per capita was then below 20 kilograms a year. During this decade, the population grew by 3.5 percent annually, and urban migration increased by 5.5 percent a year. In response to these demographic changes and a price decline in rice, total rice consumption rose, but per capita consumption remained steady. In the 1960s, per capita rice consumption grew slightly as wages and the prices of corn, plantain, beans, and other peasant-grown foods rose. But by the 1970s, rice had become firmly established as a working-class food. Average per capita consumption increased to 36 kilograms a year, and by 1978, 71 percent of Colombia's rice was eaten by those making less than 20,000 Colombian pesos (about $570 dollars) a year. In Bogotá, working-class families consumed 18 kilograms of rice a month. But while they ate more rice, sugar, and chocolate, between 1950 and 1970, these families put less corn, bread, potatoes, bananas, and plantain on their tables (see fig. 4.5).[50]

Rice became the food of the poor because prices for alternative foods went up and real wages declined. The costs of other foods continued to rise because the Colombian government systematically favored producers of commercial crops over peasant growers. To be sure, rice and wheat were cheap, but scarcity drove up the urban prices of other foods grown on Colombia's small farms. While peasants produced most agricultural products in 1973, by 1977 the production of food crops grown by peasants was falling as rice production increased.[51] In addition, a 30 percent decline in real wages during the international recession forced low-income Colombians to eat rice. According to a report published by Colombian businessmen in 1977, Colombians earning the minimum wage would have to work two hundred hours a week just to cover basic living expenses.[52]

Figure 4.5 Working Class Family Consumption of Food Items, 1953–1970 (Bogotá, pounds per month).

Item	1953	1970
Rice	18.0	24.2
Corn	9.5	5.6
Bread	20.5	14.3
Potatoes	122.0	58.0
Plantain	21.0	11.0
Bananas	12.0	9.0
Milk	55.0	48.7
Sugar	3.5	11.6
Panela	23.0	19.4
Chocolate	9.5	10.0

Source: Instituto Interamericano de Ciencias Agricolas, *Estudio del proceso de generación*, chap. 2, 40.

By 1982, the Rice Growers' Federation voiced concern that per capita consumption had declined slightly to 35 kilograms a year because cheaper products made from imported wheat were becoming popular. But when it sponsored a consumer survey, the Rice Growers' Federation found that rice remained the most important carbohydrate and that its price had increased by less than that of the potatoes and plantain that Colombians prefer. One-fourth of all consumers ate more rice in 1983 than in 1982, and the increase was highest among the poorest groups, some of whom purchased more than one kilogram a day.[53]

Today, it is uncertain whether commercial rice farming can adequately and regularly meet Colombia's growing urban food needs. Like other commercial crops, rice is subject to the cost-price squeeze, which hurts consumers and producers alike. For consumers, price declines leveled off in the mid-1970s, and as early as 1978 imported rice would have been cheaper than Colombian rice to the consumer. Since then, the gap has widened.[54]

As for producers, rice farmers now feel the pinch of both the increased costs and the low prices that checked the growth of other commercially grown crops. Where imports destroyed the profitability of many commercial crops, rice profits are threatened by both overproduction and the government's "cheap food" policies for the urban poor. After the cotton market collapsed in the late 1970s, rice production increased by 46 percent between 1977 and 1982 because it appeared to be the only crop with a secure market. But, while yields remained steady and production costs increased by 6 percent, the real prices paid to farmers declined over those years by 16 percent. Now, Colombia's farmers want to *raise* internal prices by creating an "export-led" scarcity.[55]

Regardless of how such scarcities affect Colombia's poor, for now the Colombian government may not want to encourage the export of what has become an essential urban food, especially because the international market for rice is thin, competitive, and unstable. (Only 5 percent of the world's rice is traded internationally, compared to 20 percent for wheat.) Then too, Colombian rice cannot compete with that of the United States, where over half of the crop is grown for export and where farmers depend on government programs to purchase and place the crop.[56]

Faced with high costs and low support prices, rice farmers may have little choice but to stop producing until prices rise. In 1976, prices were low, and in 1977 farmers reduced their hectareage, forcing the government to import rice. In 1982, increased world rice production brought international prices to their nadir. In 1983, Colombia faced a tight supply-demand situation, although rice exports to Peru and Ecuador had been authorized earlier in the year.[57]

By almost any reckoning, new rice-production technology has strengthened Colombia's commerical agriculture. But it has also displaced small farmers, concentrated wealth, and generated unemployment and poverty. Making the most of international support, Colombian rice farmers have achieved great yields. Yet, with unstable international commodity markets and Colombia's current agrarian structure and priorities, new rice-farming technologies will not necessarily continue to provide cheaply what has become an essential staple for the poor.

AS GOES META

The story of the development of Meta in southeast Colombia shows in human terms that Colombia's land policies (which re-created on the frontier the inequitable conditions of the country's central valleys) are the root of Colombia's food insecurity and land mismanagement. Along with the Amazon jungle, Meta was one of the two eastern frontiers that Colombian landowners pegged as new homes for the landless (see fig. 4.1). Meta was eventually drawn into the national economy largely because of its commercial rice farming. Until mid-century Meta and all the Llanos Orientales comprised Colombia's most extensive cattle-raising region. In the 1950s, Meta's Piedmont region produced only 5 percent of Colombia's rice. But by 1974, Meta had become Colombia's second largest rice-producing region, exporting 70 percent of its crop to the rest of the country and supplying most of Bogotá's meat as well.[58]

Villavicencio, Meta's capital, is 120 kilometers southeast of Bogotá. Meta stretches from the Andes' Eastern Cordillera in the west and across the Llanos Orientales in the east. The rice-growing piedmont area is in what used to be moist tropical forest extending north along the Andes from the Amazon Basin.

Commercial agriculture's success in the Piedmont depends on the land's slope and soil quality. Save for the mountainsides, Meta's land is flat and easily worked by machines, but most of the land is not fertile. The plains east of the Metica River—worked extensively as cattle ranches because of their low rainfall and infertile soils—cover over half of Meta, whereas the western third of the land is mountainous and forested. Eighty-seven percent of Meta's best farming land is in the Piedmont, which covers less than an eighth of the region. But even here, almost half the Piedmont land is acidic, loaded with toxic aluminum, and low in organic matter and phosphorus. Until the 1950s, this *savanna,* as it is popularly called, was used for cattle raising. In contrast, a little more than a third of the Piedmont's land consists of fertile alluvial soils, or *vega.* These rich soils lie along the principal rivers that flow away from the mountains: the Upia, Humea, Guatiquia, Guayuriba, and especially the Ariari. The Piedmont gets enough rain, on average, 2,788 millimeters a year, to produce corn and rainfed rice on vega soils during the wet months and such crops as cotton or sorghum during the drier months.[59]

Rice has been planted in the Piedmont's vega soils since 1900 by land-hungry *colonos* moving down the Andes. For decades, rice and corn were used as "civilizing crops" to replace the tropical forests with pastures. Once the forests were felled and burned, local rice varieties were planted in the rainy season and families harvested them by hand. When soil exhaustion caused yields to decline after two or three harvests, the crops were interplanted with pasture grass. Thus, ranches developed in the Piedmont of Meta and Casanare, much as they have traditionally throughout Colombia. In time, the region's vega pastures became fattening stations for cattle raised on the arid Eastern Plains or the acidic savanna lands of the Piedmont.

But in the 1950s, two migratory currents increased Meta's rice production: peasants and workers came to Meta fleeing La Violencia; and wealthy rice farmers arrived in Villavicencio from Tolima and Huila seeking cheaper land.[60] Ironically, the runaway workers and peasants settled on the Piedmont's best soils because the wealthier farmers bought or rented vast tracts of land to make irrigation and mechanization work. Richer farmers could work the cheap but infertile savanna soil because irrigation raises the soil's pH, increases the phosphorus available to the plant, and lowers toxic aluminum levels.[61] The peasants and workers could not acquire large parcels of land, so some bought and most simply took, small parcels of vega lands by the rivers, where they planted subsistence crops, rice, corn, and plantain.

Another actor in this drama was a pioneer colony established in the Ariari Basin—a virtually unpopulated virgin forest in the 1950s. In 1961 the Agrarian Bank with AID support (and later, in 1968, with World Bank support), founded a colony in the Ariari. While unmechanized upland rice production declined elsewhere in Colombia, the immigrants who came to the Ariari region received 50-hectare parcels and produced impressive agricultural yields. Between 1965 and 1973, an estimated 20,000 hectares a year were planted in unmechanized upland rice, most of it in the basin's vega soils.[62]

Roads were built and the Ariari River bridged. But, the colony failed anyway because the credit, the roads, and the marketing did not meet farmers' needs. In the early 1970s, just as high-yielding rice varieties were introduced, land reform was abandoned and new emphasis was given to increasing the commercial crops grown by wealthy farmers. The ensuing competition bankrupted most pioneer farmers, while those who stayed for the excellent 1974 harvest were ruined when a disastrous land-slide at Quebrada Blanca closed the market road from Villavicencio to Bogotá for six months. Prices plummeted and most of the original pioneers sold their holdings, returned to cities, or moved south to open new lands. In their wake came another wave of immigrant peasants and workers, as well as investors or wealthy entrepreneurs from Bogotá or Tolima.

Within just a few years, irrigated and mechanized production dominated rice growing in Meta, especially after HYVs were successfully introduced. Farmers grew rice on irrigated savanna soils, while the remaining pioneers and others grew corn rotated with cotton on the vega soils, and ranchers began to use corn instead of rice to "civilize" new fattening pastures. Neither pioneers nor ranchers could compete with mechanized irrigated rice farming on savanna soils.

But in 1978, a now-legendary rice variety, CICA-8, was introduced, and rice made a comeback on vega soils. Total costs fell as the labor needed for irrigated production was eliminated, and yields were at least those achieved on irrigated fields. Between 1978 and 1982, the hectareage in upland rainfed rice (now mechanized) increased from 6,400 hectares to 39,000—over one-third of all ricelands in Meta in 1982.[63] The decline in markets for corn and cotton, which were being imported, added momentum to the shift. Mechanized rainfed rice production on Meta's vega lands allowed others to grow rice—among them, ranchers who again used rice to prepare or renew pastures on vega soils. Meantime, doctors, lawyers, agronomists, fumigation pilots, veterinarians, accountants, and other professionals invested in rice. These new-comers entered the farming business in droves because the Agropecuarian Finance Fund's proviso that all crops receiving credit had to be supervised by licensed agronomists diminished the importance of previous agricultural experience. At the same time, some *colonos* and other farmers with relatively small plots switched from corn and cotton back to rice.

CICA-8's broad appeal notwithstanding, the distinction between small-farm production and commercial farming held fast. Meta's smallest farms didn't have enough money or land to grow rice. As elsewhere in Colombia's, the bulk of Meta's rice production now stems from large farms, whether on savanna or vega soils. In 1982, the average irrigated rice plot was 74 hectares, compared to 35 hectares for upland rice. Meta's plot size distribution mirrors the national pattern: the largest proportion of plots (32 percent) are between 20 and 60 hectares, and these cover 17 percent of all ricelands. Another 28 percent of the plots (5 percent of the area) are smaller than 20 hectares, while 56 percent of the area is planted on the 19 percent of plots over 100 hectares each.[64] Modern rice farming helped draw a frontier region into the national economy, but on what terms? Land holdings were unequal, the agrarian structure dual, and unemployment high.

These trends had roots in the 1960s. From 1960 to 1970, Meta's small farms, like those throughout Colombia, decreased in number and in area, while farms of all other sizes increased. Relative increases in size and area were greatest for farms between 100 and 500 hectares. By 1970, farms below 20 hectares represented 49 percent of Meta's farms, a loss of 28 percent in number and 12 percent in area since 1960. Not surprisingly, all these small farms reported a 15–76 percent decrease in the area available for fallowing, while farms between 50 and 1,000 hectares left most of their land fallow or unused.[65]

As land distribution and use changed in Meta, so did farm administration. In 1960, not 5 percent of Meta's farms were managed by a *mayordomo* for an absentee owner. By 1970, 11 percent were. The number of 1,000-hectare ranches run by absentee landlords increased by 65 percent, and the size of these ranches grew only slightly. But in the Piedmont, where farm sizes are smaller (5 to 1,000 hectares), the increase in absenteeism was another story. Absentee farms of between 50–99 hectares increased by 216 percent in number and 225 percent in area. Those between 100–499 hectares increased by 124 percent in number and 141 percent in area, and those between 500–999 hectares grew by 102 percent in number and 108 percent in area.[66] The new owners were not peasants or pioneers expanding their landholdings, but urban entrepreneurs and speculators.

As flatland farms of the Piedmont get smaller, rice production is abandoned and the split between commercial crops and
small-farm crops deepens. Thus, Integrated Rural Development
Programs aimed at the Piedmont's small farms don't include rice
with its rotation crops of sorghum or cotton. On the flatlands,
mixed farming systems developed based on corn, cassava, plantain, beans, coffee, and cocoa and some milk and beef cattle. But
most of Meta's small farms are dairy farms clustered on the eroding Andean foothills—land that machines cannot work even if
farmers could afford them.[67] These dairy farmers supplement
their incomes by working on irrigated farms, taking part-time or
seasonal jobs in cities, or periodically migrating south to work in
the coca fields.

Figure 4.6 Occupational Structure in Meta, 1964 and 1980.

Employment	1964	1980
Agriculture and Ranching	64.51	13.0
Manufacturing	5.67	9.0
Construction	3.53	7.0
Commerce and Services		
Commerce and Finance	6.31	no data
Government	5.82	no data
Municipal and State Government	1.96	no data
Professional and Technical	2.44	no data
Total Commerce and Services	16.53	43.0
Other	9.76[1]	28.0
Total	100.00	100.0

[1]Not accounted for.

Sources: For *1964*, Berry, A. and M. Urrutia, *Income Distribution in Colombia*, 140–
141. For *1980*, Banco de la República, *Situación economica del departamento del
Meta, 1981*, 60–61.

This troublesome cycle has changed Meta's demographic profile. Because of heavy immigration, Meta's population swelled from 67,000 in 1951 to an estimated 441,000 people in 1982. By 1980, fully 75 percent of the population in the Piedmont lived in towns. Colombia's national employment service estimates that 10 to 12 percent of Villavicencio's population is unemployed and that 60 percent of the positions available are for unskilled labor, especially for cheap female labor.[68] Rough estimates for Meta show rural employment dropping from 65 percent of total employment in 1964 to 13 percent in 1980 (see fig. 4.6).

Rural and urban unemployment and underemployment have obviously contributed to the Colombian cocaine trade. In Meta, airplane flights from Villavicencio to San José Guaviare in Meta and Miralfores, Vaupes, were filled in the early 1980s as men searched for work harvesting and processing coca leaves. A side result of the cocaine trade is that the Piedmont malaria rates have doubled in some municipalities, because migrants contract malaria while clearing or working in recently cleared forests in coca-producing regions and return to the Piedmont for treatment. Of course, no official figures exist on cocaine employment. Still, in 1980, the Bank of the Republic estimated that 28 percent of the population worked in "informal," "illegal" (cocaine-related) activites.[69] Even if coca production and distribution employ only, say, 14 percent of the population, the cocaine economy has probably brought more jobs, wealth, and demand for services than has commercial farming. Small wonder: in 1982, the Piedmont's daily agricultural wage was about $5.00, while coca workers in Meta, Caqueta, and Vaupes earned $18.00.[70]

The development of the Meta Piedmont encapsulates the history of Colombia's settlement: pioneers clear land that is later absorbed by *latifundia* while *minifundia* proliferate. New commercial technologies combined with underfunded, hit-or-miss colonization programs, as in the Ariari Basin, accelerate the process. In the end, national and international successes in increasing rice production have helped deprive Meta's people of their farms and ranches, fostering political instability and expanding the cocaine trade.

SO GOES THE FRONTIER

If commercial rice production has brought to Meta many of the inequities that beset the rest of Colombia, how have new rice farming technologies affected food security and land management at the local level? A look at upland rice farming in the Meta Piedmont's rich soils shows why rice production can be unstable, and environmentally and socially unsound. Essentially, these technologies have resulted in increased production, but they have contributed new mechanisms for the concentration of land and its conversion to pasture.

Since the early 1960s rice production in Meta has increased in steeply oscillating cycles (see fig. 4.7). Such variations in the amount of land put in production reflect not only the market forces that affect the cost of inputs and the price of rice, but the region's land tenure system as well. According to the Rice Growers' Federation, 75 percent of all of the rice lands are rented in six-, twelve-, and thirty-six-month periods. This arrangement encourages boom and bust production cycles: land is rented for a quick profit and then abandoned when prices decline. But while production variations can cause shortages as well as gluts, rice price oscillations frequently benefit landowners.

On irrigated savanna lands, many rice landlords are absentee ranchers or land speculators. They collect rent, have their pastures leveled and plowed free, and occasionally reap the benefits of the soil-boosters that some renters apply. When the contract expires, the field is ready to be seeded in pasture grass. Indeed, some rental contracts specify that the land must be returned in pasture.

To appreciate these benefits fully, consider what happened in the early 1970s when *Brachiaria decumbens,* a hardy, invasive, and drought-resistant pasture grass, was introduced. This grass, which grows well on infertile savanna soils that receive little late-season rain, dramatically increases the carrying capacity of the pasture. At first, farmers planted only small fields. But by the mid-1970s, the Colombian Agricultural Research Institute raised the germination rate of these seeds from 20 to about 80 percent.[71] Then, when paid labor was no longer needed to plant, collect, and transplant grass shoots, expanses of land were seeded in *Brachiaria,* often after the land had been rented and worked by a

Figure 4.7 Hectareage Planted in Rice, Meta Piedmont, 1965–1983.

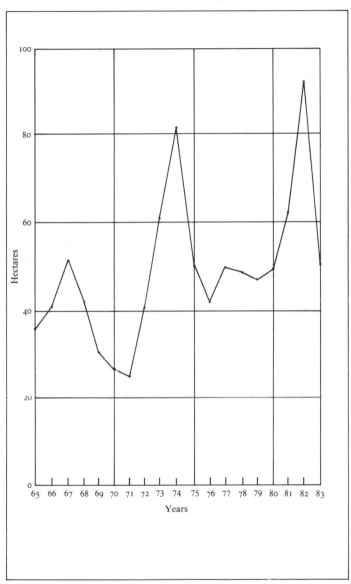

Sources: *ICA*, 1982, Area Inscrita por Cultivos Hasta Mayo 30 de 1982. Llanoticias. Boletin Informativo No. 09:1. *ICA*, Regional No. 8, Villavicencio; *ICA*, 1982, Regional 8, Llanos Orientales, Distrito de Transferencia de Tecnologia No. 1. Villavicencio. Informe Annual de actividades, March 1982; *ICA*, 1983, Inscripcion de Cultivos. Semestroe A de 1983. Llanoticias, Boletin Informativo No. 011, *ICA*, Regional No. 8. Villavicencio.

rice grower. Because pasture preparation is now mechanized, much savanna land in irrigated rice has been switched from rice production to *Brachiaria* pasture.

What will happen to the richer vega soils over time is not as clear. These lands were settled by land-hungry pioneers, as well as ranchers and others, and their management by various owners, renters, and entrepreneurs is more complex. Differences in entrepreneurial goals and social class within the commercial rice growing sector have led to less consistent land management.

A study of the land and soil fertility management among upland rice farmers undertaken by the author for the International Fertilizer Development Center in Alabama and the Centro Internacional de Agricultura Tropical in Colombia helps put the land-mangement issue for vega soil into perspective.[72] As a group, the rice growers surveyed as part of the study were wealthy, literate, educated, and urban, like most of Colombia's commercial farmers. Three-quarters were affiliated with powerful farming and ranching associations of Villavicencio. Eighty percent had farmed for over ten years in the Meta Piedmont and had permanent employees on their farms. Over 60 percent planted more than 50 hectares of rice on farms that averaged 99 hectares in size. Only the largest farmers owned one or two combines, though four out of five owned at least one tractor. The average number of hectares worked by this machinery was 111, although the range varied from 2 hectares to 400. Eighty-five percent drew on the Agropecuarian Finance Fund's commercial credit and the assistance of licensed agronomists.

While the history of rice farming in Colombia and Meta makes it obvious that rice farmers have greater access to land, credit, and machinery than do the small mixed dairy farmers of the Piedmont, Meta's farmers of upland rice are not a homogeneous group. Four kinds of entrepreneurs grow upland rice on Meta's vega soils and their land management is affected by their entrepreneural goals. *Rice-only* farmers, for whom rice is their main source of income, tend to grow rice on large (100+ hectares), owned, and mainly irrigated savanna plots. But, because the labor costs of irrigated rice are higher than those of upland rice on vega plots, they will rent vega plots for upland rice in off years. *Ranchers,* in contrast, grow rice only on their own land. They grow it primarily to prepare fattening pastures for cattle.

The amount of land they put in rice in any given year depends on the market for rice, but the long-term direction of their vega land is into pasture.

Such is probably also the case for much of the vega land used by *Investors and Income Supplementers,* who farm exclusively on rented land. As their label indicates, they grow rice to supplement incomes derived from professions, business, and even wage labor. Like Rice-only farmers, the wealthier among these tend to farm large (100+ hectares) irrigated savanna plots, and to rent vega lands or increase the proportion of rented vega lands for upland rice on off years. Finally, *Mixed Farmers* also grow upland rice on vega soils. For Mixed Farmers cattle raising is an integral part of enterprises that often include growing crops other than rice and its rotation crops of cotton and sorghum. Like Ranchers, Mixed Farmers use crops to prepare fattening pastures on some of their land. Because a high proportion of the land owned by Mixed Farmers is in pasture (about 45 percent in the sample studied) the largest growers among them rent additional land on which to grow rice, both irrigated and upland.

Two points related to land management emerge from a review of the kinds of entrepreneurs that grow upland rice on Meta's vega soils. First, is that the traditional "civilizing pattern" of clearing frontier or new land with crops for conversion to pasture remains an explicit goal for many of Meta's upland growers. Second, is that as with irrigated rice, a very large proportion of the land on which upland rice is grown is rented. The study took place in 1983, an off year for production. Even so, over half of the hectares surveyed by the study were rented, and nearly three-quarters of the farmers rented some land for rice. We have seen that rentals for rice on savanna lands often results in preparing the land for the pastures of absentee landlords or ranchers. Such is also likely to be the case on Meta's vega soils, but the process is less direct, and is likely to involve putting people off the land as well.

This is because on vega soils the largest groups of landlords for plots rented for growing upland rice are not ranchers, absentee landlords or speculators of the savanna lands: here they are farmers who are described as being "too poor to plant rice." In fact, they are the pioneers, sons of pioneers, or second generation buyers who colonized Meta's vega soils in the 1950s and 1960s when irrigated rice was beginning its expansion on vast plots of savanna land. The advent of varieties like CICA-8 allowed such small farmers—all of whom are Mixed Farmers—to grow upland rice, now with machines, on vega fields again. But in the long run the effects of social class—relative poverty, less access to credit and technology—make it difficult for such small, landowning rice growers to remain in production.

Figure 4.8 Rotations on Owned Alluvial Land (in percent, by farm size).

Farm Size (Hectares)	Crop	Stubble	Pasture	Nothing	Other/ No Answer	Total
1–49	74.5	10.5	15.0	0	0	100.0
50–99	81.9	0	0	2.7	15.4	100.0
100+	43.7	42.2	3.0	11.1	0	100.0
Total (all farms)	57.7	27.2	5.2	7.0	2.9	100.0

Figure 4.9 Rotations on Rented Alluvial Land (in percent, by) farm size.

Farm Size (Hectares)	Crop	Stubble	Pasture	Nothing	Other/ No Answer	Total
1–49	38.1	30.4	2.2	5.5	23.8	100.0
50–99	86.5	5.7	0	7.8	0	100.0
100+	27.8	55.0	0	15.0	2.2	100.0
Total (all farms)	43.1	40.2	0.3	12.1	4.3	100.0

Source: E. de G.R. Hansen, *Land Management and Phosphorus Fertilizer Use Among Upland Rice Farmers in Meta. Colombia: Executive Summary of Research.* International Fertilizer Development Center, May 1984.

Ironically, these are the steadiest producers of rice. The study was able to show that while small Mixed Farmers (growing fewer than 100 hectares of rice) grew rice year in and year out on owned and rented plots, large Investors and even Rice-only farmers could respond dramatically to adverse market conditions and simply stop producing rice by not renewing their rental contracts. It is probable that a longitudinal survey would confirm the study's one year finding that the largest entrepreneurs who rent land for rice are responsible for the bulk of variation in Meta's rice production.

As social class affects the amount of land put in production, so it takes a predictable toll on land management. Even though the smaller Mixed Farmers appeared to be the most reliable and efficient suppliers, none of the smaller farmers (growing on fewer than 100 hectares) could afford to fallow their rice fields on vega soils "even for 10 minutes." Unlike growers with over 100 hectares of rice, the fields of Mixed Farmers growing on fewer than 100 hectares, both rented and owned, were used for crops most intensively (see fig. 4.8).

Unfortunately, the farmers who use their land most fertilize least.

The study was able to show that among the growers surveyed, all fertilizer practices including the sources of phosphorus to the timing of its application were correlated to the farmers' social class as indicated by the number of hectares farmed. The most important finding was the high proportion of farmers who used no phosphorus at all, or only very small quantities of complete (nitrogen, phosphorus, and potassium) fertilizer.[73] Almost 40 percent of the farmers in the sample applied no phosphorus at all, 20 percent used a complete fertilizer, and 40 percent used diammonium phosphate (DAP) or slow-release sources, such as basic slag or ground phosphorus rock. Significantly, the proportion of nonusers declines as the number of hectares rises, and among users, the amount of phosphorus applied increases with the number of hectares.

The scant use of phosphorus, an important indicator of soil-fertility, is especially telling. According to one specialist in Latin American tropical soil management, "the decline in available phosphorus may be one of the most important reasons for abandoning field(s) to forest regrowth."[74] Soils will degrade if the phosphorus that crops naturally deplete is not replaced. In Meta's fertile vega soils, phosphorus levels are generally high enough to grow several crops of rice. However, the traditional shift from food crops to pasture on vega soils occurred precisely because yields decreased as the soil became exhausted. With mechanization, far larger fields have been cleared and continuously rotated, first in corn and cotton and now in rice and cotton or sorghum. Today, vega soils that have been regularly worked have phosphorus levels well below 10 parts per million (ppm)—a sign of probable soil degradation.[75]

Although greater access to credit and technology explains why the richer growers of upland rice make more use of fertilizer, that "the wealthy have more" is not a novel discovery. More interesting are the mechanisms, both formal and informal that ensure differential soil management. In principle, Colombia's Law 5 requires all commercial rice growers to follow uniform and optimum cultivation practices, and the enforcement of the law depends on its connection to credit for rice growing. Thus, to receive credit from the Agropecuarian Finance Fund, farmers must show a receipt for certified seed and a signed contract with a licensed agronomist who is to oversee fertilizer use, pesticide applications, and other technical procedures.

In practice, the law can't work equitably unless these licensed agronomists can reach all social classes and all are in a position to use sound advice. Regrettably, Law 5 makes no special provision for fertilizer, and the first credit installment does not arrive until the crops are already in, too late for the optimal time for phosphorus fertilizer application. In fact, for small growers the cost for certified seed is so high, even for just 20 hectares,[76] that from the moment of seed purchase, they tend to protect their investments in seed with herbicides, nitrogen fertilization, insecticides, and fungicides. When the first of two credit installments comes, about fifteen days after the rice has germinated, the first herbicide and insecticide applications are due. At least one nitrogen fertilization and at least two fungicide applications follow—expensive necessities. When rice prices are declining, cash-short farmers without adequate support for fertilization skimp on phosphorus, even later in the growing cycle, and soil degradation ensues.

Most large farmers, in contrast, have a cushion of cash and other alternatives needed to weather the cost-price squeeze. They can reduce the overall hectareage planted and still make money, or they can lean on other sources of income and withdraw temporarily from production. Because they can pay the initial costs of seeds, phosphorus fertilizer, and other agrochemicals, they can time their applications for credit so the installments pay for harvesting costs, or so that the loan comes due after they have sold their rice, thus avoiding late penalty interest rates. Often, large farmers do not need credit to grow rice: one wealthy Mixed Farmer in the sample applied for credit so he could invest it at an interest higher than the rate charged by the Agropecuarian Finance Fund. At the extreme, credit for the smaller growers allows them to remain in the commercial farming arena and functions to protect their investment rather than to enhance their cultivating practices. For the wealthier farmers credit may enhance their cultivating practices, but it might equally be considered as an enhancement of their portfolios.

Just as credit means different things to rice growers of different social classes, so does access to an agronomist. For the larger growers, agronomists can perform a variety of functions. Too often, however, for the smaller growers, the hiring of these professionals only represents the price that such farmers must pay in order to receive any credit at all. This is because agronomists are not entirely neutral elements in the system.

As a group these professionals suffer from poor reputations: although there is unemployment and underemployment among them, many are reportedly "signature agronomists" who rarely visit the fields, but earn their livings by signing contracts for a price, so that the farmer can apply for credit. All the farmers studied said they had contracted with agronomists at some point only in order to get credit, and all the farmers complained that their agronomists did not visit the fields regularly. Indeed, under the best of circumstances agronomists are frequently held as scapegoats for mishaps during the growing season. But the complaints were loudest among the small growers: in the Ariari Basin, farmers frequently call agronomists *ladronomos,* a play on the Spanish word for thief because they are only seen at the time of signing the contract at the bank and rarely in the fields. Clearly, the small country grower depends more than city-based farmers do on agronomists for technical advice. But just as clearly, agronomists, who are paid by the hectare, seek out the larger growers and sign on with the smaller ones in the hope of striking more lucrative bargains later. In extreme cases, then, while agronomists act as scientific and often managerial advisers to the large growers, for the small growers who live in the countryside, they are felt to represent only an additional cost.

A particularly stunning example of the Matthew principle—to them that have shall be given—is farmers' "phosphorus connection." Before 1981, compound fertilizers made in Colombia supplied most of the phosphorus used for upland rice. But in that year, the Rice Growers' Federation announced plans to replace compound fertilizers with simple ones for rice and recommended imported DAP. At the same time, as a marketing ploy, the major phosphorus rock producer gave ground phosphorus rock free to influential rice farmers. Because the informal networks for new commercial and scientific information are exclusively urban, only urban farmers and their agronomists find out immediately about new products such as DAP and phosphorus rock.

In Meta, the poorest growers must economize on soil inputs and investments, thus depleting the soil and undercutting long-range success. Land tenure, high production costs, unstable markets, and difficulties in making optimal use of credit and technology virtually force different land-management strategies upon different classes of farmers. Whereas large Rice-only farmers or Investors are free to reduce production, Mixed Farmers feel pressured to abandon agriculture for lower-paid but more secure ranching. But, only the largest growers can switch easily from cropping to ranching because the costs of pasture grass seed, fencing, and additional cattle are high, particularly after a bad harvest. None of the farmers interviewed established a pasture in 1983, and only a fifth of them could name others who, after losses in 1982, had put their upland rice fields in *Brachiaria,* the least expensive and most invasive pasture grass.[77] Those who did switch were Large Mixed Farmers with farms of well over 200 hectares each. Small Mixed Farmers who planted less than 100 hectares of rice and lost money in 1982 sold their cattle to pay their debts, and continued to plant crops intensively, investing little or nothing in the soil. Others, not captured by the survey (but spoken of by the farmers surveyed), sold their farms, or became "farmers too poor to grow rice," and rented rice land to investors or others. Ultimately, such farms are likely to be sold and incorporated into large holdings where the land will be underused or seeded in pasture.

The story doesn't end here. Future land use depends partly on which pasture grasses are selected. Because it is extremely invasive and difficult to destroy without water to flood the fields, *Brachiaria decumbens* is not a good selection for vega soils. It will not grow on the wettest land, and on drier vega land the grasses that Ranchers traditionally used for the fattening pastures—*yaragua* (*Melinis minutiflora*), *puntero* (*Hyperania ruffa*), *guinea* (*Panicum maximum*), and *kudzu* (*Pueraria phaseoloides*)—are more nutritive grasses. Unfortunately, almost half of the farmers surveyed who worked vega lands planted only *Brachiaria decumbens*. If more *Brachiaria* pastures are extended to vega soils, it may no longer be possible to balance rotated crops with pastures on these lands.

Traditionally, few vega pastures have been returned to crop, partly because crops long have been used to establish pasture, partly because of the high incidence of rentals. Yet, there are exceptions. One rancher whose father ranched 700 hectares of vega and savanna in the 1930s now regularly renews his old fattening pastures with mechanized short-term crops. Others plan to do the same. In the Ariari, two Mixed Farmers with farms of about 60 hectares each reported that when the cropland of one and the pasture of the other grew weedy and infertile, they had cooperatively established a *puntero* pasture on the cropland and planted rice and cotton on the pasture field. While mechanization had short-circuited the traditional fallow cycle, they said, it also allowed them to rotate pastures and crops.

Although new rice varieties, including those planted at lower cost on vega soils, have increased production in the Meta Piedmont, they have not contributed to the efficient use of Meta's best soils. Nor will they as long as the wealthiest growers have greatest access to land, credit, and technology and underuse the land, forcing small producers to overuse their parcels. As long as most rice is produced by renters with no long-term commitment to the soil, the germs of sound management that exist in the Piedmont—irrigated rice/*Brachiaria* rotations on savannas, and rotations between field crops and fattening pastures on vega lands—merely help expand *latifundia*.

The dynamics of soil management on Meta's vega lands show why it is hard for the pioneer farmers of thirty years ago to remain on their farms, and how cattle come to replace them. Far from providing a solution for a land hungry population, the land hungry "process" frontier lands so they become incorporated into *latifundia*. In this way the inequitable conditions of the central part of the country are reproduced. Today, the Ariari is not recognizable as the colony of the 1960s in which 50-hectare parcels were given to pioneers. Ranchers, commercial rice farmers, and speculators have put together farms of well over 500 hectares by buying out the original pioneers, their descendants or widows, or other "second generation" owners. In contrast, in the same area, in 1982, 77 percent of the farms below 20 hectares were smaller than 5 hectares.[78]

Efficient land use in Meta demands limits on the amount of land any one person can own. Clearly, the productive potential and the efficient use of that land before new lands or frontiers are brought in to production and management of different lands must be considered when those limits are set, and land distribution must be buttressed by adequate credit and price-support systems. The chasm between peasant and commercial agriculture must be bridged by credit policies that increase farmers' access to fertilizer and other essential technologies. Price supports for food crops must help all farmers meet production costs and supply the population with a greater variety of foodstuffs. Low support prices for selected cheap grains to underwrite the low wages of landless and underemployed workers only make it harder for farmers to produce food, and over time such policies threaten the quality of low-income urban diets.

With equitable development and sound agrarian policies, agricultural researchers need not work around the problem of developing technologies for impoverished farms. Researchers can let go of obsessions with yields and develop technologies that don't exacerbate inequalities and inefficient resource management. In Meta, small rice growers need attention. Domestic and international resources can create farming systems to increase farm income from the food and industrial crops that can be grown on Meta's vega soils (rice, corn, cotton, sorghum, coffee, cacao, plantain, banana, cassava, beans, watermelon, citrus fruits, papaya, African palm, and many other tropical fruits). Aid can also be used to develop technologies to lessen local agriculture's dependence on imported pesticides and fertilizer and to investigate the long-term relationship among pastures, field crops, and soil fertility on vega soils. Further work on soil fertility and pasture and crop rotations on vega land can promote more varied and resilient farms and the integration of the cattle-raising savanna and Llanos ranches with the cattle-fattening vega pastures. More important, stable and mixed farming systems would allow people to stay on the land instead of migrating to cities to find work or to the jungle to seek land or a niche in cocaine production.

CONCLUSION

Most experts agree that the keys to food security and sound resource management are not technical, but political. Because the social structures of a country determine the social and ecological impacts of any agricultural technology it adopts, assessment and decisions related to agricultural development and research must take far more than productivity and investment returns into account.[79]

In Colombia, the darker side of its agricultural success story is that people are pushed off the land while agricultural employment and the production of other food decreases. Growing food insecurity because of agricultural imports is accompanied by resource abuse and degradation, emigration, and drug dealing. This downward cycle represents a deep social problem, not technological backlash.

From this perspective, U.S. support for rice research in Colombia—part of a more general support for the country's economic growth—helped Colombia's elite avoid agrarian reform. By strengthening the minority's hold over the country's best lands, American support for industrialization helped perpetuate the misallocation and misuse of Colombia's resources. Colombia's new rice-growing technologies have not been a "blunt instrument" for social redistribution, as the World Bank says, but rather sharp tools that the rich have used to get richer at the expense of political stability and long-term agricultural productivity.

Colombia's lopsided agricultural development has broad policy implications for the United States as well as for Colombia. First, it shows that providing cheap food to urban industrial workers doesn't enhance food security. Too often, such a policy turns out to be a rural subsidy to low industrial wages. Because land distribution concentrates cheap and surplus labor in cities in Colombia, the United States must look hard at all the impacts of its food policies on Colombian agricultural development. The cost-price squeeze Colombian farmers face is real, and increased productivity is no hedge against fluctuating commodity prices. Such U.S. programs as PL-480, under which wheat, corn, milk, beans, and even frozen chickens are imported, only exacerbate this insecurity. Although the PL-480 program is popularly known as "Food for Peace," too often it is used to meet short-term economic and political goals that work against broader and longer-term U.S. interests in food security and political stability abroad.[80] For Colombia, depressing a commodity's price through increased supplies (either through trade or greater production) ensured neither agricultural stability nor sound resource management.

A sustainable, equitable, and balanced growth policy must address both agrarian and industrial goals in an overall context of equity and social justice. For Colombia, the keys are legal land reform, limits on the size of holdings, and the refusal to resort to, colonization to avoid breaking up fertile but inappropriately used *latifundia*.[81] The need for Colombian land reform has been recognized by international observers, Colombian reformers, peasants and guerrillas alike, and the failure of previous reform is no secret either.[82] While only Colombia can make the political decision to redistribute land and to orient growth toward equity, the United States can politically support Colombian groups that are working toward greater justice and withdraw support from those that oppose it.

The opportunity for reform has already arrived: in May 1984, eleven years after Colombia's last land reform effort, the Colombian government reached an accord with the country's major guerilla groups and committed itself to land redistribution and other social reforms. Not only the success of agricultural policy, but also Colombia's capacity for orderly social and political change hinges on these reforms. It is in the interests of Colombia, the region, the United States, and other outside development assistance donors to help translate good intentions for food security—and political stability—into programs that give title to the land to those who till it.

When policymakers recognize that inequitable land distribution causes agricultural stagnation and resource mismanagement, realistic agricultural development goals can be set. Agrarian reform that combines the socially and ecologically sound distribution of land with research, new technologies, extension services, credit, and marketing programs can make agriculture resilient, multifaceted, and self-sustaining. For Meta's vega soils, for example, rice research should be tailored toward increasing the overall stability of the region's most reliable producers. Whereas research on yet higher-yielding varieties suits large landowners and landless investors who have access to fertilizers and pesticides, these growers may not be the most reliable market suppliers. The land-tenure system and the cost-price squeeze make it easy for those of means to produce, to stop producing, or to put fertile land under pasture and invest their capital elsewhere. In contrast, smaller growers run the twin risks of degrading their land or losing it to larger but less intensive enterprises. Besides research on high-yielding varieties, such farmers need help keeping soils fertile and a balanced mix of cropping alternatives that include both tree crops and pastures.

The interrelationships among land tenure, soil management, social class, and agricultural technology are important to the future rice research. The world's greatest disparities in land distribution are in Latin America; and in the tropical lowlands, rice may soon join cattle as a symbol of inequitable landholdings, rural and urban poverty, and pioneer encroachment on frontiers.[83] For the past twenty years, rice growth rates in area and total production have been the highest among all Latin American cereals except sorghum, which is used for cattle feed. Yet, despite the introduction of high-yielding varieties, the growth rates for yields are the lowest among the major cereals because the high yields of rice grown under irrigation and with machines must be averaged with the considerably lower yields for rice grown by peasants or pioneers under rainfed, unmechanized conditions. Indeed, irrigated high-yielding rice covers only 20 percent of

Latin America's rice area, whereas rainfed systems cover over 75 percent and produce over half the continent's rice.[84]

Recognizing the importance of upland rice, CIAT, the research center that developed the first high-yielding varieties for irrigated rice in Latin America, has shifted its research to varieties that yield well under rainfed tropical environments. As part of this research, CIAT is mapping the distribution of upland rice systems throughout Latin America. CIAT's next step should include mapping socioeconomic features. Such a map is important because, since mechanization, the area under upland rice is growing faster than that under irrigation. Indeed, the upland rice area is expected to increase by 50 percent by the year 2000. Moreover, most growth is expected to occur on frontiers as cultivation shifts to cheaper lands—Meta, Mexico's Yucatan peninsula, or the edges of the Amazon Basin in Peru, Brazil, and Bolivia.[85] Because Latin American rice-growing expands primarily along its frontiers, land management and the social and economic costs of land's absorption into *latifundia* must be matched by concern about the escalating rates at which frontier forests are being cleared. Today, high-yielding varieties to be grown under extensive and mechanized conditions on alluvial soils could speed land-clearing by pioneer farmers.

Where unjust land-tenure systems are simply accepted, the connections between improved agricultural technologies, poverty, food shortages, and resource degradation are likely to be ignored.[86] But if agricultural researchers consider socioeconomic factors as they map upland rice systems, they can identify and lend technological support to pioneer farming systems before they are incorporated into *latifundia* and forced into further encroachments on forested lands. Research oriented toward increasing such farmers' economic stability can complement new rice technologies with research aimed at giving the farmer multiple sources of income. Indeed, much research on soils, fertilizer needs, and alternative crops has already begun for portions of the Amazon Basin,[87] and research on farming systems is conducted by many international centers affiliated with the Consultative Group on International Agricultural Research.[88] Given the increasing importance of rice in Latin America, rice-farming systems research in the region's tropical lowlands is essential. Without it, "Green Revolution" rice could, as it has in Colombia, contribute to food insecurity, resource mismanagement on an ever expanding frontier, and political instability.

But such research can only be effective and should only attract funding when policymakers in Colombia, Latin America, the United States, and the international community recognize that Latin American economic and political development does not depend on the *creation* of wealth so much as it depends on the distribution of land and wealth. Policymakers must also reorient development aid to further social justice, food security, and sound resources management. The economic future of Latin America lies not in accumulating or concentrating wealth, but in satisfying basic human needs.

NOTES

1. International Food Policy Research Institute, *Food Needs of Developing Countries: Projections of Production and Consumption to 1990,* Research Report No. 3 (Washington, D.C., December 1977) 17.

2. The World Bank, Agricultural Research Sector Policy Paper (Washington, D.C., 1981); Consultative Group on International Agricultural Research, *Report on the Consultative Group and the International Research It Supports: An Integrative Report* (Washington, D.C.: CGIAR Secretariat, 1983), Annexes 2 and 3.

3. The World Bank, Agricultural Research Sector Policy Paper (Washington, D.C., 1981), 18–23.

4. The World Bank, Agricultural Research Sector Policy Paper, (Washington, D.C., 1981) 23; A. Pearse, *Seeds of Plenty, Seeds of Want: Social and Economic Implications of the Green Revolution* (Oxford: Clarendon Press, 1980); Cynthia Hewitt de Alcantara, *Modernizing Mexican Agriculture: Socio-Economic Implications of Technological Change 1940–1970,* UNRISD Report No. 76.5 (Geneva); and E. Feder, *Perverse Development* (Quezon City, Philippines: Foundation for Nationalist Studies, 1983).

5. See the Comptroller General, Report to the Congress of the United States. Changes in U.S. assistance to deter deforestation in developing countries, Government Accounting Office ID-82-50, September 16, 1982; and Bruce Rich, "Recent U.S. and International Initiatives Concerning Tropical Deforestation," *Cultural Survival Quarterly,* no. 1, 1982: 25–27.

6. G. Scobie, and R. Posada, *The Impact of High-Yielding Rice Varieties in Latin America with Special Emphasis on Colombia* (Cali, Colombia: Centro Internacional de Agricultura Tropical [CIAT], 1977) 10; and A. de Janvry, *The Agrarian Question and Reformism in Latin America* (Baltimore: The John Hopkins University Press, 1981) 131–136.

7. World Bank, Agricultural Research Sector Policy Paper, 23.

8. E. Feder, "The Odious Competition Between Man and Animal over Agricultural Resources in the Underdeveloped Countries," *Review*, vol. 3, no. 3: 463–500; J. Foweraker, *The Struggle for Land: A Political Economy of the Pioneer Frontier in Brazil from 1930 to the Present Day* (Cambridge: Cambridge University Press, 1981); B. Helmsing, "Colonización agricola y asentamentos campesinos en zonas fronterizas," *Revista Interamericana de planeación*, vol. XVI, no. 62: 146–196; N. Myers, "The Hamburger Connection," *Ambio*, 1981 vol. 10, no. 1:3–8; J. Nations and D. Komer, "Indians, Immigrants and Beef Exports: Deforestation in Central America, *Cultural Survival Quarterly*, 1982, vol. 4, no. 1: 8–12; and J. Parsons, "Forest to Pasture: Development of Destruction," *Revista biologica tropical* (Suppl. 1) 1976, no. 121: 28.

9. See U.S. Congress, Senate Committee on Foreign Relations, *Survey of the Alliance for Progress: Colombia, A Case History of U.S. AID* (Washington, D.C.: Government Printing Office, 1969) 2; M. Speck, *Colombia: Growth Without Equity* (Washington, D.C.: Center for International Policy, 1981); and R. Jimeno and S. Volk, *Colombia: Whose Country Is This Anyway?* North American Congress on Latin America's *Report on the Americas*, 1983, vol. XVII, no. 3: 2–35.

10. A. Berry and M. Urrutia, *Income Distribution in Colombia* (New Haven: Yale University Press, 1976) 115; Speck, *Growth Without Equity*, 2; and Instituto Interamericano de Ciencias Agricolas-Organización de Estados Americanos, Proyecto cooperativo de investigación sobre technologia agropecuaria en América Latina, Centro Internacional de Investigaciones para el Desarollo, Estudio del processo de generación, Difusión y adopción de tecnologia en la producción de arroz en Colombia, *Estructura y organización de la producción de arroz en Colombia* (Bogotá: Ofisel, 1981) ch. 2, 38.

11. The last census was taken in 1970. See Speck, *Growth Without Equity*, 10; S. Perry, *La Crisis agraria en Colombia, 1950–1980* (Bogotá: El Ancora Editoras, 1983) 78, 565; and A. Posada and B.C. de Posada, *Bases para un desarollo harmónico del valle* (Cali, Colombia: Libreria Nacional, 1982) 32.

12. R. Cardona, et al., *El Éxodo de Colombianos: un estudio de la corriente migratoria a los Estados Unidos y un intento para proporcionar el retorno* (Bogotá: Ediciones Tercer Mundo, 1980) 51.

13. Speck, *Growth Without Equity*, 4; and Jimeno and Volk, "Whose Country Is This?", 16–18.
    Since the assassination in May 1984 of Colombia's minister of justice, Rodrigo Lara Bonilla, pressure on drug mafias has increased. Following the largest M-19 guerilla attack in several years on Florencia, Caqueta, in March 1984, a counter-raid by the military seized $1.2 billion worth of cocaine in a processing factory that operated under the protection of a guerilla group. See *El Tiempo*, July 5, 1984, 1–2; *El Tiempo*, March 18, 1984, 1; and *The New York Times*, March 21, 1984, 1.

Let Them Eat Rice?

14. See E. Duff, *Land Reform in Colombia* (New York: Frederick A. Praeger, 1968) 138ff; H. Felstenhausen, *Agrarian Reform and Development in Colombia* (Madison, Wis.: University of Wisconsin, 1970); and Perry, *La Crisis agraria 1950–1980*, no. 13, 79–80.

15. Perry, *La Crisis agraria*, 62, 17–20, 173–174.

16. R. Marsh, *Development Strategies in Rural Colombia: The Case of Caqueta* (Los Angeles: University of California, Latin American Center Publication, 1983) 8; J. Ashby, "Socio-economic Factors in Soil Erosion: A Case Study of Pescador and Mondomo, Cauca Department, Colombia", forthcoming in E.G. Hallsworth (ed.), *Socio-Economic Factors in Soil Conservation* (Boulder, Colo.: Westview Press) 1; R. Howeler and L.F. Cadavid, *El Cultivo de yuca con conservación del suelo en la región de Mondomo* (Cali, Colombia: Centro Internacional de Agricultura Tropical, mimeo, 1982) cited in Ashby, 1982, *Socio-economic Factors*, 8; and Perry, *La Crisis agraria*, 12, 62, 94.

17. Colonial and other precapitalist forms of institutionally coerced labor include *encomiendas, repartimientos,* slavery, and various forms of *colonato;* or sharecropping. See R. Stavenhagen, *Agrarian Problems and Peasant Movements in Latin America* (New York: Doubleday, 1970); K. Duncan, I. Rutledge, and C. Harding, *Land and Labor in Latin America* (New York: Cambridge University Press, 1977); A. de Janvry, *The Agrarian Question;* and J. Foweraker, *The Struggle for Land.*

18. The most succinct accounts of Colombia's land reforms and their relation to pioneer frontiers are to be found in Marsh, *Development Strategies,* and Duff, *Land Reform.*

19. C.A. Machado, "Políticas agrarias en Colombia," in D. Fajardo et al. (eds.), *Campesinado y capitalismo en Colombia* (Bogotá: 1981), 57–88.

20. P. Oquist, *Violence, Conflict and Politics in Colombia* (New York: Academic Press, 1983), 89–99, 227.

21. Berry and Urrutia, *Income Distribution,* 21; Machado, "Políticas agrarias," 68–78; Instituto Interamericano de Ciencias Agricolas, Estudio del proceso, ch. VI, 10.

22. Colombia was among the first Latin American countries to sign Mutual Defense Assistance agreements with the United States in 1952. That same year the first Latin American counter-insurgency training school was established in Colombia, and these soldiers were sent to battle against the peasants during La Violencia. Between 1961 and 1967 Colombia received about $60 million in military aid and almost $100 million more in military equipment. See Jimeno and Volk, "Whose Country Is This?" 10–12.

23. Marsh, *Development Strategies,* 14–22; Duff, *Land Reform,* 171–174; and A. Molano, *De La Violencia a la colonización: Itinerario social de una illusión campesina* (Bogotá: CINEP, ms., preliminary version, 1981).

24. Duff, *Land Reform,* 168.

25. Marsh, *Development Strategies,* 19–22.

26. de Janvry, *The Agrarian Question,* 132.

27. Perry, *La Crisis agraria,* 121.

28. Marsh, *Development Strategies,* 23–24; and B.M Bagley and F.B. Botero, Organizaciones contemporaneas en Colombia. Un estudio de la Asociación Nacional de Usuarios Campesinos in *Estudios rurales Latinoamericanos,* 1978.

29. A discussion of the complement of measures taken to promote industrialization is beyond the scope of this chapter. They include tariffs against imported manufactured goods and low foreign exchange rates, as well as the emphasis on cheap food and labor discussed above. de Janvry, *The Agrarian Question,* 132; Scobie and Posada, *The Impact of High-Yielding Rice Varieties,* 81–83. Perry. *La Crisis agraria,* passim.

30. Perry, *La Crisis agraria,* 126–9: 159–160.

31. Instituto Interamericano de Ciencias Agricolas, Estudio del proceso, ch. 3, 11–12.

32. Perry, 1983, *La Crisis agraria,* 126–129.

33. Perry, *La Crisis agraria,* 125–6; Speck, 1981, *Growth Without Equity,* 5, 9; Marsh, *Development Strategies,* 25; de Janvry, *The Agrarian Question,* 251.

34. de Janvry, *The Agrarian Question,* 133–136.

35. Perry, *La Crisis agraria,* 66.

36. Perry, *La Crisis agraria,* 21–53.

37. Perry, *La Crisis agraria,* 26–29.

38. C.E. Alvarez, "La Agricultura moderna: Contra la pared," in Sociedad de Ingenieros Agronomos del Llano (SIALL) 1983, ed. #3, 40.

39. Perry, *La Crisis agraria,* 24–27, 35–37, 144–149.

40. Scobie and Posada, *The Impact of High-Yielding Rice,* 82.

41. P.P. Leurquin, *Rice in Colombia: A Case Study in Agricultural Development.* Food Research Institute Studies, 1967, vol. 7 no. 2: 217–303; and Instituto Interamericano de Ciencias Agricolas, 1981, Estudio del proceso, ch. 6, 9.

42. Instituto Interamericano de Ciencias Agricolas, 1981, Estudio del proceso, ch. 6, 10, ch. 2, 7; CIAT, *CIAT in the 1980's:* A Long-Range Plan for the Centro Internacional de Agricultura (Cali, Colombia: 1980) 7, 16–33.

43. E. Sin Clavijo, 1983, "Producción de arroz en Colombia," *Arroz,* vol. 32, no. 327, 9–340 (Bogotá).

44. Instituto Interamericano de Ciencias Agricolas, Estudio del proceso, ch. 6, 27–30, 35, ch. 3, 12.

45. Scobie and Posada, *The Impact of High-Yielding Rice,* 32, 78.

46. Scobie and Posada, *The Impact of High-Yielding Rice,* 32–37; and Instituto Interamericano de Ciencias Agricolas, Estudio del proceso, ch. 6, 33.

47. Fedearroz, *El Arroz en Colombia* (Fedearroz [the Colombian rice growers' federation] Bogotá, 1981).

48. Instituto Interamericano de Ciencias Agricolas, Estudio del proceso, ch. 6, 36; and Sin Clavijo, "Producción de arroz," 23.

49. M.L. de Leal and C.D. Deere, "La mujer y el desarollo del capitalismo en el agro," in M.L. de Leal (ed.), *Mujer y capitalismo agrario.* Estudio de Cuatro Regiones Colombianas. (Bogotá: Associación Colombiana para el Estudio de la Población, 1980); Perry, *La Crisis agraria,* 78; and Instituto Interamericano de Ciencias Agricolas, Estudio del proceso, ch. 3, 10.

In addition to changes in land tenure and employment, commercial agriculture brought other consequences to Tolima country people that remain incompletely understood in their long-range implications. In 1974, Dr. Marco Micolta, the director of the hospital in Guamo, Tolima, called attention to an "epidemic" of spontaneous abortions and premature and malformed births. Rural workers had apparently been exposed to heavy spraying with herbicides based on toxic components (2,4D and 2,45D). Subsequent investigations brought to light the dangers of pesticide intoxication, its harmful effect on the male reproductive system and libido, and the high rates of contamination of commercial foods with organochlorides such as Aldrin, Endrin, Dieldrin, and DDT. The dangers have received journalistic and sensationalist treatment and they require serious and long-term investigation.

50. Instituto Interamericano de Ciencias Agricolas, Estudio del proceso, ch. 2, 37–38.

51. Fedearroz, Informe Anual, Bogotá, 1977.

52. Cited in Jimeno and Volk, "Whose Country Is This?" 20.

53. O. Lombana, "Estudio sobre las causas de la disminuición del consumo del arroz en Colombia," *Arroz,* vol. 32, no. 327: 51–64.

54. Instituto Interamericano de Ciencias Agricolas, Estudio del proceso, ch. 2, 44.

55. Sin Clavijo, "Producción de arroz," 22.

56. United States Department of Agriculture, Economic Research Service, *Rice: Outlook and Situation,* September 1983, 6; S.H. Holder and W.R. Grant, *U.S. Rice Industry,* U.S. Department of Agriculture, Agricultural Economic Report No. 433, Washington, 1979; and J.L. Flora and C.B. Flora, *The State and Rice Production, Marketing and Research in the United States* (Unpublished manuscript. University of Kansas, 1982).

57. Foreign Agricultural Service, Attaché Report: *Colombia: Annual Grain and Feed Report,* February 28, 1983, 1–12; and Perry, *La Crisis agraria,* 29.

58. Instituto Interamericano de Ciencias Agricolas, Estudio del proceso, ch. 2, 10; and Hartford and Reed, 1980, *Caracterización del Sector Ganadero de Colombia, 1950–1975.* CIAT, Cali (in press).

59. E.J. Owen, and L.F. Sanchez, 1979, "Uso y Manejo de los Suelos de la Parte Plana del Departamento del Meta," *ICA,* Bogota.
   In the Piedmont the popular distinctions for soil types are *vega* and *savanna*; technically, the soils of Meta are classified in types ranging from I (the most fertile *vega* soils) to VI, VII, and VIII, which are extremely acid, infertile, and of limited use.

60. Instituto Interamericano de Ciencias Agricolas, Estudio del proceso, ch. 2, 4.

61. L. A. León, "Fertilización fosfórica del Arroz" (Cali, Colombia: CIAT, 1981) 14.

62. A. Molano, 1981, "De la violencia a la colonización"; S.D. Giraldo and L. Ladron de Guevara, 1981, "Desarollo agricola y distribuición espacial de la Población. Analisis del proceso de colonización reciente en Colombia." Asociación de Facultades de Medicina y Corporación Centro Regional de Población Informe final presentado; and D. Leal, C. Coral, and J. Neta, "Diagnosticó sobre el cultivo del arroz en el Departamento del Meta," (Instituto Colombiano Agropecuario [ICA], Villavicencio), ms.

63. Instituto Colombiano Agropecuario (ICA), Regional 8, Llanos Orientales, Distrito de Transferencia de Tecnología No. 1, Villavicencio, Informe Anual de Actividades. Villavicencio, 1982; ICA, 1982, Area Inscrita por cultivos hasta mayo 30 de 1982. Llanoticias. Boletin Informative No. 09:1; ICA, Regional No. 8, Villavicencio.

64. Fedearroz, *El Arroz en Colombia.*

65. Censo Nacional Agropecuario. Boyaca y Meta. (Bogotá: Departamento Nacional de Estadística, 1971) 115.

66. Censo Nacional Agropecuario. (Bogotá: Departamento Nacional de Estadística, 1971) 109, 112.

67. CECORA, 1981, Diagnostico de la explotación y el mercadeo de la leche en el Pie de Monte Llanero. Central de Cooperativas de Reforma Agraria Ltda. Programa de Desarollo Rural Integrado, DRI. Subprograma de Comercialización. Villavicencio, agosto 1981; Departamento de Planeación Nacional, 1980, Programa de Desarollo Rural Integrado, DRI, Departamento del Meta. Selección de Areas a Incorporar. octobre 1980, Villavicencio; Instituto Colombiano Agropecuario, 1982. Analisis de la situación general de familias PAN del Distrito Ariari. Documento de Trabajo. Instituto Colombiano Agropecuario. Granada (Ariari).

68. Interviews with Marta Alvares, Director, Servicio Nacional de Empleo, August 1983, Villavicencio.

69. Banco de la República, Situación Economica del Departamento del Meta en 1981 (1982) 60–61.

70. It is frequently asserted that the explosion of working-class housing in Villavicencio took place in response to the cocaine economy: either from wage workers—who harvest cocaine—participation in the repression of cocaine farming, which brings its own opportunities for profit; or from delivery runs. In the countryside, especially in the area north of Villavicencio, the small dairy farms of the Piedmont are managed by women and children because the men have gone to work in the coca fields. It is believed by local agronomists that the need to launder monies obtained from cocaine sales was responsible for as much as 10 percent of the upland rice hectares in 1982.

71. N.A. Ramos and C. Romero, "El pasto Brachiaria: caracteristicas y establecimiento en los Llanos Orientales," Boletin Tecnico, no. 4 (Bogotá: ICA, 1976); and N.A. Ramos and C. Romero, "Efecto del almacenamiento y la escarificación en la germinación del Pasto Brachiaria (*Brachiaria decumbens* stapf)," (Villavicencio, Meta: ICAAA).

72. The socioeconomic component of the Phosphorus Project in the Meta Piedmont was supported by International Fertilizer Development Center and CIAT, and a postdoctoral grant from the Rockefeller Foundation. See E. de G.R. Hansen, *Social Relations of Land and Fertilizer Use and Frontier Integration: Upland Rice in the Llanos Orientales of Colombia*. Report to IFDC, Cali, December 1983; and E. de G.R. Hansen, *Land Management and Phosphorus Fertilizer Use Among Upland Rice Farmers in Meta, Colombia: Executive Summary of Research*, International Fertilizer Development Center, May 1984.

73. Because they are planting HYVs that are highly responsive to nitrogen, all farmers used an average of over 130 kilograms of urea on their fields, applied at the crop's critical growth stages, 20–30 days after germination and 50–60 days after germination. Predictably, the larger farmers used somewhat more urea than the smaller ones. In addition, most use at least 50 kilograms potassium chloride mixed in with the first application of urea.

74. On acidic soils much of the phosphorus that is present in the soil is not available to the plant because the aluminum and iron react with phosphorus to form relatively insoluble—and so unavailable—aluminum and iron phosphates. Midwestern American soils average 3,000 parts per million (ppm) phosphorus in the top soil; older North American soils range between 200 ppm and 500 ppm. In Latin American soils total P ranges from only about 200 to 600 ppm. See Sanchez, *Properties and Management of Soils in the Tropics*, 259–274; and W. Fenster and Leon, "Management of Phosphorus Fertilization in Establishing and Maintaining Improved Pastures on Acid Infertile Soils of Tropical America," in P. Sanchez and L.E. Tergas (eds.), *Pasture Production in Acid Soils of the Tropics* (Cali, Colombia: CIAT, 1979). P. Sanchez, *Properties and Management of Soils in the Tropics* (New York: John Wiley and Sons, 1976) 253.

75. International Fertilizer Development Center/CIAT Phosphorus, Project, Meta, Colombia. See also, L.F. Sanchez and E. Owen, n.d. "Situación actual de los suelos arroceros del Piedmonte Llanero," Regional 8,

Villavicencio, for the high variability of Piedmont soils after years of rentals for rice growing.

76. There is a discreet black market for receipts for certified seed. In addition, when farmers are not planting all of their hectares with credit, they can buy cheaper uncertified seed from local rice growers.

77. One very large farmer turned his farm over to 250 head of recently purchased cattle, and may in the next season, rent fields out with pasture establishing clauses.

78. DRI 1982. Inalisis de la situación general de familias PAN del Distrito Ariari. Documento de Trabajo. Instituto Columbiano Agropecuario. Granada (Ariari).

79. See Pearse, *Seeds of Plenty,* 108–110; de Janvry, *The Agrarian Question,* 264–268; S. George, *Feeding The Few, Corporate Control of Food.* Institute for Policy Studies (Washington, D.C.: Institute for Policy Studies, 1980) 69; F.W. Lappe, J. Collins, and D. Kinley, *Aid as Obstacle* (San Francisco: Institute for Food and Development Policy, 1980) 13, 41.

80. Public Law 480, the Agricultural Trade Development Act, was passed in 1954, and later named the Food for Peace Program. Its essential purpose was, and is, to dispose of United States agricultural surpluses so as to prevent price declines at home, and to create markets for American products abroad. Title I sales are made on concessionary terms (long term, low interest) and the proceeds of sales are used by receiving governments for their own support. Title II grants the products to U.S. voluntary agencies, the U.N. World Food Program, and less frequently to governments in need of food relief. In 1975 amendments to PL-480 decreed that three-quarters of PL-480 loans were to go to countries with low per capita GNPs, and not be given to countries that consistently violated human rights. See Lappe et al., *Aid as Obstacle,* 63–79, and R. Burbach and P. Flynn, "Agribusiness in the Americas," *Monthly Review Press* (New York, 1980), 93–120, for evidence that PL-480 food loans (1) have driven foreign farmers out of production and made countries like India, South Korea, Colombia, and Bolivia dependent on the United States for basic foods; (2) promote the economic interests of U.S. grain dealers and food processors at the expense of food security; (3) have used food as a political weapon in support of U.S. military allies, such as Israel, Turkey, South Korea, Pakistan, South Vietnam, Cambodia, and Chile under Pinochet, but against governments like Allende's Chile; and (4) serve to feed urban middle-income populations rather than the urban or rural poor. Even disaster relief (Title II) shipments, either do not reach the poor (Ethiopia, Upper Volta, Ghana) or stand in the way of reconstruction efforts (Guatemala).

81. See S. Eckstein, G. Donald, D. Horton, and C. Carol, *Land Reform in Latin America: Bolivia, Chile, Mexico, Peru and Venezuela* (World Bank Staff Working Paper No. 275, Washington, D.C., 1978), for evidence of generally greater output and more efficient land use following redistributive reforms.

82. Duff, *Land Reform;* Perry, *La Crisis agraria;* Felstenhausen, *Agrarian Reform;* and U.S. Congress, Senate Committee.

83. World Bank, *Land Reform,* Sector Policy Paper (Washington, D.C., 1975) 5.

84. CIAT, *CIAT Report 83* (Cali, Colombia: CIAT, 1983) 5205; D.R. Laing, R. Posada, P.R. Jennings, C.P. Martines, and P.G. Jones, *Upland Rice in the Latin American Region: Overall Description of Environment, Constraints and Potential.* Paper presented at Upland Rice Workshop, Bouake, Ivory Coast, October 1982, 305; and P. Jones, *Upland Rice in the Andean Region.* Presented at the International Rice Testing Congress, August 1982 (Cali, Colombia: CIAT, 1983).

85. CIAT, *CIAT Report 83,* 52.

86. In determining its commodity choices and research strategies, for example, CIAT essentially accepts and so intensifies the fundamental inequities of land distribution in South America. Recognizing the "very skewed distribution of land, a particular characteristic of Latin America," four commodities were selected for research: pasture grasses, cassava, beans, and rice. These correspond to different types of land and land use strategies by different socioeconomic groups: (1) intensification of production by large farmers who control the more fertile areas, primarily through mechanization and higher input use, with irrigated rice production; (2) expansion of agricultural production on the less fertile frontier land, with pastures whose establishment is paid for by increased productivity in crops, such as upland rice and cassava; and (3) intensification of production by small farmers through higher, more stable yields, with crops like beans and cassava.

   In this context (in which control of most of the land by large landholders is assumed), the justification for small-farm intensification is primarily political, not economic. While small farmers are recognized to be more efficient producers in terms of their use of land, labor, and capital, their contribution to total production is limited because they control so little land. Small farm intensification, then, represents an attempt to control urban migration and to increase rural employment. Frontier expansion with ranching systems is seen as a necessary complement to large farm agricultural intensification, without regard to the fact that in Colombia, most of the best lands are still given to cattle rather than people, that "in developing countries with rapid increases in incomes, the total use of cereals for livestock feed has increased considerably faster than the use of cereals for human consumption," and that lags in production of food crops arise not from lack of technology, but from socioeconomic conditions that encourage the development of dual agrarian structures, the misuse of land, and the expansion of *latifundia.* See CIAT, *CIAT in the 1980's.*

87. See, for example, Hecht, S.B., ed. *1982 Amazonia Investigacion Sobre Agricultura y Uso de Tierras, Memorias de la Conferencia Internacional,* April 1980, CIAT, Cali.

88. CGIAR, 1979. *The 1979 Report on the Consultative Group and the International Agricultural Research System: An Integrative Report.* Washington, pp. 15-20. Zandstra, H.G., E.C. Price, J.A. Litsinger, and R.A. Morris, 1980. *A Methodology for On-Farm Croppings Systems Research.* The International Rice Research Institute, Manila, Philippines.

CHAPTER 5

Banking on Oil in Venezuela

GENE BIGLER AND
FRANKLIN TUGWELL

───────────────*Editors' Preface*───────────────

In Colombia's next door neighbor, Venezuela, development—driven by a different natural resource, oil—has taken a quite different direction. Venezuela's foresighted government determined to use oil profits to fund diversification and modernization of the economy, so that growth and prosperity could be sustained when oil reserves were gone.

In Venezuela, as in Mexico and Brazil, the importance of the national leadership's basic decisions on development policy and the creation of institutions to carry out development tasks, becomes very clear. The vitality of contested elections creates, in our opinion, more opportunity than problems. The parastatels invented to modernize the country include some excellent models, and some inefficient and corrupt ones. And the Venezuelan investment in education and training is a necessary ingredient for success.

Yet the discouraging lesson of this chapter by Gene Bigler and Franklin Tugwell is that even national control of rich resources, foresight and planning, a tradition of responsive, flexible political leadership, and inventiveness in organizing for development cannot guarantee good resource management. If Venezuela with its wealth and awareness of the need to plan for the sustained exploitation of resources does not succeed, what nation can? This chapter suggests just how difficult the problems of rational development are.

Bigler and Tugwell analyze some of the shortcomings in the Venezuelan experience: postponement of conflict through government largesse, insufficient accountability in the autonomous industries, tardy recognition of the importance of management and coordinating skills, and even the ambitious scale of development.

But another very important lesson in the Venezuelan experience is the problem of indebtedness, and the extent to which that problem may lie beyond a nation's ability to respond. Debt, very large debt, is obviously a heavy burden in any country. It may be even more tricky to manage in a nation that is dependent on the world price of its single commodity. Every aspect of Venezuela's situation is affected by world oil supplies and prices, by the world monetary situation, by the overall health of the world economy and the U.S. economy, and particularly by U.S. interest rates. Fluctuations in any of these can have major effects on developments in Venezuela. Venezuela and other debtor countries are tied to the success or failure of U.S. monetary and economic policies. As this chapter points out, a 1 percent increase in the U.S. interest rate adds $2.5 billion to Venezuela's debt. The irony is a bitter one: even if Venezuela pulls off a miracle of reform and management, U.S. failures could still cause the Venezuelan development efforts to fail.

The United States also has a big stake in Venezuela, despite the relative size, resources, and power of the two states. Sixty percent of all foreign investment in Venezuela is American, as is most of its foreign debt. U.S. firms have invested heavily in Venezuela's iron and steel industry. Venezuela's new generation of technocrats will be largely educated in the United States, and Americans cannot forget that Venezuela in 1984 was the source of approximately 10 percent of U.S. imported oil. Beyond these strictly economic interests is a more transcendent concern: that this friendly democratic society succeed as a model of good governance in the hemisphere.

A s MOST observers of hemispheric affairs know, Venezuela today is in the grip of the most serious economic crisis it has faced in modern times. The economy is very nearly paralyzed. The Gross National Product (GNP) has not grown in more than four years. Internal investment is suffering from "capital flight." Unemployment is at a forty-year high. Inflation is chronically in double digits. Disagreements with the International Monetary Fund (IMF) over the management of the country's foreign debt are worrying Venezuela's lenders.

This crisis is all the more serious because it threatens the viability of the country's development program and, by implication, its democratic institutions.[1] The next few years may well determine whether Venezuela can continue to develop as a stable democracy, a valuable trading partner to the United States, and a champion of the resource-exporting underdeveloped countries.

Venezuela's experience with resource management and its efforts to discover a pattern of sustainable economic development differ in many ways from the experiences of other Latin American countries. For its size and population, Venezuela is the country best endowed with those resources generally considered necessary for industrial development—petroleum, natural gas, iron ore, and bauxite. Its hydroelectric potential is second in South America only to Brazil's.[2] Moreover, its deposits of "unconventional" oil, tar-like heavy and ultra-heavy crude, in the Orinoco Basin represent one of the largest remaining unexploited hydrocarbon resources on earth. Indeed, for the last fifty years the development challenge facing the country's elite has been how to manage abundance—not scarcity—and thereby appropriately limit the role of foreign organizations and technology in the exploitation of that abundance.

Venezuela is also a thriving democracy. During the 1960s and 1970s, when many elected governments fell to military dictatorships, Venezuelans were building, step-by-step, a party-based democracy that has withstood violent challenges from the right and left, and has permitted peaceful transfers of power to the opposition.[3] The most recent occurred early in 1984 when Jaime Lusinchi, the candidate of the Social Democratic party, Acción Democrática (AD), took office. Venezuela was, and remains, however, a democracy whose character has been shaped strongly by the availability of periodic "bonanzas" of government income from the petroleum industry— and whose survival may well be at stake in the struggle to manage the current crisis.

U.S.-Venezuelan relations have sometimes run aground precisely because Venezuela is so rich in resources and so proud of its democratic tradition. Bristling with "resource nationalism," and a commitment to democratic governance that goes beyond its borders, Venezuela has more than once taken issue with Uncle Sam's realpolitik. The principal challenge for the United States has been preventing short-term "irritants"—such as Venezuela's role in creating OPEC (Organization of Petroleum Exporting Countries)—from obscuring the long-term interests that the two countries share as fellow democracies and trading partners.[4]

How did Venezuela's current crisis originate? In a sense, the nation was a victim of its own petroleum. Oil dominates Venezuela's politics and economy far more than it dominates those of Texas. Since the 1920s, the country's economy has relied increasingly on oil exports. By 1982, the industry accounted for about 20 percent of the GNP, 70 percent of the government's budget, and over 95 percent of the country's export earnings. What these dramatic figures do not reflect, however, is how extensively unstable oil earnings have shaped the way Venezuelans live, make economic decisions, and settle conflicts. This "institutionalization" of dependence on income earned by so few is the root of the ongoing crisis.

For decades, most far-sighted Venezuelans have been acutely aware of the unsustainable character of their oil-based development. As early as the 1930s, the phrase *sembrar el petróleo* (to sow the oil) became the government's motto—a commitment to use oil earnings to support self-sustaining growth when the wells run

dry. The country's more astute leaders also realized that oil earnings were partially a curse, arriving erratically and sometimes in
quantities too great to absorb, thus defeating private initiative
and creating habits of dependence that were difficult to alter.
One of these leaders was Juan Pablo Pérez Alfonzo, the "father"
of OPEC, whose conservationist doctrines received acclaim for
decades, but whose advice was almost never heeded on nonoil
matters. To reduce the economic dominance of oil, the governments began in the 1950s and 1960s to invest in other national
resources, including iron ore, hydroelectricity, and, later, aluminum. But these resource sectors grew too slowly to supplant oil's
economic role, especially after the price increases that followed
the 1973 Arab oil embargo.

A critical juncture was reached, in two stages, in the early
1970s. Exploitable reserves of conventional oil finally ceased to
grow as the foreign oil companies, seeing the approach of nationalization, reduced their investments in exploration and drilling.
Production peaked and declined. But the oil crisis of 1973–1974
intervened, and even without new production Venezuela had another income "bonanza" on its hands.

This time the government's reaction was different, partly because the sums of new money were so large, and partly because it
was now clear that the career of conventional oil production was
on the decline.[5] Led by newly elected President Carlos Andres
Pérez, Venezuelan policymakers made it quite clear that they understood this to be the last chance: the last chance for the country
to begin to earn its way and the last chance for the democratic
system to prove its worth. To begin, they nationalized the oil industry, hoping thereby to domesticate decisions about the
country's principal source of revenue. Policymakers then designed and implemented a dramatic program of state investments in human and physical capital—education, iron and steel,
aluminum, mass transit, hydroelectricity, and housing—striving
to create within a few short years the basis for self-sustaining industrial and commercial development. The depopulated
Guyana region, already targeted for new industry, received much
of the new investment. However, as the projects multiplied, the
government lacked capital and decided to borrow internationally, using Venezuela's large reserves as collateral. The management of this program was placed largely in the hands of an

innovative system of powerful public sector enterprises—what we have termed "the entrepreneurial state."[6]

The program was breathtaking in scale and conception. But would it work? Could the country modify its unbalanced economy by exporting finished and semifinished products to pay for imports? Could Venezuela accomplish this and tackle poverty and inequality at the same time? Did the country have the necessary human skills? Could it overcome the economic and political habits that had hamstrung it in the past?

By 1981 the answer, it seemed to many, was no. Venezuela was caught in a deepening economic crisis that fed growing fears that the country would never recover. When a second wave of petroleum earnings, the result of price increases following the Iranian Revolution, flooded the country in the late 1970s, no new growth was generated at all. By 1981, the oil market had slumped again, and government income from petroleum exports fell suddenly. When short-term loans came due in late 1982, payment was postponed. Capital flight had begun, and evidence mounted of managerial incompetence, corruption within state agencies, growing private fortunes, and worsening social conditions for the majority. The subsequent Christian Democratic administration of Herrera Campins vacillated, unable to act decisively. The vicious cycle of underdevelopment seemed to have triumphed; the historic development "lcap" seemed to have failed.[7]

Fortunately, this story can be interpreted differently and could have a very different conclusion. Despite bad timing and implementation problems, Venezuelans may in fact be groping toward a new but more viable political economy—one that promises to ease the grip of oil dependence. The obstacles to success remain formidable and will take years to overcome. But Venezuela's inherited institutions, flexible leadership, problem-solving orientation, and capacity to learn and experiment give ample grounds for hope. Clearly, the most innovative aspect of Venezuela's developmental experiment lies not in its speed or scope, themselves extraordinary enough, but in Venezuela's unusual synthesis of public enterprise, private sector initiative, and democratic politics—all backed by major investments in "human capital."

The closest parallel to Venezuela's approach is probably Chile's attempt to promote development via its innovative Chilean Development Corporation (CORFO) in the late 1930s. The path followed by India and other Latin American countries (Colombia, Mexico, and Uruguay), combining democracy and state enterprise, also bear some resemblance. Yet Venezuela differs because of its great and continuing resource abundance, its emphasis on experimentation and innovation, and its public sector predominance without private-sector exclusion. Venezuela also differs in its support of higher education in technical fields, and, above all, the growth of its two-party democracy.

OIL REVENUES AND PUBLIC SECTOR GROWTH

Venezuela's peculiar development pattern and the Venezuelans' remarkable sense of self-awareness are both personified by Juan Bimba. A national caricature, Juan is a hungry peasant bumpkin of the 1940s who became a consumer-happy social cynic by the 1980s.[8] Particulars of the story vary, but Juan Bimba's world is shaped, often vicariously, by such overpowering forces as big oil, the government, political parties and bosses, family business empires, generals, politicians—or sometimes just "oligarchs." Bimba traipses through this world, suffering assorted misadventures, but always, somehow, ending up just a little better off.

Modern Venezuela's development, like Juan Bimba's, has been remarkable and lucky. At the end of World War I, the country was a rural backwater governed by a brutal dictator. Fewer than 15 percent of the people lived in cities, per capita income was roughly equal to Bolivia's, and almost 80 percent of the population was illiterate. Today, the mostly urban population has a per capita income of $4,500, the highest in Spanish-speaking America, and five or six times that of Bolivia. The country boasts generous civil rights and liberties and about as high a per capita university enrollment as England, Germany, and the leading countries of Latin America. Comparable social and economic change took nearly a century and a half in England and the United States.

Oil has been the engine of Venezuela's growth. From 1917 to the Great Depression, hundreds of thousands of people migrated from rural areas to burgeoning oil camps and regional centers of oil development, such as Maracaibo. Oil companies bid up the price of labor. The rapid influx of dollars and sterling drove the value of the currency up and, together with the rural labor shortage, helped ruin the traditional agricultural export economy. Concession and royalty payments to the government, though meager at first, paid the national debt, enlarged the bureaucracy, and strengthened the armed forces, thus ending regional challenges to government authority in Caracas. In short, the petroleum industry provided the foundations of a strong centralized national government in Venezuela.

As the petroleum industry grew, the oil companies, often in collaboration with dictator Juan Vicente Gómez, sought to limit the industry's impact on the country. They imported more "manageable" English-speaking workers and built their refineries off-shore, on the Dutch-held islands of Aruba and Curaçao. Even so, the industry's impact was enormous. Fully 96 percent of the nonpetroleum growth in Venezuela from 1942 to 1948 stemmed from the oil industry's domestically retained earnings (domestic purchases of goods and services, plus taxes). The Gross Domestic Product (GDP) grew at an incredible 13.5 percent a year over that period. As late as the mid-1950s, retained earnings from petroleum still accounted for about 70 percent of growth, and from 1917 to 1977 oil underwrote one of the most rapid and sustained periods of economic growth in modern history.[9]

While Venezuelans benefited from this economic growth, they realized that it was not a healthy, sound, enduring growth. In some ways, it was like living on welfare. As they watched their world change, the country's democratic leaders grew increasingly concerned about relying on the exploitation of nonrenewable natural resources, the consequent lack of control over matters of national interest, and the consumption-oriented pattern of private enrichment and indifference to cultural and other values that seemed to come with repeated fiscal bonanzas.

After Gómez died in 1935, the new government in Caracas issued the first national plan to "sow the petroleum." Seven national plans have been issued since then, all of them proposing essentially the same thing. First, the wealth from exhaustible foreign-dominated resources must be used by the state to foster new sources of renewable and nationally controlled income. Second, the benefits from national resources must be spread equitably. Third, the state must nurture the country's cultural and social growth by providing scholarships, subsidized housing, transportation, cultural and athletic opportunities, better health care, and improved living conditions.[10]

Such expectations were not unrealistic, because Venezuela had the money. By the late 1940s, Venezuelans were already collecting 50 percent of the profits earned by foreign companies; by the 1970s, just before the industry's takeover by the government, the share had increased to 90 percent.[11] The income bonanza created by the Arab oil embargo made it possible for the government to "purchase" the industry, although several companies have claimed that the compensation paid, totaling about $1 billion, was insufficient.[12]

Although government revenues from the private petroleum industry in earlier decades were huge, they did fluctuate unpredictably as new deposits were discovered, international oil demand varied, and competition (especially from the Mideast) arose. Because Venezuela's government couldn't control the country's major source of wealth, the state and society had to adjust constantly.[13] Between 1936 and 1981, revenue fluctuations of 30 percent or more were common from one year to the next—changes of a magnitude seen in the United States only at the start and finish of World War II. Nor did nationalization bring stability. The petroleum tax income of 1976 (33 billion bolívares) increased 5 percent in 1977, and then fell 9 percent in 1978.[14] Collections then rose 65 percent, 37 percent, and 6 percent to an historic high of 75 billion bolívares in 1981, only to plummet by 22 percent in 1982 and another 18 percent in 1983, to a level below that of 1979 (48 billion).

Successive governments have responded pragmatically to this problem. Before nationalization, when income was down, democratic governments usually increased oil production or the country's share of oil revenue. At the same time, they cut spending, increased borrowing, and sought more foreign investment. Military dictatorships before 1945 and again during the 1950s bucked a national consensus by selling to foreign oil companies.

Until 1976, when oil production was nationalized, the need for fiscal revenue tended to prevail over the government's conservationist concerns. From the mid-1950s on, the state pushed foreign companies to increase production as world prices declined. Pressure intensified after the late 1960s when taxes on industry profits had become so high that taxes could no longer be increased when new funds were needed. As nationalization approached and world oil prices improved in 1972–1973, the state enforced a stricter conservationist policy. Production levels were cut by almost a quarter from 1974 to 1976, and then reduced another 20 percent after the price increases of 1979–1980. More recently, to help keep OPEC prices stable, Venezuela further stanched output. Thus, production has dropped from its peak of more than 3 million barrels per day in 1970 to just over 1.5 million barrels per day in 1984. This reduction, along with increased investment in new reserves, will make Venezuelan conventional crude oil deposits last at least forty more years.

When the treasury was full, the Venezuelan government typically spent some windfall earnings to create or expand public enterprises, public service corporations, development finance banks and institutes, and other autonomous institutions. Thus was born the decentralized public administration—the entrepreneurial state—that, especially since the 1970s, has become a distinctive feature of the Venezuelan development world.[15] The government's hope was that generous initial endowments and management autonomy would allow these new institutions to prosper even when no new government transfers were available. In contrast, funding for ministries tended to change more slowly. As revenues grew, the agencies of the decentralized public administration thus took on more and more responsibility. Many outgrew their original focus on development projects, and some even found themselves in the business of providing basic human services—housing, sewage and water, education, recreation, and employment.[16]

THE POLITICS OF FISCAL SATURATION

The state's growing importance as a source of income and employment, along with Venezuela's economic vulnerability to international events, also shaped Venezuelan political development. On the one hand, oil revenues empowered the central government in Caracas, reducing state and local governments to secondary status. They also buffered many "classic" political clashes common in other nations. Schisms between urban modernizers and rural landholders, squabbles between the state and the middle and upper classes over taxation, conflicts between workers and managers over income redistribution, and disagreements between public and private economic managers over productivity and international competitiveness all lost their edge.

On the other hand, the economic growth that petroleum development stimulated made the burgeoning middle class clamor for more control over the government and the distribution of largesse. Oil revenues also heightened the stakes of political competition: because the government controlled such a large percentage of available funds, losing an election or being toppled in a coup spelled economic as well as political catastrophe. (Indeed, a key step in consolidating a democratic system was the realization of the Social Democratic party, Acción Democrática, that stability required a coalition government—in effect, sharing access to government—with opposition parties.) Oil revenues also increased corruption. Governments tended to rely heavily on the distribution of revenues to garner support—one explanation for the large numbers of public employees, regional patterns of public spending, and historical overinvestment in urban construction projects as elections approach. But the same things have made Venezuelan governments vulnerable to income fluctuations.

In sum, petroleum revenues have created a political system that, though democratic, has had little experience in handling and overcoming the "classic" social conflicts of political evolution. To be sure, Venezuela has run into peculiar difficulties of its own, mostly associated with the heightened conflict over control of public revenues. But what has emerged is a polity heavily oriented toward managing largesse, a system in which control of the government is all-important, and in which conflict is "managed" simply by distributing more benefits. A cardinal rule of Venezuelan politics is to avoid politically costly, visible redistributions. Except in elections, there are few overt losers in the political game.

Such an arrangement, of course, tends to feed on itself, increasing the size of the state and the appetite of political leaders for ever-increasing sums of money. It also creates an ensemble of institutional and personal dependencies—hangers-on expecting protection and support—as well as optimism about the future and specific expectations about the availability of money for, say, an industrial project, an irrigation system, or a hospital. Government is too often seen not as an arbiter of conflicting demands but as Santa Claus.

THE PRIVATE SECTOR AND THE STATE

Venezuela remains a capitalist country despite the crucial importance of the public sector in the economy. Domestic taxation levels have remained low, and government concern for such matters as productivity and export potential has been episodic. Politicians have regulated private business closely, tolerated individual enrichment, and helped preserve the private sector's traditional concentration in services, import management, and production for private consumption. In general, government has stimulated development by investing public funds in infrastructure and "social overhead projects" rather than promoting productivity.[17]

Partly because Venezuela's economic growth has been so rapid, the private sector is relatively young. A surprising number of new businesses have first and second generations of entrepreneurial families at the helm. Only thirteen of the country's thirty-one commercial banks (in 1983) existed before 1950, and only 10 percent of all manufacturing firms were formed before 1940. (Even so, these firms are highly concentrated, with most of the markets for domestic goods and services dominated by a few firms that restrict competition.)

The private sector is also quite "foreign." The history of foreign corporate involvement in petroleum and iron ore, at least until the 1970s, is well known. But the degree to which products and services, technology, production and marketing methods, and consumption patterns reflect international standards is not. Although the relative importance of direct foreign investment in Venezuela has declined greatly in recent years, from about $9 billion in 1974 to just over $2 billion today, there are still over a thousand foreign-owned enterprises and about five hundred of mixed ownership. Twenty-five of these number among the seventy leading manufacturing outfits in the country. Sixty-five percent of these investments are from the United States, but Canadian, Japanese, German, Swiss, English, and Spanish businesses have important stakes in Venezuela as well.[18] Many of businesses' leading families are headed by or descended from recent immigrants, as are many executives of the large companies.[19]

As might be expected, the key to survival in Venezuelan business is access to public authorities. Private businesses, which profess ideological commitment to markets and free enterprise, are nonetheless heavily subsidized and protected. They depend on the government to enforce market-sharing arrangements and to restrict competition. With government its protector, business has neglected productivity. With business its ward, government has gotten deeply into market affairs.[20]

The "boom and bust" pattern of economic growth, and the unpredictability of government actions, have also left Venezuela's private sector with a short-term investment mentality—even compared to the United States—and an obsession with security. Yet, Venezuelan private businesses and agricultural producers have been as pragmatic as the country's democratic politicians. Extensive foreign participation and the tendency of new businesses to spring up in response to product diversification or market development also indicate the openness and adaptability that commercial success requires.

Who gives out the stronger signals—the market or the government? When government revenues are swollen, public sector influence dwarfs that of the market, and businesses respond to it. But this influence can shift overnight. In the early 1980s, with oil revenues flowing and the bolívar overvalued to increase importers' advantage, everyone got into the import sales business and the country's total imports jumped about 20 percent in a year. Meanwhile, domestic production shrank even as easy credit made it possible to expand. Since the February 1983 devaluation, however, the tables have turned. A cheap bolívar has induced many firms to export for the first time and imports had fallen by almost half by late 1984. New production incentives to substitute for imports have arisen from this situation, and in many economic sectors production has risen dramatically. Thus, the market has its impact, but within a framework—sometimes rapidly fluctuating—of public economic policies.

GUYANA DEVELOPMENT AND THE ORIGINS
OF THE ENTREPRENEURIAL STATE

Venezuela's resource wealth extends well beyond the rich petroleum deposits that have made the country famous. The government's main efforts to diversify the economy and begin to "sow" oil income focussed on iron ore (discovered in large quantities in the late 1930s), the hydroelectric potential of the Caroní River system (a source of power that was recognized in the late 1940s), and bauxite (which was confirmed as commercially exploitable only in 1977). As fate would have it, all three are located in Guyana, near the confluence of the great Caroní and Orinoco rivers and the story of their exploitation is also the tale of one of the largest regional development schemes ever attempted in Latin America.[21]

The Guyana region comprises almost a third of Venezuela, but in the 1930s only about 2 percent of the population lived there, congregated in Ciudad Bolívar, a few isolated settlements, and Indian villages. Investment in the region began in the 1930s and 1940s, when military governments granted concessions to Bethlehem and U.S. Steel to exploit iron ore. These two U.S. companies built camps for their workers at the mines and railroad facilities to carry ore to new docks on the Orinoco, from which it was shipped to Sparrows Point (near Baltimore) and other major U.S. steel plants.

The potential for a different kind of development in Guyana was recognized during the brief tenure of a social democratic government from 1945 to 1948. Junta President Rómulo Betancourt and his minister of development, Juan Pablo Pérez Alfonzo, had begun to search for inexpensive energy—natural gas or hydroelectricity generated by the region's huge rivers—needed to develop Venezuela's domestic iron ore and energy industries. But before they could implement their plans, the military again seized power.

The Pérez Jiménez dictatorship also sought to develop the region—the mines were beginning to pay significant taxes—and formed two special commissions to oversee projects in Guyana: one, run directly out of the office of the presidency by an Italian consortium, was to build a steel mill; the other, under the Ministry of Development, was to dam the Caroní for hydroelectricity.

165

The results were a study in contrasts. When the dictatorship fell in 1958, the steel project proved a disaster, its management corrupt and incompetent. The dam project, on the other hand, turned out to be a great success, and the engineer who supervised its construction, MIT-trained Major Rafael Alfonzo Ravard, launched a career that has become a model for Venezuelan development managers.[22]

Under President Betancourt and Alfonzo Ravard, the iron-steel-hydroelectric project was redefined as a program for regional growth, urbanization, and industrialization to establish a new "pole" for national development rather than an isolated enclave of export production. To make good on this tall order, the government created new public corporations to operate under the Corporación Venezolana de Guyana (CVG), headed by Alfonzo Ravard. Steel projects were incorporated as SIDOR (Siderúrgica del Orinoco), and the hydroelectric project became EDELCA (Electrificación del Caroní). A short while later, Reynolds Aluminum agreed to a joint aluminum-producing venture, ALCASA (Aluminio del Caroní), with the CVG to take advantage of the cheap electricity and nearby Caribbean sources of raw material. During the mid-1960s, the urban area serving the region was rechristened Ciudad Guyana, and the sleepy port towns quickly consolidated into a city of more than 110,000 people. The area's industrial base also grew when U.S. Steel built an iron-ore briquetting plant, and several new mixed enterprises appeared along with new private metal-mechanical manufacturers and service companies, including an intercontinental hotel.

By the early 1970s, the industrial expansion based on the conversion of iron and hydroelectric natural resources—the strategic development element that was the state's responsibility —seemed right on schedule, and observers dreamed about the region becoming a kind of Venezuelan "Ruhr." In the process, the government had backed the first major expansion of the state (and mixed-) enterprise system, which would increasingly serve as the administrative mechanism for the country's publicly financed development activity, and it seemed to be functioning reasonably well. To be sure, industrial activity in Guyana was far from unseating oil, but many were optimistic that the first steps had been taken.

THE PETROLEUM BONANZA OF THE 1970s

Despite the success of the Guyana program, the early 1970s saw considerable anxiety in Venezuela because of the troubled condition of the oil industry. Production peaked in 1970, then gradually declined. Although prices started rising in 1971, foreign oil corporations, taxed to the limit and tightly regulated, were unwilling to make major new investments. More important, the many decades of increasing production had so depleted proven reserves that production rates would gradually have to fall—as would the income earned by oil. Prospects were further dimmed by industry's failure to discover new deposits of more valuable lighter oils.

At this point, however, the world oil market tightened and the Arab oil embargo caused a sudden price increase. OPEC took advantage of the resulting panic and raised prices. As the Venezuelan Treasury's share of oil income shot up from $1.72 per barrel in 1972 to $9.43 in 1975, total revenues jumped from 8 billion to 32 billion bolívares. Total domestically retained value (taxes plus company spending for wages, goods, and services) from the oil industry jumped from 9.6 billion to 41 billion bolívares in 1974 and then dropped with declining production to 33.2 billion bolívares just before nationalization in 1976.[23]

This bonanza coincided with the inauguration of Acción Democrática's Carlos Andrés Pérez, who used the opportunity to try to accelerate rapidly Venezuela's move to self-sustaining economic development. Venezuelans were by then deeply concerned about the nation's future, and Pérez called the windfall the country's "last chance" to prove the worth of its democracy by setting the nation on a new path.

The "last chance" development strategy had several features. The government decided to exert total control over the basic raw materials industries, iron ore and petroleum. On January 1, 1976, the president raised the Venezuelan flag on the rusty remains of the first commercial oil derrick erected in the country. The already nationalized iron ore companies became part of the state-run Guyana complex while the petroleum industry came under the management of a national holding company, Petróleos de Venezuela (PDVSA).

The government also decided to invest much of the new income in large-scale industrial development projects in Guyana and elsewhere, to be managed by autonomous and semiautonomous public corporations and agencies. In effect, Pérez instituted a massive, state-directed industrial development program as a platform for the country's development.[24]

The Pérez administration also sought to accelerate the "domestication" of Venezuela's private sector by further restricting foreign investment, as other Latin American nations were doing. The goal was to attune private enterprise to the government's development ideas and to decrease the emphasis on short-term repatriable profits.

Almost overnight the government expanded and accelerated the Guyana projects. As one official put it, they were the only projects that were more than "back of the envelope" schemes when the petrobonanza swept the country. The SIDOR complex and the Rául Leoni hydroelectric dam were enlarged in scope, and their projected completion date was brought forward by more than a decade. The VENALUM project, originally to be 10 percent public and 90 percent private became 80 percent state-owned, and plant capacity was raised from 100,000 to 250,000 tons. Before long, plans for even more megaprojects were hatched—among them, a state-owned plant, Interalumina, scheduled to produce 1 million tons of alumina, and another, Bauxiven, slated to produce 3 million tons of bauxite. There was also a huge tractor-truck diesel motor plant—a joint venture with the Mack Truck Company—called Fanatracto; a new cultivated wood plant intended to inaugurate a pulp-and-forest products industry; and an expanded regional cement facility. The old Guyana gold mines were also reopened and enlarged. Once completed, the theory went, the Guyana complex would displace imports of key industrial materials and supply vast surplus resources and electricity enough to electrify all of central Venezuela.

Alone, the Guyana program was breathtaking in scope. And it might have worked better in the short term if Venezuela's leaders had not taken on so many other programs and projects: its most ambitious scholarship program ever (designed to provide technical and administrative education to any Venezuelan willing and able, including 10,000 students who were to be sent abroad for study each year); an acclerated and expended agricultural assistance program; new credit programs for small- and medium-sized businesses and farms; a Caracas subway; an enormous urban housing program; naval expansion; new aircraft and shipbuilding industries; a new national railway; and new foundations to sponsor research, cultural activities, environmental protection, and health and welfare. At the same time, many old projects and institutions that were not operating properly, including the Agrarian Reform Institute, the National Petrochemical Institute, and the Agricultural and Livestock Bank, were reorganized or recapitalized, or both, and many of their outstanding debts were simply liquidated.

Almost from day one there was trouble. Skilled workers and managers were in short supply everywhere. A private study in 1974 identified gaps of tens of thousands of managers, engineers, and skilled craftsmen. As the boom progressed, private employers soon competed with state enterprises for personnel. In SIDOR and a few other technical enterprises, annual worker departures surpassed 30 percent. The pace of work in some places, such as the Ayacucho Scholarship Foundation, was so hectic that records had to be piled in hallways and contractors were accepted solely on a convenience basis. In 1972, ships reaching Caracas' main port, La Guaira, had a turnaround time of a few short days; by 1976, they had to wait in line for months.

To speed up development, autonomous entities—public or mixed-enterprise institutes or foundations—were preferred. In theory, such new entities would not have hardened arteries like central government departments; in practice, many escaped civil service regulations and conventional spending constraints.[25] Between 1928 and 1973, ten Venezuelan administrations had created several hundred such bodies, but fewer than two hundred had survived within what was called the "decentralized public administration" (DPA). With the 1973–1974 petrodollar boom, however, the DPA's size and importance grew dramatically: 163 new entities were created in four years, and 42 were giants. By 1978, it accounted for about 36 percent of the country's GNP, for over half the annual fixed investment, and for 12 to 15 percent of employment. The DPA was spending about 50 percent more than the federal, state, and local governments combined.

VENEZUELA'S DEVELOPMENT MODEL IN CRISIS

Signs of trouble appeared well before the Pérez administration ended. As a result of the helter-skelter growth of projects and investments, the government quickly lost control of its industrial development program. Many projects suffered mismanagement. Construction delays, noncompliance with contracts, cost overruns, shortages of skilled manpower—all threw timetables into disarray and delayed profitability. Evidence of widespread waste and corruption mounted as the spending spree continued. By the late 1970s, it was clear to all that Venezuela simply was unprepared to handle such an incredibly ambitious agenda.

Ironically, while the Pérez administration tried to wrestle its new commitments into order, many of the public corporations and agencies began running short of funds. But rather than retrench, many took advantage of their autonomy, the lack of central accounting, and the country's strong rating in international financial markets to borrow from private foreign banks—*independently*—obligating the Venezuelan government to repay huge sums. What is worse, they borrowed for short terms at high interest to escape controls or to expedite access to funds. Soon, 70 to 80 percent of the country's public foreign debt was held by the decentralized public administration. Many of these enterprises, such as SIDOR, are still so indebted and constrained by government price controls that they suffer huge operating losses each year despite noteworthy industrial efficiency.[26]

In the 1978 electoral campaign, the Christian Democratic opposition sharply criticized the megaproject frenzy, denouncing the misuse of funds and blaming the government for the mounting inflation. Even within the ruling party, divisions arose over growing corruption in the bloated public sector. Few were surprised, therefore, when the electorate retired Acción Democrática leaders to give the opposition a chance. By the time the new president, Herrera Campins, took office early in 1979, oil earnings had begun to decline and a recession was on the way.

The new government's first line of defense was to institute reforms to revitalize the private sector. If the state could not generate economic growth in the short term, maybe private domestic and foreign entrepreneurs could. Accordingly, the government eliminated price controls and, in the few areas where it was politically feasible, reduced protectionism to open the economy to international competition. Unfortunately, the private sector did not come to the rescue. Nor could it: on the one hand, the government measures provided few incentives attractive enough to stimulate revitalization; and on the other, the private sector would not abandon the familiar security of its established patterns of operation to achieve productivity improvements and generate exports. Besides, government's weight in the economy was by this time so massive that no recovery could occur without some success in the public development domain. Consequently, Herrera's measures worsened stagflation, cut the purchasing power of lower-income people, supplanted domestic production with imports, and united the opposition in a chorus of criticism.

Herrera's Christian Democratic party had never been as enthusiastic about the Guyana regional development program as the AD, and its policies only fueled the chaos that prevailed. People from everywhere in Venezuela had flocked to Guyana, drawn by the thousands of jobs at SIDOR, EDELCA, and other enterprises. Technicians came from Europe and the United States, along with thousands of Peruvian steel workers and Brazilian dam construction workers. The housing shortage grew so severe by 1976 that an ocean liner was rented to sit in the Orinoco River as a floating boarding house. Most of the housing that was available was located in mushrooming squatter *barrios* outside city limits on the river's west bank. The two sides of the river were connected by a single two-lane bridge that became so congested it sometimes took workers three hours to get to work. Ciudad Guyana, with about 3,000 people in 1950, had grown to more than 400,000 by 1979, and the quality of life in perhaps the most carefully planned city in South America had deteriorated deplorably.

But Herrara's answer to Guyana's problems was not so much to solve them as to put everything into suspended animation. Many projects simply were halted; others were scaled back dramatically. Work ground to a standstill on almost every project except the last stage of the hydroelectric dam. By early 1983, regional unemployment had reached 35 percent. Shuttered businesses, abandoned factories, and scores of empty or half-finished high-rise apartments and office buildings dotted the landscape; it seemed almost like the aftermath of war.

The economic policies instituted by Herrera were firmly in place when the second energy crisis, created by the Iranian Revolution, brought still another infusion of petroleum revenues. Inflation and imports both surged while the economy failed to grow at all, even though revenues increased by almost 100 percent over two years. Venezuela's government was simply unable to invest such sums usefully when short-term loans demanded such high interest and consumption had to be subsidized. The public sector was in disarray, and the private sector had lost its confidence. The outflow of capital to banks in Miami and Zurich grew panicky by February 1983.

In the meantime, the full extent of public indebtedness began to emerge. Lavish borrowing by public sector enterprises only was exposed when creditor banks, more than four hundred of them, began to request repayment and discuss Venezuela's financial situation with the International Monetary Fund. A debt that many estimated at $15 billion in 1982 had mounted to more than $25 billion by late 1983, with more to be disclosed. The debt was aggravated even more by rises in interest rates during the world recession. Loans originally underwritten at 7 or 8 percent interest had to be refinanced at 12 to 14 percent just as petroleum revenues began to decline. A cumulative increase of 2 percentage points in 1982–1983 cost Venezuela, in added interest, about 20 percent of the principal it had borrowed in the first place. This increase was a major cause of the increase in total debt after August 1982.

In desperation, the government turned once again in 1981–1982 to the standard Venezuelan revival formula: another group of public works managed by still more state enterprises. It announced a huge coal and steel project for the western state of Zulia, a new Caracas tunnel and railroad to the coast, a new bridge linking the mainland to the Caribbean island of Margarita, and a new natural gas (cryogenic) plant with a thousand kilometers of pipeline. To help manage the debt crisis, it called again on the oil industry, wresting control of the state company's financial reserves from the holding company and placing them under Central Bank management. As a result, the country's international reserve status increased by some $8 billion, though it further frightened investors who had counted on the political (and financial) autonomy of the oil industry as a measure of the country's continuing creditworthiness.

In February 1983, with the opening of an election year and the precipitous decline of the country's international reserves, the Herrera administration finally acted. The need for emergency measures was heightened when revenues began falling as oil exports dropped and prices eroded in the glutted world oil market. Once again, the Venezuelan economy experienced the consequences of heavy dependence on a single commodity. In response, the government began rationing currency, drastically devalued the free exchange rate, suspended foreign debt payments, and instituted a new price-control system.

Herrera did succeed in cutting imports, helping to stem the drain of reserves, and the revival of rigid price controls leveled off inflation at about 8 percent. But the economy as a whole continued to decline: the Gross Domestic Product dropped by 4 percent in 1983 and unemployment hovered at nearly 20 percent. Private investment came to a standstill. The failure of several private and public entities to make scheduled debt payments and the lawsuits prompted by these failures seriously damaged Venezuela's reputation and stiffened the terms it would have to meet to settle its accounts.

No one was surprised when, in December 1983, opposition AD candidate Jaime Lusinchi defeated the Christian Democratic candidate, former President Rafael Caldera, by the largest margin in any election since 1948. The election itself went smoothly and on schedule, attesting to the strength of the democratic system, and early in 1984 a new government set out to solve the country's seemingly intractable crisis. Once again, the Venezuelan voters sought new leadership and new solutions to the country's problems.

PROGNOSIS

Where can Venezuela go from here? Is the current crisis in some sense the end of the line? Does it reflect intractable habits of life formed by decades of economic life tied to oil exports? If it does, must Venezuelans settle for a future of economic stagnation and growing social and political conflict? Will Juan Bimba end his life despondently in Caracas, the capital of a country whose elites, perhaps again ruled by a military dictator, quarrel bitterly over earnings from the sale of ever dwindling natural resources?

Venezuela's history of bonanzas and the remarkable accomplishments of its leaders in building a stable democracy—one of Latin America's few political success stories of the postwar era— have nurtured both optimism and pessimism among foreign analysts. Prophets of gloom and doom have emphasized the waste, corruption, and inefficiency that prevail in Venezuelan society. Those taking a longer view, on the other hand, note that predictions of failure have never proved right.

In our view, grounds for guarded optimism still exist, even after five years of stagnation. Venezuela, despite the decline of oil, is still resource rich. Its economic infrastructure remains impressive. Its population is far better educated than before. Then why *guarded* optimism? Because these ingredients are not enough; other Latin America countries, such as Argentina and Chile, have foundered despite impressive material and human resources. True progress also requires a country's leaders and institutions to work together to solve problems, allocate resources efficiently, and frame an image of the future that can inspire confidence.

The best way to answer the questions posed here is to determine whether the broad entrepreneurial approach that Venezuela has chosen for the necessary task of "sowing" its oil can overcome the deficiencies of its development process to date. Obstacles include: a large and growing public sector committed to equitable and self-sustaining development, but currently lacking skilled technical and managerial personnel and successful mainly in extracting revenues from the international sale of natural resources; a political system with strong public support but addicted to distributing funds as a way of solving problems; and a risk-shy private sector heavily oriented toward making profits on the state's extractive and distributive activities, instead of increasing productivity or participating aggressively in international commerce. All these elements are, in turn, very much the products of Venezuela's distinctively rapid but erratic growth.

With luck, Venezuela's current crisis could shock Venezuela's leaders and institutions out of their complacency. After all, time and again they have demonstrated their flexibility and adaptability, their capacity to innovate and to learn from experience. Even under difficult conditions, Venezuelans show great willingness to cooperate, openness to new solutions, and a capacity for debate and self-criticism quite unusual in developing countries. These attributes are both the products and the foundations of the democracy.

Consider first the entrepreneurial state. The development strategy chosen by the Venezuelan government is one thing and its performance in implementing it is another. Indeed, implementation has been seriously flawed. However, the system of autonomous and semiautonomous state-owned and mixed enterprises is a natural outgrowth of Venezuela's distinctive experience, and, there is no reason, in principle, why it cannot succeed.[27] Indeed, many success stories in Venezuela attest to the operating efficiency of the entrepreneurial state, even within the context of a highly populist democracy.

The best example is the petroleum industry itself, which performed surprisingly well in its first ten years under state ownership despite difficult political and economic conditions. PDVSA sustained production levels after nationalization while it reorganized and consolidated the component companies into a more effective administrative system. The company did lose its financial autonomy when the government incorporated its reserves into the Central Bank, and the appointments of the new president in 1983 and members of the governing board were politically influenced.[28] But PDVSA has established a diversified market, gained access to foreign technical skills, modernized and restructured its refining system, and mounted an exploration-and-drilling program that has added greatly to proven reserves of conventional petroleum.

In the eight years since nationalization PDVSA has raised its proven reserves by the equivalent of the total oil in the North Slope of Alaska—close to 11 billion barrels. Proved reserves now stand at about 25.5 billion barrels. This amount equals almost thirty-nine years of production at current rates, or sixteen years at the time of nationalization. By substituting natural gas and hydropower for petroleum in electricity generation and by increasing the price of domestic gasoline, the industry has saved some 150,000 barrels per day of petroleum that it is free to export under the OPEC production quota. PDVSA has also redirected the use of the country's natural gas resources. (Natural gas exploitation started in the 1940s in Venezuela, but the resource was used inefficiently for electricity production or simply flared into the atmosphere.) In the last five or six years, natural gas is being used more efficiently in a growing petrochemical industry, a cryogenics industry, as a substitute for exportable petroleum for electricity generation, and as an experimental substitute for gasoline. Overall, the company's performance has been solid and its commitment to technical efficiency, within guidelines set by the democratic system, remains strong. Most experts agree that its future is bright.

The petrochemical industry has also been rejuvenated since 1978. For twenty-two years, the petrochemical complex operated as a nonprofit institute with accumulated operating losses equal to four or five times its initial capital. After nationalization, however, PDVSA executives convinced the government to approach this basic industry as a corporate venture, giving it operational autonomy (apart from public control of broad policy). By late 1984, the new organization had proven itself. It had maintained a successful export program for two years, reinvigorated the domestic plastics industry, and begun to explore the potential for further internally financed expansion. Most important, it operated well in the black for the first time.

In addition, the government has significantly improved the management of other important natural resources—among them, the country's forests. Interest in exploiting the nation's forestry potential dates only to the 1960s in Venezuela, but investments made in the last decade have begun to pay off. The National Forestry Corporation (CONARE) and the Corporacíon Venezolana de Guayana have just begun harvesting large-scale plantations of Caribbean pine and eucalyptus, many of them planted on marginal lands or reclaimed acreage in the Orinoco delta area. An Inter-American Development Bank loan in 1984 to extend these projects for the pulp and paper industry and to improve forest-management practices represents the country's first foreign public development financing in almost fifteen years.

On July 5, 1985, President Jaime Lusinchi affirmed a more explicit commitment to a conservationist policy than had any of his predecessors. In his Independence Day speech, Lusinchi noted that the country's natural resources were not unlimited. He declared that for the sake of future generations all resources should be developed and managed more efficiently. This announcement culminates the increasingly conservationist stance that Venezuela's democratic governments have taken since the late 1950s.

The Lusinchi administration holds public sector reform a principal goal and has pursued this objective flexibly and inventively. With the help of private consultants, the government has carefully defined sectors in which the state will retain a "strategic" or "basic" interest—primary exploitation or transformation of natural resources and infrastructure production and services—and has tried to clarify policies governing public enterprises. Experimentally, it is also closing some entities, "privatizing" others, using "fire brigade" management teams from the private sector for ailing enterprises, and cutting the workforce of inefficient organizations. In short, the government appears finally to be serious about order and administrative efficiency in the entrepreneurial state.

Also to the good, the Venezuelan public and private sectors can count on a new generation of well-trained technical and administrative personnel. These beneficiaries of the scholarship program of the mid- and late 1970s and of the newly created graduate and scientific institutes and programs are now entering the workforce and rising through the ranks of organizations, agencies, and enterprises.

It is more difficult to generalize about the ability of Venezuela's democratic political system to manage the problems for which easy "distribution decisions" aren't enough. Indeed, how can political habits nurtured in abundance be adapted to the greater self-restraint and discipline that greater productivity requires?

Historical precedent gives grounds for some hope. Near the end of the Pérez dictatorship in 1958, the leaders of Venezuela's major political parties agreed to moderate their rivalry to assure democracy's success. This agreement became official in the Pact of Punto Fijo before the dictator left office. The pact was especially important in the case of the AD, because it had failed before to share responsibility for and access to government with other parties—a key weakness of its reformist rule from 1945 to 1948.

Accordingly, when Rómulo Betancourt took office, he formed a coalition cabinet, sharing administrative duties and access to government with opposition parties. His successor, Raul Leoni, after lengthy discussion within the party, decided to do the same. This spirit of cooperation helped Venezuela's government ride out violent challenges from the left and the right as well as the economic crisis that gripped the nation in the early 1960s.

The record shows that Venezuelan leaders have demonstrated their ability to rise above destructive competition and to invent cooperative mechanisms when the political system's survival is at stake.[29] This lesson was learned at considerable cost and current leaders won't soon forget it.[30] A recent sign of political stability is labor's restraint: despite the loss of subsidies for many basic consumption items, the Venezuelan Labor Confederation recently abandoned demands for across-the-board cost-of-living raises in exchange for government commitments to increase employment.

Another cause for optimism is the understanding that Venezuelan political leaders appear to have for the character and dimensions of the challenge they face. They know that tough measures (including the reduction of public employment levels and salaries) are needed to trigger recovery and restructure the economy. Characteristically, Venezuelans have adopted an American cliché to describe the cutbacks: *cinturación,* the tightening of the belt.

While the government has already taken some difficult steps—devaluing the bolívar, raising the prices of gasoline and other subsidized products, refusing to meet labor's demands for wage increases—the list of needed, but politically difficult, reforms is still long. Not only must the government seek new income through taxation, but it must also improve efficiency, while responding to, or at least managing, the demands of international debtors and lower-income groups who justifiably have felt ignored in recent years.

Finally, there is the troubling complacency of the private sector. Will private sector elites shed their protected—but now less secure—economic cocoons, begin to take risks, and help the country make its way in international commerce? They continue to wield considerable political influence, amounting often to a veto power where their interests are directly affected. But, at the same time, they suffer a heavy burden of regulation, including selective wage and price controls, as well as cumbersome licensing requirements—reflections of the power of other contenders in the political process.

The critical factor in a field of countervailing currents may be intelligent public policies to bolster private initiative. Under Pérez and Herrera Campins in the 1970s and early 1980s in particular, such policies often were confused and self-contradictory. Regulatory restrictions were tightened and then relaxed, price controls imposed and lifted, international competitiveness demanded and then foreclosed, foreign investment courted and then restricted. To a great extent, of course, this "yo-yoing" reflected Venezuela's ongoing internal political struggles and the ability of successive leaders to bend policies to their personal will. But it also reflected an uncertainty about the future role of private enterprise, domestic and foreign, in the country's development scheme.

In contrast, Lusinchi's "social pact" has gone a long way toward clarifying the limits of the entrepreneurial state and restraining purely personal policy-making. What remains now is the need for continuity in regulatory policy, adequate incentives for foreign investment and export promotion, and greater public confidence in government and the economy.

Venezuela's political leaders are increasingly aware of the urgent need to achieve economic efficiency and export competitiveness throughout the economy. While many remain suspicious and critical of the private sector, politicians and technocrats alike are placing a new emphasis on defining and strengthening business' contribution to the country's growth.[31] Some private-sector actions have been promising too. Nontraditional exports are growing, agricultural production is increasing despite a drought, and long, drawn-out negotiations over such issues as debt rescheduling and price controls have moved along calmly and cooperatively. If such achievements, and their own resolve, sustain the commitment of enough political leaders, they may bring forth from domestic and foreign investors the constructive response that would restore economic growth.

In many respects, Venezuela finally has come to the turning point about which its more insightful leaders and intellectuals have been writing for half a century. There may be more bonanzas, but no one counts on them any more. Unless Venezuelans can begin to earn their way, gradually displacing imports or at least diversifying and increasing exports, the country will founder: growth will not resume, expect perhaps fitfully; social and political conflict will intensify; the government will encroach further on the oil industry's autonomy; the private sector will disinvest; violence will increase; and the democratic system will lose its legitimacy. None of this will happen overnight because the country is still too wealthy; but its money cannot long protect it from failure.

Acknowledging this bleak prospect, Venezuelan leaders in the last decade have fashioned an alternative model with three key components. First is a productive, responsible, but now more limited, entrepreneurial state charged with initiating and administering large-scale resource exploitation and transformation projects. Second is a democracy capable of managing more intense social and economic conflicts and supporting leaders committed to allocating resources more efficiently and to improving the welfare of the poor. Third is a private sector increasingly able and willing, with public support, to face the challenge of domestic and international competition.

Taken together, these add up to an approach for which there are few direct precedents and little clear ideological guidance from left to right. Each component of this model has already proved extraordinarily difficult to achieve; making the components complement each other is harder still. The country's first efforts, buffeted by another cycle of income fluctuations in oil and damaged by a worldwide recession, were quite disastrous. But one failure does not prevent it from gradually making the combination work—replacing bit by bit the habits and institutions nurtured by decades of deepening dependence on the unstable earnings from the export of exhaustible natural resources. Control of those resources is now in Venezuelan hands, and the prospects seem good that the income they produce will continue for many years. Venezuelan managerial competence is increasing, especially in the petroleum industry. Close to the 400,000 Venezuelans are enrolled in universities, and some 20,000 are seeking degrees in technical and administrative fields in the United States and other countries.[32] At home, the country boasts an impressive physical infrastructure, an informed population, and political and technical leadership aware of many of the remaining obstacles.

THE ROLE OF THE UNITED STATES

What does this imply for U.S. interests and policies? What can or should the United States do? To answer, look first at how U.S. interests—ranging from direct economic ties and security interests to concerns about political relationships in the hemisphere—have changed in the past fifteen years.

Venezuela is best known to Americans as a source of imported oil. In recent years, the amount of oil and other oil products coming to the United States from Venezuela has declined significantly—the result of reduced production and PDVSA's efforts to diversify its markets. The country remains an important supplier, however, sending over 400,000 barrels of crude and oil-based products directly to the United States every day and many thousands of barrels more indirectly via Caribbean refineries. It ranks second only to Mexico as a source of U.S. imports of crude oil and oil products.[33]

Equally important, Venezuela continues to be the United States' most secure and reliable source of offshore petroleum. During the Arab oil embargo, for example, Venezuela immediately increased its shipments to help make up for the lost supplies.[34] The national oil company's success in discovering new reserves of conventional oil, plus the commitment of the government to develop the unconventional reserves in the Orinoco gradually, suggest that Venezuela will also remain the United States' most reliable source of oil for years to come.[35]

Venezuela also has strong trade and financial ties with the United States. Forty percent of Venezuela's imports come from American shores, 65 percent of all direct foreign invement originates in the United States, and American banks hold over a third of the country's foreign indebtedness.

Important as these direct economic links are, more far-reaching common interests transcend them. Venezuela has become a regional leader in promoting international cooperation and the peaceful resolution of conflict. Venezuelan diplomacy has been instrumental in such regional policy initiatives as the

Contadora process (a group formed by Mexico, Colombia, Venezuela, and Panama in January 1983 to promote peace in Central America) and the creation of the special Venezuela-Mexico oil facility to help oil-importing countries in the Caribbean and Central America.[36] During the postwar years, Venezula has also been one of the world's most outspoken defenders of democracy.

This is not to say that the two countries agree on all issues. At the regional and global level, Venezuela has led developing countries' efforts to promote their economic interests in conflicts with the developed countries. It was a cofounder of OPEC, and it remains a supporter of high petroleum prices.[37] Moreover, the United States and Venezuela occasionally find themselves opposing each other on such important issues as the Falklands War. Yet, Venezuela's importance to the United States does not stem from trade or the U.S. need for natural resources. Instead, Venezuela is important because it is a vibrant working democracy and a civil, open society and because its foreign policy has promoted the kind of world *all* Americans would like to live in. If, as such a society, Venezuela can take advantage of its resource abundance to build an efficient industrial and manufacturing base, both countries stand to benefit.

This pinpoints a key challenge to American statecraft posed by Venezuela's economic crisis and the country's attempt to start the transition to self-sustaining development. The United States must distinguish between its deeper, long-term interests in the quality of world and hemisphere civilization and short-term irritants that can be expected to crop up in the day-to-day conduct of foreign policy with any proud, nationalistic democracy.

The record of the U.S. government has been mixed in this respect since World War II. During the first difficult years of Venezuelan democracy, when U.S. fears of the spread of Cuban communism were intense, the State Department downplayed conflicts over Venezuela's treatment of American oil companies and offered Caracas some foreign assistance under the Alliance for Progress. However, Venezuela's pleas for special treatment— or even treatment equal to that of Canada and Mexico—in the U.S. petroleum import program fell on deaf ears in Washington. Nor did Venezuela subsequently receive much foreign aid, especially compared to other Latin American countries.[38] The

Venezuelan government simply didn't have the leverage that the United States' larger and closer neighbors could exert.[39]

While the executive branch of the U.S. government has tended to appreciate Venezuela's importance as an ally and reliable supplier of oil, Congress sometimes has not. No doubt, future relations and sources of conflict between the two countries will also involve Congress: trade relationships, in particular the treatment of steel and aluminum imports; financial arrangements for managing outstanding debts; U.S. positions regarding the activities of the World Bank, the International Monetary Fund, and the Inter-American Development Bank; and the still more touchy issue of U.S. involvement in Central America. While Venezuela can hardly expect favoritism, it might suffer if rising U.S. protectionism forces it away from its most obvious export market. In the near term, growing pressure from the U.S. refining industry for limits on imports of refined petroleum products and pressure for the imposition of a tax on oil imports also pose threats.

Both branches of government in the United States pay limited attention to complex issues of this kind and Venezuela isn't big enough to get the sort of treatment that, say, Germany or even Brazil gets. While more than half Venezuela's foreign investments come from the United States, they represent less than 1 percent of total American foreign investment.

The problems between the United States and Venezuela reflect a deep asymmetry. For example, from May to June 1984, U.S. prime interest rates increased about 1 percent. This was cause for U.S. concern because it threatened to hurt the housing industry and slow economic recovery. But in debt-ridden Venezuela, it was a major disaster: a single percentage point could add $2.5 billion a year—the equivalent of 21 percent of the federal budget—to the country's debt repayment burden amid the worst economic crisis in fifty years.

Another serious problem is that perceived short-term threats to national security, such as the conflict in Central America, tend to dominate American attention at the expense of deeper development problems that may have equal or greater long-term implications. During the Falklands crisis, for example, Venezuelan sympathies for Argentina deeply irritated Washington. And while Caracas has pleased the United States by supporting the government of El Salvador, an American decision to invade Nicaragua would almost certainly find the countries on opposite sides once again.

On the other hand, Venezuela's economic problems, like those of Costa Rica and other Latin American democracies, become important only when the repayment of foreign debts is jeopardized or when economic failure leads to political collapse. Washington does not understand that the promise of liberal democracy means little to the leaders of developing countries if democracy brings little national improvement.

The growing power of conservative economic ideology in American foreign policy may also pose difficulties. The "entrepreneurial state," in which the public sector, albeit highly decentralized, manages large-scale industry, evokes little sympathy or understanding at a time when promoting the private sector has become a major objective of American diplomacy. As it is currently conducted, this campaign exhibits a certain ideological blindness about the quality of "private sector" economies whether they are efficient or inefficient, competitive or monopolistic.

To promote its interests in Venezuela, the United States will need to pay more attention to problems that may seem minor against a global backdrop but may nevertheless be vitally important for a small and struggling democracy. In trade, this will mean resisting protectionism. In energy policy, it may mean granting preference to Venezuelan products if import limitations become politically unavoidable. In international finance, it will mean being more flexible about debt renegotiation if world oil prices continue to fall. Venezuela, like all debtor countries, is extraordinarily vulnerable to changes in interest rates; in this respect, its fate also remains tied to the success or failure of American economic policy and to the success or failure of efforts to reduce the U.S. budget deficits. Finally, in the conduct of its security policy, the United States should accept the prospect that, like its European and Pacific allies, democratic countries in Latin America may hold differing views about threats to their security and consequent responses. Like many smaller countries, Venezuela can be expected to resist most American military intervention.

In the end, the United States cannot determine the outcome of Venezuela's struggle to break its overwhelming dependence on resource exports. This is a job for Venezuelans. However, an American appreciation of the far-reaching significance of Venezuela's economic crisis—and of its struggle to redesign its development path along quite original lines—will become increasingly important as the two countries conflict, as they will, over trade, finance, and national security issues in the next decade.

NOTES

1. For an analysis that focuses on the question of political viability, see John D. Martz, "The Crisis of Venezuelan Democracy," *Current History*, February 1984, vol. 83, no. 490: 73–77, 89.

2. The country's resource endowment also includes modest amounts of gold and diamonds, a large share of Amazon rainforest, a semitropical savannah, and some of the world's great rivers. An excellent overview of these can be found in Ruben Carpio Castillo, *Geopolítica de venezuela* (Caracas: Editorial Ariel-Seix Barel Venezolana, 1981).

3. The most comprehensive work in English on Venezuela's political system is John D. Martz and David J. Myers (eds.), *Venezuela: The Democratic Experience* (New York: Praeger, 1977). The editors are now completing a second, completely new collection of similar scope. See also John V. Lombardi, *Venezuela: The Search for Order, The Dream of Progress* (New York: Oxford University Press, 1982); David E. Blank, *Venezuela: Politics in a Petroleum Republic* (New York: Praeger, 1984); and Judith Ewell, *Venezuela: A Century of Change* (Stanford: Stanford University Press, 1984).

4. The basic background on international issues is provided in Robert Bond (ed.), *Contemporary Venezuela and Its Role in International Affairs* (New York: New York University Press, 1977). See also John D. Martz, "Ideology and Oil: Venezuela in the Circum-Caribbean," in H.M. Erisman and J.D. Martz (eds.), *Colossus Challenged: The Struggle for Caribbean Influence* (Boulder, Colorado: Westview, 1983); and Janet Kelly Escobar, "Venezuelan Foreign Economic Policy and the United States," in Jorge Dominguez (ed.), *Economic Issues and Political Conflict: U.S.-Latin American Relations* (London: Butterworth Publishers, 1982). For a Venezuelan perspective, see the papers of a recent colloquium edited by the Instituto de Estudios Políticos, *La agenda de la política exterior de Venezuela* (Caracas: Ediciones de la Biblioteca de la Universidad Central de Caracas, 1983).

5. Venezuela's proven reserves did not increase beyond the level of about 18 billion barrels for about a decade before nationalization in 1976. In the early 1970s, there was less than a twenty-year supply on hand. Since

nationalization, proven reserves have been increased to over 25 billion barrels. This would last for about forty years at the much lower current rates of production. For a slightly dated, but excellent technical synopsis, see U.S. Department of Energy, Energy Information Administration, *The Petroleum Resources of Venezuela and Trinidad and Tobago* (Washington, D.C.: U.S. Government Printing Office, July 1983).

6. This term is becoming fashionable in Venezuela; it draws attention to the fact that the state has gone beyond the provision of services and has taken responsibility for a basic function, entrepreneurship, that in the United States is associated almost exclusively with the private sector.

7. The "vicious cycle of underdevelopment" represents the traditional institutionalist view that Gunnar Myrdal and others advanced in the 1950s. In contemporary dependence analysis, this is the expected fate of peripheral capitalism under state domination. See Fernando Coronil and Julie Skurski, "Reproducing Dependency: Auto Industry Policy and Petrodollar Circulation in Venezuela," *International Organization,* vol. 36, no. 1 (Winter 1982): 61–94; and James F. Petras and Morris H. Morely, "Petrodollars and the State: The Failure of State Capitalist Development in Venezuela," *Third World Quarterly,* January 1983, vol. 5: 7–27.

8. The story of Juan Bimba was first related in English in Loring Allen's overview, *Venezuelan Economic Development: A Politicio-Economic Analysis* (Greenwich, Connecticut: JAI Press, 1977) 4–6.

9. See Jorge Salazar-Carillo, *Oil in the Economic Development of Venezuela* (New York: Praeger, 1976). Such rapid development has spread the benefits of modernization unevenly, but not as unevenly as might be expected, especially since the advent of democratic government in 1959. For data on these changes, see, among others: Oscar Altimir, *La Dimensión de la pobreza in America Latina* (Santiago: Cuadernos de la DEPAL, 1979) no. 27, 63; Inter-American Development Bank, *Economic and Social Progress: Natural Resources, 1983,* (Washington, D.C., 1983) 41; James Wilkie and A. Perkal (eds.), *Statistical Abstract of Latin America* (Los Angeles: UCLA, 1984); and Gene E. Bigler, *La Política y el capitalismo de estado en Venezuela* (Madrid: Editorial Technos, 1982) 89–94.

10. Bigler, *La Política,* 78–9. See also Allan-Randolph Brewer Carias, *Cambio político y reforma del estado en Venezuela* (Madrid: Editorial Tecnos, 1983).

11. Indeed, the nationalization continues today, although in a different form, as the industry seeks to maintain its autonomy and to retain control of its earnings for future investment, and the government demands access to financial resources and ample support for the public budget from the industry. For thoughts on this problem, see F. Tugwell, "Venezuela's Oil Nationalization: The Politics of Aftermath," in Robert Bond (ed.), *Contemporary Venezuela and its International Role* (New York: New York University Press, 1977).

12. See F. Tugwell, *The Politics of Oil in Venezuela* (Stanford: Stanford University Press, 1976). The nationalization is described by John D. Martz in "Policymaking and the Quest for Consensus: Nationalizing

Venezuelan Petroleum," *Journal of Inter-American and World Affairs,* December 1977.

13. For more on this, see Gene E. Bigler, "The Politicization of Trade and Venezuelan Economic Development," presented at the Meeting of the Latin American Studies Association, Pittsburgh, April 1979.

14. These comparisons were calculated in constant prices; that is, they are controlled for inflation.

15. The most detailed account of the creation of Venezuela's public enterprises is found in Bigler, *La Política.* See also Enrique Viloria, *El estado empresrial* (Caracas: Editorial Juridica Venezolana, forthcoming); José Antonio Gil Yepes and Luis Eduardo Brizuela, *¿Que hacer con las empresas del estado?* (Caracas, forthcoming). Gene E. Bigler and Enrique Viloria, "The Political Economy of State Enterprises," in Martz and Myers (eds.), *Venezuela,* forthcoming, provides an overview.

16. For an analysis of the U.S. experience, where private contracting, quasi-governmental organizations, and revenue sharing have also expanded the role of the state, see Ira Sharkansky, *Whither the State: Politics and Public Enterprise in Three Countries* (New York: Chatham House, 1979).

17. The most comprehensive study of government-business relations is José Antonio Gil Yepes, *The Challenge of Venezuelan Democracy* (New Brunswick, N.J.: Transaction Books, 1981), originally published as *El Reto de las Elites* (Madrid: Editorial Tecnos, 1977).

18. Much of the preceding is drawn from a new study of Venezuelan private business behavior by Moises Naim, "La Empresa privada en Venezuela, o que pasa cuando se crece en medio de la riqueza y la confusión?" in Moises Naim and Ramon Piñango (eds.), *El Caso Venezuela* (Caracas: Ediciones, IESA, 1985).

19. A study by Fred Jongkind of the Netherlands found, in a sample of 109 manufacturing firms of moderate or large size, that the principal executives were foreign born in 70 percent of the cases. See *Venezuelan Industrialization: Dependent or Autonomous?* (Amsterdam: CEDLA, 1981).

20. A related problem is the weakness of Venezuela's private agriculture and the country's consequent need to import food. This reflects a rational response to broad economic policies rather than some perversity of private producers in Venezuela. The overvaluation of the bolívar for most of the country's modern history has made food imports cheap and created a huge disadvantage for Venezuelan growers. Government subsidies concentrated on infrastructure or preparation for planting, or focused on cooperatives or agribusiness, or on price controls—but contributed little to actual harvests. Each time oil revenue has accrued, old debts have been condemned and new credit extended. As a result, farmers, whether peasant beneficiaries of land reform or traditional *latifundistos,* concentrated on generating credit or transfer payments rather than on producing crops.

21. Not in this list, but also qualifying as a "new" resource is the Faja Bituminosa, the heavy, unconventional petroleum deposit located in a wide belt that stretches across the center of the country near the Orinoco River. Its potential was recognized in the 1970s and its development is part of the government's long-range development program.

22. See John R. Dinkelspiel, *Administrative Style and Economic Development: The Organization and Management of the Guayana Region Development of Venezuela* (Ph.D. diss., Harvard University, 1967).

23. Oil revenues pushed total government revenues from 14.8 billion bolivarés in 1972 to 46.6 billion bolivarés in 1974 and permitted spending to rise from 15.1 billion bolivarés in 1972 to 42.4 billion bolivarés in 1974. This all took place before inflation started to erode the value of the currency in 1975–1976.

24. Bigler, 1982, *La Política.*

25. For example, several ministries had existing foreign scholarship programs, but each had large staffs and took months to manage a few hundred students in foreign universities. In contrast, the Ayacucho Scholarship Foundation was able to use about twenty people and contractors to send nearly 9,000 students to educational programs in just over a year. The costs were high, but the emphasis was on short-term results. Moreover, the medium-term results indicate that the costs may not have been as high as thought earlier, because the much higher retention and graduation rates of the Ayacucho scholars in comparison with national university students meant that costs per degree earned were comparable. Then too, during at least its earlier years, the program tended to favor students of lower socioeconomic status than the typical student able to complete a degree program at a national university.

26. On the role of public enterprises in the current debt crisis, see Gene E. Bigler and Alfred E. Saulniers, "The Public Enterprise Sector," in Jack Hopkins (ed.), *Latin America and Caribbean Contemporary Record* (New York: Holmes-Meier, 1984) vol. II.

27. There is a point of ideological contention, here, clearly, for those who feel that public ownership is a priori inefficient and therefore undesirable. Accumulating evidence suggests, however, that other variables, such as the nature of management incentives and the degree of market discipline, are more important than ownership per se. See Bigler and Saulniers, "The Public Enterprise Sector," 204.

28. Loss of control over its investment funds caused PDVSA a serious cash flow problem in 1983. A repeat of this problem was averted in 1984 when the government allowed the company access to some of the funds, increased gasoline prices, and brought the industry additional income by instituting a preferential exchange rate. Politicization also seems to have been reduced greatly by the 1984 change back to a technocratic administrator, Brigido Natera, heading PDVSA.

29. Another exmaple is the successful pacification effort undertaken by presidents Leoni and Caldera in the late 1960s and early 1970s to persuade leftist guerrillas to return to the democratic process.

30. As so many of his political generation had, Jaime Lusinchi suffered imprisonment and enforced exile at the hands of Pérez Jiménez. Indeed his understanding of the United States is extensive as a result: as a young pediatrician he interned in a hospital in Manhattan.

31. This is true of both parties, but is more pronounced in the case of the Social Democratic party, Acción Democrática, which took office in 1984.

32. The importance of this investment in human capital cannot be overemphasized. In the mid-1950s the country had only about 7,000 university

students and fully 60 percent of the population over twenty-five years of age had received no schooling at all.

33. Even if Venezuelan petroleum and petroleum products do not reach the United States, its output is important in keeping the world oil market well supplied and, therefore, in keeping prices down.

34. Venezuela cooperated with the allies in World War II and by increasing production helped reduce the seriousness of supply interruptions during the Iranian and Suez crises in the 1950s.

35. Although the cutbacks forced by the crisis have slowed the development of Orinoco hydrocarbons, the deposit, with between 1,000 and 1,300 billion barrels, is one of the largest remaining petroleum deposits in the world. The government now plans to be producing significant quantities from these fields by the turn of the century. Venezuela is also working to substitute natural gas and hydroelectricity for petroleum for domestic consumption, leaving more for petroleum export.

36. See George Grayson, "The Joint Oil Facility: Mexican-Venezuelan Cooperation in the Caribbean," *Caribbean Review,* Spring 1983, vol. 12.
    Venezuelan foreign assistance in the energy field includes concessional energy project financing in eleven countries and joint efforts such as the Latin American Energy Organization (OLADE), Petrolatín (a joint venture in Panama with Brazil and Mexico for international project development), and the Latin American Energy Program (PLACE).

37. But its role in OPEC has changed from that of a militant critic of the international majors to that of a conciliator between the conflicting interests in the cartel. It has always been an outspoken promoter of international agreements to stabilize price and supply.

38. Total U.S. foreign aid to Venezuela since 1949 has totaled only about $65 million, next to the lowest in absolute and per capita terms in the Western Hemisphere. Almost all of it came to assist the fledgling democracy from 1959 to 1966. The low level of foreign assistance stems mainly from the U.S. decision to concentrate its foreign assistance funds on countries that are the poorest in the world or involve significant security interests (such as Israel). The survival and welfare of democratic governments, per se, has not been a major determinant in the distribution of largesse. In recent years Venezuela has also benefitted more modestly from Eximbank loans to support U.S. exports, which from 1973 to 1981 averaged about $22.8 million per year. During this period Argentina received more credit even though the value of its trade with the United States was lower and it proved unwilling to support the American grain embargo against the Soviet Union. See, for more data: *Statistical Abstract of Latin America* (Los Angeles: UCLA, 1984), Tables 3119–3121.

39. For more on the diplomacy of oil resources, see Tugwell, *The Politics of Oil in Venezuela.*

Figure 6.1

CHAPTER 6

Brazil's Amazonian Frontier

TAD SZULC

————————————Editors' Preface————————————

Nine of South America's eleven nations (plus France's colony of Guyana) share common borders with Brazil. Most of Colombia and Venezuela also lie in the vast Amazon Basin. Brazil is the giant in South America, with 45 percent of the continent's land, 50 percent of its people, and a comparable giant share of the plans, programs, and problems (see fig. 6-1).

Tad Szulc's enthusiasm for things Brazilian appropriately conveys a sense of the nation's weight and influence. Brazil is very much its own ruler, a leader in the hemisphere, and a potential world power.

Like Mexico, Brazil has its population problems and its urban megalopolises, but it also has an enormous wilderness. It contains the largest undeveloped piece of land in the Third World. Brazil's "solution" to its population pressures is bound to be directed to this vast underpopulated, richly endowed expanse. As Mr. Szulc points out in the historical background of this chapter, the goal of development of the Amazon has tempted Brazilians, and their North American compatriots, for almost a hundred years.

If we accept the author's assertion that the Amazon *will* be developed, that it is only a matter of *how*, then what principles of resource management should apply? Everything that is undertaken in the Amazon—logging, mineral extraction, hydro development, agriculture, and the infrastructure necessary for it all—has major implications for the environment. Indeed, from a North American environmentalist's point of view, the scale of the Brazilians' assaults on the fragility of tropical Amazonian ecosystems gives development in the region a nightmarish quality.

The Amazon raises unique questions: when one single nation owns such a large portion of the remaining natural resources of the world, especially species of fauna and flora, does it have the exclusive right to make decisions over that territory? Does it have obligations to develop its resources in ways that preserve the earth's heritage of biological diversity? And what, if any, is the appropriate role of the United States and other outside interests? We may assert that Brazilian tropical forests are the "lungs of the world," but what impact ought that fact have on Brazilian farmers' need to grow food (for whom the greenhouse effect and global climate warming is surely an abstraction), on Brazil's national pride and her determination to be a great power? And how can it be explained that Brazilian behavior, so much like that of the United States with regard to its nineteenth-century frontier, may not be appropriate or affordable in the late twentieth century?

Brazil's considerable experience with sophisticated industries, construction projects, and development of virgin areas, demonstrates how difficult it is to control resource use, environmental hazards, and population growth even when the will and money are there. This is a region-wide problem: throughout Latin America national governments struggle with the question of how to change the behavior of thousands of small farmers who live far from the seats of government. In part it is a reflection of the inadequacy of government institutions developed thus far to plan and manage the very difficult problems associated with rapid development and change in the twentieth century.

Mr. Szulc concludes that the Ford, Ludwig, and other United States-sponsored enterprises in the Amazon failed because outsiders tried to impose their culture and values on the Amazon, and that Brazilians must develop their country in their own way. Perhaps the more meaningful lesson to be drawn from these experiences is that such projects failed, and will fail, not just because of the importation of foreign ways and institutions, but because the enterprise does not respect the resources, both human and natural, with which it must work.

No matter how badly Brazilians want to appear independent of other powers, our two nations remain inextricably involved with each other. As Mr. Szulc points out, the United States has shaped Brazil in important ways, and we continue to be vitally important to one another. U.S. investments in Brazil are large. Trade is very important to both nations. U.S. banks hold most of Brazil's debt. Yet, there are real limitations on what the United States can do in Brazil. Brazil's orientation in world politics is very important to the United States. Brazil is the richest and most powerful country in Latin America. Brazil is the United States' greatest adversary or friend in the hemisphere.

B RAZIL stands, in the closing years of the twentieth century, at a crossroads in its economic and social development: can Brazil, a dynamic society now led by a democratic government, successfully incorporate the vast Amazon River Basin that covers the North and the Northwest into the nation's economic structure? Can Brazilians develop the 2.5-million-square-mile Basin, which represents two-thirds of the country, without causing an ecological disaster?

With Brazil's ever-expanding population and endemic unemployment, the country's fate seems inexorably linked to the agricultural and mineral wealth of the North. Enormous as the country is, geography and climate leave few, if any, alternatives to a human and economic expansion into the Amazonian North and Northwest. But a failure to direct and control the opening of Amazônia—a truly historic process that is already well under way as millions migrate spontaneously from the Brazilian South—could distort and even subvert Brazil's economic development process. Thoughtless, over-ambitious, or ill-conceived development policies could also imperil the ecology and environment of the Amazon Basin itself, quite possibly damaging global ecological systems permanently. The Basin's tropical rainforest has been called the "lungs of the world," and even moderate deforestation could have serious effects.

By any reckoning, the problem of the Amazonian North and Northwest represents an extraordinary challenge to Brazil. Not surprisingly, it is also becoming a major international controversy. Amazonian ecology and the destiny of the earth's last-untouched Indian tribes are concerns that, rightfully, fall well beyond Brazil's borders. The fate of the Amazon Basin prompted hearings before the U.S. Congress in 1984, and the Amazonian controversy has already produced a large body of literature, ranging from the scholarly and technical to the polemical and romantic. This concern, some of it well-informed, some of it ignorant, is carried to an extreme by some foreigners. Yet, even Brazilians long involved with the Basin admit that true understanding is just beginning to emerge. At the moment, we still know little about what is to be gained and what is to be lost in the development of Amazônia.

THE AMAZON AND BRAZIL'S POPULATION

Any discussion of the Amazon Basin must begin with a look at the demographics of Brazil. In 1985, there were about 140 million Brazilians; a population of 180 million is projected for the year 2000. Close to half of the 1985 population was clustered in and around the great cities, and the flow of people from the hopeless and destitute rural zones, especially in the Northeast, to the metropolitan areas has gone on uninterruptedly for a half-century. That the dream of a better life in the cities turned into the nightmare of the *favelas* (slums), unemployment and underemployment, and crime and violence, has not stemmed the tide. Evidently, each generation has to discover anew the horrors of urban existence.

Nowadays, the population of metropolitan São Paulo, which stretches across fifty miles, approaches (or exceeds) 20 million. Given the widespread unemployment caused by the nation's chronic economic crisis, the new industry that attracted migrants cannot fully employ the population already there, let alone the millions of unskilled workers arriving from the countryside. Rio de Janeiro, the former capital, whose economy is based on services, has around 10 million inhabitants. Brasília, the new capital, and the satellite cities immediately around it account for some 5 million more. Belo Horizonte and Goîania in central Brazil, and Recife, Bahia, and the other ever-growing urban centers of the Northeast, add 10 million or so. The metropolitan areas of Pôrto Alegre, Curitiba, and the other cities of the once-rich southern agricultural region have some 10 million inhabitants as well. The urban population is thus spread among towns that keep springing up and growing all over the map.

The most critical problem facing Brazil is what to do with all its people. In the Northeast, where the rural population is estimated at 50 million, the prospect for most is bare subsistence. Indeed, this has been true throughout the region's entire history: the land is basically poor, and punishing cycles of drought and flood further undermine production.

In April 1985, for example, destructive rains and floods hit the Northeast after five years of withering drought. Half a million *nordestinos* were left homeless when torrential rivers suddenly smashed their miserable shacks. In sugar-growing Paraíba state alone, seventy-four towns were totally cut off when the waters flooded some two thousand miles of roads and highways. In the state of Ceará, twenty-four towns found themselves under water. A region so frightfully exposed to flagellation by nature can do little to develop its economy, be it agriculture or sugar refining (the only important industry). SUDENE, a federal government agency formed in the late 1950s to create an economic foundation for the northeast (and an agency that received considerable assistance from the United States under the Alliance for Progress programs in the 1960s), has provided no miracle cures for a region cursed by nature and occupied by a population that nonetheless grows by leaps and bounds.

As things stand, *nordestinos* have little choice but to go on migrating in great numbers, and the great cities to the south will remain their natural destiny—unless the flow is redirected before urban Brazil's otherwise inevitable collapse in the coming decades. One of the main considerations behind the development of the Amazon Basin is, obviously, to lure migrants to the Northeast region.

Northeast-to-Amazônia migrations were first attempted during and after World War II. But these small-scale migrations were disastrous because no real employment or infrastructure awaited the migrants. (And, on top of this, hundreds of thousands died en route.) In the 1980s, however, proponents of Amazonian development argue that the situation has changed to a marked degree. They believe that both governmental and private capital resources are available to absorb and assist the new settlers, and that in time the Basin can offer at least a partial answer to the northeastern dilemma. What remains unclear is the real extent of these resources, given the scope of Brazil's economic crisis which, in the mid-1980s, still shows no signs of abating.

The point, of course, is that Brazil's overflowing population has no other place to go. The cities are approaching social explosion. Since the 1970s, most migrants to the Amazon Basin—anywhere between 5 and 10 million people—actually came from the southern provinces of Paraná and São Paulo, the country's wealthiest region, because even there they could no longer make a satisfactory living. Coffee and modern industry, the chief employers there, are labor-*intensive* but not *extensive,* and jobs are increasingly scarce; also, family farms are shrinking in number through the inheritance dynamic, or are being purchased by agribusiness. The depth of the Brazilian economic crisis, then—which may persist indefinitely without higher employment and a more equitable distribution of national wealth—is a powerful motivation for millions to move, from the South as well as the Northeast. In fact, the migrants from the South to the Amazon area include a large number of nondisenchanted *nordestinos* who are dislocating themselves a *second* time.

The actual percentage of unemployed and underemployed in Brazil is impossible to estimate, though it must run into extremely high and socially dangerous numbers. Some observers report that 50 percent or more of the labor force is underemployed. For years inflation has run at annual levels beyond 100 percent, preventing the poor from acquiring much purchasing power and eating away at the wealth of the Brazilian middle class. The system of indexation has become self-defeating, because it perpetuates the cycle of inflation. Perhaps the best summation of the underlying Brazilian social crisis was made in April 1985 by the National Conference of Bishops of Brazil (CNOB), which declared that 80 percent of the nation's 60 million youth live in misery. In their "Pastoral of Youth," the three hundred Roman Catholic bishops said that Brazil's young people "work from sun-up to sun-up for their very survival without any hope of leaving the vicious circle in which they were born."

Not surprisingly, millions of desperate Brazilians are determined to colonize (or invade) the Amazon Basin, which looms as a modern El Dorado to those who want to get rich quick and as a last hope to those who simply want to improve their lots and leave their children some kind of future. Many of these Brazilians are seeking economic salvation in agriculture, turning away from the once-brilliant promise of industry. This appears to mark a significant historical turnabout in Brazil, where (as in most developing nations) governments have emphasized modernization in industry at the expense of agriculture. It is surprising how a society can instinctively reach out for its own solutions, even if it means contradicting the vaunted decision-making of the national elites.

CONQUERING THE NORTH

To understand the Amazônia issue, bear in mind that the Brazilians are seeking to conquer no less than 65 percent of the national territory. Although the Basin comprises two-thirds of Brazil, it is essentially empty, except for a few thousand Indians, a handful of old cities, and the new towns and settlements at the jungle's edge. In this sense, the enterprise is heroic in scope and has a dimension or romanticism that fuels its march.

Until just a generation ago, the North and the Northwest were essentially separated by topography—dense rainforest and huge rivers—from the rest of the nation. The region was never a factor, except sporadically, in the national economy and development. Even in the mid-1980s, that isolation persists. But when the Amazonian Basin, with its formidable natural resources, becomes firmly linked to the rest of Brazil—within a generation or so—the country will be fully integrated for the first time in its five hundred-year history, a Colossus of the South. Then, Brazil will loom as a world power, comparable only to the United States in the Western Hemisphere.

In the meantime, the great controversies surrounding the northern surge hinge principally on how the Brazilian government will direct, manage, and supervise this expansion by millions of people, and on whether and how serious ecological damage can be averted. In the past, even the recent past, hundreds of millions of development dollars—nobody can estimate the actual amount—were wasted through inexperience, incompetence, greed, and corruption. Official policies for land settlement were often unrealistic, ill-planned, and poorly executed. Frequently, ownership of newly opened lands was left unclear, leading to virtual warfare between real owners and claimants, legal and illegal settlers, and squatters and bandits. Legal settlers often lost land to heavily-armed squads recruited by business interests seeking to acquire large parcels for cattle-raising (which is highly profitable, though damaging to the land) and speculation. And, of course, the few remaining Indian tribes were pushed away from their lands despite government agencies and laws to protect aboriginal rights.

The ecological ramifications are even more ominous and wide-ranging. Deforestation and desertification are feared, partly because some scientists believe that both on an Amazonian scale could significantly alter the earth's atmosphere and climate. The argument has also been advanced that most rainforest soils are not suitable to farming—not suitable enough, anyway, to justify the wholesale destruction of the forest. Others argue that disturbing the Amazonian environment will cause thousands of plant, bird, fish, and insect species to vanish forever.

The reality is that millions of Brazilians will continue streaming into the Amazon Basin because in their opinion they have no alternatives. Inevitably, they will vote with their feet, so the current learned discussions as to *whether* the Basin should be opened to development are sterile. Day-to-day, however, the entire controversy and the options available are falsely presented by many economic and environment experts, particularly abroad. Brazilians, too, take exception to much of the unsolicited advice from foreign countries as to how *they* should go about building and protecting *their* country.

Clearly, the Brazilian government must play an attentive and highly responsible role in Amazonian development. The herculean task cannot be left entirely to land-scheme promoters or inexperienced settlers. An overall development strategy, one more coherent than the plans devised and implemented in the 1970s by the ruling military regimes, is urgently required. Recalling the grandiose projects of the departed generals, projects that cost billions of dollars and left little to show for the expenditure, the government must balance adequate investments to maintain steady development with ecological considerations: in other words, a strategy that will be fruitful for migrants and the overall economy without a destruction of resources that will mortgage the future.

The most immediate obstacle, as many Brazilians themselves know, is continuing ignorance about the Amazonian Basin in all its economic, natural, and human dimensions and complexities. The government in Brasília has always lacked knowledge, expertise, adequate personnel, and basic infrastructure to support land settlement. All too often the government has cut roads through the jungle to allow settlers to reach their new land, but did almost nothing to help them farm and market their crops.

THE BRAZILIAN ECONOMY

Meanwhile, in the mid-1980s, Brazil is still beset by fearsome pressures—inflation, foreign debt, import dependency, and so on—that bode uncertainty for Amazonian development. Will the basin be given the attention and priority it deserves and desperately needs?

On the brighter side, on March 15, 1985, Brazil welcomed back political democracy after almost twenty-one years of dictatorial military rule. Unfortunately, however, Tancredo Neves, the highly popular seventy-five-year-old president elect, became critically ill on the eve of the inauguration and, after hovering for five weeks between life and death, died without having been sworn in. This uncertain interregnum seriously damaged political and economic stability before José Sarney, elected to the vice-presidency, could assume the nation's highest office.

Sarney inherited a $104-billion foreign debt that the previous government had been unable to reschedule during the past two years, despite continuous negotiations with the International Monetary Fund and hundreds of private creditor banks. Though inflation remained rampant, reaching an annualized rate of 255 percent for 1985, Sarney doubled the minimum salary in Brazil to restore a modicum of social peace. Even so, hundreds of thousands of workers, from São Paulo automotive workers to airline pilots and post office handlers and teachers, went on long strikes to demand higher wages.

At the end of February 1986, inflation was running at a 500 percent annual rate, and Sarney dramatically declared a "war of life and death" against inflation, ordered a price-and-wage freeze, and created the *cruzado,* a new currency to replace the old *cruzeiro;* a *cruzado* is now worth 1,000 *cruzeiros.* Instantly, international banks reduced interest rates on about one-third of the Brazilian debt, to help Sarney survive and to express their faith in the economic reform.

Sarney regarded himself as simply a transitional president. Soon after taking office, he asked the Congress to reduce his own presidential term to two years—meaning universal suffrage elections in 1987. (Tancredo Neves and Sarney had been elected by an electoral college set up by the outgoing military regime.) Under the circumstances, Sarney is unlikely to launch any bold long-range plans for the Amazon or anything else, and at least until the late 1980s, the North and the Northwest will most likely go on growing and developing on their own, probably still in a disorderly fashion, without paying much heed to significant structural and ecological issues. Even though the Brazilian economy grew at an encouraging 7.4 percent in 1985 despite inflation, the country clearly cannot plan major development strategies in the foreseeable future.

Sarney did announce in late May 1985 that he would advocate an agrarian reform plan to grant land to 1.5 million peasant families, a plan based on legislation approved twenty years earlier. Once it created an Agrarian Reform Ministry, however, the Sarney government let it be known that the reform would be conducted "smoothly and gradually," suggesting that it would be implemented over many years, if at all.

Critics of Amazon Basin agricultural-settlement programs have argued that if a *real* agrarian reform were introduced in Brazil to disperse the huge private holdings, peasants and others would not need to farm in the North. However, while President Sarney himself has admitted that 45 percent of Brazilian farmland is owned by 1 percent of the landowners, a reform program in the South would not resolve the basic land-hunger problem. In the first place, Brazilian politics of the foreseeable future rule out a comprehensive reform program, as Sarney has indicated. Then too, creating small landholdings would greatly disturb the Brazilian farm economy in the South, which is geared to modern agribusiness methods; it would also inevitably result in further land acquisition by big producers. Either way, peasants would still not have title to adequate land in the South, and the appeal of the Amazon Basin would grow.

Given all the aspects and variables in the Amazon Basin equation, the inevitable conclusion is that as long as penetration and colonization cannot be reversed (and history suggests that it never will be), Brazilian and international efforts should center on how best to protect Amazônia's people, environment, and economy.

BRAZIL AND THE AMAZON: A HISTORICAL VIEW

In turning to the Amazonian Basin, Brazil is reaching out for the second time in this century for its historic destiny, and once again its approach is grandiose, romantic, and very controversial. Modern Brazil's first great enterprise was the construction in the late 1950s and the early 1960s of Brasília in the central plateau to replace seaside Rio de Janeiro as the nation's federal capital. The opening of Amazônia is a second heroic undertaking flowing logically from the first a generation later.

The urge and surge to conquer the North will cost countless more millions of dollars in huge errors and miscalculations. But as history teaches us, the price paid for new civilizations is always great. In the end, immense Brazil may well absorb the mistakes, enabling future generations to look back with gratitude at the great national adventure of the closing decades of the twentieth century.

The origins of great events, whether in the lives of people or the history of nations, are often unpredictable. In Brazil's case, President Juscelino Kubitschek de Oliveira's decision to build Brasília stemmed from an idle campaign promise. To be sure, Brazilian constitutions since the nineteenth century had stipulated that the national capital be located in the hinterland and as close to the country's geographic center as possible, but such a capital had always seemed too difficult, too remote, too costly.

Once Kubitschek took office in 1956, he resolved to proceed with Brasília. Then, as now, Brazil was beset by large foreign debts and crippling inflation. But Kubitschek forged ahead with Brasília for various reasons, ranging from his growing belief (long *after* he made his campaign pledges) that the only way to open up the country's hinterland was to move the capital, to his political instinct that Brazilians as a people were ready for world power status.

Unquestionably, Kubitschek, the physician-politician from the inland state of Minas Gerais, had seized a psychologically ripe moment in the history of Brazil. But his decision must also be placed in historical perspective. From its discovery in 1500, the country—first as a Portuguese colony, then as a Brazilian empire and a Brazilian republic—had been settled principally along the Atlantic coast, where most of the wealth became concentrated. Development had, of course, reached into the immediate hinterland—into the Minas Gerais and São Paulo regions—but for all practical purposes the Interior (as Brazilians call it) had remained untouched in all its geographical immensity. The Amazonian North, for instance, lacked overland links with the Atlantic coast, existing almost as a separate entity from the rest of Brazil. At the peak of the great Amazonian rubber boom at the turn of the century, the rubber capital of Manaus found it easier to communicate and trade with Paris and London than with Rio de Janeiro. The entire territory had been crisscrossed over the centuries by trail-blazing *bandeirante* expeditions in search of riches, but few *bandeirantes* became settlers or pioneers. Instead, they created a tradition of romantic adventurism reignited in the present-day surge into Amazônia and did nothing to lure development away from the coastal cities and areas.

Kubitschek's decision was also influenced by a particular Brazilian mentality. Discovered by the Portuguese, who were the first settlers after the Indians, and home to a million or more African slaves who arrived between the sixteenth and eighteenth centuries, Brazil historically had trouble defining its own identity. Perhaps partly because of frequent changes in the country's racial mix, Brazil's national indentity problems grew especially intense after waves of European immigrants arrived in the twentieth century.

Vianna Moog, probably Brazil's greatest social historian, wrote in the late 1950s that some of the most outstanding Brazilian thinkers of the nineteenth century rejected their country as a shameful and hopeless backwater. According to Moog, "There was no acceptance of Brazilian reality, nor sufficient detachment to accept it just as it was in fact. Some rationalized, concealing the painful aspects of the country, to present the reality they desired, that is, a Brazil for the consumption of chauvinists. Others, face to face with Brazil, grew despairing, regarding all as lost . . . . These Brazilians all ended up by either rationalizing in defense of Brazil or despising her for being the Brazil she was."

Indeed, this was, psychologically, the Brazil just before the midcentury mark, a society whose educated classes made derogatory jokes about the country in front of foreigners, as if to beat them to the punch. During World War II, Stefan Zweig, the exiled Austrian author, published *Brazil, the Country of the Future*; Brazilians readily agreed that, yes, Brazil would always be the country of the *future*, but never of the *present*.

This, then, was the Brazil that Juscelino Kubitschek, a second-generation Brazilian of Czech origins, inherited in 1956. Change, however, can rarely occur until the ground is cleared, and a grown-over but important path to modernization had been opened for Kubitschek a quarter-century earlier. The pathbreaker was Brazil's first real modernizer, Getulio Vargas, who emerged from his native Rio Grande do Sul to launch a revolution in 1930 and to lead the country on and off for twenty-four years.

As it developed, the Vargas revolution ended Brazil's feudalism. Prior to 1930, the economy was mainly agricultural, with coffee as the chief cash and export crop. There were great estates, a small middle class (compared to that in neighboring Argentina), and masses of poor and deprived. Vargas, a dictatorial "president," conducted the nearest thing to a social revolution in Brazilian history. He inherited a rural economy dismantled by the abolition of slavery in 1888 and not yet rebuilt. A born populist, Vargas initiated some of the world's most advanced social legislation (starting with social security). A patriot, he began to instill in Brazilians a sense of national pride. He nationalized

Brazil's then-limited petroleum reserves and encouraged exploratory drilling in the Northeast. He helped to usher in the modern industrial age by obtaining U.S. financing for constructing the nation's first large steel mill complex at Volta Redonda. All of this, in turn, encouraged the growth of the middle class.

To make so many changes and still stay in power, Vargas instituted a quasi-Fascist dictatorship known as the "New State," complete with a Mussolini-like constitution, secret police, and censorship, but without the corresponding brutality. In World War II, he fought on the side of the Allies, dispatching an army division to Italy to join U.S. forces. Ironically, the democratic spirit of the returning Brazilian troops led to a coup d'état and his ouster in 1945. Then, in a further irony, Vargas was elected president in 1950 under Brazil's new democratic system, although his term ended with his suicide in August 1954.

Juscelino Kubitschek, elected a year after Vargas's suicide, pledged to continue the old president's developmental policies. His most valuable campaign asset was a photograph showing him and Vargas embracing. Moreover, there was a historic logic in Kubitschek becoming, in effect, Vargas' successor. As Moog wrote, the 1930 Vargas revolution represented "a first capturing of a consciousness of the national reality, a collective desire to seek out the unknown quantities of Brazilian destiny." But it was left to Kubitschek to define this Brazilian destiny and to give it force.

THE BUILDING OF BRASÍLIA

Juscelino Kubitschek launched his presidency in 1956 under the slogan "Fifty Years of Progress in Five Years," the length of Brazil's presidential term. The slogan captured its author's ambition, and Kubitschek's achievements unquestionably were impressive. Kubitschek changed Brazil's face and its soul, and his presidency was perhaps the turning point in modern Brazilian history.

When Kubitschek appeared on the scene, a postwar technocratic generation was coming into its own in Brazil. This generation strongly believed that new directions were needed if the country was to be yanked out of stagnation. Unlike their ancestors, those described by Vianna Moog, the new Brazilians were optimistic and enthusiastic and—as befits inhabitants of a continent-sized nation—they thought big. Kubitschek was their natural and ideal leader. He too thought big, and he may have been the most optimistic and enthusiastic national leader in the world at that moment. His ideas and his personality won him instant rapport with his countrymen. Suddenly, the national inferiority complex was gone, pride was ensconced in its place, and nothing seemed to daunt Brazilians.

I have a personal recollection of the day, in December 1956, when Kubitschek took me to a spot in the central plateau where Brasília was to rise from the savannah. Our small plane landed on a grassy strip, and the only structure in sight was a two-story shed where engineers and architects were drawing blueprints at improvised desks. For miles around, however, the plateau was marked with small white pennants, and Kubitschek drove me to each of them in a jeep. "This *is* the presidential palace, this *is* the supreme court, this *is* the cathedral," he kept saying, pointing to clusters of pennants. Frankly, I had scant faith that, almost magically, marble-and-glass buildings, plazas, and freeways would materialize on the empty plateau.

But, it was done—and in record time. Early in 1960, a year before Kubitschek completed his presidential term, Brasília was inaugurated as the capital of Brazil, presumably the equivalent of fifty years' progress in five. Naturally, the whole idea was regarded with skepticism and withering criticism by Brazilians and foreigners alike. Many believed that Brazil, poor and inflation-ridden, could not afford and did not need a new capital in the middle of nowhere, particularly a city of such grandiose dimensions. Indeed, at the outset, bricks and lumber had to be *flown* to Brasília at almost criminal expense. Kubitschek's family and friends, it was said, were lining their pockets from the huge profits constructing a city entailed. The president of the government corporation in charge of building Brasília, NOVACAR, was, after all, Kubitschek's close friend, and so on.

Despite these troubles and criticisms, Kubitschek simultaneously set in motion two great Brazilian trends that complement each other: the growth and expansion of the hinterland through the construction of Brasília and other new cities and towns, and the establishment of modern industry. As he broke ground for the new capital, Kubitschek also laid the foundations for what is today one of the world's large and most self-sufficient automotive industries. It took a combination of political courage and stunning initiative to create an automotive industry overnight, and both paid off. Today, Brazilians produce all their trucks, buses, and passenger cars, and even export some to the United States.

What Brazil did—and is still doing, especially in the Amazonian North—was make the first move toward a system of integrated economic development. Much of this development is incomplete, much is flawed, and some even occurred unplanned, but Kubitschek's basic equation remains sound. Making Brasília the country's center and constructing highways radiating from it in every direction, Kubitschek created a civilization where before there was only emptiness. The highways gave birth first to lonely country outposts, then to villages, then to farm settlements, towns, and cities. The newly-developed areas instantly attracted people from Brazil's drought- and flood-ravaged and overpopulated Northeast; and they created markets and new demand for goods and services. The northeastern overpopulation problem, like the urban overpopulation problem along the Atlantic coast, is far from being solved, but the opening of the hinterland is the only major alternative. Northern highways are so important in terms of economic development that administrators and mapmakers define regions and subregions as "under the influence" of this or that road.

Road construction and new towns have increased demand for automotive industry products too. Now dominant in the state of São Paulo and expanding into Minas Gerais, the automotive and related industries—steel, aluminum, rubber, glass, and so on—provide hundreds of thousands of jobs. As a result, the economic situation there continues to improve as some of the excess northeast population is absorbed gradually by the automotive industry and the Brazilian middle class keeps expanding.

A ROAD NORTH

Before Brasília was built, the central plateau held the agricultural centers of southern Minas Gerais and São Paulo and the industrial centers to the east and the south: settlement ran diagonally from the northeast to the southwest. To the west lay virtually un-inhabited savannah and forest. In the state of Goias, the site of the future Federal District, the principal city was Goiânia, a sleepy provincial capital of cattle traders and merchants serving the region's farmers. In the west, Mato Grosso abutted Paraguay and Bolivia along the Paraguay River; except for the old towns of Cuiaba and Corumba, there was little activity in this hot, steamy province. There were practically no roads, but plenty of forest and swamp.

When congress approved and Kubitschek ordered the construction of Brasília, Brazil's population had reached nearly 90 million, a small number of inhabitants for the world's fifth largest country (after the Soviet Union, Canada, China, and the United States). Yet, although Brazil houses a small number of people for its geographic size, government policies and patterns of resource distribution could not adequately support Brazil's population. More than one half of them lived in the ever-growing urban slums—notably those of Rio de Janeiro, São Paulo, and Recife—and over 30 percent in the rural Northeast. The rest lived in the more prosperous southern and eastern regions outside the metropolitan areas. The vast Amazonian North held just 3 percent of the population. With such a bizarre and debilitating population distribution, no nation could evolve into a great power, no matter what natural resources it possessed—especially if there was no communication among its different regions, no access to God-given wealth, a labor shortage, and no infrastructure in such a promising region as the Amazon.

The construction of Brasília changed all this. Kubitschek concluded that the new capital should be linked immediately with Belém, the port city in the North at the mouth of the Amazon River. An overland link between the North and Center-South had been a centennial dream in Brazil, slashing through the world's greatest rainforest to unify the country. A major highway running west from Belo Horizonte, the capital of Minas Gerais, to Brasília had been started in 1956, but this was fairly simple—at least to the Brazilians—because the bulldozers had only to mow through the low growth of the savannah and lesser rock formations. Soon roads led to Brasília from Belo Horizonte, Rio de Janeiro, and São Paulo/Santos. Buses and trucks carrying building materials, merchandise, and people streamed toward the new capital day and night. The flow increased when a railroad connected Belo Horizonte and Brasília, and a modern airport was quickly built.

Going to Belém by road was still a trek. Although long tunnels and cliff-hugging highways had been built, no such enterprise—a 1,200-mile road through virgin rainforest—had ever been attempted anywhere in the world, so the Brazilians devised their own means and techniques. The favorite device in building BR-14, as the highway was then known, was for trailblazing teams to push into the jungle on foot and clear just enough space for a small landing strip. Light planes would bring more workers and equipment, and deforestation would proceed in both directions: north toward the next spot where a landing strip would be cleared and south toward the main "front" ahead of the chain-linked bulldozers and motor-graders advancing from Brasília. It was a game of leapfrog that greatly accelerated an otherwise painstaking pace of construction.

I visited the jungle highway several times during its construction. What always impressed me was this huge undertaking proceeding in the heat and the intense tropical rain. When it was dry, blinding clouds of red dust rose from the roadway where the machines and the axes had torn away the huge trees and the foliage. When it rained, the dust and the sand turned into a sea of ooze in which machines, trucks, and jeeps constantly bogged down. Often, the jungle would reinvade the highway behind the advancing machines and workers, narrowing a wide swath to a red footpath, and it was cut away again and again. The massive project cost many lives; even Bernardo Sayão, a friend of Kubitschek who was in charge of the highway, was among the victims, killed by a falling tree.

After the road link was finally made, pessimists argued that there would never be enough traffic and maintenance to keep it pen, even after it was paved. Jânio da Silva Quadros, elected in 1960 to succeed Kubitschek as president, predicted that "jaguars" would soon reclaim BR-14. As it happened, Quadros resigned after several months in office, but the Brasília-Belém highway prospered. Truck and bus traffic rose rapidly and outposts of civilization bloomed along the road. Old towns south of the Amazon River, like Carolina and Imperatriz in the western corner of the state of Maranhão, quickly doubled in size, wealth, and population. And scores of new towns, villages at first, appeared like mushrooms after a rain.

Such prodigious undertakings as Brasília, the creation of an automotive industry, and BR-14 also changed Brazil psychologically. Ancient inferiority complexes gave way to pride and self-assurance—but not arrogance or jingoism. Brazilians seemed comfortable as they approached big-power status and renown. At the same time their music was sweeping the world, Brazilian airlines extended their routes beyond the United States to Europe, the Middle East, and the Far East. Modern Brazilian architecture was becoming famous thanks largely to Brasília. Brazil, in short, was suddenly fashionable and admired. Its image had progressed fifty years in five years; bursting from the nineteenth century directly into the second half of the twentieth: Brazil was no longer a nation eternally fated to be one of the future.

THE GREAT BEYOND: AMAZÔNIA

The Amazon River Basin, covering 2.5 million square miles and accounting for 66 percent of the entire 3.3 million square miles of Brazilian territory, is the world's last major frontier with great potential for human and economic development. It is the planet's largest undeveloped region, and it seems immensely rich. Yet, too little is known about Amazônia to quantify its potential wealth. The soil may not be sufficiently fertile in much of the Basin, but forestry is unequalled. Amazônia's mineral resources are incalculable: Amazônia possesses the world's greatest deposits of iron ore, vast reserves of manganese and nonferrous metals, plenty of gold, and possibly a great deal of oil. In the rivers lies the potential to develop at least 100,000 megawatts of hydroelectricity.

The Basin is formed geographically by the North and Northwest regions of Brazil, stretching from the Colombian, Peruvian, and Bolivian borders in the west to the Atlantic coast (between French Guyana and northeastern Brazil) on the east. Venezuela, Suriname, and Guyana are the northernmost limits of the Basin; Goias and southern Mato Grosso lie at the southern extreme.

For administrative purposes, the Basin is formally called "Legal Amazônia"; it is composed of the states of Amazonas,

Para, Mato Grosso, Mato Grosso do Sul, Rondônia, the west of Maranhão, and the north of Goias, as well as the federal territories of Acre, Amapa, and Roraima. The World Bank defines the basin more succinctly, as "The Frontier," and refers to Brazil's two other main regions as the Northeast and Southeast.

The Amazon River and its basin have fascinated, attracted, repulsed, and swallowed up explorers and conquerors for nearly half a millennium. As far as is known, the Spanish explorer Vicente Yanez Pinzon was the first European to discover the fantastic river, sailing fifty miles upstream from its mouth in 1500. Francisco de Orellana, another Spaniard, followed the full course of the Amazon from Peru to the Atlantic. It was probably Orellana who named the river after the giant female warriors of Greek mythology.

THE RUBBER BOOM

From the seventeenth century on, the Amazonian region became a Portuguese preserve, the Portuguese having colonized all of Brazil east of the dividing line drawn with the Spanish at the Treaty of Tordesillas. The first settlers, hardy military men and Jesuits, succeeded in navigating the river and establishing several forts and settlements. Belém, for example, was founded as early as 1616 by the Portuguese explorer Francisco Caldeira Castelo Branco. About the same time, other Portuguese built forts far to the west on the Madeira, near Pôrto Velho, which now is the capital of Rondônia. Amazônia soon became a legend, but the region boasted nothing of economic importance until around 1870. Predatory *bandeirantes*, hunters, and adventurers haunted the area over the centuries, but it took the rubber boom to put Amazônia on the map.

The boom stemmed from a fast-rising world demand for natural rubber late in the nineteenth century—a result of the Industrial Revolution in Europe and the United States. Amazônia's stands of rubber trees were the largest in the world. When the boom came, almost overnight, Amazônia became Brazil's most affluent region. During most of its history, Brazil had experienced unrelated boom periods interspersed with long economically unproductive lapses. There was a sugar boom in the seventeenth century (until sugar could be produced more easily and cheaply in the West Indies); a sputtering hundred-year gold boom in the eighteenth century (mainly in Minas Gerais); then a coffee boom, which petered out with the abolition of slavery late in the nineteenth century.

But, because Amazônia was so isolated from the rest of Brazil, the new rubber wealth stayed in the region. Belém, the old port, aspired to opulence; Manaus, the sleepy port town on the middle reaches of the Amazon, became a fashionable tropical version of a European city, boasting a marble opera house with a gold-leaf ceiling and an array of legendary orchestras and singing stars. Belém and Manaus were the first Brazilian cities to have electricity and telephones; Manaus was the first in all of South America to have streetcars. Parisian department stores opened branches in Amazonian towns; mansions, museums, libraries, and botanical gardens were designed and built. Because the Amazon River was navigable some 2,300 miles upstream from its delta, ocean-going liners linked Manaus and Belém with the great European port cities. In truth, it was not Brazil as a nation, but Amazônia as a principality that traded rubber with the outside world; it was a Brazilian paradox.

The Amazonian rubber boom, however, ended as suddenly as it began. Even before World War I, British botanists were quietly transporting tree cuttings to Malaysia, Ceylon, and other parts of Asia where rubber was easier and cheaper to produce. The Asian plantations killed the Amazonian affluence with cruel swiftness, and the Basin reverted to its stagnant ways.

An unexpected rubber renaissance seemed possible in 1928, when Henry Ford was seized with the notion of growing his own rubber in Brazil to produce tires for his automobiles. Ford obtained from Brazil a concession for 2.47 million acres (about five-sixths of Connecticut in area) on the banks of the Tapajos River in the state of Para. The town of Fordlândia was literally transported to Amazônia from the United States—it was moved to Brazil from Michigan lock, stock, and barrel rather than built on its site—and served as the center of the plantation empire. It had a refrigeration plant where food for two thousand persons could be stored for six months; it had hospitals, clubs, and company housing. Rubber prices were skyrocketing, and at first Ford appeared vindicated in his heroic enterprise. But Fordlândia lasted for all of ten years. One day the *caboclo* (white-Indian mixed-blood Brazilian) rubber workers rebelled against the strict and alien North American living standards, smashing most of the town in wild riots. In the words of social historian Vianna Moog, "In one night the officials of the Ford Motor Company learned more sociology than in years at a university ... they learned that the *caboclos* detested, simply detested, the tiled houses in which they lived and the Puritan way of life the officials wished to impose upon them."

All of this should have been a lesson in the folly of transplanting civilizations instead of creating them from local roots, but it was not learned—at least not by Henry Ford. He sold the Tapajos plantations only to purchase new land in Belterra in 1938, and continued to pursue his obsession. Once again, the beginning was auspicious. When Japan's conquest of Asia at the outset of World War II deprived the allies of natural rubber, demand exploded for Amazonian latex; Ford's Belterra operations were combined with additional production efforts financed by the U.S. government through the Rubber Credit Bank. In one of the least-known tragic odysseys of modern times, tens of thousands of northeastern workers and their families perished from starvation, disease, and exposure as they were transported—cattle-like—by truck and on foot from their coastal homes to the Amazonian rubber plantations, a thousand or more miles distant. However, wartime rubber extraction ceased when peace returned; Asian natural rubber and new synthetic rubber now sufficed. In 1946, Ford ceased his Brazilian operations, leaving little behind but broken dreams.

I visited parts of Amazônia in the early 1950s. Belém had returned to its sun-baked somnolence, and decay had set in; the beautiful Portuguese mosaic tiles that graced the fronts of the great mansions and downtown structures were disappearing, either stolen or sold for pennies. To me, this symbolized the ignominious end of the rubber cycle. In Manaus, the opera house had not been used in long years; the great mirrors inside were smashed, and cobwebs draped the stage. Black *urubus*—vultures—congregated along the riverbank and elsewhere, searching for edible garbage, dead dogs, and whatever else they could find. It was another symbol of an end. Of the 1 million hectares of the Ford Belterra rubber plantation, only 30,000 hectares are still being worked by the government, though the hope now is to settle the rest of the Ford land with small farmers.

When the rubber market vanished, it was logical to ask whether Amazônia had any economic future at all. Even in the 1950s, Amazônia was a difficult destination to reach; besides, Brazil had neither the money nor the incentive to inject the region with economic development. Some Japanese immigrant families were planting jute and vegetables around Belém and Manaus, but plans and profits were limited. Cattle ranchers began expanding north and northwest in Mato Grosso, but an integrated concept for Amazônia had not yet emerged. The word Amazônia summoned images of the huge river and the rainforest, and nothing else.

DEVELOPING THE BASIN

President Getulio Vargas was the first to breathe new life into the region. In 1953, he established the first regional development organization in the basin, the Superintendency for the Economic Evaluation of Amazônia (SPVEA). But the Congress would not approve its funds, and SPVEA was forgotten after Vargas' suicide a year later. Still, SPVEA sparked modern thinking about the basin, and the old revolutionary deserves some credit for today's transformations.

For about twenty years after the Ford Motor Company sold Belterra, the Basin remained in oblivion. But things began changing slowly in the early 1960s. The initial development was the Brasília-Belém overland link. In the west, settlers and ranchers discovered the quality lands of northern Mato Grosso and of what, at the time, was the Federal Territory of Rondônia. (The state, once known as Guapore, was renamed after Marshal Cândido Mariano da Silva Rondon, this century's greatest Brazilian pioneer, who strung telegraph lines to the furthest confines of Northwest Brazil and created the first federal agency to protect the country's rapidly disappearing Indian population.) Primitive roads were hacked through northern Mato Grosso and into Rondônia for the first settlers, but nobody paid much attention to these stirrings.

Brazil's dictatorial military regimes really initiated the current spectacular phase in the development of the Amazon Basin.

The military seized power in April 1964, vowing to arrest the spread of "leftist" ideas and movements in the country and to do away with the incredible inflation and corruption that were eroding Brazil's social cohesion. To be sure, the military most likely would not have been able to launch the Amazon development projects if Juscelino Kubitschek (whom their "revolution" forced into exile abroad) had not erected Brasília, begun to open the hinterland, and connected the North with the rest of Brazil. Kubitschek and the military may have had profound differences over the meaning of representative democracy—the former president, certainly not a leftist, simply believed in democratic government at all costs—but they thought very much alike in terms of economic and social development. In a way, the military leaders, who also encouraged new foreign investments, picked up where Kubitschek left off.

By definition, military thought is strategic thought, and the Brazilian generals and admirals were strategic experts. Unlike other military establishments in Latin America, the Brazilian armed forces had evolved an intellectual nationalist tradition in their upper ranks, mainly through the influence of their Superior War College, where the strategic approach to economic development was studied even more seriously than war and the idea of national security was superimposed on theories of development. Marshal Humberto Castello Branco, the first military president after the 1964 revolution and an intellectual who had served for years as deputy commander of the Superior War College, had very firm notions about Brazil's economic growth. As it happened, Castello Branco had also commanded the Amazônia military region, which made him familiar with northern problems.

Castello Branco and his colleagues concentrated immediately on expanding and improving the Amazon Basin highway system as a natural prerequisite for regional development. Gradually, they molded a fairly systematic development program. Castello Branco revived SPVEA, assigned funds to upgrade the Brasília-Belém highway, and ordered a review of all Amazônia policies. In September 1966, the president, predictably using military jargon, launched "Operation Amazônia" as a national priority. Eventually, SPVEA was replaced by SUDAM, which is the Superintendency for the Development of Amazônia, and by the

Bank of Amazônia. A duty-free industrial zone was established in Manaus, where goods are manufactured from domestic or imported components for export abroad or to other parts of Brazil. (In 1982, the free zone would employ 60,000 workers and produce 1.25 million television sets, 6 million radio receivers, 2 million calculators, 1 million telephones, 300,000 bicycles, and 50,000 video cassettes.) The government planned to diversify Amazônia by creating industry and employment in an agricultural and mining region so the region would be less vulnerable to the vagaries of weather or international commodity prices. More important, however, were the successive five-year plans aimed at integrating the Amazon Basin as much as possible into the larger Brazilian economy.

All the while, the fundamental dilemma facing this new economy and region was Brazil's population explosion. The World Bank summarized the problem in its 1979 "Special Report" on human resources in Brazil: "With 120 million people in mid-1979 and a growth rate estimated at 2.8 percent, Brazil is currently adding some 3.4 million to its population each year— more than a third of Latin America's contribution to world population growth." Ominously, the report added that "the pattern of income distribution associated with the growth process appears to have worsened in the 1960s."

The situation was worst, as usual, in the Northeast. A study on "Extreme Poverty in Brazil" by José Pastore of the University of São Paulo and Archibald O. Haller of the University of Wisconsin showed that whereas the absolute number of impoverished families in the Northeast had decreased between 1970 and 1980, the region housed a larger percentage of the Brazilian destitute than previously—the percentage of destitute had risen in a decade from 41 to 50 percent. By 1980, the authors said, more than a fifth of Brazil's population—over 25 million people— lived in absolute poverty, most of them in the Northeast. The poorest families in the Northeast were usually the largest; heads of households held precarious farm jobs or were "self-employed," finding occasional work as day laborers.

The classic pattern is for the Northeast to export its excess population to the southeast's great cities. These migratory flows, however, seldom lead to anything except an urban version of the destitution left behind. In a 1982 doctoral dissertation, urban specialist Celine Sachs reported that the squatter population in Rio de Janeiro slums rose from 7 percent of the total in 1950 to 32 percent in 1980. In absolute numbers, she noted, slum population increased tenfold. São Paulo had virtually no squatter slums until 1972, but, according to Sachs, had attracted 1 million squatters by 1982. While São Paulo's overall population grows by 4.5 percent anually, the squatter population has been rising by 30 percent per year in the last decade. As a result, cities cannot accommodate new rural migrants.

Brazilian poverty rules out adequate education to a significant degree. A special World Bank study on Brazilian school quality revealed, for example, that "a typical youth in rural Brazil is exposed to fewer than four years of primary schooling." While primary school enrollment in Brazil jumped from 10 million pupils in 1965 to 21 million in 1978, national government expenditures per pupil (for nonwage items) dropped, in real terms, from $9 to $7. (The corresponding U.S. figure is $220.) In the Northeast, the expenditure per pupil was four times less than in the Southeast.

If national agreement exists in Brazil on any issue, it is on the future of the Northeast: the nation will never achieve orderly economic development if the Northeast is left to fester. But by the mid-1960s, many analysts had come to see Amazônia as Brazil's only solution to the horrendous problems of the Northeast. As the World Bank report emphasized, "Urban population growth [in the Northeast] . . . will continue to be much faster than the national average, with correspondingly surging demands for urban infrastructure." The Northeast simply cannot accommodate such growth; it has to be shipped out.

Waves of migrants from the Northeast are already having quite an impact on Brazil's settled lands. While Brasília itself is being held down to 750,000 inhabitants, as provided in the original plan, 2 to 3 million people live in the ramshackle satellite cities around the capital. Initially, these camps were "temporary" construction camps for the workers, mainly northeasterners, who built Brasília, and were to be demolished afterwards. But the planners underestimated the tenacity of migrants who, having sampled a somewhat better life, will simply not return to abject poverty, even if the alternative is life in squalid slums. So the population of the Central Plateau rose from almost zero in

1955, when Kubitschek decided to construct Brasília, to somewhere around 5 million in 1985. And it may keep growing geometrically as the center, west, and north of Brazil become increasingly integrated with the spontaneously emerging towns, settlements, farms, and trading centers along highways and feeder roads.

A few statistics illustrate the dimensions of the Brazilian population problem, as well as the rate of migration to the Frontier. Between 1970 and 1980, the population of Conceigão do Araguaia in Para state rose from 27,372 to 112,357; Tucurui, also in Para, where a huge power dam was erected on the Tocantins River, went from 9,936 to 61,319 people; Imperatriz in Maranhão (along the Brasília-Belém highway) increased from 80,827 to 220,469; and Porto Velho, the capital of Rondônia state, grew from 64,522 to 138,289. These figures represent unplanned, unchecked, spontaneous movements of people who left their homelands and took their chances with a generally wretched transportation system and an almost complete lack of infrastructure to receive, settle, and employ them.

Obviously, grand-scale development of the Amazon Basin, whether workable or not, is already a reality. Arguing about whether it should have happened is less important than administering Amazônia to produce the best results for the settlers, to protect the land and the forest, and to prevent harming the few remaining Indian tribes and the Amazonian ecological system. Furthermore, how will Amazonian development be financed? That is an overarching question in debt-ridden Brazil.

THE BRAZILIAN PSYCHE

Successive Brazilian governments—from Kubitschek's democratic administration to the subsequent military regimes—were often accused of waste and profligacy, of "gigantism" or "triumphalism." In many cases, such criticisms were warranted, and the development process has certainly not escaped the temptations of corruption. On the other hand, a giant of a country like Brazil, growing at a rapid rate, cannot be managed by a committee of accountants. Brazil's triumphalism in nation-building posed risks worth taking given the payoff for future generations. What is not justified, however, are important decisions that have

217

not been adequately thought out or were made for reasons of political ideology. The military regimes that followed Castello Branco, an intelligent moderate tragically killed in a 1967 plane crash, were guilty of taking stands based on ideology or expediency. These led to extremely serious errors in overall economic policy, and the impact of these errors on the Amazon Basin could be severe.

Brazil's military rulers believed that sufficient foreign capital would create jobs, markets, and prosperity. The left-leaning regime ousted by the 1964 revolution had been wary of too much foreign investment and control (as was that quintessential nationalist Getulio Vargas, who coined the slogan "Petroleum is Ours" to keep out the oil companies), but the military turned promptly to overseas banks and multinationals for help.

The Brazilian economic "miracle" that was the planned result of this policy was stymied by runaway inflation and excessive foreign borrowing. Clearly, foreign investments did help foster production, employment, and consumption, but they tended to be concentrated in "safe" areas such as São Paulo, Minas Gerais, and the south. Brazil badly needed development capital in the Amazon Basin, but the region was too risky for foreign venture capital; only the U.S. Export-Import Bank, the World Bank, and the Inter-American Development Bank would approve loans for infrastructure projects. Big mining companies with long experience in Brazil, such as U.S. Steel, became partners with Brazilian firms in promising ore areas, but these were exceptions. Other foreigners acquired cattle and forest land, primarily on speculation and to little profit. Amazônia's would-be developers dreamed of finding investors with great resources and staying power.

One such investor did appear in the person of Daniel Keith Ludwig, the octogenarian American shipowner and billionaire. A mysterious man who had long nurtured Ford-like dreams about the Amazon, Ludwig planned to become the world's principal producer of cellulose; to that end, he purchased 1.63 million hectares of jungle from a grateful Brazilian government in 1967. The Ludwig jungle was in the state of Para on the Jari River, immediately northwest of where it flows into the Amazon, several hundred miles east of Belém. The land of the Companhía do Jari, Ludwig's holding company, was on the western border of the

Federal Territory of Amapá, just below the Maracanaquara Plateau. Macapá, the Territory's capital, was not too far away, but Ludwig, like Henry Ford, chose to build his own company town, Monte Dourado. The town, built where nothing had existed before, reached a population of 20,000 (mainly workers and their families from the state of Maranhão to the east), and a huge slum, hopeful and dependent, grew up in Beiradão on the Jari River.

Ludwig planted 300,000 hectares of fast-growing trees from West Africa and the Caribbean. He cut down 100,000 hectares of native trees, which fed the immense pulp mill that cost over $200 million and stands seventeen stories high in the middle of the rainforest. After a deep-river port was constructed in Monte Dourado, Ludwig had the pulp mill built in Japan and towed on barges to Jari across two oceans and up the Amazon. (The mill was, according to reports, built to high standards of pollution control.) It is impossible to estimate Jari's overall cost—it had to be billions—but at the height of the operations, local expenses averaged $12 million monthly. Monte Dourado, a classical company town transplanted from the United States, had a hospital, U.S.-styled municipal services, four schools for Brazilian children, an American school with English-speaking teachers for the children of Jari executives, a hotel, and a staff club.

Jari's failure was as spectacular as the project itself: Ludwig and his advisers simply did not know what they were doing. Although hired scientists were convinced that African and Caribbean seedlings should do extremely well in Amazônia— even better than native varieties, some said—they didn't. Theoretically, the scientists were probably right, having carefully studied the local climate and the soil quality. But, Brazil is different. Something about the soil or climate around Jari prevented the imported trees from flourishing. Meanwhile, world cellulose prices had collapsed, and Ludwig's other Brazilian operations— bauxite extraction, exports of precious Brazilian hardwoods, cattle-raising, and rice farming—were doing just as poorly. A hydroelectric power project at Santo Antonio on the Jari River, which would have obviated the need to burn expensive imported petroleum or local wood for energy, was abandoned when Ludwig realized that his project was doomed. In January 1982, he sold almost all of the Jari operation to a group of 23 Brazilian investors for a pittance and vanished. (Ludwig still owns and operates a $52-million rice planting and milling operation at the mouth of the Jari River.) The new investors would now like the government to administer the town of Monte Dourado, and to help preserve as much of the gigantic enterprise as possible.

When I toured the Brazilian North in 1983, Jari in a new scaled-down form seemed to have a chance to survive. The cellulose mill was working, although at much reduced capacity. (During the first year of Brazilian ownership, the world cellulose price fell from $520 per ton to $250, forcing a vast operational retrenchment.) The new management was also excavating and selling gravel, for which demand in Brazil is considerable, and trying to increase rice production. But nobody wants the millions of acres of forest that Ludwig had purchased, and the Brazilian owners have no idea what to do with the land.

Although no two experiences are identical, the Ford and Ludwig failures—their great resources notwithstanding—stemmed in part from a common error: transplanting an alien civilization to a strange and generally unknown environment. In retrospect, the collapses of Fordlândia, Belterra, and Jari seem inevitable. Social and cultural conditions cannot be superimposed on local populations with much hope of success. Change in Brazil must begin in Brazil.

My own sense, after recent visits to the Frontier, is that the conquest will work because Brazilian society, consciously or unconsciously, has decided to make it work. (The Brazilian move north resembles the winning of the American West more than a century ago; and, interestingly, the Brazilians I have met in the North are pleased and fascinated by the comparison, which they had noted themselves.) It should succeed because it is being done by Brazilians for Brazilians. If nothing else, Brazilians fully understand each other, and can communicate among themselves on almost every level. Also, Brazil in the 1980s has superior technology at its disposal, ranging from jet aircraft and satellite communications to sophisticated radar map-making and road-building equipment. Brazilians themselves now have to make it work; in 1983, the government agency in charge of Amazonian forestry banned foreigners from operating in the region.

Of course, Brazilians can make stupid and costly mistakes, too. A good example is Capemi, a timber, cattle, and agricultural corporation that went bankrupt in 1982 after failing to deforest the area around the huge hydroelectric Tucurui project on the Tocantins River, in the state of Para. Capemi owes Brazilian investors millions of dollars, and the project may have caused grave ecological damage because such defoliants as 2,4,5-T (Agent Orange) were used to try to clear the "taking area" for the 243,000-hectare artificial lake. The defoliation program became one of the decade's greatest ecological scandals in Brazil, and government teams spent months searching for discarded drums of defoliant before the area could be flooded.

THE ECOLOGICAL RISK

The Amazon Basin covers 2.5 million square miles, a piece of terrain so huge it remains an abstraction to most people, including Brazilians. Swooping low in a small plane over the rainforest is like flying over an endless green ocean. And across the mouth of the Amazon River, one bank is not visible when flying a thousand feet over the other, even on a clear day.

The Amazon River is slightly shorter than the Nile, but it is the world's most colossal river system by far. It flows 3,900 miles from the Andes to the Atlantic (2,300 miles are easily navigable, all the way from the Brazilian north coast to Iquitos in Peru). With its tributaries, the Amazon system holds over 15 percent of the world's fresh water, and two-thirds of all the world's *river* water. The Basin has 1,100 tributary rivers and streams, including six large secondary basins formed by the Madeira, Araguaia, Tapajos, Xingu, Tocantins, and Negro rivers. The Tocantins, Araguaia, and Madeira rivers are themselves navigable over hundreds of miles, providing natural transportation links throughout the Amazon Basin, complemented by the new highways and railroads.

The Amazon rainforest is equally huge. It is the largest intact forest in the world—Brazil, in fact, has 31 percent of the world's total forested area—and has changed little in the 100 million years since the Gondwanaland supercontinent in the Southern hemisphere broke up. Only now is the rainforest being seriously disturbed (and not only in Brazil), and some severe ecological problems may be difficult to avoid.

Some scientists consider the Amazonian rainforest a critical influence on world climate. Burning off 20 percent of this forest would noticeably increase the rate of carbon-dioxide build-up in the atmosphere and accelerate a global warming that scientists call the greenhouse effect. The sea level rise that would accompany a global warming—in some worst-case scenarios, even melting the polar ice caps—would threaten low-land coastal areas throughout the world. Writing in *Foreign Affairs* in 1984, British forestry specialist Nicholas Guppy observed that such a scenario cannot be ruled out, "disasters of equivalent magnitude have occurred in historical and recent prehistoric times, as the ruined desert cities of North Africa and Asia testify." And Guppy speculates that "in the destruction of tropical rainforest a crisis-point may be approaching between human activity and life-support systems."

As Guppy and other experts have noted, the rainforest system is not only the largest net terrestrial producer of oxygen, but is also a sponge for rainfall and groundwater, which it evapotranspires and later releases as rain in other areas. Fifty percent of Amazônia's rainfall comes from forest transpiration. By absorbing sunshine, the forest combines carbon dioxide gas with water to form sugars, starches, oils, fats, and ultimately, proteins. The forest is thus an important part of the global web of life and, according to Guppy, "it is inconceivable that technology or engineering could replace the functions that rainforest performs for us free, without human inputs of energy, time, money or materials."

The consequences of losing a forest so vast and little understood are difficult to predict. However, in *The Primary Source—Tropical Forests and Our Future*, Norman Myers, an expert on endangered species, says that deforestation has already engendered severe drought-flood cycles in Asia. The rainforests, and chiefly the Amazon Basin, are widely believed to contain several million plant and animal species, many still uncatalogued. According to Guppy, maintenance of "this genetic diversity is ultimately the most important [responsibility] because ... it is irreplaceable." Myers has written that the rainforests produce not only food, wood, fuels, and raw materials, but crucial drugs, including 1,400 anticancer compounds. (The anti-leukemia drugs Vincristine and Vinblastine, for example, are manufactured from the tropical rose periwinkle.) Amazônia has more than an estimated 1,500 species of fish alone, as well as 8,600 species of birds. It has 319 different types of hummingbirds alone. The destruction of the rainforest would mean the disappearance of much of this extraordinary genetic heritage—an ecosystem catastrophe beyond reckoning.

Today, we are not even sure how quickly the rainforests in Brazil and elsewhere are being cut down. A 1983 report by the U.S. Office of Technology Assessment estimated that 0.4 percent of the Brazilian rainforest is cleared every year. (The figure is 1.2 percent in Malaysia, but that country accounts for only 1.8 percent of the world's tropical forests.) Henrique Bergamin Filho, the director of the Amazon Research Institute in Manaus, reports that satellite observations show that 1.5 percent of the Amazonian rainforest has already been cleared, most of it for farming and cattle-raising. Infrared photographs from Landsat (a NASA land satellite program) show that, between June 1976, when the first satellite pictures were taken, and May 1981, about 220,000 hectares of tropical moist forest had been cleared for agriculture and pasture in the state of Rondônia alone. Although such figures are sobering, there is little agreement on how much rainforest may be safely cut. It can be misleading to simply extrapolate current trends, but doing so, says Nicholas Guppy, "gives a date 74 years ahead [2057] for the final demise" of the world's rainforests.

In Brazil's case, the government and private farmers and ranchers must resolve the fundamental conflict between the need to preserve the rainforest ecosystem and the human and economic drive to develop the Basin. Laws requiring reforestation exist, but in practice they apply only to government and large corporations. With hundreds of thousands of prospective small farmers rushing into the Frontier, ecology and environmental protection measures simply cannot be enforced. It is also true that even if every settler is convinced that the polar ice caps will melt if he burns a hectare of forest to plant rice, the rush to colonize will not be reversed. Ecological balance is an abstraction; it may take another generation before the terrible consequences of rainforest destruction are widely comprehended, even in the developed nations. The young government land-settlement agents I met in Rondônia are as aware of such dangers as the Environment Ministry in Brasília, but they know the uselessness of preaching ecology to a destitute family.

Even today, extremely little is known about Amazônia. Mario Andreazza, who as Interior Minister in the last military government supervised and coordinated all Amazonian development activities, told me in Brasília in 1983 that "the truth is that we know almost nothing about the Amazon, that we are learning something new every day, and that this is why we sometimes do not know what we are doing." But he also said that there were never enough funds, materials, experts, and time to keep up with the development needs. Only recently, after the new highway was built and hundreds of thousands of families went to live in the Amazon, did experts gain some rudimentary knowledge of soil quality in various parts of the Basin—a prerequisite, in most cases, to successful settlement.

Satellite and radar observation in the early 1980s surprised even Amazon experts by discovering unsuspected large rivers and high plateaus in the region. It had been long assumed that Amazônia is so flat that the river falls only a quarter of an inch per mile, on the average, as it descends from the Andes to the Atlantic. Landsat photography now shows that the Basin is far from flat and that the great river drops quite precipitously in some sections.

THE JUNGLE HIGHWAY NETWORK

Given the lack of information about Amazônia, and the fact that settlement manages to stay several steps ahead of current knowledge, how can the Brazilian government promote wise patterns of settlement and development? Settlement in the Frontier—or "occupation," as planners in Brasília say—has always depended, and will continue to depend, on highways and roads. The whole matter of where roads should be built, and how fast, remains highly controversial in Brazil.

Aside from Kubitschek's Brasília-Belém highway, probably the most important road in settling the Basin was the one linking Cuiaba in Mato Grosso with Pôrto Velho in Rondônia. A 900-mile highway, now known as BR-364, was begun in the late 1950s by local authorities and business interests as word spread in southern Brazil about available northwestern lands. In the mid-1960s, the first military government decided to improve and ultimately pave BR-364. Using this road, buses and trucks carting settlers from São Paulo and the southern states of Paraná, Santa Catarina, and Rio Grande do Sul progressed to the promised land of northern Mato Grosso and Rondônia, still a virtually empty federal territory. Many migrants stayed in northern Mato Grosso, founding the new towns of Sinop, Indeco, Canarana, Alta Floresta, Colider, Carmen, Vera, Celeste, Contribuacu, and Copercan. Most were developed by private capital, and towns like Sinop and Alta Floresta today have populations approaching 100,000, schools, hospitals, hotels. They even have direct-dial long-distance telephone systems linked to the new Brazilian communication satellites over the Amazon Basin; it's just as easy, in fact, to dial New York directly from Alta Floresta, Pôrto Velho, or Carajas as it is to dial the next Brazilian town or Rio de Janeiro and São Paulo. Other migrants, more and more of them, continued past Mato Grosso and into Rondônia where the federal government was selling land at a pittance and encouraging settlement with feeder roads and a government-supported infrastructure.

There was never any real controversy over the Cuiaba-Pôrto Velho highway, which was built with U.S. assistance, because it served its purpose (even if some disagreed with facilitating migrations to Rondônia). But there was—and is—plenty of debate over other road projects, particularly the 1,900-mile Trans-Amazon highway.

The *Transamazônica* was launched in 1970 by President Emilio G. Medici to link western Maranhão with Benjamin Constant, a somnolent town located where the Brazilian, Colombian, and Peruvian frontiers converge on the Amazon River. Running south of the river, this extraordinary highway was to cross the immense rainforest in the states of Para and Amazonas, bringing settlements and civilization to the center of the Basin. As a part of the National Integration Highways (PIN) system, the Trans-Amazon highway also served an unspoken military purpose. The military leaders were concerned about the security of rich Amazônia (perhaps they feared future leftist influences in Venezuela, Guyana, and Suriname). The army began training and stationing jungle regiments throughout the Amazon, and a highway appeared necessary to give the troops overland mobility. (Actually, Brazil gently invoked its jungle regiments in 1983 to convince Suriname's leftist regime to oust Cuban advisers.) But, overall, economic development was paramount.

Critics of the highway accused the Medici administration of "gigantism," "triumphalism," and megalomania; Brazil, they said, had other priorities. The Trans-Amazon, however, was intended to create a transportation corridor from the impoverished Northeast to the Amazon Basin, where new opportunities would materialize as the region developed. To that end, the highway was worthwhile. Near the Para-Maranhão border, the highway was to intersect with the north-south road between Brasília and Belém, cross the Cuiaba-Santarem highway, another main north-south artery, meet the Pôrto Velho-Manaus highway, and feed into the Peruvian jungle highway system (which does not yet exist). The cost was initially estimated at $450 million, although an additional $760 million was available from the World Bank for Brazil's overall highway program.

To encourage farming, the government planned to establish *agrovilas*, sixty-six-house settlements, along the highway; again, the concept was imaginative and novel. Nigel J. H. Smith, a professor at the University of Florida who spent thirty months studying the Trans-Amazon and the *agrovilas*, wrote in *Rainforest Corridors* that "the 1970 drought, which seared the backlands of the Northeast and uprooted 3.5 million people, was the triggering factor behind the decision to build the Transamazon . . . [it] was perceived as a safety valve for the densely settled (Northeast) region, by creating access to the well-watered demographic void of Amazônia."

Was the Trans-Amazon highway even a partial success? Did it justify the effort and the expense? As with everything else in Brazil, this is a matter of opinion and interpretation. The two-lane highway was completed except for the relatively unimportant final leg to Benjamin Constant in the west, but most of it remains unpaved, and it is self-inflicted torture to travel even on the best stretches. By and large, the *agrovila* settlements failed, mainly because of poor soil quality and ineffective land distribution. Nigel Smith's conclusion is that "the Transamazon scheme has proved too costly to serve as a model for other developing regions . . . . it is a mistake to open up substantial areas of the interfluves of Amazônia for settlement by either the government or private concerns." Smith added, "considering the potential dangers of regional or even global climatic change as a result of accelerated deforestation, as well as the problems of erosion and access to markets, most of the *terra firma* should remain under permanent plant cover." He also believes that "the North should not be viewed as a convenient depository for the excess population from other regions," and that the Northeast's problems could be alleviated with land reform. The last conclusion, however, is overstated because the climate and poor soil quality are the Northeast's worst problems—even worse than maldistribution.

Smith's arguments have been contested in Brazil, and even he concedes that large-scale migrations to Amazônia will continue indefinitely. He also admits that due to new development trends, the Trans-Amazon is serving a partially useful purpose—one more point of view in this hot controversy.

The region's most encouraging indication is the breathless economic and social expansion in the area of eastern Pará and western Maranhão, crossed by the Trans-Amazon. This activity is the result of large mining complexes in the area. The Carajas iron mines, exploiting perhaps the world's largest deposit of high-grade ore, will begin operating in 1986, ahead of schedule. The $4 billion enterprise includes the Carajas company town, near Maraba (which is on the Trans-Amazon highway), and a 500-mile railroad, completed in 1984, to carry the ore from the mines to a new deep-water port on the Atlantic coast in Maranhão. Not far away is the Serra Pelada gold mine, employing 80,000 men, who are helping to make Brazil the world's third-largest producer of gold. (Gold is also being extracted by divers from the bottom of the Madeira River, upstream from Pôrto Velho in Rondônia, and taken out of streams all over the Basin.) There is also the Tucurui hydroelectric project on the Tocantins River immediately north of Maraba. Moreover, Maraba, the latest center of Amazonian wealth, is approaching 200,000 people—up from 27,000 in 1970. Before the Trans-Amazon, Maraba hardly existed at all.

It is the small farmers, however, who may yet have the biggest impact on the region. In conversations with new settlers in Mato Grosso and Rondônia, I was repeatedly told that a man who owned five acres of land in the South can buy 100 acres in the North—and prosper in two or three years. Other migrants are farmhands who never owned land in the South and were attracted by the prospect of owning a few miserable acres. In Rondônia, coffee can be harvested in the first year; cocoa and bananas grow much faster there, too, and rice can be harvested several times a year. I have visited many of these new landowners, still living in lean-tos and walking miles each day between home and field, but ecstatically happy over their new lives.

Of course, there are problems. Land titles are often delayed or are flawed, and in some areas legal colonists occasionally shoot it out with squatters. This is especially acute in southeast Para, in the Maraba region. Brazil must find a fair way to protect squatters who have lived on the land for many years.

INDIAN DISLOCATION

Indian rights are another delicate and painful issue. Only 200,000 Indians remain in Brazil, most of them in the Amazon Basin. Once as many as 5 million Amerindians lived in the country; they were decimated by disease and the white settlers. A recent World Bank study noted that "more recently, the progressive occupation and economic development of Amazônia has placed the Amerindian population in an increasingly precarious position ... diseases transmitted by the new settlers have decimated whole tribes and illegal seizures of Indian lands have reduced the area available for traditional hunting, fishing, and agricultural activities."

Federal laws theoretically protect Indian interests, and a government agency, FUNAI, is responsible for Indian welfare. FUNAI has the power to "interdict" an area inhabited by Indians, keeping out all strangers. FUNAI can also resettle Indians. But, why not just leave the Indians alone? FUNAI teams penetrate the rainforest to "contact" or "pacify" tribes that have rarely seen whites, then study Indian culture and needs to determine government policy. The remaining tribes might survive better and longer if they have no contact with whites at all. That FUNAI should intervene if Indian rights are violated is obvious, but the policy of seeking out Amerindians should be suspended. In Mato Grosso and Rondônia, there are thirty-two known Indian tribes now totaling only 10,000 people—a sad and pathetic situation. The smallest tribe, the Jaboti, is down to ten members.

AMAZON POLICY AND THE U.S. ROLE

The Brazilian Amazon Basin, under both spontaneous and organized development for over twenty years, has an uncharted future. Past governments have experimented with Amazonian development, sometimes achieving positive—and historic — results, sometimes committing dreadful errors and miscalculations. The military regimes, in the absence of democratic checks and balances, promoted policies ranging from the Trans-Amazon highway construction to the establishment of the duty-free industrial zone in Manaus. Concessions were granted wisely and unwisely to foreigners, such as Daniel Ludwig. Even so, the region has registered impressive growth, and sound economic investments have been made, from the Carajas iron mines to the tin mines of Rondônia. An enthusiastic and optimistic young generation now runs Amazônia. Most themselves are Amazonians.

Since March 1985, a new civilian government has been trying to create order amid an enormous, Hydra-headed economic crisis. The fragile Sarney government has some difficult decisions to make. Among them is the quandary of electric power development. Specifically, the new government must decide when to complete the troubled Tucuruí project on the Tocantins River, designed to supply power for the big Alumar aluminum enterprise in Para. Severe budget cuts in 1983 and 1984 slowed the construction of the power plant, which is to generate 3.9 million kilowatts. Under the so-called Plan 2000, the Brazilian government has scaled back its power-generating plans, eliminating among others two hydroelectric projects in the Amazon Basin—Couto Magalhães on the Araguaia River and Peixe on the Tocantins River. Brazil's power requirements were seriously overestimated in the last decade. The Itaipu plant on the Paraná River on the Paraguayan border is now by far the world's largest hydroelectric project, but Brazil may not need its installed 12.6-million kilowatt capacity. Under the agreement with Paraguay, power from Itaipu is already flowing to that country, but there have been budgetary delays in sending Paraná River power to São Paulo. Moreover, because Paraguay does not need much Itaipu power, this single dam alone may have been overbuilt in relation to Brazil's foreseeable needs.

Likewise, the new government must evolve a policy for coordinating Amazonian development, which from 1974 to 1984 was conducted by the Interior Ministry under the name of Polamazonia. This implies fundamental decisions on how much Brazil should, and can, spend on an expanded highway network, while improving land-settlement projects, assisting agriculture, studying the Basin's soil (a monumental undertaking), and making a necessary commitment to ecological surveys and environmental protection.

In facing this dilemma, Brazil must be able to depend on two things: a resolution of its debt crisis and continued economic growth. During 1985, however, U.S. policies paradoxically turned against Brazilian trade, a pattern that could continue for the rest of the decade. The country is being hurt by U.S. import restrictions—or, as some commentators prefer to put it, U.S. protectionism—to the point where its economic growth is seriously affected.

While Brazil's record $13-billion trade surplus in 1984 helped it pay off some of the debt and allow a 4.4 percent growth rate, the drop in exports in 1985 indicated that the trade surplus would be halved. This, in turn, would slow the growth rate and cause additional unemployment. World Bank projections during 1985 suggested a heavy drop in the Gross National Product (GNP); other sources report that private investment in Brazil was the lowest in thirty years. The continuing reduction in the world price of commodities (for Brazil, the ones that count are coffee, sugar, soya, and orange juice) was also a factor in the cutback of Brazilian exports. In addition, the national trade balance was hit by the over-valued dollar and by U.S. barriers against Brazilian manufactured goods—increasingly, the mainstay of the country's export trade.

Brazil must decide what kind of assistance—and how much—it desires for development in the Amazon Basin. Considerable U.S. private capital is invested in the region's major mining ventures, notably in iron ore and manganese. Market conditions as well as Brazilian internal politics will determine the need for additional monies. (At the moment, foreign investment is not politically popular in Brazil.) The United States can support Amazonian development through its vote in the World Bank, which finances highways and other development projects in the region. However, the U.S. government is being pressured to discourage such financing because these highways may threaten the area's remaining Indian tribes, or lead to forest clearing of soils unsuitable for agriculture.

Besides direct development assistance, limited so far, the United States can be helpful to the region in other ways. One is supporting Brazilian radar and satellite surveys to provide better information on what is happening on the ground in Amazônia. Indeed, if the United States assists in the region's development, it may have more influence on policies with ecological impacts. Thomas E. Lovejoy, a vice-president of the World Wildlife Fund-U.S., believes that to protect natural resources in countries that carry a heavy foreign debt (such as Brazil) the United States should "explore the possibility of instituting debt credits for natural resource protection and management in these countries." In testimony before a congressional subcommittee in September 1984, he noted that the foreign debt "is not resolvable in ordinary terms." He added that "not only would proper environmental safeguards ensue, but, also in analogy to our Civilian Conservation Corps, the activities would contribute to the national economies and hasten the resolution of the rest of the debt."

No central organ in Brazil monitors or directs Amazonian development. The Interior Ministry, the regional development corporation (SUDAM), the colonization and land reform institute (INCRA), and the Indian protection service (FUNAI) supposedly coordinate their activities and consult frequently. But the Brazilian private sector plays as vital a role as the government in opening up the region, and the government has little control over private sector activities—especially over the tens of thousands of small farmers pouring into the Basin.

Without attempting to teach Brazilians about Brazil, Americans could contribute significantly to Amazonian growth through a jointly-established research foundation or institute. The initiative for such research could come from the two governments; private organizations in the two countries could then create an appropriate institution. In the United States, the National Academy of Science, for example, could play a leading role, and scientific and technological back-up could come from American universities with agricultural or tropical research programs, scientific and environmental groups and societies, and corporations involved in farming, forestry, or food processing.

Public health is another area in which Brazil could profit from international cooperation. The Brazilians made major contributions to tropical medicine through the work of such outstanding scientists as Dr. Oswaldo Cruz and Dr. Carlos Chagas. They also have a well-functioning public health network. The sheer size of the Amazon Basin, however, could strain the country's public health resources—especially if rapid and large-scale migrations contribute to the spread of diseases. This is particularly true with northeasterners, many of whom carry serious disease contagions. The experience and resources of U.S. institutions—from the U.S. Public Health Service to medical schools with specialized research—and the World Health Organization and the Pan American Health Organization could be applied to Amazon needs through a well-organized system. Vaccines, preventive serums, and antibiotics should be made available through public health services in Amazônia. Financing must be found to put Brazilian medical-sanitary teams in the field to vaccinate and medically assist the new populations.

Only 55 percent of Brazil's population has access to clean drinking water, a high percentage by Third World standards, but still too low. Only one out of four Brazilians has decent sanitary facilities, which is obviously inadequate. While no figures are obtainable, the situation is much worse in the Amazon region, and the rapid growth of the population has already created a serious public sanitation and pollution problem. It may be worth considering U.S. support for a public health infrastructure—treatment plants and outdoor latrines—in the Amazon Basin. At present, Brazilian authorities cannot keep pace with the demand for anything in the region—even something as critical as health—and this is unlikely to change anytime soon.

The United States can help:

1. As much as possible, the United States should relax trade restrictions that hurt Brazil's export marketing strategies and inhibit its economic growth. Economic growth in developed areas, especially the industrial sector, will raise employment levels and help stem the tide of migration to Amazônia.

2. Through its voting power at the World Bank—which is financing a number of Amazonian development projects, especially highways—the United States can help ensure that ecology, native Indians, and potential development problems (such as poor soils) are not ignored.

3. The United States, as Brazil's chief lender, should consider a system of "debt credits," by which some of Brazil's outstanding foreign debt would be erased in exchange for serious efforts to protect natural resources in Amazônia.

4. A U.S.-sponsored foundation or institute devoted to the study of Amazonian resources and development could influence policy and events in Brazil, without offending the Brazilians' national pride.

5. A U.S.-sponsored satellite tracking and high resolution photography unit might reveal much about the Amazon that needs to be considered to ensure sound development.

6. A major U.S.-sponsored public health program for Amazônia—where yellow fever, malaria, and other tropical diseases are rampant—would not only be a goodwill gesture but could give the United States a kind of moral credibility that would help us influence Brazilian policy.

The United States' potential influence on Amazonian development is limited. We are not a keystone to the region's future. Massive projects such as Tucuruí Dam are now being built by Brazilian engineers, using Brazilian technology. The financing often comes from abroad, but the United States is no longer such a dominant lender; huge sums have been lent by Europe, Japan, and the multinational banks, in whose policies the United States plays an important but limited role. The best the United States can do is try to help the Brazilians not repeat their past mistakes, or those elsewhere, like the intensive plowing and dryland farming that led to the Dust Bowl in the United States. Meanwhile, Brazil has a population crisis; an urban crisis; an economic, trade, and debt crisis; a drought and poverty crisis in the Northeast; a settlement, development, and ecological crisis in the Amazon; and an intense desire to achieve great-nation status. The decisions Brazil makes will have impacts far beyond Brazil.

REFERENCES

Arns, Paulo Evaristo-Cardinal. *São Paulo 1975-Crescimento e Pobreza* (São Paulo: Pontifical Commission for Justice and Peace of São Paulo Archdiocese, Ediciones Loyola, 1976).
Brown, Lester R. *State of the World 1984* (New York: W.W. Norton & Co. Inc., A Worldwatch Institute Report, 1984).
Cambridge University of Latin American Studies. *Land, People and Planning in Contemporary Amazônia.* Proceedings of the Conference on the Development of Amazônia in Seven Countries (Cambridge, England: University of Cambridge Press, 1980).
Caufield, Catherine. *In the Rainforest* (New York: Alfred A., Knopf, Inc., 1985).
International Energy Program, Brookhaven National Laboratory. *Renewable Energy in Brazil: Opportunities, Barriers, and Remedies.* 1981.
Kandell, Jonathan. *Passage Through El Dorado* (New York: William Morrow and Company, Inc., 1984).
Kelly, Brian, and Mark London. *Amazon* (San Diego, New York, London: Harcourt Brace Jovanovich, 1983).
Lutzenberger, José A. Who is Destroying the Amazon Rain Forest? A statement before the Committee on Science and Technology, Subcommittee on Natural Resources, Agriculture Research and Environment. U.S. Congress. Hearings: September 19, 1984.
Ministry of Interior of Brazil. *The Brazilian Center-West* (Brasília: Center-West Region Development Superintendency (SUDECO), 1981).
Moog, Viana. *Bandeirantes and Pioneers* (New York: George Brazilier, 1964).
Moran, Emilio F. (ed.). *Developing the Amazon* (Bloomington: Indiana University Press, 1981).
Moran, Emilio F. (ed.). *The Dilemma of Amazonian Development* (Boulder, Colo.: Westview Press, 1983).
Raine, Philip. *Brazil—Awakening Giant* (Washington, D.C.: Public Affairs Press, 1974).
The Rockefeller Foundation. *Amazônia—Agriculture and Land Use Research* (Cali, Colombia: Proceedings of the International Conference of the Centro Internacional de Agricultura Tropical, 1982).
Roett, Riordan. *Brazil and the United States: Beyond the Debt Crisis.* University of Miami Conference on U.S.-Latin American Issues. 1985.
Salati, Eneas, and Peter B. Vose. "Amazon Basin: A System in Equilibrium," *Science Magazine* (July 13, 1984).
Smith, Nigel J. H. *Rainforest Corridors—The Transamazon Colonization Scheme* (Berkeley: University of California Press, 1982).
Stone, Roger, D. *Dreams of Amazônia* (New York: Viking, 1985).
Subcommittee on Natural Resources, Agriculture Research and Environment of the Committee on Science and Technology—U.S. House of Representatives. Hearing on Tropical Forest Development Projects; Status of Environmental and Agricultural Research. (Washington, D.C.: U.S. Government Printing Office, September 19, 1984).
Superintendency for the Development of Amazônia (SUDAM). *Amazônia—New Universe* (Brasília: SUDAM, 1980).
The World Bank. *Brazil—Human Resources Special Report* (Washington, D.C.: World Bank, Latin America and the Caribbean Regional Office, 1979).

234

CHAPTER 7

AT SEA IN THE CARIBBEAN?

LAWRENCE MOSHER

―――――――――――――*Editors' Preface*―――――――――――――

It is on islands that one experiences the obviously finite limits of nature. For the small islands of the Caribbean, the ocean is the frontier. The importance—and vulnerability—of marine resources to the economies and ecology of the area are appreciated by Caribbean people. When hillsides are denuded and soil eroded, when the resources are exhausted, the people have nowhere to look except across the seas. When there is no longer opportunity or hope at home, islanders look for refuge to other islands, to Central America, and to the United States.

The contrast of these states with Brazil could not be more stark, either with respect to size—most of the Caribbean nations are mini-states—nor with regard to their national psychology and relations with other states, especially with the United States. It is not coincidence that the islands have adopted birth control measures more readily than the mainland countries, or that Cuba—a big island as Caribbean islands go but isolated and cut off from neighbors in a political as well as a physical sense—has the lowest birth rate in Latin America. It is not coincidence that many islanders think of the United States as the promised land, and emigration as their only real hope of a future.

It is the proximity of the Caribbean states to the United States and the amount of U.S. cargo and ships traveling the Caribbean sea lanes that make the area of such importance to the United

States. Many North Americans may think of the Caribbean primarily as the romantic site of the winter vacation they would someday like to take. Our tourist dollars are important to the island economies, but the United States' primary interest in the area is and will remain a strategic one.

Relative size, resources, and power make it inevitable that U.S. relations with the Caribbean states will be very one-sided. The North American predominance is overwhelming. When the United States coughs, these tiny countries break a rib. Even though the U.S. AID programs are very small in U.S. terms, they can have major effect in recipient countries. The lack of U.S. contribution to an important regional program like the Caribbean Action Plan could mean its failure. Private U.S. dollars also, although a miniscule fraction of overseas investment and spending, are crucial to many island economies where they have a greater relative importance than in other countries in Latin America.

Some of these countries are so small and so strapped that they have neither the experience nor the technology to deal with pollution and other forms of environmental degradation. They are unable to make pollution control and resource management a priority, sometimes because there is no existing institutional niche to which responsibility can be assigned. The very difference in scale between us and them even makes it hard for the United States to deliver help, as Lawrence Mosher points out in this chapter.

Mosher analyzes both the necessity and the difficulty of organizing multinational efforts to control pollution and degradation. United States-Cuban intransigence, which holds up cooperation in the region, is just one part of the problem. Much more persistent are the restrictions on natural and human resources available to solve the problems. Working collectively through multinational regional associations is an important way of overcoming the size/power differences between the Caribbean nations and the United States, but even to do that puts a strain on human resources in the area. An important contribution may be U.S. training assistance.

What is, for most North Americans, the protection of some favorite vacation playgrounds is for the islands themselves a matter of survival. Yet, it is clearly in the U.S. strategic interest to maintain friendly relations with the island communities through which so much U.S. commerce must pass. The alternative is a scenario none of us wants: an isolated, prosperous United States surrounded by a score of small, miserable, hostile countries, who may have no great power but a large nuisance capacity. These tiny states can create pollution and health problems for the United States via export of fresh produce laden with pesticides, or pesticide-resistent bugs. They can create immigration problems and tension in neighboring states and the United States. They can have dangerous and costly oil spills and other industrial accidents, and even promote sabotage. Some are vulnerable to the appeals of demogogues and could easily become the site of revolutions and a small epidemic of "Cubas."

On the larger scale of things, the islands' positive economic value to the United States may be very small, but, even without malevolent intent, negative costs could be huge. It behooves U.S. policymakers to think what kind of attention and investments would lead to a more favorable outcome.

A SPECTER haunts the glittering Caribbean Sea. The region's abundance of sunshine, white sandy beaches, brilliant aquamarine waters, and carefree resorts make it difficult to discern. But it is there, increasingly visible now to a newly-independent people, and it is growing.

That specter is us. We mainlanders are in the process of radically transforming the region. We are doing it with new oil refineries and transshipment depots, with more international airports, hotels, and marinas, with a continuing demand for the fruits of its plantation monocultures, with the pesticides and fertilizers that support that practice, and with the increasing pressure of ourselves, pouring out of a proliferation of cruise ships and widebodied jet airliners that are turning tourism into the Caribbean's primary economic mainstay.

But the Caribbean is now increasingly at ecological risk. As Edward L. Towle, a St. Thomas-based expert on island resource-management observes, the islands of the Caribbean are suffering from the often well-meant but nevertheless erroneous development strategies of "mainland" planners, developers, and consultants. These "outside interests," Towle believes, fail to understand that islands are intrinsically different from continental countries because of their relationship to coastal and marine resources.[1]

This distinction is—or ought to be—the linchpin to any U.S. approach to the region. Those who fashion American policy in the Caribbean should be aware of its particular environmental fragility. Furthermore, they should recognize the relationship between the Caribbean Basin's ecological health and its political stability. However, the United States is still putting environment last, both in how much it spends and where. U.S. policy has yet to appreciate the region's greatest threats, which are more environmental than political.

The United States is not, of course, changing the region without the region's own complicity. The Caribbean people want progress too, although they might define that differently than mainlanders do. Their newly-independent governments welcome the new oil refineries, airports, hotels, and industries. But in doing so they are, for the most part, ignoring the environmental safeguards that their more developed neighbors to the north have adopted. In their sometimes desperate struggle to survive economically, the region's islands are suffering from self-inflicted wounds; some, if not healed, could be ecologically fatal.

The United States cannot avoid assuming a major responsibility in this process. It is U.S. economic and political power that encourages this transfer of technology and lifestyles. U.S. institutions, policies, and, most significantly, its continental biases will shape the Caribbean's future. But the United States has so far failed to grasp fully a unique opportunity to help the peoples of the Caribbean Basin begin to help themselves, which is both tragic and instructive. The president and his chief policymakers have taken a traditional American approach to this region, which includes Central America, that focuses on short-term political and economic goals to the detriment of longer-term environmental (and economic) viability.

238

It is, admittedly, harder to relate environmental degradation to its economic and political consequences; to fasten on more immediate political explanations of the region's problems is easier. In the Caribbean, the U.S. government has focussed on Cuba's Fidel Castro and the spread of Marxist-Leninist dogma to such other "hot spots" as Nicaragua, El Salvador, and Grenada. If Castro is the disease, this thinking goes, then the United States should quarantine it.

The United States, however, needs to get beyond these narrow political definitions. Castro may or may not be a destabilizing curse. The Nicaraguan Sandinistas may or may not be worthy of the president's fury. But we do know that an environmentally degraded country becomes an economic and political problem both for itself and its neighbors. It is usually only a matter of time before ecological disintegration leads to political chaos. In the Caribbean Basin, that variable is measured in double-time. While continental land masses can tolerate immense environmental abuse and still survive, islands cannot.

The smaller the island, the faster things can go wrong. In a 1984 study conducted for the U.S. Agency for International Development (AID), Towle again is compelling: "Failure to understand distinctive differences between island and continental systems has often had unanticipated and undesirable results for both private developers and public sector funding agencies engaged in island development activities. Evidence of mistaken, ill-advised, inappropriate, sometimes naive development schemes abound in the island world."[2] Most failed, Towle found, even though similar approaches had worked well on mainlands.

That policymakers usually overlook such relationships is seen in the 1984 National Bipartisan Commission on Central America, chaired by Henry A. Kissinger. The Commission, in recommending a doubling of U.S. economic aid, did not address the region's high rates of population growth, deforestation, and soil exhaustion as part of the problem.[3] A later University of Miami study, reflecting the views of U.S. business interests with ties to the region, took issue with any U.S. Latin American policy that considers Marxist subversion the principal cause of political unrest. The study, edited by Ambler H. Moss, Jr., a former U.S.

ambassador to Panama, concluded: ". . . rural peasant movements in opposition to an oligarchic regime are not necessarily a
function of external subversion. There is a real danger in seeing
such opposition as only a result of 'enemy' actions, a view which
tends to support responses such as military aid, as opposed to aid
aimed at eradication of some of the basic economic and social
problems of the affected societies."[4]

But like others before it, the Reagan administration, determined to confront subversion both in Central America and the
Caribbean, relies heavily on the traditional diplomatic tools of
military assistance and economic aid. From 1984 through 1986,
the United States committed more than $4 billion to the region.
Of this, however, less than 1 percent is for direct environmental
protection. Seventy-six percent is for economic development
and 23 percent is for military support.[5]

During this same period, however, the U.S. government has
steadfastly refused to contribute any money to a new United Nations Regional Seas trust fund established by all twenty-seven
Caribbean Basin countries and territories (including the United
States) to protect and restore the Caribbean's environment. Although the United States did commit nearly $1 million in
bilateral foreign aid for certain environmental projects, the failure of the U.S. government to support the Caribbean Basin's own
structure has hurt American credibility and fostered Caribbean
cynicism about U.S. motives. As one official who has worked
closely with the Regional Seas program put it: "They [the Caribbean members] feel the money needed here does not even
compare with the military aid given by the United States to countries like El Salvador. And they feel this environmental
assistance is vital to them. For some of them, it could even be a
matter of survival."[6]

ISLAND DEGRADATION

The most tragic example of ecological disintegration in the Caribbean is the island of Hispaniola. The island, which
Christopher Columbus discovered five centuries ago, was then
almost totally forested. Today, most of its forests are gone. Now
the region is witnessing the consequences: flight of the poorest
from Haiti by boat and food riots in the Dominican Republic.

Hispaniola offers a grim view of what the rest of the Caribbean Basin could become if the region's fragile ecological balances are not safeguarded.

Less than 9 percent of Haiti, which occupies the island's western end, is now forested. The Dominican Republic, Haiti's neighbor to the east, is only marginally less denuded. The country faces "a bleak future," an AID field study states, because of its already "substantial environmental degradation."[7] When land loses its trees, it generates and holds less rainfall, loses its topsoil, grows less food, and destroys its littoral marine life (a result of the soil erosion). In the Caribbean Basin, trees provide more than shade.

Haiti is worse off than the Dominican Republic because of its higher population density. Their populations are about the same, around 6 million in 1981. But Haiti has more than twice as many persons per square kilometer of arable land as the Dominican Republic does (see fig. 7.1). In terms of national poverty, Haitians are four times poorer than their island neighbors. Thus, the Dominican Republic's food price riots of April 1984, in which 60 were killed and 4,300 were arrested, should be seen as an omen for the entire island and beyond. Deposed Haitian President Jean-Claude (Baby Doc) Duvalier's carrot-and-stick rule wasn't able to mask his country's worsening environmental condition.

Deforestation is the Caribbean Basin's primary environmental threat. Since 1975, its rate of deforestation has nearly doubled to 4.5 million acres a year. By the year 2000 the region's forests are expected to shrink to some 432 million acres, down from 571 million acres in 1966—a loss of about a quarter of its trees.[8] Barbados, once completely covered with forests, now has none. St. Lucia's tree coverage has dwindled alarmingly since 1959, from 49 percent coverage then to only 29 percent as of 1984.[9]

St. Lucia, a dramatically beautiful volcanic island in the Windward chain of the Lesser Antilles, typifies what is happening to many of the smaller islands of the Caribbean Basin. Much of its forest loss stems from the monoculture export of bananas. In addition to degrading the island's fragile topsoil, such plantation practices have forced many farmers off the best land and into the hills, where they "slash-and-burn" to raise food as well as grow more bananas. This exacerbates soil loss through erosion,

Figure 7.1. Population Data Sheet for the Wider Caribbean Region.

Region or Country	Population Estimate Mid-1981 (millions)[1]	Crude Birth Rate (per thousand)	Crude Death Rate (per thousand)	Rate of Natural Increase (annual, %)	No. of Yrs. to Double Pop. (at current rate)
Caribbean Archipelago	30.0	27	8	1.8	38
Bahamas	0.3	22	5	1.7	41
Barbados	0.3	16	8	0.9	80
Cuba	9.8	15	6	0.9	77
Dominica	0.1	21	5	1.6	43
Dominican Republic	5.6	37	9	2.8	25
Grenada	0.1	24	7	1.8	39
Guadeloupe	0.3	17	6	1.1	65
Haiti	6.0	42	16	2.6	26
Jamaica	2.2	27	6	2.1	33
Martinique	0.3	16	7	0.9	80
Netherlands Antilles	0.3	28	7	2.2	32
Puerto Rico	3.2	22	6	1.6	44
St. Lucia	0.1	32	7	2.4	29
St. Vincent and the Grenadines	0.1	35	7	2.8	25
Trinidad and Tobago	1.2	26	6	2.0	36
Central America	93.0	35	8	2.7	26
Belize	0.2	40	12	2.8	25
Costa Rica	2.3	32	4	2.8	25
El Salvador	4.9	39	7	3.2	22
Guatemala	7.5	43	12	3.1	22
Honduras	3.9	47	12	3.5	20
Nicaragua	2.5	47	12	3.4	20
Panama	1.9	28	6	2.2	31
Wider "Basin" Countries	—	—	—	—	—
Colombia	27.8	29	8	2.1	33
Guyana	0.8	28	7	2.1	33
Mexico	69.3	33	8	2.5	28
Suriname	0.4	30	7	2.3	30
United States	229.8	16	9	0.7	95
Venezuela	15.5	36	6	3.0	23

[1]Based on a population total from a very recent census or on the most recent official country or UN estimate; for almost all countries the estimate was for 1979 or 1980. Each estimate was updated by the Population Reference Bureau to mid-1981 by applying the same rate of growth as indicated by population change during part or all of the period since 1975.

[2]The total fertility rate (TFR) indicates the average number of children that would be born to each woman in a population if each were to live through her childbearing lifetime (usually considered ages 15–49) bearing children at the same rate as women of those ages actually did in a given year. A TFR of 2.1 to 2.5 depending upon mortality conditions, indicates "replacement level" fertility—the level at which a

Population Projected for 2000 (millions)	Infant Mortality Rate (per 1000 live births)	Total Fertility Rate[2]	Population under Age 15 (%)	Population over Age 64 (%)	Life Expectancy at Birth (years)	Urban Population (%)	Persons per Sq. Km. of Arable Land	Per Capita Gross National Product (US$)
42	74	3.5	38	5	65	52	276	1,480
0.4	28	3.5	44	4	69	54	1,488	2,780
0.3	27	2.2	32	10	70	39	692	2,400
12.3	19	1.9	32	7	72	65	185	1,410
0.1	20	—	—	—	58	27	416	410
8.5	96	5.4	45	3	60	51	205	990
0.1	15	—	—	—	63	15	700	630
0.4	35	3.2	32	6	69	44	435	3,260
9.9	130	5.3	41	4	51	25	425	260
2.8	16	3.7	43	6	70	50	463	1,240
0.3	15	3.0	33	6	69	66	592	4,680
0.4	25	3.1	38	6	62	90	3,162	3,540
4.1	18	2.7	34	6	74	70	652	2,970
0.1	33	—	50	5	67	17	610	780
0.1	38	—	—	—	67	—	626	490
1.4	24	2.6	33	5	69	49	702	3,390
142	71	5.0	43	3	64	60	81	1,430
0.2	—	—	49	4	—	50	133	1,030
3.5	22	3.8	39	4	70	43	113	1,810
8.7	53	5.8	45	3	63	41	383	670
12.8	69	5.7	45	3	58	36	282	1,020
7.1	103	7.1	48	3	57	36	104	530
4.6	122	6.6	48	2	55	53	52	660
2.7	47	4.1	43	4	70	51	109	1,350
—	—	—	—	—	—	—	—	—
42.8	77	3.9	41	3	62	60	120	1,010
1.2	46	3.9	44	4	69	30	61	570
101.8	70	4.8	42	4	65	67	71	1,590
0.8	30	—	51	4	67	44	753	2,360
258.9	13	1.8	22	11	74	74	53	10,820
25.9	45	4.9	42	3	66	75	70	3,130

country's population would eventually stop growing (or declining), leaving migration out of account. Most TFRs shown here refer to the 1975–1980 period for less developed countries and are from the UN, *World Population Trends and Prospects* . . . or survey estimates such as those of the World Fertility Survey. For more developed countries, rates are the latest officially reported as shown in the sources noted above or from Alain Monnier, *L'Europe et les pays développés d'Outre-mer. Données statistiques.*, Population, 35:4–5, Institut national d'études démographiques, Paris, 1980 and refer to 1979, in most cases.
Source: World Population data sheet, published by Population Reference Bureau, Inc, Washington, D.C., 1981.

which in turn forces the farmers to move on to other areas after several growing seasons when their crop yields diminish. The vicious cycle can ultimately change the microclimate, transforming farmland into desert.

The Caribbean's mainland members also are losing their trees. Venezuela's forests are disappearing at the rate of 617,750 acres a year. Colombia is losing nearly 2 million acres a year. In Mexico, the annual forest loss is nearing 1 million acres. From 1961 to 1978, the forests of Central America and Panama shrank by 39 percent.[10]

Plantation monoculture farming is not the only cause of deforestation, however. The market for timber, conversion to pastures for raising beef cattle (primarily for U.S. fast-food chains), and the Caribbean Basin's own voracious appetite for firewood and charcoal are also responsible. In Haiti, for example, even well-to-do families cook with charcoal.

FORESTS, FOOD, AND FISHERIES

In the Caribbean, the relationship between forests and economic health is critical. Trees keep the soil from eroding; an unleached soil grows better food crops; littoral zones free from mountain sediment support healthy beds of seagrasses, corals, and mangroves; a healthy coastal ecology provides the needed nursery habitat for a thriving fishery and encourages tourism. Mountains, forests, oceans, settlements—all are linked. This ecological relationship is more at risk in the tropics because of the higher annual rainfall there compared to the temperate zones. In the tropics, hurricanes (common in the Caribbean) and ten-inch downpours can cause severe erosion on deforested hills. Because the nutrient cycle is very rapid in humid zones, Caribbean soils can be degraded quickly. And they are.

"On most islands," reports Allen D. Putney, a forester and natural resources manager based in St. Croix, "the agricultural, fisheries and timber resources have been over-exploited and are on the decline . . . . Beach and sailing tourism is near or over capacity on most islands where the resource exists, while tourism oriented to historic sites, volcanic features, reefs, rain forests, wildlife, landscape diversity and interesting cultural traditions has generally been neglected."[11]

244

Putney and a colleague based in St. Lucia, Yves Renard, work with the Eastern Caribbean Natural Area Management Program, which surveyed conservation priorities in twenty-five islands or island groups in the Lesser Antilles. The data atlases, published by the Caribbean Conservation Association in 1982, identified the largest remaining areas of relatively unaltered ecosystems in the region for "areas of particular concern." They also identified specific endangered species.

One of the lesser-known consequences of deforestation is a particularly Caribbean phenomenon—the destruction of island coastal seagrass beds, coral reefs, and mangroves by the soil eroded from island mountains. The soil chokes these marine assets by blocking the sunlight. Seagrasses also are destroyed by chemical pollution, urban runoff, oil spills, and increased use of fertilizers.[12]

Caribbean seagrass meadows not only are a food source themselves, but act as sediment stabilizers, improve water quality, and, most important, nurture fisheries by providing a nursery habitat. Seagrasses are especially important to crustaceans, mollusks, and hundreds of species of fish that need their shelter and protection in the early stages of life. Shrimp and lobster particularly depend on seagrass beds as a foraging area for food. These coastal fisheries provide local Caribbean fishermen—usually the artisan-villager who sells or barters his daily catch—about 500,000 metric tons of fish a year, which is roughly equal to the region's annual commercial haul. Because of the Caribbean's stable thermocline—(small variation in temperature at different depths), it experiences little upwelling: thus its nutrients do not rise to the surface. This means most of its exploitable fish populations live in and near coastal estuaries, mangroves, and coral reefs. Most of the region's commercial fishing takes place in the relatively shallow Campeche Bank off Mexico's Yucatan Peninsula, the Mosquito Bank off Honduras and Nicaragua, in the Gulf of Paria between Venezuela and Trinidad and Tobago, and off Guyana and Suriname.

MARINE POLLUTION

The environmental condition of the Caribbean Basin's marine resources is largely undocumented. In a report published by

Ambio magazine in mid-1981, Aresenio Rodriguez of the United Nations Environment Programme's Regional Seas program, reported that information on agricultural waste—inorganic fertilizers, pesticides, the effluents from sugar refineries and rum distilleries, and silt deposits—were "fairly scarce." He found a "marked paucity of data" concerning the environmental impact of existing and planned industrial development. Information on coastal pollution from sewage outfalls was "very limited," and data on the levels of heavy metals, PCB's (polychlorinated biphenols), and chlorinated hydrocarbons was "not generally available." Information on the effects of pollutants on marine organisms and regional ecosystems also was "limited."[13] Planners and decision-makers, Rodriguez concluded, simply do not know how pollution and development activities are affecting marine ecosystems, human health, and coastal amenities.

Little has changed. Today most industrial and domestic wastes aren't treated or isolated properly. Oil pollution from routine operations and accidents is a growing threat. There are almost no water-quality or seafood standards for toxic materials suitable for tropical warm waters. Few nations have policies on marine pollution control and coastal and marine resource protection. There is still no effective regional coordination for data gathering and exchange, and no integrated marine pollution monitoring and research.

OIL: A MIXED BLESSING

During the past decade the strategic importance of the Caribbean has increased dramatically because of petroleum. Through the 1960s, oil flowed almost entirely in one direction—out of the Basin—primarily from the rich oil fields of the U.S. Gulf Coast and Venezuela. Since then, increasing United States demand for foreign oil, the advent of the supertanker, the steep rise in world oil prices, and the introduction of Mexican and Alaskan oil to Basin markets have turned the Caribbean into a giant petroleum mixing bowl. Supertankers carrying crude oil and petroleum products now crisscross the Caribbean in a spider-web complex of sea lanes.

Six years ago, Mexico and the United States somehow escaped serious harm from what became the world's biggest offshore oil spill. Ixtoc I spewed some 475,000 metric tons of crude oil in the Gulf of Campeche off Mexico's Yucatan Peninsula from June 3, 1979 to March 23, 1980. Inexplicably, much of the oil just disappeared. The Gulf of Mexico's pattern of currents could easily have carried the oil to the gulf coasts of both countries. Dr. Anitra Thorhaug, professor of marine biology at Florida International University, believes both nations were lucky to have avoided a major ecological disaster.[14] Meanwhile, the increasing flow of oil through the Basin raises the potential for environmental harm.

Crude oil moves into the Basin from the Middle East, East Africa, and North Africa to be refined, stored, or transhipped to the United States on smaller ships. Petroleum and products from Venezuela, Aruba, and Curaçao flow to markets throughout the world. Alaskan crude oil from Prudhoe Bay transits the Panama Canal to reach refineries on the U.S. Gulf and East coasts. Moreover, Mexican oil is increasingly flowing to U.S. ports, some of it for storage in Louisiana and Texas salt domes as part of the U.S. Strategic Petroleum Reserve. There also are intrabasin shipments from oil producers in Barbados, Colombia, and Trinidad and Tobago.

How much oil passes through the Caribbean, however, is not easily known. The region still lacks a clearinghouse to assemble current data. However, as of 1978, according to the London-based International Maritime Organization, an average of 4.7 million barrels of crude oil was transported through the Caribbean every day. About half was carried by supertankers that averaged 200,000 tons each. Tankers averaging 60,000 tons in size carried the rest. Two supertankers and six mid-sized tankers entered and left the Caribbean on average every day.[15] Because of the increase in Alaskan and Mexican oil shipments since then, the number of tankers plying the Caribbean today is much higher.

Since the mid-seventies, the United States has shifted its primary foreign oil purchases from the Persian Gulf to Mexico and Canada. By the end of 1983, Mexico was shipping 852,000 barrels of crude oil to the United States every day, which amounted to 17 percent of U.S. total imports of 4.9 million barrels a day. The flow of Persian Gulf crude, meanwhile, had slowed to about a third of the slightly more than 1 million barrels a day in 1975.[16]

This strategic change in U.S. energy dependency has meant an increase in reliance on oil shipments transiting the Caribbean Basin.

Oil production in the Basin totaled nearly 7 million barrels a day in 1978, with 39 percent coming from the U.S. Gulf Coast states. From 1973 to 1979, the refining capacity in the Caribbean (excluding the U.S. Gulf Coast) increased by 27 percent to reach 6.5 million barrels a day. This more than doubled the Basin's total capacity, when added to the U.S. Gulf Coast's 5.7 million barrels a day. By 1980, there were seventy-three refineries in the Basin.

Caribbean countries depend primarily on oil and gas (67 percent in 1977) for their energy needs. The remainder comes from solid fuels, mainly firewood (20 percent), hydroelectric power (13 percent), and nuclear power (less than 1 percent). In the region's rural areas, however, firewood and charcoal supply an estimated 80 percent of fuel needs. Tree cutting to feed this demand continues to be a significant cause of deforestation, which the escalation of petroleum prices has speeded.

Unfortunately, the Caribbean's vast potential to harness solar energy remains largely unfulfilled because of its higher cost. But alcohol from the aerobic fermentation of sugar cane and such starch-bearing plants as cassava (the source of tapioca) are potential energy sources. The anaerobic digestion of vegetable and animal wastes is another promising source. For the rest of this century, however, oil will remain a mixed blessing, guaranteeing the Caribbean's economic and strategic importance while threatening its environmental health.

Surprisingly, despite the Ixtoc I oil blow out of 1979–1980, overall oil spillage has been declining. The total amount of oil dumped into the Caribbean Basin decreased to 3.1 million metric tons from 6.1 million from 1973 to 1981, the International Maritime Organization (IMO) reports. One reason was a 38 percent drop in oil rig spills. But accidental and intentional spills still pose a major problem. During this same period, spills at marine terminals increased sevenfold, oil pollution from municipal waste more than doubled, and spills from tanker accidents nearly doubled. In 1981, the spillage from these three categories totaled 1.1 million tons, or a third of the region's total.[17]

"There are more congested and dangerous areas in the world," the IMO's David T. Edwards told a recent oil spill contingency planning meeting at St. Lucia, "but the Caribbean and the Gulf of Mexico might arguably be defined as having the world's most intricate pattern of tanker traffic. Add to this the transhipment terminals, refineries and offshore production in the region, as well as the ecologically sensitive and economically important beaches and coral zones, and you indeed have an area at risk."[18]

Indeed, in early August of 1984, 1.8 million gallons of Venezuelan crude oil from the grounded British tanker *Alvenus* began to wash up on twenty-five miles of Galveston, Texas, beaches, threatening both the city's tourist industry and Galveston Bay's rich beds of shrimp, crabs, and oysters. Fortunately, wind blew some of the oil back into the Gulf of Mexico. The last big oil slick to hit the Gulf Coast occurred at almost the same place in 1979, when two ships, the *Mimosa* and the *Burmah Agate,* collided. Again, luck intervened; most of the oil burned at sea.

PEOPLE, CULTURE, AND ECOLOGY

As the Caribbean Basin's environment comes under greater stress, its complex culture will dramatically influence rescue efforts. As Cuban critic Norberto Fuentes wrote of this region's unusual extremes and incongrous mixtures, "A cryptic telegraphic language is not suitable for expressing a reality such as ours. This is a violent, wild landscape."[19] The Caribbean's fragility is not just environmental; its people and culture also suggest a unique vulnerability.

The population density of the southern Netherlands Antilles (Aruba, Bonaire, and Curaçao), measured in persons per square kilometer of arable land, is more than seventeen times greater than that of Cuba. On the other hand, the average annual rainfall in the relatively flat and deforested Netherlands Antilles does not exceed 63.5 centimeters, compared to 800 centimeters on the highest peaks of Guadeloupe, 1,467 meters high.

Caribbean peoples differ as well. They represent historical infusions from Africa, Spain, Portugal, France, England, Holland, China, Indonesia, India, Syria, Lebanon, the United States, and Canada. Such a heritage, combined with the region's

Amerindian culture, has produced a rich racial mixture: Mulattoes (African and white), Mestizos (Amerindian and white), Zambos (African and Amerindian), Dooglas (African and East Indian), and Chinese-Creoles (African and Chinese). Then there are such local ethnics as the Barbados Redlegs, the Black Caribs of Belize, and Jamaica's Maroons (the descendents of runaway slaves).

The Basin's people, resources, and politics have forged contrary patterns. Martinique leads the region with a per capita Gross National Product of $4,680, which is eighteen times higher than that of the Caribbean's poorest country, Haiti ($260). Cuba's main export is sugar, while Jamaica's is aluminum ore, El Salvador's is coffee, and Trinidad and Tobago's is oil. Some of the governments are dictatorships (Haiti), some are democracies (Barbados), some are "associated states" (Puerto Rico and the Netherlands Antilles), some are dependencies (British Virgin Islands), and some are actual parts of other countries (Martinique and Guadeloupe are departments of France). Cuba has the region's largest military force, while Costa Rica has no army at all. Venezuela's population is growing at 3 percent a year, compared to Cuba's 0.7 percent. Barbados is the most crowded; Nicaragua the least. A Puerto Rican can expect to live seventy-four years, a Jamaican seventy years, and a Haitian fifty-one years.[20]

The Caribbean's most significant population characteristic, however, is the distribution disparity between its islands, with their limited carrying capacities, and the mainlands. Only the island states of Cuba and the Dominican Republic have fewer than 100 persons per square kilometer. On Barbados, the population density is more than 550. The Basin's continental countries, in contrast, average just above 25 persons per square kilometer, with the exception of El Salvador.[21] (Although El Salvador faces the Pacific Ocean, its high density of 170 persons per square kilometer coupled with its rugged terrain makes it similar to the overburdened islands of the Caribbean.)

To understand the Caribbean's environmental problems is first to understand that its history acted to cut off its people from their environment. Until very recently, there has been no grass roots basis for the growth of an environmental ethic as there has been in the United States and Europe. The land was not theirs. To go home was to "return" to somewhere else. Caribbean writer

John Wickham put it well in an essay published by the Caribbean Conservation Association: "The dispossession that followed the European discovery of these islands had the effect of a massive brainwashing. As the Barbadian poet Edward Braithwaite says in his *Islands*: '. . . . the land has lost the memory of the most secret places. We see the moon but cannot remember its meaning. A dark skin is a chain but it cannot recall the name of its tribe. There are no chiefs in the village.' Given the history of the Caribbean and its colonial experience, it is entirely understandable that the Caribbean personality should carry a burden of self-destruction and uncertain identity. But what cannot be useful is the continuing reluctance to use the elements which are at hand to repair the ancient disadvantage."[22]

This is as much an admonition to the Caribbeans themselves as it is to those outside interests that would still manipulate the region to their own ends. But the Caribbean's unique background, as Wickham describes it, does suggest that its new stirrings of environmental connection should be supported rather than patronized or ignored.

A REGIONAL SOLUTION?

On April 8, 1981, at Montego Bay, Jamaica, twenty-five of the twenty-seven nations and territories that form the Caribbean Basin adopted a program—the Caribbean Action Plan (CAP)—to protect the region's natural resources. "The Caribbean Sea is certainly not as polluted, say, as the Baltic or the Mediterranean," declared United Nations Regional Seas director Stjepan Keckes. "But there are hot spots, usually near concentrations of population and industry. Fortunately, there is still time to limit and control them."

The Regional Seas office, part of the United Nations Environment Programme (UNEP), was created in 1974 to encourage nations to cooperate in controlling pollution in bodies of water they share. CAP's area extends from French Guiana, 600 miles southeast of Trinidad and Tobago, through the Lesser and Greater Antilles, up Central America's east coast, and around the Gulf of Mexico to Florida and the Bahamas.

With the help of the Economic Commission for Latin America and a number of other U.N. and regional groups, UNEP's

Regional Seas program developed a long-term goal of sixty-six environmental projects. They represented a comprehensive attempt to deal with the Caribbean's growing vulnerability to oil spills, unmonitored marine pollution from human and industrial wastes, rapid deforestation and soil erosion, lack of protection for fragile natural areas and endangered species, lack of trained environmental specialists, and scant public understanding of the region's critical ecological issues.

For UNEP's Regional Seas office and its director, Yugoslav marine biologist Stjepan Keckes, Montego Bay marked an auspicious beginning, especially when Colombia and Honduras later joined to make the initiative unanimous. But the plan's execution developed one major flaw; the United States and several other countries, including Great Britain, refused to contribute to the action plan's trust fund. The U.S decision particularly dismayed many of the regional representatives, who had pledged an initial $1.2 million toward a three-year, $8.2 million program. Even tiny Marxist Grenada pledged $16,450. Without U.S. financial support, CAP faced an uncertain future.

Why the United States decided not to contribute any money to the CAP trust fund is one of those policy-making episodes that reflects both bureaucratic rigidity and inertia. The basic problem was that no one at the top policy-making levels in the government really paid any attention to the issue. It wasn't—and still isn't—that important among the concerns that animated either the Carter or Reagan administrations as well as Congress.

The State Department's Bureau of International Organizations, which manages U.S. participation in trust funds, opposed any U.S. contribution to the CAP fund. A few State Department career officers tried to reverse this policy, but could not overcome both the bureau's bias and a rigid procedural attitude "to keep accounts straight" in the Senate Appropriations Committee. The one person in Washington who openly fought this decision, Senator Claiborne Pell of Rhode Island, the ranking minority member of the Foreign Relations Committee, labored in vain.

When Mary Elizabeth W. Hoinkes, the deputy assistant secretary of state for environment, health, and natural resources, returned from the Montego Bay conference in the spring of 1981, she tried to keep the door open for a policy shift. "The new Administration has not had a chance to fully assess this thing in respect to our own financial contribution," she then said.[23] Both Hoinkes and Donald R. King, who replaced her in late 1981, tried to interest either State's Bureau of International Organizations or AID to put up a nominal $300,000.

"Nobody had any quarrel with the CAP," recalled A. Daniel Weygandt, the action officer for the U.S. Environment Programme at the State Department's Bureau of International Organizations. "After all, we did sign the Caribbean convention, and that does have financial implications. But it was not a high-level issue. The trouble was the congressional restriction over Cuba, and nobody wanted to be the one to get around that!" The State Department, Weygandt explained, thought trust funds were inefficient and often duplicated other activities. "Some never get enough money to get off the ground, and thus the dollars never get used," he said. "Our policy is not to encourage them."[24]

AID, however, still tried to keep the door open. During the winter of 1981–1982, it considered making a contribution to the CAP trust fund as development assistance under a Foreign Assistance Act slot called "voluntary funds." But the agency is primarily a vehicle for bilateral foreign assistance, and without a clear policy directive no AID bureaucrat would take this risk.[25] Albert C. Printz, AID's environmental coordinator, blames both Congress and the State Department's Bureau of International Organizations for killing U.S. participation in the CAP trust fund.[26] Printz said AID was blocked both legally and politically from contributing to it, and that the Senate Appropriations Committee staff opposed his attempt to make it possible. "When Pell showed an interest in making a contribution to the trust fund, we sent a one-page informal note to the Hill suggesting $300,000," explained James S. Hester, AID's chief environmental officer for Latin America and the Caribbean. "But committee staffers turned it down without further ado."[27]

James D. Bond, majority staff aide to the Senate Appropriations Subcommittee on Foreign Operations, could not remember either the meeting with Printz or Hester's note. But he said his panel would have objected because "multilateral accounts should be funded by State, not AID."[28] This was corroborated by

Senate Foreign Relations Committee staff member Peter W. Galbraith, who did remember the episode. Galbraith said that when Senator Pell urged AID administrator M. Peter McPherson to contribute to the trust fund, Senator Robert Kasten of Wisconsin, the Appropriations panel chairman, objected. Because of that, Galbraith said, AID developed its current "hybrid" approach to the Caribbean Action Plan.[29]

THE AMERICAN "CONTRIBUTION"

In the spring of 1982, a ruffled Senator Pell summoned McPherson for a not so friendly chat. Not only was the Reagan administration not putting any money into the Caribbean Action Plan trust fund; but the administration's minions were also being "high-handed and insulting" to some of the United Nations Regional Seas officials who continued to press for a change in U.S. policy.[30] The meeting resulted in a quick trip for Hester to UNEP's Regional Seas office in Geneva to patch things up. If Pell and CAP's few friends at the State Department could not overcome the administration's—and Congress'—policy, Washington could at least try to package a bilateral facsimile. Hester's objective was to organize an American response to CAP's priority list of projects. What resulted was the combining of one previous AID activity with several new programs for 1982 and 1983 that together came to $660,000.

AID, to its credit, had already allocated $60,000 in 1980 for a series of oil spill contingency planning workshops. As Hester later explained, this was to help the embryonic Regional Seas plan get started with something tangible. After the formation of CAP, AID allocated another $60,000 for more oil spill workshops, $125,000 for a U.S. Coast Guard officer to serve as an oil spill adviser based in San Juan, Puerto Rico, $240,000 for watershed management training, $125,000 for environmental education, and $50,000 for wildlife management training. Further allocations to extend these projects through 1985 have brought the total U.S. contribution to $939,500.

This bilateral American approach represented a laudable effort by AID to help the Caribbean Action Plan. U.S. environmental know-how is what the Caribbean needs, but U.S. bilateral aid also has drawbacks. Projects often represent one-shot efforts when what is desperately needed is continuity that could have been provided under a regional approach. Also, the U.S preference for bilateral help has tended to undermine the region's embryonic authority and spirit. AID also has earmarked $116.7 million over a ten-year period for environmental projects in the Caribbean and Central America, and agency officials contend that these sums also represent a substantial U.S. commitment to the region's environmental welfare. But these AID programs are available only to "eligible" countries, such as Haiti, the Dominican Republic, Jamaica, and all the Central American countries except Nicaragua. Many of the region's leaders, including Jamaica's Prime Minister Edward Seaga, contend that lack of U.S. participation in the Caribbean trust fund hobbled efforts to initiate the action plan and is continuing to stunt its growth. The establishment of a regional headquarters in Jamaica was delayed five years, largely because of the U.S.'s initial lack of financial support. Indeed, it was not until the fall of 1983 that the action plan's executive arm, called the monitoring committee, finally had enough money to begin any work.[31]

A DIPLOMATIC VISION

For almost three years, the Caribbean Action Plan remained merely a diplomatic vision. Its nine-member monitoring committee met twice, first in New York City and then in Cartagena, Colombia, mostly to agree that nothing could start until its trust fund grew larger. By mid-1982, a year after CAP's inauguration at Montego Bay, its trust fund had received only $25,355 out of initial pledges that totaled $1,293,000.

"If France was giving $375,000, we had hoped for $500,000 from the United States," recalled Arsenio Rodriguez, the U.N. Environment Programme official who helped organize the Caribbean Action Plan. "But because the United States consistently sabotaged the trust fund, the action plan faced a severe financial crisis. It's so petty; just to keep a few dollars from going to Cuba!"

The extent to which U.S. nonparticipation in the Caribbean trust fund has undermined regional resolves is difficult to assess. Although some countries—Dominica, Grenada, Guyana, and Nicaragua—lagged with their nominal commitments of $16,450, others since then have either met or exceeded their pledges, including the Bahamas, Barbados, St. Lucia, and Suriname. Mexico, Venezuela, and Colombia have emerged as the leaders.

By late 1983, CAP's trust fund had finally accumulated $824,700, which was considered enough to make a start. Meeting in Havana on November 10, 1983, the monitoring committee authorized eleven projects out of the sixty-six environmental jobs outlined in 1981 by the United Nations Regional Seas staff.[32] These projects, totaling $636,000, dealt with coastal protection, environmental education, marine pollution monitoring, oil spill contingency planning, tourism, environmental management, environmental training, and cleaning up Havana Bay, the region's most polluted waters.

The slow pace of contributions, however, was not to be CAP's only problem. Of the eleven projects listed above, only the first four were sufficiently organized to get under way by mid-1984. The rest were either postponed or returned to their sponsors for reworking because of basic defects. One proposal thrown back for a rewrite, according to A. Melville Gajraj, CAP's coordinator, was a plan for tourism development submitted by the U.N.'s Economic Commission for Latin America. "ECLA was told to redesign its proposal to provide guidelines to help governments to develop their tourism industries with less damage," Gajraj explained. "ECLA had ony presented an overview."[33] Gajraj, on loan to CAP from the U.N.'s Regional Seas program, helped the monitoring committee develop guidelines for drafting proposals and the criteria for then accepting or rejecting them.

Oil Spill Planning. The most successful CAP project so far is its oil spill contingency planning, which the International Maritime Organization (IMO) coordinates. The smaller Caribbean islands in particular lack the resources to deal with oil spills. The IMO, with the help of the Organization of American States and the U.N. Environment Programme, sponsored an islands experts meeting on St. Lucia May 7–11, 1984. The Swedish International Development Authority and AID also helped finance the event. Oil experts from seventeen states and territories agreed on a contingency plan for quickly reporting accidents and cooperating to minimize their impacts. U.S. Coast Guard communications facilities at San Juan, Puerto Rico, will be used initially as the hub of the island-warning network.

"This is at least a beginning," said David T. Edwards, the IMO representative. "We now have a mechanism to call in help from the outside and a means to let neighbors know a spill is coming. And that's progress."[34]

Part of the plan calls for expediting oil spill control equipment through customs. Precious time has been lost in the past because of customs holdups. One infamous case involved the oil tanker *Independente* after it blew up in the Turkish Straits in 1982. Turkish customs not only held up the oil spill equipment but also slit open the flotation gear looking for drugs.

Intentional discharges by ships pumping out their ballast residues before entering ports comprise a major part of the oil spill problem, Edwards said. The practice is outlawed under the International Convention for the Prevention of Pollution from Ships (MARPOL), although enforcement is difficult. Edwards predicts, however, that compliance will soon become "very easy" because of a new additive that makes residues usable.

Authority for CAP's oil spill contingency plans stem from the Convention for the Protection and Development of the Marine Environment of the Wider Caribbean Region, and from the Protocol Concerning Cooperation in Combating Oil Spills, which is the convention's enforcing arm. Both were adopted by CAP members on March 24, 1983, in Cartagena. The treaty becomes binding when ratified by nine members. When CAP member countries met in Cancun, Mexico, in April 1985, the United States, Mexico, St. Lucia, and the Netherlands had already ratified the treaty, and France, Jamaica, Venezuela, Panama, Barbados, Cuba, and Britain were expected to sign on soon.

About a third of the U.S. bilateral "participation" in CAP has been applied to oil spill contingency planning. In October 1983, AID assigned Lt. James D. Spitzer, a U.S. Coast Guard officer, to San Juan, Puerto Rico, as a "regional consultant on marine pollution." Spitzer immediately toured the region and found that Trinidad was "one of the more advanced countries" because it had a national contingency plan that required oil company participation. But he also noted that Trinidad's plan had little force. Its maximum fine for an intentional spill was the equivalent of U.S. $21. "The region's main problem is overcoming its inertia," Spitzer says. Most of the governments have no bureaucratic niche for dealing with oil pollution. So it is very easy for them to do nothing."[35]

As an example of such intertia, Spitzer cited his visit to Grand Cayman, an island south of Cuba. The cruise ship *Rhapsody* had gone aground on a coral reef in the harbor with seven hundred passengers aboard. When he called on the port director to inquire about the ship, he found him busy dealing with the press. It was a Friday, and the port director was ready to close for the weekend without having set up communications with the stricken vessel. The director also had not found out how much oil the ship carried and where it was located, or made salvage plans in case the ship should break up. Nor had he filed a lien against the French owners in case there was an oil spill. The next day, Spitzer located another official and persuaded him to take action. "No one in their government had this responsibility," Spitzer concluded. "That's what we're trying to do now by getting each country to allocate that responsibility. Then the prime minister will know who to finger when the oil starts coming ashore."

Spitzer's inability to visit Cuba did not hinder communication because Cuba can still participate in the region's oil spill warning network through the IMO. Even though the United States does not recognize Cuba, a Cuban environmental official attended a two-day oil spill exercise at the U.S. Coast Guard base in San Juan, Puerto Rico, following the 1984 St. Lucia conference.

Coastal Marine Environments. The most troubled of the first four CAP projects launched in 1984 concerns the protection of the eastern Caribbean's marine and coastal environment. CAP inherited a poorly run program initiated with the UNEP money by the Caribbean Community and Common Market (CARICOM) in 1981. CARICOM, with technical assistance from the Pan American Health Organization (PAHO), had devised a solid waste management plan that first required a rapid assessment of the islands' air, water, and land pollution. However, the assessment turned out to be anything but rapid. After CAP's creation, the PAHO-appointed coordinator was fired and a new man hired to finish the country surveys.

The U.N. Environment Programme hired a new senior scientist for the Caribbean Environmental Health Institute (a small laboratory in St. Lucia) who is now coordinating the CAP project.

258

With a newly acquired gas chromatograph, Dr. Joshua Ramsammy is analyzing the chemical content of St. Lucia's waters as well as their level of fecal pollution. Already, Ramsammy has detected the presence of the pesticide DDT, which is banned in the United States.

The institute is now assuming a subregional role to help the other small islands establish similar monitoring facilities. The extra equipment to allow them to start costs about $10,000 for each island. "The point is to establish a data base as soon as possible in order to assess the impact of future development," says Ramsammy. "We can train the technicians here. It all hinges on the funding we get."[36] In 1985, CAP allocated $59,413 more, which with additional funding from the U.N. Environment Programme's Environment Fund, CARICOM, and PAHO, is now allowing similar monitoring to begin at Grenada, Dominica, and St. Vincent. When more money becomes available, basic water quality monitoring also will start at Antigua, Montserrat, and St. Christopher-Nevis.

Watershed Management. The U.S. "contribution" to CAP also included $375,000 to the U.S. Forest Service's Institute of Tropical Forestry in Puerto Rico. Under the direction of Ariel E. Lugo, the AID-funded program installed river-gauging stations on three eastern Caribbean islands: St. Lucia, Dominica, and St. Vincent.[37] The gauges, which take samples from the rivers every fifteen minutes, relate rainfall and land use to river discharges and water quality—key regional concerns. Unfortunately, the one-shot program ended September 30, 1985. But AID's Hester was able to find "a few thousand dollars" to allow the islands to keep the gauges that had been supplied by the U.S. Geological Survey, which should allow the monitoring to continue. "The action is on these islands," says Lugo. "They behave completely differently from the continents. More energy is consumed per land unit on the islands; they are where the people are really impacting on their environment. In the Caribbean, unlike the Mediterranean, you have to understand the islands to see what is happening to the water. This is why our gauging stations are so important; they are measuring what's coming off the islands and going into the sea."

Lugo also initiated a forest inventory and a wildlife survey on the same three islands and on Antigua, Barbados, and

Montserrat. Twenty-seven foresters from these islands and Jamaica also trained in Puerto Rico during two three-month classes. Moreover, Lugo investigated how Dominica and St. Lucia dealt with the forest damage caused by Hurricane David in 1979. In 1986, AID assigned a full-time forester to the Caribbean to help the AID-eligible islands. These include most of the independent eastern Caribbean countries, Belize, Jamaica, the Dominican Republic, and Haiti.

Education and Training. The Caribbean Conservation Association, headquartered in Bridgetown, Barbados, is the Caribbean Basin's only "grass roots" environmental organization. It is supported by sixteen Caribbean member countries and by grants from the Canadian government and several American universities.[38] Following CAP's creation, the association published a regional environmental education directory of existing institutions, materials, and experts, which the U.N. Environment Programme financed until the CAP trust fund had enough money. The association also produced a series of radio programs and two workshops in 1984 for the media and educators.

When the United States decided to "participate" in CAP by selecting certain CAP priority projects, AID chose environmental education as one of them and allotted $125,000 in 1983 to RARE, Inc., an affiliate of the World Wildlife Fund in Washington, D.C. In May 1984, RARE initiated the first of five projects by holding a two-week training session for selected Caribbeans in St. Lucia. The five men and four women participants from seven countries were all government employees working in fisheries (Belize and St. Lucia), forestry (Dominica), health (Montserrat), housing (Barbados), education (Belize, Grenada, and St. Lucia), and natural resources (Ecuador). The point of the workshop was to teach "skills and techniques" in dealing with environment versus development issues, and the session's highlight was a simulation game called "Coastal Tourism Development." One of the trainees, a twenty-one-year-old fisheries manager from St. Lucia, summed up what he learned from the workshop this way: "We're a small island. If we lose our forests we'll see a difference in the water available to the towns. If we don't live within our resources, we'll suffer. There is just no margin for error here."[39]

James Talbot, AID's Caribbean environmental specialist based in Port-au-Prince, Haiti, stresses the value of bottom-up training. "What is needed, for example, is to get some decent environmental country profiles," he says, "and they should not be done by an outside team from Arizona that comes in and says this is what you need to know. They should be built from the inside out, using the outside team only as advisers. You could do one with a semi-trained cadre of fifteen local people who would then learn the process of environmental assessment. They would then become spokespersons for the environment with their government ministers. Instead of dumping $375,000 on Lugo [the U.S. Forest Service's project director in Puerto Rico], dump $10,000 on fifteen little island agencies locally and then provide some activities to assist them."

Happily, the AID-financed RARE program followed this advice, although initially RARE planned to hold the training sessions in the United States. The Caribbean Conservation Association's executive director, Jill Sheppard, intervened to help RARE avoid that mistake.

New Initiatives. By April 1985, when CAP members held their third intergovernmental meeting at Cancun, Mexico, the trust fund had received $1,432,401—more than before but still 45 percent short of its pledges. Nevertheless, despite continuing U.S. refusal to contribute to the fund, there were breakthroughs.

The first concerned CAP's four-year frustration over not having enough money to set up its own regional headquarters in Kingston, Jamaica, whose government had offered free office facilities. At Cancun the U.S. representative, H. Alan Krause, said the United States would pay its "fair share" of CAP administrative expenses by assigning a full-time environmental expert—Dr. John Belshe, an Army Corps of Engineers oceanographer—to the Kingston headquarters for two years. This is equivalent to about $100,000 a year, and the U.S. contribution then helped to induce CAP member countries to approve establishing the office, which was expected to open in early 1986. Dedicating operating expenses for a headquarters facility made little sense when monies were meager. But a regional program without a local nerve center—CAP had been administered from UNEP's Geneva office—faces an uphill fight to cohere and prosper.

Another breakthrough—for the United States—came when the United States was allowed representation on CAP's nine-member monitoring committee. Ironically, Cuba supported the

U.S. bid while France objected. Now, although the United States has not yet been asked, any country that "supports" the Caribbean Action Plan may serve on CAP's executive body. Previously, only members that contributed to the trust fund could be represented. (The committee, whose current members are from Barbados, Colombia, Cuba, France, Jamaica, Mexico, Panama, St. Lucia, and Venezuela, will meet next in April 1987 at Guadeloupe.)

Meanwhile, CAP's program has begun to operate more effectively after its faltering beginning. Five more projects of the original eleven have started: oil spill contingency planning for the South American subregion; case studies of environmentally sound tourism development in Colombia, Puerto Rico, and an eastern Caribbean island; a survey of environmental training needs for marine pollution and health; oil dispersion training; and development of environmental impact assessment methods in Mexico for use throughout the Basin. Also, three new projects were added, largely financed by UNEP: a water management plan for Jamaica, protection of three endangered species of marine turtles in Mexico, and publication of a Caribbean marine research directory and marine science bibliography.

At Cancun, CAP's monitoring committee also approved another eight projects costing $627,600, which included the expansion of the St. Lucia-based monitoring of island coastal waters. In addition, fourteen more projects were selected pending available funding that would cost $802,300. These include watershed management in Haiti, establishing natural resource reserves in the eastern Caribbean, a coastal and marine data atlas, and guidelines for water recycling.[40]

ECOLOGY VERSUS POLITICS IN THE CARIBBEAN

The United States now spends about $12 million a year on scattershot projects to protect the Caribbean's fragile and threatened environment. For the 1986 fiscal year, the administration asked Congress to spend a total of $1.43 billion in the Caribbean Basin, an increase of $91.5 million from 1985. Most of this—79 percent—will go to Central America, where just two countries, El Salvador and Honduras, will get almost half of all the U.S. foreign aid for the Caribbean Basin. Military assistance alone to these two countries will total $220.8 million, or more than eighteen times what the United States is spending to protect the entire region's environmental future.[41]

Meanwhile, the United States will not directly support the region's multilateral grass roots effort to ensure its own ecological health, while U.S. bilateral aid—although often well conceived—remains both unevenly applied and inadequate. Indeed, in the view of some experts, the U.S. effort in such countries as Haiti represents a classic case of "too little, too late."

President Reagan's so-called Caribbean Basin Initiative—launched in January 1984 to encourage U.S. business investments and increase trade—may or may not help raise the region's standard of living. But once again, such traditional economic strategies fail to deal with the Caribbean's essential ecological issues. If the region continues to lose its forests, soil, and fisheries while adding to its industrial pollution, no amount of new business investments and easier access to U.S. markets is going to save the Caribbean from an environmental collapse. U.S. aid suffers from the political restrictions in the Foreign Assistance Act, which limits where and how U.S. help can be applied. The U.S. government, for example, excludes Cuba from any benefits, and must consider such congressional directives as a recent House report suggesting that the Haitian government should limit emigration to the United States and improve human rights before it can receive more U.S. aid.[42] This is a defect of the bilateral approach, compared to funnelling U.S. assistance through such regional instruments as the Caribbean Action Plan. Environmental protection should be separated from political concerns.

American priorities in the region are badly warped. A government that is willing to spend $645.6 million in just two Central American countries to contain "radical" political change is, at the same time, unwilling to spend more than a thousandth of that sum to help a potentially pathbreaking regional environmental and resource management effort. The irony is that if this regional ecological fight is lost, a scarred and degraded region may produce the very economic and social ills that cause the kind of radical revolutions the U.S. government so fears.

As U.S. policymakers ponder this dilemma, they can look to Haiti as an example of how not to proceed. The United States currently allocates about a third of its local Caribbean Basin aid to the islands of the Greater and Lesser Antilles. Most of this help (86 percent) goes to just two countries, the Dominican Republic and Haiti.[43] In 1981, the U.S. Agency for International Development committed $8 million in Haiti to finance a four-year tree-growing program. The money is going to three private organizations; two of these groups, the Pan American Development Foundation and CARE, use a variety of local and religious institutions to supply seedlings to the farmers. It is, by most standards, a laudatory effort.

By the spring of 1984, the Pan American Development Foundation, which accounts for half the AID program, had planted more than 5 million trees, mostly a fast-growing hardwood called the leucaena. In eighteen months, a seedling can grow to a ten-foot height (often higher) and be ready for harvesting as a cash crop for fuelwood. These trees then sprout new shoots to repeat the process again and again. The tree-planting program has a survival rate of from 50 to 70 percent. The problem, however, is that Haitians are still cutting down their trees five times faster than they are being planted. "Our program is just a drop in the bucket," Glenn R. Smucker, the foundation's project director, admits. "If it's valid to plant trees as a cash crop, then the idea will sell itself. But you shouldn't think of this in anything less than generational terms."[44]

Some natural resource experts argue that as needy as Haiti is for more trees, it now makes little sense to fight a losing battle there while virtually ignoring other areas that are still salvageable. "With Haiti," says Dr. Carleton Ray, a University of Virginia marine scientist, "we are using an approach that is the opposite to triage. We are putting a lot of money into a bottomless hole there." James Hester, AID's chief environmental officer for Latin America and the Caribbean, admits that Haiti "is probably the most environmentally degraded country in the wider Caribbean." The question now, however, is how to keep other threatened Caribbean countries such as St. Lucia from becoming new Haitis while there is still time to act. Clearly, U.S. foreign aid spending priorities must change in the Caribbean Basin. If the United States has the resources to spend $221 million on military aid to El Salvador and Honduras, and even $8 million in Haiti on trees, it surely can allocate more than $375,000 to a half-dozen smaller islands to protect their watersheds.

AN OPPORTUNITY MISSED?

The Caribbean Action Plan still limps along without enough money to carry out its basic mandate. Imperfect as CAP is, it does offer the culturally and politically diverse Caribbean community an unusual opportunity for environmental cooperation. The United States should ally itself fully with this Caribbean movement, rather than allowing procedural and political constraints to inhibit a proper role that also promotes long-term U.S. interests.

"What will happen if the Caribbean's resources are stripped, if the top soil is lost, and the fisheries are destroyed?" asks the U.N. Environment Programme's Arsenio Rodriguez. "People won't be able to support themselves, and then they will go to Florida, or try. The islands are overpopulated now in relation to their resources. So why not invest in protecting the region's resources now, rather than sinking more money into a place like Haiti *after* the resources are gone?"[45]

This question haunts AID officials too, especially James Talbot, the agency's Caribbean environmental specialist in Haiti. Talbot recognizes that the Caribbean as a region extends well beyond AID's current list of countries the United States may help bilaterally. For this reason he argues for a broader U.S. environmental policy in the Caribbean despite the known defects of multilateral groups. "Just because UNEP [the U.N. Environment Programme] says, yea verily, sewage treatment is a good thing, what is a little island going to do?" he asks. "Create technicians out of nowhere? So they decide they have to get everybody trained. It then takes them eight months to find somebody, another six months to get the money and two years for the person to go off to school. And then usually the wrong one goes off to school because it's somebody's turn. This is the small-island top-down approach, and it is only a piece of the puzzle. It doesn't mean UNEP is doing something wrong; they aren't doing enough. They should have done a little less political protocol signing and a little more on how to get at this. Without these low and mid-level technicians, you won't have anything."[46]

Talbot recognizes one of the great developmental truths of much of the Caribbean: its individuality and the smallness of its member nations make it a difficult place for large institutions to operate efficiently. Both AID and the U.N. agencies are best at initiating oil spill contingency planning among governments. They are least effective in launching ongoing natural resource management schemes for small islands. Yet, as Dr. Michael P. Greene, the science consultant to the Organization of American States who fashioned the first Caribbean oil spill contingency plan puts it, what the United States has accomplished "is a great tribute to a few dedicated individuals at AID and the State Department, despite Congress' restrictions."[47]

"Borders do not exist concerning the environment," Juan Antonio Mateos, a Mexican Foreign Ministry official in charge of U.N. activities, said in explaining why his country supports the Caribbean Action Plan. "These twenty-seven countries have decided that this is a good program and that it will help a lot to prevent the deterioration of the environment. They also think it can create bridges of cooperation between the English-speaking countries and the others. It is a very practical approach with very few political implications. In terms of self-interest alone, the United States should participate. This would be a very simple and direct way for the United States to cooperate with the countries of the Caribbean. But in the Caribbean you have put ideology first, and now you are tripping over it."[48]

NOTES

1. Edward L. Towle, "The Island Microcosm," Island Resources Foundation, Washington, D.C., 1984.

2. Towle, "The Island Microcosm."

3. Report of the National Bipartisan Commission on Central America, Henry A. Kissinger, chairman, January 1984.

4. The Miami Report: Recommendations on United States Policy Toward Latin America and the Caribbean, University of Miami Graduate School of International Studies, Coral Gables, Florida, 1984.

5. U.S. House of Representatives Foreign Affairs Subcommittee on Western Hemisphere Affairs.

6. Lawrence Mosher, "Maybe Later, U.S. Says in Response to Bid for Caribbean Cleanup Funds," *National Journal*, May 2, 1981, 783–784.

At Sea in the Caribbean?

7. U.S. Agency for International Development, "The Dominican Republic: Country Environmental Profile," July 1981, AID/SOD/PDC-C-0247.

8. United Nations Environment Programme Regional Seas Reports and Studies No. 14, "Development and Environment in the Wider Caribbean Basin," August 2, 1982.

9. Interview with Gabriel Charles, forestry supervisor, St. Lucia Ministry of Agriculture, Castries, May 10, 1984.

10. A. Melville Gajraj, "Threats to the Terrestrial Resources of the Caribbean," *Ambio,* 1981, vol. X, no. 6.

11. Allen D. Putney, "Survey of Conservation Priorities in the Lesser Antilles, Final Report," Caribbean Conservation Association, St. Croix, U.S. Virgin Islands, October 1982.

12. Anitra Thorhaug, "Biology and Management of Seagrass in the Caribbean," *Ambio,* 1981, vol. X, no. 6.

13. Arsenio Rodriguez, "Marine and Coastal Environmental Stress in the Wider Caribbean Basin," *Ambio,* 1981, vol. X, no. 6.

14. Mosher, "Maybe Later, U.S. Says."

15. U.N. Environment Programme, "The Status of Oil Pollution and Oil Pollution Control in the Wider Caribbean Region," E/CEPAL/PROY.3/L.5, October 25, 1979.

16. Lawrence Mosher, "Next Time the Persian Gulf Shuts Down, The U.S. May Be Ready to Act," *National Journal,* February 25, 1984.

17. "Inputs of Petroleum Hydrocarbons into the Marine Environment," IMO/OAS/UNEP Government Experts Meeting on Sub-regional Oil Spill Contingency Planning for Island States and Territories of the Wider Caribbean, St. Lucia, May 7–11, 1984.

18. David T. Edwards, International Maritime Organization representative to the Government Experts Meeting on Sub-regional Oil Spill Contingency Planning for the Island States and Territories of the Wider Caribbean, St. Lucia, May 7, 1984.

19. Barry B. Levine, "Abundance and Scarcity in the Caribbean," *Ambio,* 1981, vol. X, no. 6.

20. Levine, "Abundance and Scarcity."

21. U.N. Environment Programme Regional Seas Reports and Studies No. 14, "Development and Environment in the Wider Caribbean Basin," August 2, 1982.

22. John Wickham, "The Environment as an Ingredient of Cultural Expression," in *Perceptions of the Environment,* Yves Renard (ed.), Caribbean Conservation Association, Bridgetown, Barbados, 1979.

23. Mosher, "Maybe Later, U.S. Says."

24. Interview with A. Daniel Weygandt, U.N. Environment Programme action officer in the State Department's International Organizations Bureau, Washington, D.C., April 13, 1984.

25. Interview with Donald R. King, former acting deputy assistant Secretary of State for Environment, Health and Natural Resources, Washington, D.C., August 9, 1984.

26. Interview with Albert C. Printz, U.S. Agency for International Development environmental affairs coordinator, Washington, D.C., April 2, 1984.

27. Interview with James S. Hester, Latin America and Caribbean chief environmental officer, U.S. Agency for International Development, Washington, D.C., April 2, 1984.

28. Interview with James D. Bond, majority staff aide to the U.S. Senate Appropriations Subcommittee on Foreign Operations, Washington, D.C., August 9, 1984.

29. Interview with Peter W. Galbraith, U.S. Senate Foreign Relations Committee staff member, Washington, D.C., April 30, 1984.

30. Interview with Joan Martin-Brown, U.N. Environment Programme Washington, D.C. representative, April 5, 1984.

31. U.N. Environment Programme Regional Seas document UNEP/IG.46/6, 4 and UNEP/IG.46/3, 10.

32. U.N. Environment Programe UNEP/IG.46/6, 4 and UNEP/IG.46/3, 10.

33. Interview with A. Melville Gajraj, U.N. Environment Programme Regional Seas CAP coordinator, Bridgetown, Barbados, May 15, 1984.

34. Interview with David T. Edwards, International Maritime Organization marine environment chief, St. Lucia, May 11, 1984.

35. Interview with James D. Spitzer, U.S. Coast Guard regional consultant on marine pollution, St. Lucia, May 11, 1984.

36. Interview with Dr. Joshua Ramsammy, Caribbean Environmental Health Institute senior scientist, St. Lucia, May 11, 1984.

37. Interview with Ariel E. Lugo, project leader, Institute of Tropical Forestry, Las Piedras, Puerto Rico, May 17, 1984.

38. Interview with Jill Sheppard, Caribbean Conservation Association executive director, Georgetown, Barbados, May 13, 1984.

39. Interview with Crispin d'Auvergne, fisheries assistant, St. Lucia, May 8, 1984.

40. United Nations Environment Programme document UNEP/IG.54/7, "Report of the Fourth Meeting of the Monitoring Committee on the Action Plan for the Caribbean Environment Programme," June 10, 1985.

41. U.S. House of Representatives Foreign Affairs Subcommittee on Western Hemisphere Affairs.

42. U.S. House of Representatives Conference Report, "International Security and Development Cooperation Act of 1985," report no. 99–237, July 29, 1985.

43. U.S. Agency for International Development Bureau for Latin America and the Caribbean Portfolio of Environmental Projects, March 1984.

44. Interview with Glenn R. Smucker, Pan American Development Foundation Haitian project director, Port-au-Prince, Haiti, May 21, 1984.

45. Interview with Arsenio Rodriguez, U.N. Environment Programme Regional Seas coordinator, Mexico City, May 2, 1984.

46. Interview with James Talbot, U.S. Agency for International Development environmental specialist, Port-au-Prince, Haiti, May 23, 1984.

47. Interview with Dr. Michael P. Greene, associate director, National Research Council Board on Science and Technology for International Development, Washington, D.C., January 5, 1986.

48. Interview with Juan Antonio Mateos, Mexican Foreign Ministry director general for United Nations organizations, Mexico City, May 4, 1984.

CHAPTER 8

The High Costs of High Dams

MARC REISNER
AND RONALD H. McDONALD

—————————————*Editors' Preface*—————————————

Costa Rica could not build a dam like Brazil's Tucurui Dam if it wanted to. This chapter is about wanting to—about choices. It is not just a debate over two ways to build dams. It is a discussion of two radically different approaches to development.

Big dams, in both the United States and Latin America, are symbols, statements of national pride. They support irrigation or industrialization and, it often follows, urbanization. Giant dams, however, no matter how ingeniously engineered, no matter how many megawatts of electricity they produce—are uneconomical. By almost any honest accounting, they probably should not be built anywhere in the world. Authors Marc Reisner and Ronald H. McDonald enumerate but do not detail the environmental and human health problems of other big dams around the world. A careful cost-benefit analysis—one that factored into the price of the electricity the real costs of health and environmental problems associated with the mega-structures—would show most big dams to be economic albatrosses.

Reisner and McDonald also raise the specter of a nation's dependency on a few very large, expensive projects. Should any of them fail, say from more rapid than expected silting, they could leave new industries without power and banks with very large unpaid loans. Alternatively, if anticipated industrial growth did not materialize, the banks might also have trouble recovering their investments.

Against this backdrop, the differing approaches to dam-building and development represented by Brazil and Costa Rica make a fascinating comparison. Brazil's mega-ventures are designed to serve industrial, heavily populated areas, to attract more capital and industry, and to create jobs, mostly in urban factories. Costa Rica's modest dam is meant to electrify the countryside, to improve amenities, services, and opportunities, mostly agricultural, in rural areas, and so to stem the tide of urbanization.

Some dams, even modest-sized structures, such as the one El Salvador planned, can trigger displacement, discontent, migration, and armed hostilities with neighbors. Others, such as that in Costa Rica, can further rural development programs and even perform useful environmental functions.

But even a model dam like Costa Rica's won't work if certain other conditions and policies are not in place: land reform; agricultural credit and technical assistance; appropriate rate structures; and possibly subsidization of electricity and maintenance for the poorest communities. Moreover, constructing power lines to deliver the dam's electricity can cost handsomely even in a small country such as Costa Rica if it is mountainous. These caveats about rural electrification provide reason to think more about alternative small-scale, renewable energy sources that are decentralized to serve local rural communities. These alternatives include really small-scale hydropower development (dams generating up to 500 kilowatts and requiring no major civil works), as well as wood-burning plants and other solar sources to power local enterprises and health facilities.

Of course, one kind of power can beget another. An interesting side effect of Brazil's joint dam ventures with neighboring states is that such small nations as Uruguay and Paraguay have acquired leverage with their huge dominant neighbors Brazil and Argentina, who have long appeared to the small states as competitive giants between whom they might be crushed.

Reisner and McDonald would go further than Tad Szulc does in Chapter 6 in urging a U.S. point of view where big dams are concerned. In their opinion, over $1 billion from U.S. banks, even though that's only 8 percent of Brazil's capital costs on this dam project, give the United States "the right to ask. . . ." And some of the negative social effects discussed in the chapter—destabilization and unrest, tension with squatters, genocide of endangered human species, and outright war in the case of El Salvador and Honduras—could also jeopardize U.S. security interests.

W ITHIN the past fifteen years, Latin America has assumed the title of hydroelectric capital of the world. True, North America still has many more dams than South and Central America, and the Soviet Union and China are both planning water-development projects even bigger than Brazil's largest. But for sheer ambition, passion for development, and capital investment in hydroelectricity as a percentage of GNP, Latin America is unsurpassed, and no other region has such a phenomenal, unexploited hydroelectric potential.

The three most impressive hydroelectric dams in the world are all now in South America—Itaipu, Tucurui, and Guri (in Argentina). The world's largest and most expensive hydro dam, Itaipu, began generating power in October 1984. Built jointly by Paraguay and Brazil, at a cost approaching $20 billion, the project's total capacity is 12,600,000 kilowatts. The 8-million-kilowatt Tucurui Dam, more massive even than Itaipu and the largest dam and reservoir ever built in a tropical wet forest, is now being completed solely by Brazil, which also has dozens of additional dams—several exceeding 1 million kilowatts—in the works.

Hulking waterworks are also planned for other Latin American nations. Chile, too, plans several large dams on its biggest river, the Bio-Bio. Peru is contemplating transbasin water diversions through tunnels drilled beneath the high Andes. A single dam under construction in Honduras, El Cajon, has absorbed as much as a third of that nation's annual budget.[1] In peacetime, the modern world has never seen an ambition anything like it.

Except, perhaps, for deforestation, nothing is likely to affect so profoundly Latin America's natural and human environment as this colossal program of dam and reservoir construction. Tucuruí's 200-kilometer-long reservoir, larger in surface area than Lake Mead, will inundate a swath of rainforest about the size of Delaware and displace 10,000 to 30,000 people, including several beleaguered indigenous tribes. Itaipu completely inundated what many considered to be the world's most spectacular cataract, Guaíra Falls, displacing thousands of people, flooding 580,000 acres of land, some of it productive farmland.

The sudden availability of so much power is an open invitation to mammoth industrial development in virtually untouched regions. Tucuruí, for example, will power a huge bauxite-alumina smelting operation in eastern Amazônia some three hundred miles from Belém, the nearest town of any size. The hydrologic regimes of some of the world's most powerful rivers, rivers that approach or exceed the Mississippi in size—the Parana, the Tocantins, the Uruguay, even the incomparable Amazon—could be dramatically altered. If they are, everything from fisheries to migratory waterfowl populations to the very survival of many tropical and subtropical species is at stake. And the creation of huge reservoirs and draw-down swamplands could create ideal conditions for carriers of such debilitating illnesses as malaria and schistosomiasis.

Obviously, Latin America's hydropower ambitions may also transform the region's development paths and economies, and, for better or worse, the changes will reverberate throughout the economies of the industrialized nations, notably the United States, that have lent it spectacular sums. The Itaipu Dam's $19-billion cost (capital plus interest) represents about 20 percent of Brazil's outstanding foreign debt, and the dam contributed mightily to that debt. However, Itaipu could help liberate Brazil from its onerous dependence on foreign oil, and it may create a turbo-booster effect on the national economy. More than 12,000 megawatts of new electricity (Brazil now consumes only 25,000 or so) could transform the economies of Brazil and Paraguay as significantly as Grand Coulee and Bonneville power revolutionized

273

the economy of the Pacific Northwest. If it did, Brazil could pay off its debt or at least the interest on its debt, faster. But if the power remains unmarketable for long—a distinct possibility given the country's deepening economic morass—Itaipu could easily become an albatross, like the Pacific Northwest's once-gargantuan program of nuclear power plant construction. Moreover, if silt reduces the power capacities of the great dams faster than expected—likely, in a region where slash-and-burn deforestation is proceeding at a terrific rate—the region's future economic growth may have been planted in mud.

It is not possible to trace in a single chapter all the implications of a vast, mostly uncoordinated hydroelectric development program involving dozens of nations from Argentina to the Dominican Republic. But a comparison of two projects that differ dramatically in scale, cost, and likely economic and environmental impact, and that reflect differing national policies, attitudes, and philosophies can reveal worlds. On one hand is Itaipu, a huge project built by two nations whose unvarnished goal is to foster tremendous economic growth through industrialization based on hydroelectricity. On the other is the Arenal Dam in Costa Rica, a much smaller project built in the name of rural electrification in a country whose environmental policies (in stark contrast to Paraguay's and Brazil's) are the most progressive in the developing world.

"Without Itaipu, I don't know what Brazil would become."

—former Brazilian president
Jaŏ Baptiste de Oliveira Figueiredo

Itaipu, the world's largest hydroelectric project, is a monument built of raw superlatives. The initial construction contract itself weighed 220 pounds! A huge barrier across the Parana River, which ranks seventh in the world in annual flow, it will, when fully operational, generate 12,600,000 kilowatts of power—three times the original output of Grand Coulee. The power plant consists of generating units, each with a rated output of 700,000 kilowatts—each housing enough power for a North American city of 500,000 people. Most of the electricity will go to Brazil, supplying the southern and southeastern portions of that nation—particularly the environs of São Paulo and Rio de Janeiro, which generate 75 percent of the country's gross national product. (To win Paraguay's participation, Brazil promised its partner 50 percent of the electricity from Itaipu, far more than Paraguay can possibly use. Thus overendowed, Paraguay will soon become the world's largest exporter of hydroelectricity and Brazil its biggest customer.)

Planning for Itaipu began in 1967, when Paraguay and Brazil began jointly studying the feasibility of launching a hydroelectric project on the Parana River that forms their common border. More than fifty plans were considered before the two governments agreed to build a single dam at Itaipu, ten miles north of the Foz de Iguacu-Ciudid Presidente Stroessner Bridge. On April 26, 1973, Brazil and Paraguay signed a treaty on the Itaipu project, and a year later they established the supervisory agency, Binacional. To a high degree for so vast and difficult a project, the engineering and construction work was indigenous. Four Brazilian firms had the primary responsibility. Engevix from Rio de Janeiro contributed the spillway and the right wing dam's final design. Promon, from São Paulo, took charge of the main dam's final design. Themag from São Paulo designed the powerhouse, and Hidroservice of São Paulo designed the earth-fill dams and the navigation routes.[2]

Before the dam was constructed, Itaipu's water level was about one 100 meters above sea level; when the dam is completed, the water level will rise another one 100 meters. For a base-load dam of such prodigious power, the reservoir is remarkably small—1,460 square kilometers at full capacity. Only because the Parana is a huge, constant river flowing through a tight, relatively deep gorge, similar to the Palisades gorge of the lower Hudson, does it work. Because of the reliable flow, a function both of natural climatic conditions and a number of smaller upriver dams, Itaipu is essentially a "run of the river" project.

To build the dam, the entire Parana River was moved to one side into an excavated diversion channel—one of the most remarkable engineering feats ever. Equally awe-inspiring is the central superstructure of the dam itself. It is formed by sixteen double blocks of concrete, each 34 meters wide and 196 meters high. Every day for five years, enough concrete was poured for a 350-story building.[3] The main superstructure, with the wing dams, will reach a width of eight kilometers, five times wider than Grand Coulee, a dam of about the same height. The generating units are built on the same scale, surpassed only by Grand Coulee's generators and turbines. A single turbine rotor weighs as much as 250 automobiles. Transporting the rotors from São Paulo, where they were made, took more than two months and required that bridges, roads, and viaducts be specially reinforced. Some of the trucks that moved the heaviest equipment used 200 tires. Over 80 percent of Itaipu's equipment was manufactured in Brazil, though many of the main hydroelectric components were designed in Europe. The rest was made in Paraguay or imported.

Filling the Itaipu Reservoir was a hydrologic experiment without precedent. Because the dam has no emergency outlet works at the base, filling could not—once started—be controlled until the spillway level was reached. For two tense weeks, the structure's fate was entirely in the hands of the Parana River. The reservoir rose thirty feet a day—far beyond the foot-per-day guidelines that the U.S. Bureau of Reclamation, the world's most experienced dam-building agency, generally follows. (A federal report blamed the collapse of the Bureau's Teton Dam in 1976 partly on a too-rapid rate of reservoir filling—four feet per day!)[4] The main risks of rapid filling are earthquakes and landslips caused by the growing reservoir's enormous weight and disintegration of the dam abutments as water infiltrates. Itaipu filled without incident in an amazing fifteen days, though critics are less amazed than leery of Brazil's reckless infatuation with water development.[5]

Hydropower already accounts for 90 percent of Brazil's electrical energy consumption. Counting Itaipu, the Tucurui Dam, and the construction of several other impressively large dams, the nation will depend utterly on huge dams for electricity—far more than Japan and France depend on nuclear reactors or Britain depends on coal. Were Itaipu to fail, the hazards of such dependence would be obvious. The cost, meanwhile, has burdened the nation's economy because constructing a large dam takes vast amounts of money and energy, but produces no revenue or electricity during long years of construction (in Itaipu's case, ten years). Brazil spent about $32 billion on hydroelectric development alone between 1982 and 1985. Another $40 billion has been committed for 1986–1990. All of this comes, or will come, from an economy of under $200 billion, and from a nation that in 1984 had a foreign debt of around $90 billion not to mention an inflation rate close to 100 percent. Then, too, Brazil has had only limited access to international financial markets over the past two years as the external financial situation has deteriorated. Yet, the prospect that Itaipu power may (by one optimistic estimate) replace 500,000 barrels of foreign oil a day and raise hydro's share of national energy consumption from 26 percent in 1979 to perhaps 36 percent in 1985 justifies to Brazil's leaders the financing troubles and accumulating debt.[6]

ECONOMIC AND POLITICAL DYNAMICS

Three-quarters of the money raised to build Itaipu was collected domestically. Still, the 25 percent raised from foreign sources, chiefly private U.S. banks, constitutes a crucial share. Whether the dam could have been built without foreign loans is debatable; at the very least, builders would have encountered substantial difficulties. (In a remarkably candid interview, former Governor Edmund G. Brown of California, who presided over the construction of the California Water Project—then the most expensive water development ever undertaken—said that raising the first $1.75 billion was relatively easy; it was the last half-billion dollars or so that the public and bond markets seemed unready to swallow. To ease the pain, the Brown administration misrepresented the cost of the project to keep it under $2 billion.)[7] The largest individual foreign creditor was Citibank, which (with various foreign affiliates) lent $612 million. The next largest was Morgan Guaranty Trust of New York, which lent $596 million. About 8 percent of the capital cost, then, came from just two U.S. banks. Other U.S. banks provided smaller loans. Other large foreign lenders included the Swiss Bank Corporation ($303 million) and Deutsches Bank ($157 million).[8]

Hydroelectric development has also linked the four main Latin American nations involved in transnational projects. Uruguay and Argentina are jointly building Salto Grande, a 1,890,000-kilowatt dam on the Uruguay River. Paraguay and Argentina are backing a second mammoth project lower on the Parana River, Yacyreta, which is expected to generate 2,700,000 kilowatts of electricity if it is completed. Because of hydropower development, relations among these four countries have changed. Historically, Argentina, the group's most affluent and developed country, has viewed the small nations bordering it—Paraguay, Uruguay, and Bolivia—as economic (if not political) colonies. It has tended to view Brazil as a rival, particularly during the past twenty years as Brazil's economic development has picked up steam. Brazil, for its part, has also had ambitions toward the three smaller nations. Uruguay has a long tradition of Brazilian investment, tourism, and influence; Paraguay shares with Brazil Latin America's number one dam site, Itaipu. Uruguay and Paraguay, which have had relatively stable (if authoritarian) regimes, skillfully have played Argentina against Brazil to their own benefit. Even unstable Bolivia has acquired this knack. Judged by size alone, these contests appear uneven, but Paraguay, Uruguay, and Bolivia have one major advantage: access to energy. As such, they can play the *chihuahua* yanking the crocodile's tail.

The hydroelectric courtship of Paraguay by the Latin American superpowers, Argentina and Brazil, has a fairly long tradition. Decades ago, Argentina reached an agreement with Paraguay to construct a relatively small (90,000 kilowatts) hydroelectric project, the Arcaray Falls Dam, which was finished in 1969. Paraguay was entitled to half the project's power, much of which it sells back to Argentina. This arrangement became the model for Itaipu and, for Paraguay, a major source of foreign exchange. Argentina and Brazil have funded subsequent projects, because Paraguay, one of the least developed Latin American nations, can generate little capital on its own.

Argentina took the Itaipu agreement between Paraguay and Brazil as a serious blow. As one observer put it, "Argentina could do nothing but sulk after the project was formalized."[9] But, amid considerable political and economic instability, the Argentines did propose their own giant joint venture with Paraguay further down the Parana River, Yacyreta, as well as a smaller one, Corpus. Such intense rivalry may lend credence to critics' claims that the dams are not "rational," but instead manifestations of national pride and jealousy, as well as the Iberian urge to conquer nature.

The economic impact of the three great transnational projects, Itaipu, Salto Grande, and Yacyreta, is still impossible to predict confidently. Yacyreta is not yet operational, Itaipu is only partially operational, and Salto Grande is new. The key questions are the extent to which the nations depend on hydrocarbons (particularly imported petroleum) to produce electricity and the rate at which their energy consumption will rise in response to economic development.

Only one of the four countries, Argentina, approaches self-sufficiency in petroleum production. Although Argentina has a developed, sophisticated, industrial economy, it has been economically stagnant for decades. Yet, hydropower will free some of its oil resources for uses other than generating electricity and should help make future industrial growth more efficient.

In Uruguay's case, the economic benefits of increased hydropower seem obvious. Oilless and utterly dependent on imported fuels, Uruguay has already been forced to buy oil from Iran, whose militant Moslem leadership stands in utter contrast to the conservative Catholic military regime that ruled Uruguay from 1973 to November 1984. Because relatively high costs for electrical energy have been an important factor limiting Uruguay's economic expansion, Salto Grande may prime its economy.

Hydropower is absolutely critical to Brazil's industrial ambitions, which helps explain why the Brazilians, having gone deeply into debt to build Itaipu, are still contemplating 66,000,000 kilowatts of *new* power dam construction in the Amazon Basin. Brazil's economy has been one of the world's most dynamic over the past two decades; in some years, its industrial growth rate reached an extraordinary 15 percent. Even as OPEC's price hikes, high interest rates in the developed nations, and the worldwide recession of the late 1970s conspired to sink Brazil, its demand for energy still doubled between 1969 and 1979.[10] Brazil's petroleum imports are few by U.S. standards, but the rate of increase in oil imports has been staggering. Today, Brazil is conducting an ambitious program to produce methanol from biomass, but it has dented oil imports by only 10 to 20 percent, and an energetic oil-exploration program has done no better. If Brazil's robust growth is to continue, hydropower will have to bear most of the burden.

Paraguay produces no petroleum, and it probably never will. Electricity, too, has always been in short supply; industries, while hardly numerous, are plagued by brownouts. Electricity has been as expensive as it has been scarce. Paraguay will equally divide the energy generated by Itaipu and Yacyreta with Brazil and Argentina, most of which it will then sell back to the two countries. This should produce enormous foreign exchange and may well stimulate the growth of energy-intensive industries. In the meantime, the increased liquidity in Paraguay's economy is already beginning to have political and social implications. By the time Itaipu is fully operational, the value of Paraguay's share of its output will roughly equal 50 percent of the nation's traditional exports. Yacyreta, when operational, will add to that amount. All of this will occur during the next five to ten years, a period of significant political change in Paraguay. As the long regime of aging President Stroessner ends, hydropower may profoundly affect the country's politics and social order.

In terms of trade with countries outside the region, Argentina will benefit least from the massive hydroelectric program because it alone of the four is almost self-sufficient in petroleum production. Uruguay, thanks to Salto Grande, has already cut foreign oil imports by 40 percent, allowing it to use that foreign exchange to purchase other materials and goods from abroad. For Brazil, Itaipu will at the very least retard the rate of increase of its trade deficits because it now spends so heavily on imported petroleum.

The one immediate impact of the new dams has been the creation of new jobs. In the beginning, Itaipu employed more than 20,000 Brazilians and 20,000 Paraguayans around the clock. Many were poor farmers who learned their skills on the job. By 1983, employment had fallen to 23,000, but the population of Foz de Iguacu had risen from 30,000 to 135,000, and the municipal budget had increased by 22,000 percent. Unfortunately such bonanzas are ephemeral; when a dam is finished, operating and maintaining it requires only a small workforce. Thousands of people are apt to be suddenly unemployed—and poor again—after the dam's completion.

On the other hand, if Brazil's hydroelectric program remains as ambitious in reality as it is on paper, it will for many years support a large roving army of *barrageiros.* These are the nomadic laborers and engineers who move from project to project, usually with families in tow, and know no other life than building dams. The *barrageiros,* who number in the tens or hundreds of thousands, can have a substantial impact—at least locally—on social and economic trends. In the beginning, they infuse cash into frontier towns, making small fortunes for both established and aspiring merchants. As a project is completed, however, things can change quickly. "There is a devastating psychological impact as the projects near their completion," one project personnel director told the *Washington Post.* "Our clinic and hospital attendance goes way up. There is a rise in criminal delinquency. When we are about to make a sizeable cut in our labor force, we let the local police know a month ahead of time so they can prepare themselves for the bar brawls and petty robberies that are bound to follow."[11]

Although dams have created new jobs in Latin America, dam-building, as a rule, has a poor ratio of capital to jobs created. In fact, it is one of the least labor-intensive industries. One typical Corps of Engineers dam in Maine, according to an economic study performed in 1978, would have created one job for each $137,000 invested. The average for U.S. private industry at the time was $20,000.[12] The electricity produced by the dams can, of course, create many jobs. But it can also make existing jobs disappear.

It is still too early to speculate about whether electric power will create new jobs over time. It probably will in Paraguay, if industries crop up to exploit its mineral resources and timber. Brazil may be different. Its industrialization for the past ten years has generated huge demands for capital, technology, and energy—but not labor. In fact, some economists argue that Brazilian industrialization has actually *reduced* job opportunities by replacing labor-intensive industries with other modes of production.

Risk, both political and economic, will probably limit Argentina's industrial growth for some time. Argentina is already fairly industrialized, given its domestic market. Uruguay's future in further industrial growth lies primarily in export, because of its small population and market and because those industries that may expand or arise (clothing and shoe manufacturing, electronics, and so forth) are not energy-intensive. The new electric energy will ease the strain on existing industries, as well as consumers, and eliminate at least one barrier to further expansion. It may also lower production costs, which are high. Whether hydropower will increase employment in the long run remains to be seen, but it seems unlikely in the near future.

More electricity at lower cost will definitely benefit energy-intensive industries—steel, nonferrous metallurgy, petrochemicals, and heavy machinery. It could also foster new ones, particularly as power prices rise in places such as the U.S. Pacific Northwest. So far, such industries have been the engine behind Brazil's rapid growth. In the 1970s, Brazil's demand for electric energy increased by 12 percent every year, compared to less than 4 percent in the United States.[13] Uruguay has virtually no natural resources to exploit with new energy, and Argentina has only a few.

The net economic advantages of the new projects, then, seem to be four. First, in Brazil, the new energy will help sustain further industrial growth in basic industries, currently a critical factor in the country's economic development. Hydropower will also help Brazil sustain an industrial sector that by Latin American standards is relatively efficient. Second, for Uruguay, the Salto Grande project will make energy supplies more plentiful and reliable. It will reduce Uruguay's cost for imported petroleum, freeing foreign exchange for other purposes. Third, for Argentina, the new electric energy will help reduce a growing deficit, allow its marginal petroleum production to be put to uses other than energy (such as petrochemicals), and perhaps make existing industries more cost-efficient. Fourth, Paraguay's long-run revenues will increase, eventually making Paraguay one of the world's major exporters of energy, all of it hydroelectric.

The project's social impacts are harder to assess. In all likelihood, however, they will increase the odds for future unrest, mainly in Paraguay and Brazil. Urbanization, education, nonagricultural employment, and mass communications—all of which grow as a society becomes electrified—are potentially destabilizing, at least initially. The almost religious belief that more electricity will improve everyone's life may well be a myth, and this realization may engender widespread disillusionment and resentment. In Paraguay, the benefits of the power projects have done nothing to narrow the gap between rich and poor. Polarization along class lines is especially dangerous in Paraguay. In Brazil it may follow racial lines as well. (About 44 percent of Brazil's population is black, but blacks are excluded from most political, military, business, and other decision-making positions.)[14] If Brazil's hydro program proceeds according to plan, the huge, migratory, on-again-off-again workforce could also seed turmoil.

Are the benefits of hydroelectricity worth the costs—economic, human, and environmental—of very large dams? Before trying to answer this question, consider a country whose approach to hydropower development is markedly different from that of the four nations discussed here.

COSTA RICA: A DIFFERENT DRUMMER

Superimposed on Brazil, Costa Rica would look like a beetle on a plate. Smaller than West Virginia, the country is extremely mountainous, and some regions receive 300 inches of rainfall a year. Topography and precipitation have thus given Costa Rica a hydroelectric potential far out of proportion to its size. Jorge Figuls, the chief of planning for Instituto Costarricense de Electricidad (ICE), the national utility, estimates his nation's hydroelectric potential at 6 million kilowatts, although other estimates have put it twice that high. (Figuls may have been speaking only of projects that are economically feasible today.)[15] In any case, Costa Rica's 700,000 kilowatts of installed hydroelectric capacity represent a rather small fraction of the nation's potential. Its newest and largest dam, Arenal, generates only 22 percent of the energy of *one* of the eighteen turbines at Itaipu.

Costa Rica's approach to hydropower development has diverged significantly from that of Brazil, Paraguay, and to a lesser extent Argentina. Asked why his country has not developed the resource more aggressively, Figuls simply said, "We don't need it." Coming from a high executive of a national utility, that is quite a statement. Figuls, in fact, looks on Brazil's frenetic effort to exploit the power of Amazônia's rivers with bemused disdain. "They want to develop 60,000 megawatts there and they only use 25,000 in the whole country," he said. "I hope they know what they're doing."

Figuls's remark reflects Costa Rica's unusually cautious attitude toward resource development. Why such an attitude, almost unique in Latin America, exists in Costa Rica is difficult to say. According to one U.S. Agency for International Development official stationed there, the country has the highest per capita debt in the world after Israel—about $2,000, twice the size of Brazil's—and looks with skepticism on expensive projects that would bury it even deeper.[16] Gary Hartshorn, an American-born ecologist at the Tropical Science Center in San José, has another explanation. "Costa Rica has had enough American and North European influence to moderate the Iberian obsession with conquering nature," says Hartshorn. "It is markedly different from every Latin American country I have visited in this regard." Another reason may be that Costa Rica, a democracy, has not had to endure authoritarian leaders with "monument complexes." One U.S. hydrologist with long experience observing hydropower projects in the developing world finds a strong correlation between authoritarian regimes and large, controversial projects.[17]

But perhaps the most important reason for Costa Rica's go-slow hydroelectric policy is its conscious rejection of rapid industrial development. Whereas the country is fairly industrial compared to, say, El Salvador—it has automobile assembly, aluminum, textile, roofing, fertilizer, and cement industries—it is primarily agricultural and seems determined to remain that way. Because of successful land reform, many Costa Rican farmers have enough land to earn modest cash incomes. Moreover, Costa Rica has no masses of impoverished peasants and urban unemployed—the cheap labor that attracts multinational industries. Several recent presidents have been ranchers or farmers, and the dream of most every Costa Rican boy is not to become an industrialist or a lawyer but a small land baron. Like Switzerland, Costa Rica has (by Latin American standards) a sophisticated, modern economy delicately superimposed on a fundamentally agrarian society. And, like the Swiss, Costa Ricans seem intent on preserving their country's supreme natural beauty and peacefulness, even at the expense of industrial growth.

Costa Rica's one flirtation with Brazilian-style hydroelectric development occurred a few years ago, when it considered constructing what would have been the world's fifth-highest dam—the 267-meter, 1 million-kilowatt Boruca Dam on the Rio Grande de Terraba, the nation's largest river. The dam's purpose was strikingly similar to Tucurui's in Brazil: the Alcoa Corporation expressed interest in building a very large aluminum smelter in the southwestern corner of the nation and promised to buy much of the Boruca Dam's power. Jorge Figuls says the dam was scrapped, aluminum prices fell, and Alcoa lost interest but the plan was reportedly controversial from the beginning.

Arenal, the dam built in Boruca's place, is on the Rio Arenal, one of the larger tributaries of the Rio San Juan, which forms the border with Nicaragua. It is an earth-and-rock dam of moderate size—about forty meters high—and generates 150,000 kilowatts of primarily base-load power. The reservoir inundated a shallow, marshy lake, several thousand acres of farmland, and two towns. In contrast to many hydroelectric projects— even in the United States—the government spent considerable effort and money relocating and providing for those who were displaced. The new village that replaced the two flooded towns seems to belong more in southern California than in the Costa Rican countryside, and it compares favorably with San José's newer suburbs. Ironically, ICE sells thirty megawatts of Arenal power to Nicaragua at the same time that it allows *contras* to use the old construction camp as a staging ground for attempts to overthrow the Nicaraguan government.

Although small, Arenal is a multipurpose transbasin project, highly efficient in design. The dam was built high in the Rio Arenal watershed, to be near the divide of the Cordillera Central. Some of the water is piped out of the back end of the reservoir through tunnels to the Cordillera's west slope, where, after running through turbines, it enters the Rio Bebedero and irrigates the seasonally dry Guanacasta province. The worst environmental problem afflicting Costa Rica (and especially Guanacasta) is deforestation, caused mainly by ranchers who want more pastureland for grazing cattle. By providing additional irrigation water enabling a given amount of land to generate much more income, Arenal should at least retard the rate of deforestation in Guanacasta. As such, it is one of the few dams ever built with a specific environmental goal in mind.

The most important distinction between Costa Rica's hydropower program and those of its more ambitious neighbors to the north and south is that it is intended to *meet* electrical demand, not *create it*. Tucurui is a perfect example of a project designed to encourage resource exploitation in a mostly virgin region. If, for some reason, the aluminum industry never materializes in Amazônia, as it did not in Costa Rica, the dam's output may become grossly superfluous—a locomotive engine in a Volkswagen bus. Neither Itaipu nor Salto Grande nor Yacyreta is likely to see its full power potential absorbed for years, perhaps decades, if continuing high interest rates and staggering foreign debts preclude rapid economic growth. Nearly all Arenal power, by contrast, can be absorbed today, as soon as Costa Rica's transmission grid is expanded.

Another difference between Costa Rica and most, if not all, other Latin American nations is its electricity rate structure. It uses an "inverted block" rate structure for pricing electricity—the exact opposite of the world's most common system. Most nationalized utilities, and most private and public utilities within the United States, use "declining block" rates, charging less for each incremental unit as a customer consumes more. Obviously, such volume discounts discourage conservation and encourage energy-intensive industries to move in. Costa Rica's inverted block rates, on the contrary, *discourage* energy-intensive industries and punish frivolous use, stretching each installed kilowatt of generating capacity to the maximum. "Our obvious intent is to husband the resource," says Jorge Figuls. "Ten years ago, we used the other system. We are treating hydroelectricity now as if it is a scarce resource, even though we are not yet close to developing our full capacity."

The inverted rate structure is actually a part of a grander, and, for Latin America, very unusual social policy, which is to electrify as much of the countryside as possible. In 1981, electricity began to reach the poorest and remotest sections of the Guanacasta coast; the only parts of the country not scheduled to receive electricity are very high, remote, swampy, or otherwise inaccessible areas. "Rural electrification is actually a bad business for ICE," says Figuls. "It may end up costing a lot more to distribute the power from Arenal than it cost to build the dam and powerhouse." Because ICE also operates the country's profit-making telephone service, however, it can use phone revenues to subsidize electrification—just as it uses electricity revenues earned from big users to subsidize peasants in Guanacasta, whose sole appliances may be a couple of light bulbs and a battered fan.

The country's interest in rural electrification betokens a national social and economic strategy that is quite the opposite of Brazil's. In Brazil, new surges of hydroelectricity from Itaipu are to be directed to São Paulo and Rio de Janeiro to encourage even greater industrial (and population) growth in those already industrialized and populous cities. Tucurui and other remote Amazonian dams will encourage concentrations of people and industry in regions that are now nearly devoid of both. Costa Rica's rate structure, its policy of rural electrification, and its go-slow approach to dam construction, in contrast, represent a well-thought-out effort to eschew the urban migration syndrome afflicting much of Latin America—a huge, uncontrolled exodus from the countryside to large cities that will become unlivable unless something drastic is done to alleviate water, sewage, employment, and transportation crises.

A city of 13 million such as São Paulo, which most Brazilians regard with pride, is viewed with horror by residents of San José. In Costa Rica, avoiding uncontrolled urban growth is a national objective that seems to transcend party affiliation and ideology; policies designed to thwart urban growth have passed virtually unchanged from the liberal regime of former president Rodrigo Carazo to the more conservative one of Albert Luis Monge. Land reform, rural electrification, an inverted rate structure, national health care—these are all part of Costa Rica's strategy for preventing San José from soaking up the country's poor, its disaffected, its disenfranchised, and turning into another Mexico City. So far, it appears to be working. Despite an ideal climate and ample room to grow, San José contains only a tenth of the country's population. Mexico City, if it continues to grow at its current spectacular rate, will soon be home to one out of every five Mexicans—although "home" to millions may be on the streets.

The fruits of rural electrification can already be observed in villages. One is Nosara, a tiny hamlet of two hundred people located on the far Pacific coast of Guanacasta province—a beautiful natural setting that, ironically, happens to be the poorest region in the country. Guanacasta's poverty stems largely from its climate, which resembles California's. For about five months each year, the region is visited by a seamless succession of hot, rainless days. During the rainy season, downpours make transportation on its poor roads a nightmare. As a result, farmers cannot easily raise cash crops without irrigation, which is too expensive for most to use. Nor, for that matter, can they easily transport crops to market much of the year. California overcame its habitual drought and became prosperous by building 1,280 irrigation and power dams to capture the winter rains and Sierra snowpack: without them, it would resemble Mexico much more than Californians care to believe. But Guanacasta lacks a good site for a sizable dam, and the country lacks the funds to build one there. As a result, most farmers live only a few rungs above subsistence by raising cattle, working on big cattle ranches, or growing fruit or crops for market.

The first economic bonanza to hit Nosara in its three-hundred year history came in 1970, when a New York developer bought 3,000 acres nearby and began building a vacation community similar to California's Sea Ranch. Hundreds of lots were purchased, but only four dozen or so homes had been built by 1980, and many of those were unoccupied most of the year. Most property owners chose not to build because of the unstable political situation in Central America and the lack of reliable electricity. Even the unreliable electricity that the Playas de Nosara project did have, by virtue of its small private generator, caused friction with the villagers who were jealous of the "lavish" life-style of "*los ricos*" (mostly middle-class American pensioners).

Eager to reduce tensions, the property association finally decided, in 1979, to sell highly subsidized electricity to the village. The result was a sudden jump in the fixed minimum annual rates (to $600–800 in most cases), which prompted a number of part-time residents to abandon the project—thus reducing the number of service jobs, and at the same time driving electricity rates even higher. By 1981, so few homeowners remained at Playas de Nosara that those remaining thought of leaving too; the project seemed destined to turn into a "ghost resort." (The arrival of armed squatters in 1981, who, encouraged by resentful villagers, camped on Playas de Nosara land, added to the mess.)

In 1980, however, ICE announced plans to run a transmission line from Arenal Dam to the Guanacasta coast. Almost immediately, an Italian developer began planning a luxurious resort a few miles down the beach, and a number of Americans who had decided to abandon the Playas project changed their minds. In 1982, ICE, unable to produce enough money for a transmission line, hastily erected a temporary 750-kilowatt diesel generating plant at Nosara. The power line is now expected some time in 1986. Electricity is more expensive than it will be when Arenal power arrives, but it is still subsidized—enough so that all but the very poorest farmers have hooked up.

According to both villagers and their vacationing neighbors, the electricity has transformed life at Nosara dramatically. Relations between the town and the Americans have improved considerably and the panicky exodus has ended, creating more service sector jobs. Several dozen jobs could be created at the Italian resort, just now being completed. For the first time, low-lying farms in the region can pump irrigation water; Nosara now has irrigated acreage for growing oranges, papayas, beans, corn, and rice. Recently, a small cabinet and boat-building factory was established by a resident Panamanian who employs several local men; without government-subsidized electricity, he says, he could not have built a business.

In Nosara, rural electrification has promoted more profitable, environmentally sound farming and tourism. The destructive deforestation and cattle overgrazing that have plagued other countries do not have footholds here. According to local residents, rural electrification will retard the rate, at best. Electricity may have even helped to change the political climate. When the squatters first appeared several years ago, some villagers, out of bitterness, encouraged them to stay. (The *guardia rural* eventually escorted them out.) When they returned recently, the villagers banned them themselves—partly because the squatters carried Soviet flags, but also, perhaps, because rural electrification has made everyone more content with their lives.

In the United States, in the 1930s, a mammoth program of rural electrification across the American West reduced the extent of the migration that followed in the wake of the Dust Bowl. One historian estimates that tens of thousands of rural families might have abandoned their hardscrabble subsistence farms on the great plains had electricity not arrived.[18] Subsidized electricity also permitted irrigation on a grand scale, discouraging the overplowing and overgrazing that precipitated the dust storms in the first place. Residents of California, Oregon, and Washington had rural electrification to thank, too; without it, their states would have become dumping grounds for even greater numbers of despairing and uprooted Okies than actually arrived.

Some would argue that it is unfair to contrast Costa Rica's rural electrification with that of Brazil (or the United States) when one nation is so huge and the other so small. What the United States did in the depths of the Great Depression, was what Costa Rica is doing now. Our own experience, and the experience of Nosara described above, suggest that rural electrification— perhaps above all other potential applications of hydroelectricity—best conforms with environmentally sound resource management and U.S. interests in sustainable development in Latin America.

By all accounts, rural electrification helps stabilize, diversify, and decentralize economies. In nations blessed with natural beauty, as most Latin American countries are, it also encourages low-impact, high-value tourism. The environmental impacts of great industrial-oriented hydroelectric schemes aside, the more modest objective of rural electrification does seem more conducive to the type of orderly social change and stable economic growth the United States would want to encourage.

THE ENVIRONMENTAL COSTS OF LATIN AMERICA'S HYDROPOWER PROGRAM

Besides the chronic burden that giant hydroelectric schemes could become to debtor and lender nations alike, the most serious concern about these projects, from the U.S. point of view, ought to be their environmental consequences. The amount of hydropower development that Brazil alone is planning in the Amazon Basin would inundate an area the size of Montana and help open the last great intact tropical rainforest ecosystem to rapid exploitation. Some climatologists are now convinced that the Amazon Basin's deforestation could foster worldwide climate changes, contributing massive amounts of free carbon to the biosphere and altering evapotranspiration dynamics on a continental scale. One likely consequence, according to recent theories, would be a warmer, drier climate not only in south central Brazil, but ultimately in the western and middle western United States—especially in California, which grows one-third of U.S. table food.[19] The Amazon is also the planet's last great reservoir of species diversity, which no country can afford to lose.

Some 200,000 Indians are currently living in Amazônia, some untouched by modern civilization. If 66,000 megawatts of hydropower, or even half that amount is constructed in the Basin the Indians will either be unhappily assimilated or, if present trends continue, annihilated. For the sake of humankind's vanishing cultures, and for simple humanitarian reasons, the United States cannot let either happen.

The construction of giant reservoirs in other tropical or hot climes has led to epidemics of parasitic diseases, notably malaria and schistosomiasis (a debilitating snail-borne disease that painfully rots internal organs and is often fatal). By one estimate, Egypt now spends $560 million a year treating and preventing schistosomiasis, which became epidemic only after the construction of the two Aswan dams. It also spends $100 million a year on fertilizer, because nutrients formerly provided by the silty Nile have been stopped by the Aswan High Dam. Do the human and environmental catastrophes attributable to that one dam, outweigh its benefits?[20] U.S. policymakers owe the American people an answer to this question.

Also, because many Latin American hydroelectric projects have been built, and will be financed in significant part with U.S. money (both private and public), the United States needs to be concerned about the long-term wisdom of such investments. Ironically, the resource development that a large project can encourage may shorten the lifespan of the project itself. The worst threat by far is deforestation. If forests disappear, erosion rates can accelerate and reservoirs silt up prematurely. Some reservoirs in the developing nations have silted up *before the dams were even finished.* In irrigation projects, salt build-up in agricultural lands is also a serious threat. That, too, has become a gigantic problem in the Nile Valley as a result of the Aswan High Dam.

The United States can do little to mitigate this syndrome if Latin America's population continues to grow at its current rate. (Brazil's population, for example, has almost quadrupled since the beginning of World War II.) But, it has to decide whether, as the most generous lender nation in the world, it should *encourage* the current use of hydroelectric energy. At the very least, the United States should use its influence and money to steer hydroelectric development onto the soundest possible course.

Consider here the environmental mitigation effort at Itaipu. Compared with the utter disinterest of some developing nations in the past, Brazil's concern about the environmental effects of Itaipu was fairly impressive. Before construction began, ecological surveys revealed that 92 percent of the area on the Paraguayan side of the river was dominated by mixed forests, whereas only 24 percent on the Brazilian side was forested. (Much of the Brazilian forest had been converted to agricultural land.) Some 625 species of trees were cataloged, the most abundant being uncultivated fruit trees such as the guabiroba, piuma, apepu, and inga. Trees with commercial value included cedar, ipe pau-margim, peroba, and cinnamon. The fauna population surrounding Itaipu was equally diverse: 252 bird species belonging to 54 families; some 1,600 insect species of 19 orders; 23 reptile species; and some 129 species of fish from 25 families. These, in turn, were cataloged according to their geographic distribution and their feeding and breeding habits.

After this survey, Bela Vista and Santa Helena were established as wildlife sanctuaries—in all, some 2,000 hectares on the Brazilian side of the river. The Itavo and Limoy sanctuaries have added 24,000 hectares on the Paraguayan side. All the sanctuaries protect dislocated animals, and the Bela Vista site also has veterinary services and facilities for studies. On the Brazilian side, another small facility was created to preserve and promote the growth of native herbs.[21]

Before the diversion channel was opened in 1978, when the water elevation rose from 100 to 142 meters, stranded animals were removed from both sides of the Parana River. Because the reservoir was filled so rapidly, many animals were stranded and drowned, although some were rescued by boat at the last minute. Still, the effort to capture and relocate animals was begun six months before the reservoir's filling.

The forest along the river edge and overall reforestation have received some attention, especially from Brazil's Gralha Azul project. Broadleaf varieties of some 50 separate species have been planted—over one million trees in all. Before the reservoir was flooded, controlled logging operations were carried out to salvage some timber. As many as 15 million fruit trees may be seeded on the Brazilian side, which will benefit both the area's people and wildlife. Reforestation in a so-called protected belt is also planned for the cleared areas on the Paraguayan side.

How effective will all these precautions and activities be? Deforestation is epidemic in Brazil, as it is throughout most of Latin America. Ferdinand Budweg, chairman of the Brazilian Technical Commission on Dams and the Environment, has written, "[Many] large dams [in Brazil] have been built in regions with sparse vegetation, in bush land or amidst extensive areas used for farming or pasture. The open landscape is mostly the result of the action of man, who indiscriminately and incautiously eliminated the woods when moving into the country's interior. Wind and heavy tropical rainstorms act strongly on the uncovered or scarcely protected soil, and thus surface erosion became a serious problem in many parts of Brazil."[22] On the Brazilian side, the "taking area" of the Itaipu reservoir obviously has been extensively deforested. According to one of Brazil's leading environmental scientists, Jose Lutzenberger, the silt volume of the Parana River reaches one to two kilograms per cubic meter at peak flows—a concentration much like the Mississippi's. Lutzenberger's unofficial hunch is that the reservoir may silt up within thirty years.[23]

In contrast to Lutzenberger's grim prognosis, Robert Goodland, a World Bank ecologist familiar with Itaipu, discounts the sedimentation threat to the dam. "Itaipu is essentially a run-of-the-river dam," he said in an interview late in 1984. "It doesn't depend on storage capacity to equalize the flow, as most bigger dams do. If sediment fills up Lake Mead, then you've got real problems, because the Colorado flow is extremely erratic and you need tremendous carryover storage. At Itaipu, the reservoir bottom could be raised a lot by sedimentation and I don't believe it would affect the power output of the dam." Goodland is also more sanguine than Lutzenberger about erosion in the Parana basin. "The geomorphology of that area is very senile," he says. "It's very ancient rock. It's also quite flat. You just don't have the kind of erosion problems you get in the Andes." Goodland admitted, however, that erosion rates can be quite serious even in very flat regions—the American Midwest, for example—if they are intensively farmed.

If one looks beyond Itaipu and considers Latin America as a whole, however, rapid sedimentation caused by deforestation could well threaten the longevity of dams. In the Dominican Republic, an extreme case in Latin America, the equivalent of up to 80 percent of the country's export income has been spent annually on hydropower development. However, with erosion rates reaching 600 tons per acre per year—thirty times higher than in the intensively farmed American Midwest—the reservoirs are collecting silt at appalling rates. The 80,000-kilowatt Tavera project, the country's largest, was completed in 1973; already, it has eighteen meters of sediment behind the dam, which reduces dead storage capacity by 40 percent and active storage by 10 to 14 percent. The government tends to blame sedimentation on huge floods caused by hurricanes Frederick and David—thereby shirking responsibility for the wholesale deforestation on steep slopes, which is the real reason the floods wreaked such destruction.[24]

Even worse examples can be sited. In China, where deforestation is extremely severe, the Sanmenxia Dam was completed in 1960 and decommissioned in 1964 when the reservoir had silted up completely. The Laoying Reservoir, also in China, filled with silt before the project was finished. The Tehri Dam in India, when operational, will be the sixth highest dam in the world, and an extremely expensive one. Taking horrific deforestation in the Himalya foothills into account, however, the Indian Geological Survey recently reduced the dam's estimated life from one hundred years to between thirty and forty.[25]

Even Costa Rica reportedly does little to enforce the strong forestry laws on its books: the government doesn't have the money, the manpower, or, according to some, the inclination. However, it made an intelligent decision in building the Arenal Dam in a high, small basin with heavy precipitation. Deforestation will be easier to control there, and the massive silt loads that can ruin lowland reservoirs are unlikely to occur even with heavy deforestation. According to tropical ecologist Gary Hartshorn of

Costa Rica's Tropical Science Center, Brazil's forest-protection program is "nowhere near as strong as Costa Rica's." Even so, on a scale of ten, Hartshorn gave Costa Rica a rating of only two compared to the most effective silvicultural policies in European countries. "Suriname and Guyana are the best—I think because of north European influence. The colonial imprint is very strong in Latin America. Ecuador I'd rate a three. Then Costa Rica. The problem in a lot of countries isn't even lax enforcement or the absence of laws. It's policies that *promote* rapid deforestation. Even Costa Rica has squatter laws that permit people to claim undesignated land after they've felled the trees and put in one crop of corn."

If a reservoir designed to function for eighty years silts up within twenty-five, then all economic equations are tossed into a cocked hat. The shrinking power revenues may never pay off the cost, and industries that were established on the promise of hydroelectricity are stranded. The government must then build new dams or find energy elsewhere. According to one prominent hydrologist, removing the silt is economically out of the question.[26] Based on Los Angeles' experience with small reservoirs, to pump out the silt that has accumulated within fifty years behind Hoover Dam would cost some $640 million, several times more than the dam itself cost, and the sediments have claimed only about 7 percent of dead storage capacity. Moreover, as this same hydrologist asks, "Even if you can afford to pump it out, where are you going to put it?"

Three-fourths of Brazil's large dams were built within the past thirty years. Much the same applies to other Latin American nations. In just three decades, the effects of erosion and siltation haven't made themselves felt, but those of explosive population growth and rapid deforestation have. (After Africa, Latin America has the highest population growth rate.)

Reservoir-induced disease is also potentially catastrophic. Malaria, which kills about a million people worldwide every year, has proliferated with rice irrigation in Africa.[27] Worldwide, about 200 million people suffer from schistosomiasis—double the afflicted number in 1947, despite great advances in medical treatment and disease control. According to one expert, "The incidence and extension of schistosomiasis and other waterborne diseases can be directly related to the proliferation of irrigation schemes, the stabilization of the aquatic biotope [environment] and subsequent ecological changes.... When agriculture depended primarily on seasonal rainfall ... infection rates were low."[28]

Most water projects in Latin America are hydroelectric, not irrigation projects, so the swampy land that the mosquito vector loves may not occur in abundance. Then too, acidic Amazonian rivers, the site of many planned projects, are inhospitable environments for the disease's snail vector. But carriers of both malaria and schistosomiasis occur throughout much of Latin America, and the creation of large reservoirs and waterlogged lands might help them proliferate. In Suriname, the Brokopondo Reservoir was built on an acidic river whose water was neutralized after remaining for long periods in the reservoir.[29] Robert Goodland of the World Bank believes that the acidity of Amazonian waters will continue to deter schistosomiasis and that a reservoir such as Itaipu, located in a more temperate latitude, is unlikely to breed either that disease or malaria. "Brazil is also very aware of the problem," he says, "and is taking measures to prevent it." What measures? "Well, it has to very carefully screen all workers around reservoirs, backfill any site where the vector is found, and stop people from urinating and defecating in the water." Is that possible? "I don't know, but the government is very aware of the problem." What if it fails? "Once the schistosomiasis snail is in the reservoir, forget it. That's the end."

Another environmental problem, one unique to South America on such a scale, is the sudden decomposition of flooded tropical moist forests. "[In] dense tropical rain forests," Ferdinand Budweg has written, "... the deterioration of such a huge amount of biomass would unavoidably result in a serious threat to all living things in the reservoir and downstream of the dam, and the badly decayed and aggressive quality of the water may even damage the mechanical equipment of the dam and power plant."[30]

Brokopondo Dam, built on the Suriname River in a biome much like the one invaded by Tucurui, exemplifies Budweg's fears. Five hundred and seventy square miles of rainforest (about 7 percent of the entire nation) were flooded when the reservoir was filled. As the trees and underbrush decomposed, they produced enough hydrogen sulfide gas to raise a howl of complaint many miles downstream. For two years, workers at the dam wore gas masks. The decomposing vegetation made the water so harshly acidic that it corroded the dam's cooling system, which cost $4 million to repair—about 7 percent of the dam's total cost. The oxygen-deficient water stunned and killed fish for fifty miles downriver. Within ten years of filling, however, 50 percent of the reservoir surface was infested by water weeds, which subsequently were given massive applications of pesticide 2,4-D.[31]

Filling Tucurui, which could ultimately flood an area twice the size of Brokopondo, threatens to start the same chain of events. Because the reservoir will be shallow, decomposition will be even more immediate and severe though the reservoir should return to "normal" sooner. After Robert Goodland sounded a warning of sudden, massive biomass decomposition, a contract was given to CAPEMI, a diversified company inexperienced in forestry, to clear as much of the vegetation within the taking area as possible. Lazard Frères, which planned to market the timber, lent the company $100 million to fell the trees. CAPEMI proved more adept at handling Brazil's military pension fund (one of its other contracts) than at clearing the reservoir area; after two years, its work was proceeding at one-tenth the expected rate. Finally, Electronorte, the construction company, grew impatient and announced plans to defoliate the area with 2,4-D and 2,4,5-T (Agent Orange). This produced an international outcry joined by Dr. Paulo Nogueira-Neto, Brazil's environmental minister. CAPEMI finally went bankrupt, leaving men and equipment stranded in the forest. In late 1984, Electronorte, defying the environment minister and worldwide protest, began spraying with 2,4,5-T and other defoliants.[32]

A veil of secrecy has been thrown around the spraying operations. But it has been penetrated by numerous reports of deaths and miscarriages from defoliation along the transportation routes and of local people using empty drums of ultratoxic defoliant to store food and water. The minister of agriculture in Para state, João Bastos, has severely criticized the whole operation, and Brazilian environmental lawyers have called on the United Nations for help.

Tucurui also symbolizes the disruptive effects of dam-building on people and the ecosystems on which they depend.

According to one report, one- to two-thirds of the people occupying the taking area will not satisfy the "uninterrupted tillage" clause in the Codigo Civil, which allows them compensation for loss of land. Their only compensation will be for the loss of flooded structures—primitive, easily replaced buildings. According to Goodland, "The treatment of squatters could provoke enormous hardship for the large numbers—possibly 10,000—of already impoverished people to be displaced by the reservoir.[33]

Similar situations are arising throughout Latin America. In fact, reservoir construction may now be the foremost usurper of indigenous peoples' lands. In Panama, the first stage of the Teribe-Changuinola Project will flood land supporting 2,000 indigenous people; the next stages could inundate 58,000 more. The Itaipu Dam may ultimately displace 50,000 people, including 5,500 Guarani Indians—for whose language, ironically, the reservoir is named.[34] In the United States, native lands were flooded repeatedly by reservoirs (against tribal will) until well into the 1950s, and federal dams that would drown the last homelands of extremely depopulated tribes are still being proposed.[35] There is no reason to expect that indigenous Brazilians will be treated any better: "We still massacre our Indians down here," says Jose Lutzenberger.

The consequences of flooding out indigenous people may go far beyond the expected or obvious. In at least one case, an entire nation's political future is at stake. The Casa Grande Dam in El Salvador—a large project in a tiny, overpopulated country—inundated a substantial valley worked by several thousand subsistence farmers. The peasants, with literally nowhere to go, squatted on the estates of wealthy landowners and were forcibly evicted. A group of local priests then took up the peasants' cause and tried to organize the dispossessed into an effective political force. Soon afterwards, several of the priests were murdered by death squads, triggering Salvadorean archbishop Oscar Romero's vocal campaign against the death squads and the radical right wing. Romero's reward was to be murdered in his own cathedral, like Thomas à Becket. The legacy of Romero's murder was universal condemnation of the Salvadorean right, greatly enhanced legitimacy for the rebel forces, and an intensified effort by the United States to install a centrist government. The fate of this misery-ridden nation is still beyond anyone's ken, but historians won't be able to ignore the influence of a dam.

This is by no means an exhaustive list of the negative environmental and human consequences attributable to large dams. For instance, many Amazonian species occupy such tight ecological niches that one reservoir could wipe them out or drastically diminish their numbers. (If deforestation continues in tropical forests, for example, over one million species could be lost by the year 2000.) All estuarine species are likely to suffer from the loss of delivered silt; in Egypt, for example, the rich sardine fishery at the mouth of the Nile has declined from 18,000 tons in the 1950s to 500 tons today because of the Aswan High Dam.[36] California's 1,200 major dams have stopped so much silt and sand from going out to sea that some beaches have been severely denuded, leaving seaside homes and towns more vulnerable to tides and storms.

Of course, some water projects help compensate for the harm they cause to natural ecosystems. Among others, the Arenal Reservoir in Costa Rica and Lake Mead in the United States support excellent sport fisheries that did not exist before the dams were built. Reservoirs also sometimes provide good wet habitat for species—alligators, in the southeastern United States, for example—whose natural haunts are disappearing.

On balance, however, the colossal dams now being built in Latin America will do far more environmental harm than good. Most important, the reservoirs' useful lives may be shortened by the very resource development the dams are meant to encourage. In the United States, the Forest Service, the Bureau of Land Management, the dam-building agencies, and the states cooperate closely to protect the watersheds above critical reservoirs. No similar coordination exists in any Latin American country. Logically, water projects would seem to *decrease* pressure on forests by offering people alternative employment, a source of energy other than firewood, and (in some cases) an opportunity to practice irrigated farming instead of slashing and burning land for cattle grazing. In fact, though, the high costs and debt service large dams entail not only preclude extensive rural electrification programs, but often keep power rates too high for the poor. Moreover, because big construction programs may draw tens of thousands of poor, rootless people into a small area, many of whom decide to remain, pressure on forests may actually *increase* once the project is finished and people have to find another way of subsisting.[37]

The price paid by the poor and by the environment could be viewed as a tradeoff for necessary economic growth. But no immutable law says that a big hydropower project *always* brightens a nation's economic picture. A country such as Paraguay, about to reap bountiful foreign exchange from power sales, is apt to emerge a winner unless the money ends up in the pockets of its military or economic elite or buried in senseless development projects. But what about Brazil? Itaipu makes sense only if it can attract enough investment and generate enough electricity demand to absorb most of the new power fairly soon. But with foreign investors cramped by the debt crisis and electricity growth rates down, how likely is this to happen? Tucurui is an even dicier case. What are the odds that a debt-ridden country, with a history of unsuccessful, large-scale Amazonian projects, can adequately finance enough electricity to power the likes of Sweden and Finland? The world's largest aluminum plant uses only eight hundred megawatts, a tenth of Tucurui's ultimate capacity, and a radically new Japanese smelting process requires no external electricity at all![38]

Chances are that Brazil has *already* overbuilt its hydroelectric capacity—even forgetting about the multitude of new dams it seems determined to add. One consultant to the World Bank says that Brazil's energy situation may be analogous to that of the U.S. nuclear industry, which has had to mothball or cancel—at tremendous cost—dozens of plants, some nearly completed, for lack of electricity demand.[39]

The question, then, is how the United States can help steer hydroelectric development in Latin America onto a less destructive and less costly course. Remember here that much hydroelectric development has been financed with U.S. money, and that the negative consequences of overdevelopment may be felt in the United States as energy-intensive industries head south. (Itaipu's power rates may be cheaper than new rates scheduled in the Pacific Northwest.) Then too, unpaid Latin American debt is mounting and adverse climatic effects are distinct possibilities. Certainly, the United States has a *right* to ask such a question and to act in our own best interest.

TOWARD BETTER BALANCED POWER

U.S. policymakers can't call the shots in Latin American hydro-electric development. But they can influence the lending policies of the two major international banks: the World Bank and the Inter-American Development Bank. The World Bank lent some $17 billion worldwide in 1983, and it funds more than three hundred new projects each year, along with hundreds already in progress. According to its published reports, about a third of its loans finance water-developed projects.[40] One of the two principal U.S. lending institutions, the Export-Import Bank, finances little water development, and the other, the Agency for International Development, has more progressive environmental policies but lends far less. Today, the United States contributes about 20 percent of the World Bank's budget and exercises a proportionate vote on grant proposals. This may seem meager, but just as a stockholder owning 20 percent of a corporation's shares can exercise effective control, power and influence are not defined by simple arithmetic. In a recent report on U.S. influence in multinational lending, the Department of Treasury claims that the government achieved its policy-changing goals in about 80 percent of the cases where it made a concerted effort, even when it acted unilaterally.[41] It may be simply a question of having clear goals.

Rural Electrification Should Be a High Priority. In Chapter 2, the overwhelming problems of Mexico City, soon to become the most populous metropolis on earth, are chillingly portrayed. By the end of the century, Mexico City is projected to have a population of 31 million. São Paulo will be close behind, and Itaipu will be a major factor in its growth.

The potential of rural electrification to slow urban migration in the developing world is too often overlooked. In Costa Rica, the record shows, electrification has promoted economic decentralization and diversification, and the same approach could work elsewhere. While the multinational banks do fund rural electrification projects, loans are paltry compared to those for dam-building. This imbalance should be redressed considering that rural electrification almost automatically promotes social justice and perhaps even defuses political unrest.

Small Is Worthwhile.   In the early 1970s, the U.S. nuclear industry suddenly traded its 300-megawatt reactors for 1,200-megawatt models. This leap turned out to be one of the most costly mistakes of the century because electricity demand declined just as the first generation of huge reactors went up. Of five such reactors under construction in the Pacific Northwest, only one has been completed; the other four were cancelled or mothballed despite $6.5 billion in sunk costs. Forty years earlier, a similar mistake was almost committed. Had it not been for World War II and its tremendous demand for aluminum for aircraft, Grand Coulee Dam's power might have remained unsold for decades and the dam could have become a financial debacle.[42]

Today, the United States has the capability and (perhaps) the money to dam the world's most powerful rivers. But in today's mercurial economic climate, with huge U.S. deficits threatening to keep interest rates high for at least several more years, the dangers of over-building hydroelectric capacity are especially acute. If a dam's cost represents 10 percent (Itaipu) or even 50 percent (El Cajón in Honduras) of national GNP, markets for its power must be found soon. But with money tight, the markets may never develop, at least not soon enough. Having learned an expensive lesson from its own nuclear industry, why should the United States finance a similar folly in Latin American dams? The argument that economies of scale favor larger projects is demonstrably untrue in the case of nuclear plants, in the case of wind machines, in the case of coal-fired power plants, and quite probably in the case of dams.[43] (Itaipu power, for example, cost $1,200 per kilowatt to build; Arenal cost $800 per kilowatt.) And even if it were true, the *threat* of winding up with expensive idle capacity seems to outweigh a few additional mills per kilowatt-hour. Also, large dams are, for the most part, considerably more environmentally destructive than smaller ones.

New Terms for Loans.   When the U.S. Agency for International Development approved a loan for a project in Peru, it demanded that all Indian lands in the area be legally titled, thus assuring the Indians adequate compensation. The agency has also begun to insist that countries take watershed-protection measures as a precondition for approving water-development loans or grants. The World Bank, by contrast, rarely makes watershed protection or relatively fail-safe humanitarian contracts between the government and the dispossessed conditions of lending.[44] Its intentions may be the best; whether they stand up in practice is another matter. The World Bank tends to use a *quid pro quo* approach with projects that would cause serious ecological disruption: at Tucurui, for example, it is helping to fund a national park near the site. On balance, however, such an approach may do more to appease the lender's sense of guilt than to protect the watershed, or preserve the flora and fauna, or prevent the spread of schistosomiasis, or otherwise help the dispossessed.

Second Opinions. The World Bank has a staff of 5,200 plus a fluctuating number of consultants. It has but one Ph.D. ecologist, Robert Goodland, on its permanent staff. According to Bruce Rich, a lawyer at the Environmental Defense Fund who has watched the bank's activities closely, "Goodland can't begin to keep up with all the projects they fund. He hears about one that sounds like it might have some pretty adverse impacts and he runs off to look it over, but he can do that with maybe half a dozen projects a year. And since they're all in the pipeline already he can't do much about them except say, 'Well, they're going to harm this and hurt that, and maybe we can help things a little if we do thus and such.' He's like an ambulance whose territory is a whole state. So he has to practice triage like they do in wartime, letting dozens of projects go by that might have some pretty substantial environmental impacts which no one has looked at carefully. The pre-project environmental impact review process that we've institutionalized in this country is utterly foreign to the way the multinational banks do their business. Few foreign countries have it, either."

A first step might be for the United States to finance an *independent* multidisciplinary team of environmental experts within the World Bank. If the World Bank wants an affirmative vote from the United States, it would have to review all major projects when planning begins. U.S. agencies have learned to live with this requirement and have even profited from it, for economically costly mistakes have often been flagged in the review process. Lately, the U.S. directorate at the World Bank has begun to cast more negative votes on projects at odds with U.S. policies or which, in its opinion, simply do not make sense.[45] Now, it also needs to consider voting "no" when projects involving large dams will harm the environment and when a project is presented without an environmental impact report prepared by an independent, institutionalized review process.

Reward Energy Conservation. Any nation with a flat or inverted block rate is not only defying conventional wisdom; it is boldly encouraging energy conservation and stifling its electricity growth rates. As the late Dr. Rene Dubos was fond of saying, "Energy shortages are not the greatest problem of mankind. We use too much energy already. The real problem is finding work for all the marginal people of the earth."[46] Priority should also be given to alternative hydroelectric power: small, run-of-the-river water turbines that could be employed by the thousands with little negative environmental impact on, for example, swift Amazonian rivers.

For some reason, lending institutions set up by the industrialized nations rarely oppose *any* kind of development in the Third World—good or bad. Such an attitude probably stems from a sense of guilt or *noblesse oblige;* because the developed nations enjoy the fruits of technological advancement, they seem to feel stingy if they keep them from Belize, Guatemala, or Brazil. Yet, despite millions lent or granted to African nations for agricultural development, the world is now witnessing one of the worst famines of modern times—a famine that, according to some, was made worse by misdirected lending policies.[47] Remember too that the United States' path to industrialization and wealth was littered with many grievous ecological mistakes—the Dust Bowl, the eradication of coastal wetlands, the erection of marginally useful dams on fabulously productive salmon rivers. It seems senseless—even cruelly shortsighted—for Americans to help other nations reproduce our own mistakes.

Lending institutions seem to believe that development projects, especially dams, enjoy universal support in the countries where they have been proposed. Is this a result of talking exclusively to those people proposing the projects? There is, in fact, very responsible and thoughtful opposition, even in superambitious Brazil. Marcel Nuñez de Alencar, the president of the State Bank of Rio de Janeiro, recently said that in "The last twenty years, the Brazilian elite went crazy with this kind of economic development. They wanted to turn Brazil into the United States. They adopted a model that is absolutely incompatible with Brazilian reality. Their great projects were all done with foreign loans. They accepted what the international banking system rammed down their throats."[48]

A final myth that could stand revision is that industrialization is the only—or the straightest—path to prosperity and happiness. In the United States, Ohio, one of the most industrialized states, has the same per capita income as Nebraska, one of the least industrialized states. And Ohio's unemployment rate (as of 1982) is more than double Nebraska's.[49] Costa Rica is one of the most advanced, healthiest, and (per capita) wealthiest nations in Central America; yet, it is primarily an agricultural nation with modest hydropower development and electricity demand growth. In the United States, the 1970s proved that energy growth and economic growth can be decoupled.[50] It is time that Latin America and the world's lending institutions absorbed that great lesson. Also, the economic value of carefully exploited but intact tropical rainforests—for hardwood lumber, for medicines, for fruits and nuts, for fish, for biomass, for watershed regulation—has been demonstrated beyond doubt.[51] To submerge vast areas of such forests under (potentially short-lived) reservoirs, and to encourage their rapid destruction to create electricity markets, is a policy that should give Latin America's chief lender, the United States, considerable pause.

NOTES

1. *World Water,* February 1984, 9.

2. This information is reviewed in a pamphlet published by Itaipu Binacional, "Sculpture for a New Era?" (Asunción, 1982).

3. "Itaipu: A Dam to Humble All," *Geo,* November 1981.

4. *Disaster at Teton Dam,* Congressional House Government Operations Committee, Washington, D.C., 1976.

5. Private communication between author Reisner and Phillip Williams, consulting hydrological engineer in San Francisco, California.

6. Statement by José Costa Cavalcanti, head of Electrobras, quoted in "Brazil's Hydroelectric Project," *New York Times,* November 14, 1983.

7. See *California Water Issues,* University of California Oral History Program, 1980; interview with former governor Edmund G. Brown.

8. "Brazil's Hydroelectric Project," *New York Times,* November 14, 1983.
9. Paul H. Lewis, *Paraguay Under Stroessner* (Chapel Hill: University of North Carolina Press, 1980) 162.
10. Bess Gillelan, "Time and Space in the Development of Amazon Water Resources" (New Haven, Conn.: School of Forestry and Environment Studies, Yale University, 1984).
11. Jonathan Kandell, *Passage Through El Dorado* (New York: William Morrow and Company, 1984) 279.
12. Natural Resources Defense Council, *Newsletter,* July/August 1978, 20.
13. Nelson de Franco, "The Superelectrification of Brazil," *I.E.E.E. Spectrum* (New York: Institute of Electrical and Electronics Engineers, May 1982) 58–60.
14. Roy A. Glasgow, "Brazil's Black Underclass: Almost Half a Nation," *New York Times,* November 30, 1984.
15. Personal communication between author Reisner and Jorge Figuls.
16. Personal communication between author Reisner and David Kitson, senior program officer with U.S. Agency for International Development in San José.
17. Personal communication between author Reisner and Phillip Williams.
18. Michael Robinson, *Water for the West* (Salt Lake City, Utah: Public Works Historical Society, 1980).
19. See, for example, Encas Salati and Peter B. Vose, "Amazon Basin: A System in Equilibrium," *Science,* July 13, 1984; also Dr. George M. Woodwell, Natural Resources Defense Council, *Newsletter,* July/August 1978.
20. E. Goldsmith and N. Hildyard, *The Social and Environmental Effects of Large Dams* (Cornwall, England: Wadebridge Ecological Center, 1984).
21. De Franco, "The Superelectrification of Brazil," 57.
22. F.M.G. Budweg, "Environmental Engineering for Dams and Reservoirs in Brazil," *Water Power and Dam Construction,* October 1980.
23. Personal communication between author Reisner and José Lutzenberger, September 1984.
24. JRB Associates, *The Dominican Republic: Country Environmental Profile,* McLean, Virginia, 1981 (produced under contract with U.S. Agency for International Development), and also personal communication between author Reisner and Gary Hartshorn, who participated in the report.
25. Phillip Williams and Associates, "Planning Problems in International Water Development" (San Francisco, California, undated).
26. Personal communication between author Reisner and Rafael Kazmann, professor emeritus of hydrology at Louisiana State University.
27. Goldsmith and Hildyard, *The Social and Environmental Effects.*
28. Asit Biswas, "Environmental Implications of Water Development for Developing Countries," in Widstrand (ed.), *Water Conflicts and Research Priorities* (Oxford: Pergamon Press, 1980).
29. Goldsmith and Hildyard, *The Social and Environmental Effects.*
30. Budweg, "Environmental Engineering."

31. Catherine Caulfield, "Dam the Amazon, Full Speed Ahead," *Natural History,* August 1983.

32. Caulfield, "Dam the Amazon"; The World Bank, "The Tucuruí Hydroproject," undated; "Soviet Scientists Attack 'Chemical War' in Brazil," *New Scientist,* November 22, 1984; and "Amazon Dam Challenged," *Ecoforum* (Nairobi, Kenya: Environmental Liaison Center).

33. Quoted in Goldsmith and Hildyard, *The Social and Environmental Effects.*

34. Goldsmith and Hildyard, *The Social and Environmental Effects.*

35. See, for example, Arthur H. Morgan, *Dams and Other Disasters,* (Boston: Porter Sargent Publications, 1971), also Marc Reisner, *The Cadillac Desert* (New York: Viking Press, 1985).

36. Goldsmith and Hildyard, *The Social and Environmental Effects.*

37. Personal communication between author Reisner and Gary Hartshorn.

38. Tsuchiya Haruki, "Aluminum Smelting Method by Blast Furnace," *Soft Energy Notes,* June/July 1983.

39. Personal communication between author Reisner and Theodor More, November 26, 1984.

40. The World Bank, *A New Environmental Policy* (Washington, D.C., 1984).

41. U.S. Department of the Treasury, *U.S. Participation in Multinational Development Banks in the 1980s* (Washington, D.C., 1982).

42. Reisner, *The Cadillac Desert.*

43. Charles Komanoff, *Power Plant Cost Escalation* (New York: van Nostrand Publishers, 1981) 20.

44. See, for example, testimony of Dr. David Price, consultant to the World Bank, before the U.S. Congressional Subcommittee on International Development Assistance and Finance, 1983.

45. "U.S. Votes No At World Bank More Often Under Reagan," *New York Times,* November 25, 1984, 1.

46. For an extensive illumination of Dubos' views on this subject, see "The Despairing Optimist," an interview in *The Amicus Journal,* Winter 1980.

47. For an illustration of another kind of hydropower alternative—water turbine machines that can utilize the flow of tiny streams with sharp drops—see Marc Reisner, "Power, Profits, and Preservation," *Wilderness,* Fall 1984.

48. "Brazil's Hydroelectric Projects" *New York Times,* November 14, 1983.

49. Newspaper Enterprise Association, *The World Almanac and Book of Facts* (New York: 1983) 116, 619, 623.

50. See, for example, Solar Energy Research Institute, U.S. Department of Energy, *A New Prosperity* (Andover, Massachusetts: Brick House Publishers, 1981).

51. See, for example, Norman Myers, *The Primary Source* (New York: W.W. Norton Publishers, 1984).

CHAPTER 9

The Caribbean—
More People and
Fewer Resources

ROBERT PASTOR
AND SERGIO DIAZ-BRIQUETS

—————————————*Editors' Preface*—————————————
Population density by itself does not inevitably mean poverty.
On islands as different in approach as Barbados and Cuba, government policies and programs have lifted the poorest of the
poor, provided basic health services and education, and increased job opportunities for men and for women, thus helping
to reduce birth rates. But in most other countries the story is
quite different: the demands of growing populations press
against dwindling resources. As a result, people are forced to live
on smaller and smaller plots and newly deforested steep slopes.
Commercial crops for export are allowed to drive out domestic
food crops and large holdings concentrate in the hands of fewer
and fewer people. In the end, the numbers of people may outweigh the land's capacity to support them. Nor do the politics
and political institutions of Latin America appear prepared, any
more than those of the United States, to tackle the real problems
underlying poverty and discontent.

    Authors Robert Pastor and Sergio Diaz-Briquets illuminate
the subtle relationships between social unrest and revolution, on
the one hand, and poverty, deprivation, and rising expectations

on the other. Their view contrasts with the oversimplified standard geopolitical explanation of Latin revolutions so tiresomely repeated by U.S. politicians and the media.

While the contrasts between the realities of life in the Caribbean countries and opportunities in the States could not be greater, close proximity and the prominent attention to U.S. media and values mean that North American hopes and expectations pervade the Caribbean cultures. The United States, often innocently or unknowingly, promises more than it can— or will—deliver.

CRISES in the Caribbean consistently demand U.S. attention. Sometimes, a crisis flashes on and off quickly, as in Grenada in October 1983. In contrast, the Panama Canal Treaty negotiations lingered for a decade. And sometimes, despite efforts to resolve the conflict, the United States is drawn in deeper, as in El Salvador and Nicaragua today.

Too often, the United States tries to "master" a problem and "solve" it without examining the problem's underlying causes. U.S. policymakers rarely explore history to find how their predecessors addressed similar crises.[1] When force is contemplated, U.S. policymakers are finally compelled to ponder deeper questions: What causes instability in the region? What interests are at stake?

President Reagan answered those questions very clearly and simply. He described the region's problems as a "Soviet-Cuban power play—pure and simple." "The national security of all the Americas is at stake in Central America," the president told a joint session of Congress on April 27, 1983. "If we cannot defend ourselves there, we cannot expect to prevail elsewhere. Our credibility would collapse, our alliances would crumble, and the safety of our homeland would be put in jeopardy."[2]

Although provocative, this perspective omits and confuses more than it illuminates. To suggest that a communist government in Central America would shatter the NATO alliance is, at best, gross exaggeration. The Soviet Union and Cuba clearly have a stake in the region, and the strategy they are pursuing is antithetical to U.S. interests. However, U.S. influence in the Caribbean dwarfs that of the Soviet Union and Cuba. Moreover, Reagan's explanation implies that people who fight and die for a political cause do so under instruction from foreign powers rather than for their own reasons.

An alternative approach is that Caribbean problems result from underdevelopment, decades of poverty, social injustice, and oppression. A proper U.S. role, according to this theory, is to promote development and help change the oppressive social structure because U.S. security is debilitated when advocates of change are forced to ally with Cuba and the Soviet Union.[3] But this analysis, too, is flawed. If poverty sparks the crisis, why is the worst violence in El Salvador and Nicaragua rather than in poorer Haiti and Honduras? And why didn't the crisis occur three decades ago, before the region's dramatic economic progress? From 1950 until 1978, Central America witnessed unprecedented economic growth—5.3 percent per year—along with a doubling in per capita income, a huge trade increase, and a vast expansion in education, health services, and infrastructure.[4] Furthermore, the Sandinistas' early request for Soviet aid is adequate proof that the region's leftists do not seek ties *only* after being spurned by the West.

What, then, is the explanation? Instability may result not so much from the absence of change, nor from outside provocations, as from the unevenness and incompleteness of change. The recurrent crises may derive from an inability of political and military institutions to adjust to social and economic changes. As Crane Brinton and others have noted, revolutions usually occur not when people are desperately poor, but when their standard of living begins to improve sporadically.[5] Those countries that allow peaceful change and access to political power—Costa Rica, Panama, even one-party Mexico—largely have avoided instability. In revolutionary Cuba, which denies political access, repression has contained potential crises that might have occurred because of economic stagnation. Those nations that

310

navigate between the two poles—maintaining heavy-handed regimes but allowing some liberalization—tend to be most vulnerable to unrest.

It is important to distinguish between the precipitating cause—the spark—that ignites instability and its underlying causes. The Nicaraguan Sandinistas had been trying to overthrow the Somoza family since 1961, but only after the murder of Pedro Joaquin Chamorro, the respected independent editor of *La Prensa,* did they gather middle-class support and become a threat. Similarly, in El Salvador, it was only after Somoza's fall that the oligarchy became vulnerable.

In the Caribbean and Central America, population expansion and resource depletion are probable triggers of change. Is it possible that the recurring crises that bedevil the region are influenced more by population and resource dynamics than by Cuban adventurism or oligarchical repression? Is there a strong—and overlooked—link between economic development and political stability on the one hand and population growth and resource misuse on the other? If such relationships exist, and the U.S. has a stake in the region's stability, then U.S. policy ought to address the issues of population and resource misuse in the region.

SIMILAR AND SHARED PROBLEMS

In this chapter, the term "Caribbean area" will refer to Central America, islands in the Caribbean sea, and Guyana and Suriname, which share a similar colonial heritage and recent independence. Until about twenty-five years ago, there were only three independent nations in the Caribbean Sea. The traditional "Caribbean" changed as Cuba turned to the Soviet bloc, Haiti turned inwards, and the Dominican Republic came to rely increasingly on the United States. As the British West Indian states became independent in the 1960s and 1970s, they increasingly appropriated the term "Caribbean" to apply to their "community."

Politically, the Caribbean ranges from Cuban communism to thirteen democracies. The Caribbean is a cultural and linguistic polyglot of English- , Dutch- , French- , and Spanish-speaking countries. Economically, the Caribbean ranges from oil-rich

Trinidad to poor Haiti, from bauxite-dependence to sugar-dependence, from tourism to semimanufacturing assembly operations.

Although it, too, is diverse, there is a "Central America" with historical roots, economic bonds, political links, and some affinity and connections with the older Latin Caribbean, but little with the newly independent English-speaking nations.

Despite the diversity, there are two reasons why one might choose to consider Central America and the Caribbean as one region. First, the region's thirty-one political entities share problems requiring cooperation and integration. All the countries are small in size and population and have open economies dependent on trade and investment. All specialize in a few commodity exports, and all depend on imports. Some are middle class by developing-world standards, but all are poor by U.S. standards.

Because internal markets are small and vulnerable to external shocks (increases in oil prices, declines in tourism), Caribbean nations must expand their markets and cushion the impact of swings in the world economy. Two approaches to reach these goals are regional integration (through the Central American Common Market and the Caribbean Community), and contributions from developed nations.[6] France and Holland fund their departments or colonies, the Soviet economy buoys Cuba's, and the British support their former colonies. But the United States is the largest donor for the entire Caribbean. The second major reason for considering the region as a unit is that the nations of the region view the United States as a common problem and source of opportunity.

U.S. INTERESTS

Although the United States overshadows the economies of the Caribbean, the economies of those countries are of trivial importance to the United States, representing less than 2 percent of U.S. trade and investment. But U.S. power and wealth, combined with the region's proximity and chronic unrest, make the Caribbean a prime U.S. interest.[7]

"For us Latin Americans," Octavio Paz wrote, "peace and democracy have been fragile curiosities; our norms are tyranny or civil war." In the nineteenth century, few government turnovers in the region were peaceful or constitutional, yet the United States ignored most of them. In the twentieth century, however, the United States has watched developments closely. What changed was the economic and political reach of North America. By 1914, the United States acquired another stake in the region: the Panama Canal, an ocean short-cut to Europe and the Orient. During the Cold War, the United States became sensitive to any changes in the region that would benefit the Soviet Union. Lately, the United States has been concerned about instability that triggers northern migration, particularly from troubled Central American nations. Regional demographic, social, economic, and political trends suggest that—without a major change in U.S. immigration policy—future migration from the Caribbean will dramatically exceed the flows of the last two decades.[8]

Like most immigrants, these new arrivals are more interested in their future in the United States than in their past in the Caribbean. But their presence forces the United States to focus on the region's violence and to insist on certain standards in our foreign policy. Thus, the migration helps change the way the United States sees itself and the region.

Even as U.S. concern increases, the central U.S. interest in the Caribbean—to promote peaceful change with justice—remains unchanged. Yet most presidents have interpreted that interest as simply promoting stability, using both military and economic aid. Clearly, a broader interpretation is needed. Because instability makes economic development impossible and opens security risks, it is in the U.S. national interest to help Caribbean nations improve the lives of their people and promote orderly change.

POPULATION TRENDS

What causes instability? How is it linked to regional population and resource trends? While most of the Caribbean area countries have small populations by international standards, many have recently experienced some of the highest population growth rates ever recorded. In some Caribbean countries, population expansion was mitigated by equally high emigration rates. In all, population growth has exacerbated problems of land distribution and environmental degradation.

The Caribbean and Central American countries vary demographically, including countries with some of the world's lowest population densities (Suriname, Belize), and with some of

Figure 9.1 Total Population, by Region and Country, Estimated and Projected (Medium Variant) Caribbean and Central America, 1960 to 2005 (in 1,000s).

	1960	1965	1970	1975
Antigua	55	61	70	70
Bahamas	113	143	177	204
Barbados	231	235	239	245
British Virgin Is.	7	9	10	12
Cayman Is.	8	9	11	15
Cuba	7,029	7,813	8,580	9,332
Dominica	59	65	71	76
Dominican Rep.	3,528	3,854	4,523	5,231
Grenada	89	92	94	105
Guadeloupe	273	311	328	325
Haiti	3,723	4,137	4,605	5,157
Jamaica	1,629	1,760	1,869	2,043
Martinique	286	307	333	324
Monserrat	12	12	12	12
Netherlands Antilles	192	208	221	240
Puerto Rico	2,358	2,594	2,718	3,105
St. Kitts-Nevis-Anguilla	57	61	65	69
St. Lucia	93	96	101	112
St. Vincent-The Grenadines	79	84	88	92
Trinidad and Tobago	843	975	1,027	1,082
Turks & Caicos Is.	6	6	6	6
U.S. Virgin Is.	32	52	63	91
Caribbean Total	20,431	22,884	25,211	27,948
Belize	92	106	120	140
Costa Rica	1,236	1,482	1,732	1,965
El Salvador	2,574	3,005	3,582	4,143
Guatemala	3,966	4,615	5,353	6,243
Honduras	1,942	2,302	2,640	3,093
Nicaragua	1,472	1,701	1,970	2,318
Panama	1,095	1,269	1,464	1,678
Central America Total	12,377	14,480	16,861	19,580
Grand Total	32,808	37,364	42,071	47,528

Source: United Nations, Department of International Economic and Social Affairs, *World Population Prospects as Assessed in 1980,* Population Studies No. 78

the highest (Barbados, El Salvador). The country with the region's largest population, Cuba (approximately 10 million), has a hundred times more inhabitants than some of the smaller countries. Mortality rates differ as well. Cuba, Costa Rica, and Barbados, for example, have life expectancies at birth comparable

1980	1985	1990	1995	2000	2005
75	84	92	00	108	117
241	268	295	320	344	366
263	277	292	305	320	334
14	15	17	18	20	21
17	19	21	23	24	27
9,732	10,038	10,540	11,152	11,718	12,174
83	89	95	101	108	116
5,947	6,715	7,534	8,414	9,329	10,331
111	118	125	133	142	153
329	334	339	345	354	367
5,809	6,585	7,509	8,596	9,860	11,284
2,188	2,358	2,535	2,705	2,872	3,063
325	328	337	350	362	378
11	12	13	14	15	17
256	285	313	340	366	397
3,675	4,345	4,747	5,043	5,312	5,605
74	82	90	98	106	115
118	127	136	144	153	65
97	103	110	117	124	134
1,168	1,252	1,337	1,416	1,483	1,557
6	6	7	7	8	9
111	123	136	147	158	163
30,650	33,563	36,620	39,788	43,286	46,793
162	184	205	223	234	243
2,213	2,485	2,776	3,075	3,377	3,684
4,797	5,552	6,484	7,531	8,708	9,926
7,262	8,403	9,676	11,109	12,739	14,392
3,691	4,372	5,105	5,953	6,978	8,142
2,733	3,218	3,778	4,422	5,154	5,965
1,896	2,117	2,346	2,583	2,823	3,060
22,754	26,331	30,370	34,896	40,013	45,412
53,404	59,894	66,990	74,684	83,299	92,205

(St/Esa/ser. A/78), New York, 1981, Table A-2, 16–21.

to those found in the developed world, whereas nations such as Haiti and Honduras are more comparable to sub-Saharan Africa. Cuba and Barbados have reached below-replacement fertility rates, but in most of Central America the average woman bears more than five children. In the Caribbean Islands, most women will have three or fewer children, although in countries such as Haiti, the Dominican Republic, and St. Lucia, reproduction rates are much higher.

Population projections prepared by the United Nations predict that if current population growth rates continue, the population of the Caribbean and Central American region will increase from 53 million in 1980 to an estimated 92 million by the year 2005 (see fig. 9.1). Approximately 80 percent of the growth will occur in the countries with already high growth rates. Because the current population is so young, the number of people will continue to rise appreciably at least for a few decades. This demographic pyramid means a high "dependency ratio": the number of people in their productive years is small relative to the number of children and elderly. In some countries, the population includes only one person of working age for each dependent. (Most developed countries boast two workers for every dependent.) A large population and a high dependency ratio could reduce already scarce employment opportunities, housing, and social services.[9]

By 1990, the number of new jobs needed to employ Central America's growing population will be triple that needed in 1960. During the 1960s and 1970s—despite high economic growth rates—new workers *far exceeded* the number of new jobs created.[10] Rural-to-urban migration has created an even more desperate need for jobs in the expanding urban areas. The urban population of Central America, Haiti, and the Dominican Republic is projected to increase from 9 to 30 million by the end of the century; this reflects an annual growth rate of 4 percent in the urban areas, well above the national rates.[11]

The statistics should not obscure underlying human frustrations. While popular expectations often reflect the consumer standards of the United States, the region's governments are unable to maintain current standards of living, and in some cases, obsolete political structures block all change. Thus, a fast-growing, increasingly aware population may collide with an

316

immovable, outdated political structure, causing instability or crisis.

Figure 9.2 School Attendance by Age Groups, Selected Countries in the Caribbean Basin: 1960 and 1980.

	Attendance Rates between Ages (%)					
	6 to 11		12 to 17		18 to 23	
Country	1960	1980	1960	1980	1960	1980
Barbados	94	99	51	65	1	9
Costa Rica	74	98	36	55	8	21
Cuba	78	100	43	83	7	30
El Salvador	49	69	40	58	9	19
Guatemala	32	53	18	34	4	10
Guyana	91	96	63	66	5	11
Haiti	34	41	16	22	2	4
Honduras	50	71	25	45	3	15
Jamaica	75	95	57	72	3	10
Nicaragua	43	61	30	54	4	19
Panama	68	96	50	83	13	43
Dominican Republic	67	82	39	64	4	21
Trinidad and Tobago	66	78	52	48	3	8

Source: Economic Commission for Latin America, *Statistical Yearbok for Latin America: 1980*, Santiago, 1981, Table 35, 102–103.

In the region, school enrollment and literacy rates rose dramatically in the last two decades (see fig. 9.2), but in some nations, even while progress was made, the absolute number of people who cannot read or write also increased. More education means the workplace will have to offer not only more but also different kinds of employment, because the better educated population will chafe in poorly remunerated, low-skilled jobs.

Providing basic needs and services is difficult in poor nations with high population growth rates. Other factors such as skewed income distribution and misallocated resources are also to blame. For example, from 1965–1967 to 1974–1976, despite impressive economic growth rates, the number of malnourished children in Central America grew by 67 percent. By late 1976, over 1.1 million children under the age of five were underfed.[12] In

this case, rapid population growth aggravated by income disparities made a bad problem worse. Population growth also
stimulates rapid urbanization, which plays havoc with health
and living conditions in cities. In the Dominican Republic,
Haiti, Honduras, and Jamaica, only an estimated half of the
urban dwellers have reasonable access to safe drinking
water.[13]

One exit for rapid population expansion is emigration. Emigration rates from many Caribbean countries (especially the
island nations) are among the world's highest: 10 to 25 percent of
several nations' populations have left the country in the last
quarter century.[14] Because many emigrate to the United States,
where even the lowest wages exceed those at home, migrant re-
mittances account for a substantial portion of some national
incomes and of the household budgets of many resident families.
However, emigration sometimes siphons off those more enterprising, thus contributing to economic stagnation.

A growing population, widespread poverty, and rising expectations obviously combine to make new and more pressing
demands on resources. For example, in already densely populated Haiti and El Salvador, further population growth seems to
trigger natural resource abuses—deforestation, erosion, and soil
exhaustion. Some of the area's more developed countries, such as
Costa Rica and the Bahamas, also misuse resources, largely to accelerate economic growth. Lately, however, a more aware public
is beginning to demand new natural resource policies.

RESOURCES

Caribbean area countries must now meet the expectations of a
larger, better-educated population with, in many cases, shaky
social and political institutions and a thin resource base. These
nations' small and open economies make them particularly vulnerable to external shocks or to internal disruption or
mismanagement. A key question, then, is how to stretch a limited natural resource base to promote long-term equitable
economic growth.

Of course, land use deeply influences any region's history.
Over the centuries, disputes over access to land—often between
powerful landed interests and a dispossessed peasantry—have

sometimes led to violence. In some countries recently, the scarcity of arable land has led to conflict; in others, maldistribution plays a more important role. Some, such as El Salvador, have both problems.

FORESTS

Land availability varies widely from country to country. Generally, the Caribbean islands are not as richly endowed as Central America and the Northern Rim of South America, where land is abundant and population densities lower. The amount of remaining forested land indicates how much land is available relative to population. In the countries of the Northern Rim of South America, where population is sparse and concentrated along the coast, about 90 percent of the total land area is still forested. Forests cover approximately 50 percent of Central America—except in El Salvador, where the figure is 13 percent. In the Caribbean islands, the situation varies. Barbados, for instance, has practically no forest; Haiti has only 7 percent of the land left in forests, and tree cover on other islands amounts to 40 percent or more.[15]

The most forested countries generally have rough topographies, complex hydrological systems, and harsh or difficult climates. In addition, in the Caribbean islands, poor soils, insufficient potable water, and the environmental effects of strong prevailing winds—not to say hurricanes—also inhibit human settlements.

If properly managed, forests constitute perhaps the region's most valuable natural resource. Worldwide demand for forest products is quickly increasing; and some rich nations—Japan and Germany among them—are desperate for wood. In recent years, however, the Central American and Caribbean countries have been deforested rapidly. Tracts of forests have been cut or burned with no effort to replant trees. Where the tropical forest cover is stripped—especially on the hurricane-prone Caribbean islands—rampant erosion can result, reducing soil fertility and silting reservoirs. Scientists have also noted the loss of unique, irreplaceable genetic material as humid tropical forests are destroyed.

The main cause of such deforestation is unmanaged or mismanaged clearing, not demand for wood or even local demand for food. One example of mismanagement is the conversion of forest land to pastures in Central America to produce more beef for export, primarily to the United States. This conversion was encouraged and financed largely by international development agencies seeking rapid economic growth. Measured exclusively in such terms, it was successful. Between 1961 and 1978, beef exports from Central America expanded more than *sevenfold,* from 20,200 tons to 151,300 tons per year.[16] Beef exports became an important source of foreign exchange for Central America, and they also helped diversify the national economies. In Costa Rica, for example, the share of beef in total exports rose from 5 to 9 percent between 1960 and 1979, easing the country's excessive dependence on coffee exports.[17]

To avoid exceeding the limits of humid tropical soils, one should consider allocating forested areas for such uses as generating wood products and their derivatives. Alternative activities would better complement economic growth and help preserve soil fertility and wildlife. Alternative approaches could also increase employment because cattle raising generally requires less labor per unit of land than other primary economic activities do.

Erosion, long a serious problem in many Caribbean countries, has been greatly exacerbated by population expansion, especially in the Caribbean islands and in El Salvador. Destruction of the forest cover is just one contributing factor. Of perhaps greater significance is subsistence farmers' intensive use of soils poorly suited for such cropping patterns. Rapid population growth magnifies the problem, but concentration of the best agricultural lands in the hands of a few is probably the main reason for soil abuse.[18] Vast expanses of land in the large estates are used for pastures or held in reserve, pushing most people onto the worst land. Strikingly similar circumstances may explain why soil productivity in Haiti has deteriorated.[19] In the Dominican Republic, erosion has reduced the life expectancy of reservoirs critically important for hydroelectricity and irrigation.

Eroded lands and fields not suited for agriculture can be reclaimed with proper soil-management practices or appropriate technologies. Fertilization, contouring, and irrigation can preserve or increase soil productivity. Irrigation is more common in the Caribbean than in Central America, where only Costa Rica irrigates more than 10 percent of its arable land and El Salvador, Guatemala, and Nicaragua irrigate less than 4 percent. In Haiti, 8 percent of the arable land is currently irrigated, but 60 percent could be.

Using irrigation during the dry season, adequate drainage during the rainy season, and other soil-conservation practices (fertilization and crop rotation, for instance), countries in the region could probably produce at least two crops per year without exhausing soils. (Such double-cropping is common in California's Imperial Valley.) More widespread irrigation would also help reduce these countries' reliance on imported foods. High costs have thus far limited irrigation to the most accessible and economical lands. But as cities grow and incomes rise, increased demand for food should make new projects economical.

Although modern agriculture thrives in some Caribbean countries, some countries overuse or misuse new agricultural technologies and techniques. Excessive pesticide use in Central America, for instance, has been linked to a resurgence of malaria.[20] Insecticide overuse may also be connected with outbreaks of dengue fever in the Caribbean in 1977 and 1981.[21] Pesticide poisonings are common, and leachates are beginning to contaminate soils and water. Throughout the region, water pollution is becoming a serious concern, largely because of agricultural runoff.

LAND USE AND OWNERSHIP

Land reform remains a central issue in the Caribbean and a policy crucible. Inequitable land holding—the main obstacle to using the region's resources more profitably—prevails in many of our neighbors to the south. Where holdings are large, relatively more land is left fallow and more capital-intensive production methods are employed. Where rural unemployment and underemployment are high, capital-intensive agriculture further limits job opportunities. Big landowners also often grow cash crops for export. Although nothing is intrinsically wrong with this approach, a nation too dependent on cash crops may grow vulnerable to world price shocks and dependent on expensive food imports.

Land tenure patterns are now being questioned. In a few cases, change is afoot. By 1970, approximately 90 percent of all farms in El Salvador and Guatemala were smaller than seven hectares, the minimum size usually required to sustain a peasant family. Comparable figures for Costa Rica and Honduras were 68 percent, and for Nicaragua 51 percent. Meanwhile, some 40 percent of the land was still controlled by 1 percent of all farms.[22] As a result, the United Nations Economic Commission for Latin America estimated that, in the late 1970s, 74 percent of Central America's rural population faced extreme poverty. The percentages ranged from 34 percent in Costa Rica, by far the lowest figure, to 80 to 82 percent in Nicaragua and Guatemala. In all countries but Guatemala, the urban poor are still better off than the rural poor.[23]

Among the Central American nations, Costa Rica has been relatively successful in redistributing land and opening new areas for agricultural settlement (although the squatter laws that have served this end are hastening the country's deforestation). To a lesser extent, Honduras and Panama have also had some success. Agrarian reform programs in Nicaragua and El Salvador have been more sweeping. In Nicaragua, reform was facilitated by the abundance of unused land and the nationalization of the Somoza family's huge holdings. In El Salvador, at U.S. prodding, a reform program began in 1980 (despite the civil war) and involves 20 percent of the country's farmland. So far, the program has benefitted nearly 35,000 peasants. As many as 150,000 families may eventually own their land. Yet, even if the Salvadorean agrarian reform is fully implemented, another 150,000 rural families could remain landless. There is simply not enough land.[24]

Agrarian reform in Guatemala has been modest and has met with only questionable success. Instead of redistributing the larger farms, the Guatemalan program has tried to open new lands, particularly in Petén. But accusations are flying that tracts of eroded lands, reclaimed with financial help from international lending agencies, have been given to military officers or their wealthy patrons instead of peasants.

Land reform is less significant in the Caribbean countries, although in Haiti and the Dominican Republic (where good farmland is scarce because the terrain is so mountainous) land concentration remains a problem. In Cuba, most large estates were nationalized and organized into state farms during the 1960s. (The 20 percent of Cuban farms that remain in private hands are reportedly the most productive.) Ironically, Cuba suffers from the same problem as some oligarchical nations: much of the best land, concentrated in huge holdings, is growing cash crops. Cuba is probably the only developing country that is *more* dependent today on a single agricultural commodity (sugar) than it was twenty years ago. Still, Cuba has done better than any other country in the region in solving its distributional and unemployment (although not underemployment) problems.

ENERGY

Nothing illustrates the Caribbean area's vulnerability so well as the impact of the 1970s energy crisis. By the time of the first oil-price leap in 1973–1974, the Caribbean area was dependent on oil imports, but was not diversified enough to cushion the price rise's impact on the rest of the economy. Thus, a region starved for investment capital was forced to divert an increasing proportion of its foreign exchange from development projects to energy imports. By 1979, when the second precipitous price rise came, Barbados and Jamaica had to spend nearly five times more money to purchase less petroleum than they had in 1973. As a percentage of total imports, petroleum purchases tripled in just seven years. An oil-subsidy program offered by Venezuela and Mexico to nine countries in the region helped, but by the early 1980s, every Caribbean nation had recognized the need to exploit whatever energy potential it had, or else to conserve, to achieve sustainable development.

At current extraction rates, Trinidad and Tobago, the region's only oil exporter, is expected to exhaust its known reserves by 1990. Natural gas is more abundant, some 240 cubic gaseous gigometers, and should last considerably longer. Excluding Mexico, Venezuela, Colombia, and the United States, no other Caribbean country harbors deposits of fossil fuels, although recent oil discoveries in Guatemala have spurred some production there. Barbados also produces a little oil, and its estimated gas reserves amount to 8 cubic gaseous gigometers. Proven oil and gas reserves in other Caribbean countries are insignificant.[25]

The expansion of hydroelectric generation in the Caribbean looks promising. Prospects for most of the island nations are limited, but not inconsequential, especially if agro-based and small-hydro technologies are employed. The mountains and rivers of the Dominican Republic, which has a strong hydroelectric potential, support twenty-eight hydroelectric facilities, and more are planned. These should help offset the $100 million trade imbalance that the country has spent by importing oil. The Madrigal Dam alone is expected to produce 50,000 kilowatts of power and to supply Santo Domingo, the capital, with potable water until the end of the century. These dams also increase the amount of farmland under irrigation.[26] The dark side to this success story, however, is that reservoir siltation caused by deforestation is becoming a critical problem.

The area's hydroelectric potential remains largely untapped. Panama and Costa Rica have made the greatest use of this energy resource. In 1979, 77 percent of all electricity generated in Costa Rica came from hydroelectric sources. Honduras will soon complete a large hydroelectric station, El Cajon (which has been absorbing up to a third of its national budget).

Central America also has some geothermal potential. But geothermal sources—estimated at one-third the hydroelectric potential—are difficult to harness. Still, El Salvador gets 30 percent of its electricity from geothermal energy, producing in 1979 some 4 percent of all Central America's electricity.

Two of the region's most important energy sources are fuelwood and charcoal. A continuing and urgent energy crisis in the Caribbean—and in much of the Third World—is the worsening shortage of fuelwood for cooking. Probably 50 percent of Caribbean households depend on fuelwood for energy. As forests are exploited and cleared, the poorer rural households most dependent on fuelwood are hurt even more than the modern economies in the capital cities by oil shortages.[27] In countries such as El Salvador and Haiti, high rates of deforestation threaten the future supply of low-cost fuel.

With planning, the fuelwood shortage can be effectively addressed. The Inter-American Development Bank (IDB) has recently financed an inventory and management plan in the Bahamas to protect the country's remaining forests and help the country produce lumber and other wood products besides charcoal. As elsewhere in the Caribbean, exploitation of the pine forests beginning in 1905 by foreign companies gradually left the islands with few forested areas. Against this backdrop, the IDB-sponsored project could be a model for other energy-oriented resource programs.[28]

Only Cuba, with subsidies and technical assistance from the Soviet Union, is trying to develop nuclear energy. Two nuclear reactors are planned or under construction. These facilities narrowly have avoided ecological disasters.[29] On the other island nations, atomic power plants are not feasible because their electricity grids are too small to absorb the power output of even the smallest plants. Given the obstacles to hydroelectric and nuclear power, and the consequences of deforestation, research into solar, wind, or biomass (bagasse and alcohol) energy could reduce the region's oil and wood dependence and make all the countries more energy self-sufficient.[30]

MINERALS

Large-scale mineral extraction in the Caribbean is limited to a few metals, such as bauxite and alumina, which have been heavily mined in Haiti, Jamaica, the Dominican Republic, Guyana, and Suriname. Cuba produces some copper, and it is estimated to have the world's fourth largest nickel reserves. Major investments are now increasing Cuba's production capacity, but other countries produce nickel more efficiently at a lower cost.[31] The Dominican Republic produces a little gold and some nickel. Although on a world scale Caribbean and Central American mining is not significant, it is an important source of foreign exchange for some local economies. Mining provides little employment, however, despite high capital inputs. Moreover, in several countries—notably Cuba and Jamaica—the environmental consequences of uncontrolled operations have been serious. Long-term ecological costs may well exceed the immediate economic payoffs.

The region's mineral resources are of marginal importance to the United States. The region's strategic importance lies instead in its geographic position—its proximity to the United States. Given the small open economies, the meager resources, and the high population growth of most countries in the region, stability depends—more than in other developing regions—on equitable growth and careful resource management.

PEOPLE, RESOURCES, AND INSTABILITY

Just how does population growth or resource use affect political instability? The first problem in addressing this central question is that "political instability" is difficult to define and even harder to measure. In a way, it is any irregular change in leadership—that is, political turbulence caused by an unconstitutional change of government. Orderly change should not be equated with political instability, nor instability with nonviolent pressures applied to increase a particular group's share of economic or political power. A strike aimed at increasing union wages does not constitute political instability, although a strike aimed at overthrowing a government would.

By the same token, it is important to distinguish between unstable regimes and stable regimes plagued by occasional political instabilities. A stable regime tries to meet its people's social and economic needs and permits peaceful and orderly political and social change. An unstable regime closes channels for political participation and social advancement. Paradoxically, a stable regime could manifest signs of political instability (say, protests and strikes), whereas an unstable regime might be quiescent. The distinction, however, is worth making because unstable regimes are more likely to have prolonged periods of unrest.

The relationship between resources and stability partly hinges on the aspirations of the people. As aspirations change—specifically, as people come to expect a higher standard of living even though the resource base remains the same or declines—the traditional system becomes fragile. This fragility increases as population expands. One overly simple hypothesis is that the higher the population density and the faster the rate of population growth, the more likely a country will become unstable. The evidence does not support this hypothesis. Barbados, with a high population density, and Costa Rica and Panama, with high rates of population growth, have all been reasonably stable politically.

Conversely, Suriname, with a low population density, and Grenada and Dominica, with low rates of population growth, have been unstable.

No single-factor hypothesis can explain the relationship among resources, population, and stability. Conclusions are even more elusive if the simple correlation between resource use and instability is examined. During the last two decades, no Caribbean nation has suffered worse deforestation or erosion than Haiti, but until deposed in early 1986 the Duvaliers had not been seriously threatened. On the other hand, the tremendous natural resources of Suriname have barely been explored, let alone exploited, even though the military violently overthrew the democratic government only five years after independence.

Put another way, rapid population growth *can* destabilize society, much as rapid economic growth can.[32] When institutions are fragile or changes are overwhelming—such as the tripling of Central America's population in the last thirty years—it becomes hard for any nation to cope.[33] A more youthful population may well increase the possibility of violent protest, as crime is higher in young populations.[34] Not surprisingly, the guerrillas in the 1978–1979 Nicaraguan Revolution were referred to as *muchachos* (boys), and the National Guard of Anastasio Somoza looked with suspicion at all young people out of uniform. Moreover, population expansion increases urbanization, because government services are more extensive in urban than in rural areas. But with additional density, demands on an already beleagured government increase; in the crucible of the region's fast-growing cities, expectations can peak as services wane.

Between 1970 and 2000, the urban population of Central America, Haiti, and the Dominican Republic is expected to increase from about 9 million to about 30 million—more than threefold. Jobs will be needed at a faster rate, though the number of young people currently entering the labor force each year already exceeds the number of new jobs.

So, population expansion has wide-ranging implications for all the region's societies. Whether the expansion triggers political instability depends on several intervening factors. Political processes and institutions may be the most important, but the economic growth rate, the location of the population, and sustainable resource patterns will also have a major impact.

Resource mismanagement causes more subtle problems. Most of the parliamentary democracies in the Caribbean have long since lost their forests, if they had any. Deforestation in Central America and Haiti, while quite severe, is only indirectly a cause of the region's political instability. El Salvador's land-tenure system increased the possibilities of resource abuse as it displaces peasants to marginal lands. At the same time, it left many people with no stake in their nation's stable growth. On balance, inequitable ownership is more responsible for the current instability than resource abuse, but neither are as important as the intransigent political structure.

This analysis is consistent with other recent findings. Robert Repetto and Thomas Holmes show that the thesis that population pressures contribute to the deterioration and depletion of resources omits critical intervening variables, particularly the impact of the social and legal system on resource management. It is not population pressure per se that leads to overexploitation of resources, but rather the breakdown of traditional legal systems and the creation of open access to public resources.[35] In a study of the causes of the Honduras-Salvador War of 1969, William Durham arrives at a similar conclusion: population growth *did* increase pressures on scarce resources, but inequitable distribution of land and economic power had far more impact on resource scarcity or abuse and, ultimately, political instability.[36]

The distribution of political power also needs to be taken into account in any assessment of how population and resource factors affect stability. A closed, authoritarian political system is more likely to tolerate, even worsen, inequitable land-tenure patterns. This, in turn, is more likely to lead to resource abuse, scarcity, and eventually political instability. Conversely, a political system that permits open competition for political power is more likely to undertake land reform, legislate economic and social equity, and address resource issues before the resources are ruined.

In most societies where social and economic power is monopolized by a few, population growth is more likely to lead to resource misuse than in societies where the power and size of the middle class is expanding. Resource misuse is more likely to lead

328

to political instability in dictatorships than in open political systems. In short, the political system is crucial to the relationship among population, resources, and instability. In Central America, as elsewhere, the shortest path to political stability is through political participation, but simply opening these channels will not solve population or resource problems.

RESPONDING TO THE CAUSES
AND CONSEQUENCES OF INSTABILITY

Stability is impossible to guarantee even if it were desirable, and, of course, it is not. In an unjust or repressive system, stability means continuing oppression. Stability in an open and dynamic system is illusory because such a system invites change. The expansion of the region's population is a continuing problem of adaptation and absorption, regardless of political regime. Given the history of some countries and the inherent vulnerability of others, instability is ever-present.

Nonetheless, the United States has a profound interest in helping the nations of the region to manage their problems, improve their standard of living, and preserve and more fully utilize their resources. Whatever the causes of regional instability, it is clear that the United States must share the consequences. First, the debate among the American people over U.S. policies toward regional crises is extremely divisive. Second, at the minimum, such crises divert attention from other important problems. Third, instability in the Caribbean area threatens to involve the United States militarily, with devastating consequences for other U.S. interests. And fourth, such instability often generates illegal migration to the United States.

Estimates by researchers from the Census Bureau suggest that up to 100,000 Nicaraguans and 500,000 Salvadorans entered the United States illegally between 1978 and 1983.[37] While the war in Central America and illegal migration capture the attention of U.S. policymakers, problems related to population and resources are accorded lower priority. But resource issues may well be tomorrow's crises, so new policies are needed to deal with them now before they get out of control.

New plans and mechanisms are needed now in the Caribbean area—from the governments in the region where the principal responsibility for resource and population policies lies. Curbing excessive growth, promoting education and employment, and improving resource planning are ways to address population growth and resource-management problems *before* they become crises. Specifically, policies aimed at three problems—future population growth, the consequences of past population growth, and resource mismanagement—are needed.

First, the region's most important long-term issue is population growth. If governments were to strengthen existing family planning programs, and, as a result, fertility levels declined, the results in terms of reduced health costs would be seen almost immediately. Withing five years, projected expenditures for education would also fall. The most positive results of population control, however, would not be evident until the turn of the century. The people who will enter the labor force between now and the year 2000 have already been born. If current Central American fertility rates (an average of about 5.6 children for each woman) continue, the region will need 411,000 new jobs in the year 2010, compared to 90,000 new jobs in 1960 and 190,000 in 1980. If total fertility rates declined to 3.0 by the year 2000, then "only" 262,000 jobs would be needed; if, by some miracle, the fertility rate declined to 2.1, then only 182,000 new jobs would be needed.[38]

These differences matter. In terms of investment needed to create jobs, one report estimates that by the year 2010 about $21 billion would be needed to accommodate labor force growth *annually* if the current trend is not reduced. If fertility rates declined to 3.0, then about $15 billion would be needed; if they fell to 2.1, about $12 billion would be required. Using optimistic economic projections (5 to 6 percent annual growth in gross domestic product through the end of the century and 15 percent domestic savings rate), the lowest fertility rate would permit governments to build up surpluses totaling $4 billion annually, whereas population growth at the current rate would create yearly public deficits of $5 billion.[39] For political reasons, regional governments and external donors now give higher priority to reducing mortality than fertility, but both need to be pursued with equal vigor.[40]

Consequences of Past Population Growth. Second, governments need to deal more effectively with the consequences of past population growth. Demographic planning units should be established or strengthened in governments to gather statistics, gauge the implications of demographic changes, and propose policies to help society adjust to the changes. The major problem is to expand employment opportunities. Perhaps the most important step Caribbean governments can take to expand jobs is to neutralize policies that discourage labor-intensive investments and undermine agricultural productivity. Unfortunately, most Caribbean governments today discourage the creation of more jobs through duty-free entry for most capital goods, high payroll taxes, subsidized interest rates, fixed and low prices for agricultural products, neglect of small or medium-scale agricultural activities, minimum wage laws where unemployment is massive, and over-valued exchange rates. Moreover, governments (including the United States) generally provide credit and inducements for companies to invest in job training, education, or retraining. A next step would be to promote labor-intensive investments and agricultural productivity.

In job creation, the social benefit of employment should be considered, not just the "cost" of production. Governments ought to provide additional benefits to businesses (through tax and tariff policies) aimed at increasing the number of jobs.[41] Governments can also create jobs by encouraging linkages among firms, industries, or sectors, and by opening new markets and giving incentives to produce and use locally produced materials.[42]

Resource Mismanagement. Finally, new policies are needed to manage resources better. Resources still offer unexplored opportunities in the Caribbean and Central America, too. Only a small percentage of the region's land has been irrigated. Reforestation is practically nil, but offers tremendous possibilities for fuelwood, timber, paper, and wood exports in virtually every country in the region. Significant petroleum, hydroelectric, and geothermal potential in the area has not yet been tapped. Conservation and planning could multiply economic opportunities now and in the future.

A number of Central America's agricultural problems have been traced to the area's land-tenure system. Peter Thacher and

Robert Wasserstrom of the World Resources Institute have offered a provocative proposal for addressing this issue—the creation of a Central American Institute for Agrarian Reform (INCARA) by the United States and other donors to support "innovative efforts to integrate land distribution with effective resource planning."[43] Of course, land distribution is essentially a struggle for power. While such a regional group could provide leverage and technical assistance, land reform success ultimately depends on the alignment of forces in each country.

The rapid loss of forests and fertile land indicates the need for broader resource planning at both national and regional levels. Technical assistance recently offered by the Inter-American Development Bank to the Bahamas to prepare a forestry plan is an encouraging step. Costa Rica's initiatives—including, for example, agricultural extension services and the conservation of virgin and nonvirgin forests as national parks—are also encouraging. If peace can be achieved, and the economic alliances of the Central American Common Market and Caribbean Community reinvigorated, the other nations may be able to look beyond their own problems, however urgent, and realize that the region's future depends on careful and cooperative resource husbandry and growth.

A COMMON CAUSE

Since the turn of the century, U.S. national security managers considered resources in the Caribbean area in terms of *access*—access by U.S. industries to bauxite, petroleum, coffee, and even bananas.[44] This obsolete vision of the region has obscured a more fundamental, long-term U.S. interest in the region's progress. Today, the United States shares with the region the consequences of bad policy and instability. When the U.S. economy founders, the economies in the region plummet. When a civil war erupts in a nation, the United States receives its refugees.

These interwoven interests demand that the United States look to the underlying and longer-term causes of instability, and particularly to issues of population growth and resource misuse. Today, the United States should be more concerned with the sustainable management of resources in the Caribbean area than with access to those resources. Rapid population growth and short-sighted exploitation destabilize societies. Those governments that cannot absorb and adapt to these changes face the prospect of violence and political instability.

It would be in the best interests of the United States and the nations of the Caribbean area to educate decision-makers and the public about the complex relations among population growth rates, resource use, and economic development. While the primary responsibility rests with the region's governments, there is much the United States and international institutions can do to reinforce appropriate efforts—by training a new generation of scientists, assisting research centers on population and resource management, and promoting better environmental standards.

Future crises are best avoided by opening channels for political change within a just and legal framework. But even a democratic country that ignores its long-term problems is destined to face cumulative crises. Curbing population growth, promoting employment, and insisting on better resource planning—these approaches are designed to leap in front of longer-term problems, and to transform future crises into current opportunities.

NOTES

1. For an elaboration of this pattern, see the following two articles by Robert Pastor, "U.S. Policies Toward the Caribbean: Recurring Problems and Promises," in Jack W. Hopkins (ed.), *Latin American and Caribbean Contemporary Record, Volume I, 1981–82* (New York: Holmes and Meier, 1983), and "Continuity and Change in U.S. Foreign Policy: Carter and Reagan on El Salvador," *Journal of Policy Analysis and Management,* Winter 1984, vol. 3, no. 1.

2. President Reagan's speech to the Joint Session of Congress was published in the *New York Times,* April 28, 1983. For his characterization of the conflict in Central America, see Francis X. Clines, "Reagan Calls Salvador Aid Foes Naive," *New York Times,* March 20, 1984, A3.

3. European Social Democrats tend to adopt this perspective. See Robert Pastor, "The Socialist International and the United States in Central America: Mirror Images," *The New Republic,* May 16, 1983. For a well-developed argument along these same lines, see *Changing Course: Blueprint for Peace in Central America and the Caribbean* (Washington, D.C.: Institute for Policy Studies, 1984).

4. Richard E. Feinberg and Robert A. Pastor, "Far From Hopeless: An Economic Program for Post-war Central America," in Robert S. Leiken (ed.), *Central America: Anatomy of Conflict* (New York: Pergamon

Press, 1984); and Isaac Cohen and Gert Rosenthal, "The Dimensions of Economic Policy Space in Central America," in Richard R. Fagen and Olga Pellicer (eds.), *The Future of Central America: Policy Choices for the U.S. and Mexico* (Stanford: Stanford University Press, 1983).

5. Crane Brinton, *The Anatomy of Revolution* (Englewood Cliffs, N.J.: Prentice-Hall, 1938); Chalmer Johnson, *Revolutionary Change* (Stanford: Stanford University Press, 2nd edition, 1982); for an application of this thesis to Central America, see Robert Pastor, "Our Real National Interests in Central America," *The Atlantic Monthly,* July 1982, vol. 250, no. 1.

6. A report written by the Bureau of Intelligence and Research of the Department of State evaluated ten regional integration schemes and concluded that the two best—the only ones which "have been unambiguously effective in integrating export-import markets"—were the Caribbean Community and the Central American Common Market. U.S. Department of State, *Evaluating Regional Schemes for the Promotion of Inter-LDC Trade,* Report No. 1362 (Washington, D.C., April 14, 1980).

7. Robert Pastor, "Our Real National Interests in Central America," *The Atlantic Monthly,* July 1982; and Jorge Dominguez, *U.S. Interests and Policies in the Caribbean and Central America* (Washington, D.C.: American Enterprise Institute for Public Policy Research, 1982).

8. Robert Pastor, "Migration in the Caribbean Basin: The Need for an Approach as Dynamic as the Phenomenon," in M.M. Kritz (ed.), *U.S. Immigration and Refugee Policy: Global and Domestic Issues* (Lexington, Mass.: D.C. Heath, 1983).

9. The Futures Group, *Central America: The Effects of Population on Economic and Social Development* (Washington, D.C., 1983), 13–14.

10. See, for example, Oficina Internacional del Trabajo, Programa Regional del Empleo para América Latina; *Necesidades esenciales políticas de empleo en América Latina* (Santiago, Chile, 1980).

11. United Nations, Centro Latinoamericano de Demográfia, *Boletin demográfico,* vol. 14, no. 28 and vol. 15, no. 29.

12. Charles Teller, Mauricio Culagovski, Juan del Canto y José Aranda Pastor, "Desnutrición, población y desarrollo social y economico: Hacia un marco de referencia," in Charles Teller, Mauricio Culagovski and Jose Aranda-Pastor (eds.), *Interrelación desnutrición población y desarrollo social y economico* (Guatemala: Instituto de Nutrición de Centro América y Panamá, 1980) 37.

13. Inter-American Development Bank, *Natural Resources in Latin America* (Washington, D.C., 1983), Table III-2, 40.

14. Robert Pastor, "The Policy Challenge," Chapter 1, in Robert Pastor, *Migration and Development in the Caribbean: The Unexplored Connection* (Boulder, Colo.: Westview Press, 1985), Table 1.5, 12.

15. Committee on Selected Biological Problems in the Humid Tropics, *Ecological Aspects of Development in the Humid Tropics* (Washington, D.C.: National Research Council, National Academy Press, 1982).

16. Norman Myers, "The Hamburger Connection: How Central America's Forests Become North America's Hamburgers," *Ambio*, 1981, vol. 10, no. 1: 3–8. See also, Norman Myers, *Conversion of Tropical Moist Forests* (Washington, D.C.: National Research Council, National Academy Press, 1980) 44–47, 131–135.

17. International Monetary Fund, *International Financial Statistics Yearbook, 1980*: 146–147.

18. William H. Durham, *Scarcity and Survival in Central America: Ecological Origins of the Soccer War* (Stanford: Stanford University Press, 1980).

19. Robert Maguire, *Bottom-Up Development in Haiti*, Inter-American Foundation (Washington, D.C.: Inter-American Foundation, October 1979) Paper #1, 12–16.

20. Georganne Chapin and Robert Wasserstrom, "Pesticide Use and Malaria Resurgence in Central America and India," *Social Science and Medicine*, vol. 17, no. 5: 273–290.

21. Pan American Health Organization, *Dengue in the Caribbean, 1977* (Washington, D.C., 1979); and Sergio Diaz-Briquets, *The Health Revolution in Cuba* (Austin: University of Texas Press, 1983).

22. United Nations Economic Commission for Latin America, Food and Agricultural Organization, and International Labour Office, *Tenncia de la tierra y desarrollo rural en Centroamerica* (San José, Costa Rica: 1973).

23. United Nations Economic Commission for Latin America, "La Pobreza y la satisfacción de necesidades básicas en el Istmo Centroamericano (Avances de una investigación regional)," CEPAL/MEX/SEM.4/12, March 1981, Mexico City, mimeo, Table 7, 23. Data for Nicaragua may be substantially different since the country's 1979 revolution.

24. Don Paarlberg, Peter M. Cody, and Ronald J. Ivey, "Agrarian Reform in El Salvador," report presented to the U.S. Agency for International Development, Checchi and Company, Washington, D.C., December 1981, 96.

25. Marc J. Dourojeanni, *Renewable Natural Resources of Latin America and the Caribbean: Situation and Trends* (Washington, D.C.: World Wildlife Fund-U.S., 1980), 400–404; also see United Nations Economic Commission for Latin America, "Energy Resources in the Caribbean Development and Cooperation Committee Member Countries" (Kingston, Jamaica, 28 May 1980), E/CEPA/CDCC/65.

26. Howard J. Wiarda and Michael J. Kryzanek, *The Dominican Republic: A Caribbean Crucible* (Boulder, Colo.: Westview Press, 1982), 118–120.

27. Don Hinrichsen, "Energy Resources in the Wider Caribbean," *Ambio*, 1981, vol. 10, no. 6: 332–334; Neil Belsen, "Agriculturally-Based Energy Alternatives for the Caribbean Basin," unpublished paper, University of Maryland, May 1984.

28. Jorge F. Perez-Lopez, "Nuclear Power in Cuba: Opportunities and Challenges," *Orbis: A Journal of World Affairs*, 1982, vol. 26, no. 2: 495–516.

29. "Bahamas to Protect Its Forest Resources," *IDB News,* May 1984: 1.

30. Don Hinrichsen, "Energy Resources," 332–334.

31. Theodore H. Moran, "The International Political Economy of Cuban Nickel Development," in Cole Blasier and Carmelo Mesa-Lago (eds.), *Cuba in the World* (Pittsburgh: University of Pittsburgh Press, 1979) 257–272.

32. Mancur Olson, Jr., "Rapid Growth as a Destabilizing Force," *Journal of Economic History 23,* 1963: 529–552.

33. Lewis Feuer, *The Conflict of Generations: The Character and Significance of Student Movements* (New York: Basic Books, 1969).

34. Richard A. Easterlin, *Birth and Fortune: The Impact of Numbers on Personal Welfare* (New York: Basic Books, 1980).

35. Other factors related to resource depletion and consequent instability include export demands, technological changes, and unequal access to resources. Robert Repetto and Thomas Holmes, "The Role of Population in Resource Depletion in Developing Countries," *Population and Development Review* 9, December 1983, no. 4: 624.

36. William H. Durham, *Scarcity and Survival in Central America: Ecological Origins of the Soccer War,* supra no. 19.

37. Linda S. Peterson, U.S. Bureau of the Census, "Central American Refugee Flows: 1978–83," mimeo., January 11, 1984, 6–9.

38. The Futures Group, *Central America: The Effects of Population on Economic and Social Development* (Washington, D.C., 1983), Tables 9 and 12, 11, 14.

39. *Ibid.* Tables 14, 16.

40. Alan L. Otten, "Population Explosion is a Threat to Stability of Central America," *Wall Street Journal,* February 17, 1984, 1, 12.

41. For an elaboration of several of these proposals, see Robert Pastor, *U.S. Foreign Investment and Latin America: The Impact on Employment* (Buenos Aires: Institute for Latin American Integration, 1984).

42. Luther Miller, "Linking Tourism and Agriculture to Create Jobs and Reduce Migration in the Caribbean," in Robert Pastor (ed.), *Migration and Development in the Caribbean: The Unexplored Connection* (Boulder, Colo.: Westview Press, 1985), Ch. 13.

43. Statement of Peter S. Thacher and Robert Wasserstrom before the Subcommittee on Western Hemisphere Affairs of the House Foreign Affairs Committee, February 23, 1984, 13.

44. See, for example, Amos A. Jordan and William J. Taylor, Jr., *American National Security: Policy and Process,* Chapter 14: "Economic Challenges to National Security" (Baltimore: The Johns Hopkins University Press, 1981); also Council on International Economic Policy, *Special Report: Critical Imported Materials* (Washington, D.C.: Executive Office of the President, December 1974).

CHAPTER 10

The Alliances
in Retrospect

WALTER LaFEBER

————————————————————*Editors' Preface*————————————————————

This chapter is about U.S. policy. It is a discouraging portrait
of how U.S. economic and security concerns have contributed
to deceptively large economic growth and to environmental
devastation—both at the expense of already impoverished
peasants. Behind Walter LaFeber's shrewd analysis of these
policies lie controversies over the development of resources—
anchovies and oil in Peru, cattle and forests in Central
America, rice cultivation in Colombia, Salvadoran dependency on coffee exports.

To LaFeber, current troubles in Latin America reflect years of
U.S. policy obsession with stability at the expense of balanced
growth and production at the expense of reform. Long before
Ronald Reagan took up the reins of government, the United
States funded and backed unwise investments, toppled "uncoop-
erative" governments, and even encouraged the flight of
indigenous capital—some of it into the private Miami bank accounts of Latin officials. The U.S. policies in question were not a
series of hapless well-intentioned mistakes, but a calculated, consistent approach in defense of perceived national interests.

This chapter raises more sharply than any other in *Bordering
on Trouble* the question: What *are* the real interests of the United
States in Latin America? Was it in the U.S. interest to protect

what LaFeber calls the "narrow interests" of a U.S. oil company in Peru, when doing so drove Peru into the Soviet Union's embrace? Can one reconcile the interests of the CIA and the Pentagon in oil—in Venezuela and Peru—with the need of those countries to increase food production? The experience of the Alliance seems to say that U.S. security interests—as perceived through seven U.S. administrations—are not identical with Latin American economic interests. Yet, throughout all those years, U.S. corporations have been making money in Latin countries. Is *that* the U.S. interest?

Sorting out these questions, LaFeber makes it clear why donor countries such as the United States so often prefer giving bilateral to multilateral assistance and loans. To be sure, it is simpler to deal with one nation at a time. But bilateral assistance is preferred over multilateral mainly because it is so much easier to attach political strings to it. LaFeber cites various instances when U.S. aid was used as a club to achieve other policy goals. Lyndon Johnson used aid as a leverage against President Goulart in Brazil. John F. Kennedy used it as a weapon against Belaunde in Peru. Jimmy Carter tried to manipulate internal politics and manage civil strife in El Salvador and Guatemala. President Reagan dangles financial relief before Mexico in the hopes of reducing Mexican enthusiasm for participation in the Central American Contadora peace negotiations. In contrast, the pluralistic base of multinational agencies makes it more difficult even for large donor states to manipulate agency programs for particular political ends.

T

WO, NOT one, Alliances for Progress developed in the 1960s. The first Alliance aimed at massive development of Latin American resources—"a vast cooperative effort," in President John F. Kennedy's words of March 13, 1961, "unparalleled in magnitude and nobility of purpose, to satisfy the basic needs of the American people for homes, work and land, health and schools."[1]

The heart of the U.S. commitment to this first Alliance, pledged at a Special Meeting of the Inter-American Economic and Social Council, held in Punta del Este, Uruguay, in August 1961, was a contribution of $20 billion from North American sources over ten years; Latin Americans were to contribute $80 billion of their own. The goal was an annual 5 percent growth in Latin America's gross national product (GNP). The Alliance, as top U.S. official Walt Whitman Rostow phrased it, aimed at nothing less than a "democratic revolution" based on an expanded middle class. By increasing the size and domestic political power of Latin America's middle class, the Kennedy administration hoped to avoid violent, especially left-wing, revolutions. In the Punta del Este Charter, all Latin American governments (except Fidel Castro's Cuba, which refused to sign), pledged themselves to "the social reforms necessary to permit a fair distribution of the fruits of economic and social progress." U.S. officials took those words to mean that the Latin Americans would ensure more equitable distribution of the projected new wealth and services.

The second "Alliance" was formed more quietly and was initially camouflaged by the grandiose objectives of the first. Its objective was political stability—immensely important to U.S. officials after Castro's rise to power in 1959 and Soviet Premier Nikita Khrushchev's famous speech of January 6, 1961. Delivered just before Kennedy's inauguration, Khrushchev's address declared that Third World wars of "liberation" were unavoidable and that Cuba's revolution "is not only repulsing the onslaught of the imperialists; it is spreading, signifying a new and higher stage of the national liberation struggle." The new president reacted strongly, reading portions of the speech to the National Security Council.[2] He also attempted to overthrow Castro at the Bay of Pigs in April 1961, just a month after outlining the Alliance for Progress.

After the Bay of Pigs fiasco, the second Alliance quickly received higher priority than the first. The first Alliance, eclipsed by the second, failed to reform and redistribute wealth. But the second Alliance also failed to create political stability and expunge radicalism. Washington officials' decisions to favor

339

short-term security over long-term resource development doomed the Alliance and undercut stability. In parts of Latin America, left-wing revolutionaries emerged from the debris of Kennedy's hopes. Their rise led Chilean dictator General Augusto Pinochet, in 1975, to condemn Kennedy for "opening a wide breach for the penetration of demagogic Marxism" in the hemisphere.[3] It was Pinochet himself who represented a typical result of the Alliance: a right-wing ruler wielding military and economic power to encourage growth and new wealth, but not rational development and more equitable distribution.

The contradictions between the two Alliances were noted early on. In 1962, economist Robert Heilbroner wrote in *Commentary* that "the process called 'economic development' is not primarily economic at all." The major handicaps to Latin American development, he argued, were "the cramping and crippling inhabitations of obsolete social institutions and reactionary social classes." Development, Heilbroner said, amounts to more than "economic growth within a given social structure." *Modernization* of that structure is needed.[4] That view, however, did not shape Kennedy's program. U.S. officials, one White House Latin American hand later recalled, "hastily pulled back when pressure for structural change threatened to produce civil conflict." (Nor did administration experts zero in on pervasive resource mismanagement or on the economic, social, and political costs of mismanagement.) The Kennedy administration, this White House official noted, was "not intellectually prepared for social turbulence," in part because "many had been lulled by Walt Rostow's model of the 'stages of economic growth' into seeing development as a bland and evolutionary process."[5]

Rostow, in fact, heavily influenced Kennedy and the whole plan. In the early 1950s, he and his Massachusetts Institute of Technology colleagues began publishing attention-getting analyses on development in the newly emerging nations. Rostow believed he had discovered an alternative to Marx: an "iron law of economic growth" (as one observer termed it) that allowed nations to evolve in prosperous, highly self-sufficient, and equitable societies without enduring bloody class revolution. When John Kennedy used the term "revolution" (as he frequently did) he meant Rostow's, not Marx's, version.[6]

The contradiction between the first Alliance's economic development and the second's quest for political stability was further blurred by Kennedy's tendency to use the wrong history as a guide and the wrong countries and leaders as models. The intellectual godfathers of the economic development plan included such key liberal Latin American leaders as Luis Muñoz Marin of Puerto Rico, Jose Figueres of Costa Rica, and Romula Betancourt of Venezuela. Kennedy and his advisors consulted closely with those leaders, but not one came from a nation facing obstacles to equitable resource development common to the rest of the region. Puerto Rico was formally integrated into the U.S. economy. Costa Rica had Latin America's most solid democratic tradition and one of the region's most equitable land distribution systems. Venezuela's oil wealth greased the political friction that resulted from, and sometimes prevented, fundamental economic reform.[7]

Nor was North American experience relevant. Rostow based his "stages of growth" model largely on U.S. and Western European history. But, unlike most Latin Americans, during the nineteenth and twentieth centuries North Americans had worked a richly endowed and seemingly limitless frontier; encountered few class-rigid political structures; feared no large, institutionalized military force; and inherited in 1776 a remarkable set of democratic institutions that provided a means for the peaceful settlement of arguments over resources. Nothing in the experiences they cited prepared Kennedy administration officials for the contradictions between rapid economic growth, which reached most Latin Americans as a meager trickle, and political stability. These unresolved contradictions explain perhaps the most important statistic of the 1960s Alliance: of each $100 increase in Latin American per capita income, only $2 went to the poorest fifth of the population.[8]

LATIN AMERICAN RESOURCES: MATERIAL AND HUMAN

That 20 percent was either the peasant population or the mushrooming urban poor who had recently left the land. In much of Latin America, these *campesinos* lived barely above the level of survival, yet belonged to the economic sector whose resources

341

were not merely the foundation of the Southern Hemisphere's economy, but in most countries the superstructure as well. Kennedy's Alliance barely touched this vast underclass. By 1965–1966, agricultural production of Latin American food and fiber was 5 to 10 percent per capita lower than before World War II. Only in Central America, Mexico, and Venezuela was per capita output substantially higher. The added income went primarily to the wealthy classes, despite a greater national capacity to distribute the income more fairly. Overall, between 1957 and 1967, Latin America's total food output increased by less than one-tenth of 1 percent per capita.[9]

As a result, many nations that previously exported grains diverted funds from other projects to buy imported food. In 1965, Peru spent $90 million on imported food, Venezuela more than $100 million, and Brazil $200 million. By one 1969 estimate, Latin America's agricultural output would have to increase by 24 percent by 1999 merely to keep pace with population growth (which, in some areas, and especially in Central America and the Caribbean, ran over 3.2 percent annually). These figures did not include badly needed earnings from food exports. The Alliance, however, gave no hope that the Latin American economy could so expand. Reforms and capital that might have increased rural agricultural output were conspicuous by their absence. Political impediments hindered reform, but the region's production also remained low for lack of chemical fertilizers, pesticides, and new high-yielding seeds. Latin American farms were among the world's most underfertilized; farmers used about one-tenth as much fertilizer per cultivated acre as those in Europe and North America. The Alliance never broke through the reflexive habits of Latin American governments bent upon allocating financial resources almost entirely to land-owning oligarchs.[10]

During the post-1945 years (especially the late 1960s), Latin American agriculture diversified into new export crops such as cotton, and the cultivation of such traditional crops as coffee and wheat was modernized. These changes, however, usually spelled disaster for most peasants. In 1960, about 47 percent of Latin America's workforce engaged in agriculture. Another 10 percent produced goods or services for the agricultural sector. Despite agriculture's concentration and mechanization, the number of Latin Americans living in rural areas grew at about 1.6 percent annually during the 1960s. Contrast this to the United States, where the rural population had been decreasing steadily since the nation's founding. In most of Latin America, the *campesinos* had little hope of owning their own land. *Campesinos* were too poor, credit was unavailable, many lacked necessary skills, and most productive land was already occupied. Laws demanding work contracts to protect rural labor were seldom enforced. In about two-thirds of the region, the laborers were largely unorganized and sometimes were suppressed. Venezuela, Bolivia, Mexico, Brazil, and Chile were the exceptions, but even there the degree of protection and organization varied.

Many peasants consequently sought refuge in cities; during the 1960s, the Latin American urban population grew at an astonishing 4.5 to 5 percent annually. In areas where industrialized plantation (*latifundia*) agriculture conditioned the cost, use, availability, and development of land, social and economic opportunities for most peasants disappeared. This type of agriculture, the prevailing system of land tenure, and the rapid population growth led to economic stress and high rates of rural emigration. Land misuse also resulted: estates were used for export crops or not cultivated at all, and land-poor peasants had no alternative but to scratch out livings on marginal plots—or become low-wage laborers.[11]

Chaotic urbanization was typical of nations with unequal land distribution. (In Chile, Peru, Bolivia, and Mexico, *minifundia* (small farms) represent 60 to 80 percent of all farms, but only 0.7 to 4 percent of the nation's agricultural land. *Latifundia* represent 0.5 to 2 percent of all farms but 75 to 95 percent of the total agricultural area). Migrants found few jobs in the cities: up to six urban laborers sought each new industrial job. Soon, slums overcrowded with new arrivals comprised more than one-third of Caracas's population, one-quarter of Lima's, and as much as 70 percent of some provincial cities. Such figures revealed another weakness in Kennedy's Alliance: the absence of regional planning. As the region's urban population grew from about 60 million in 1950 to 115 million in 1965 (or from 40 percent of the total population to 50 percent), regional and urban planning remained primitive at best.[12]

The evolving development system aimed at growth for growth's sake, not at a balanced development of human and material resources to provide widespread personal security; *campesinos* were to provide cheap labor. In Western development, agriculture provided the foundation (with excess foodstuffs, minerals, and agrarian purchasing power) for new industry, but then agriculture suffered. In the United States, both the market and the native elite determined that industry was more important than agriculture during the 1870 to 1920 era.[13] This same change occurred in parts of Latin America during the 1950s and 1960s. There was, however, a crucial difference: in the United States, agriculture generated large export earnings and triggered capital formation for the entire economy, but it also developed powerful interest groups that became more potent politically even as they became relatively less important economically. Rural interest groups ensured that some of the new industrial wealth was converted into communications, dams, electrification, credit systems, and extension services for rural areas.[14] In Latin America, however, no return flow of wealth and services occurred. The elites who controlled most agricultural sectors either kept the wealth themselves or channeled it into the cities where many of them lived. The *campesinos* thus watched resources flow out without hope for new jobs or living improvements.[15] Land and water resources benefitted from this process no more than did human resources.

The rural-to-urban exodus formed part of a larger problem: a Latin American population growth rate that reached 3 percent a year (the comparable figure in 1900 had been 1.8 percent) and threatened a doubling of population every twenty-three years. No major Latin American leader had the courage to touch the population problem until Colombia's President Alberto Lleras Camargo warned in 1960 that unless the increase was brought under control it would become "unmanageable." But he went no further, nor did the 1961 Punta del Este Charter. President Eduardo Frei attacked the problem in the mid-1960s when his government integrated family planning into Chile's national health program; then Lyndon Johnson addressed the population challenge in his 1965 State of the Union address. Finally, despite intense Vatican resistance, Roman Catholic leaders in Latin

344

America began discussing new ways to control population increase, paving the way for Peru, Venezuela, and Honduras to establish pilot programs for family planning. But meanwhile the U.S. Agency for International Development (AID) (which administered the Alliance for Progress in the United States), quietly told southern nations that it would do little about this pressing issue. In 1968, AID gave the entire region only $25 million for technical, financial, and commodity assistance related to population problems.[16]

The United States had reason to keep a low profile. If the United States publicized the population problem, it could, according to a memo to President Johnson, "unite strange bedfellows: the Church which is opposed for doctrinal reasons; the Nationalists who measure national prestige and power by size of population; the Communists who want social unrest to continue." It recommended that the United States work on population problems "quietly but rigorously (through AID and private groups)," but outside the limelight.[17]

Latin Americans who were willing to tackle the problem were assisted by multinational agencies (especially the United Nations) and some crucial but quietly-given U.S. encouragement and funds. In yet another irony, however, the United States, despite doing little, partially realized its goals in population management. The elites' interest in stability dictated lower birth rates, especially in rural areas, and the United States helped. On few other issues did Latin American initiative and successful north-south cooperation occur. This overall failure came about because the first Alliance's reformist goals posed too great a threat to the overriding objective of the second: stability.

THE U.S. APPROACH: BUREAUCRACIES
AND AN UNUSABLE PAST

The need for fundamental change in developing resources and the concomitant need to avoid revolutionary political change framed the choices that confronted the Kennedy and Johnson administrations. The dilemmas that resulted appeared quickly in perhaps the most basic and important of all the problems Alliance officials had to tackle: land reform.

345

The original Punta del Este Charter pledged the signatories to encourage "programs of comprehensive agrarian reform . . . with the help of timely and adequate credit, technical assistance, and facilities for marketing and distribution of products."[18] But the landed elites who dominated Latin American politics were hardly inclined to fulfill a pledge that was tantamount to economic and political suicide. The United States, for its part, refused to push or take any significant step toward fulfilling the pledge.

The key decision in Washington occurred immediately; Congress provided no money for land reform in Alliance funding.[19] The remaining alternative was the Inter-American Development Bank (IDB), formed in 1958 despite the apprehension of President Dwight Eisenhower who feared the IDB would usurp the funding of private investors. The bank provided government monies to supplement inadequate private sources for development projects. In 1962, the Kennedy administration told the IDB that individual countries must "bear the entire cost of land purchase" in agrarian reform projects. The IDB could then provide funds for credit, fertilizers, and roads. However, this decision blocked reform: the new infusion of U.S. and IDB funds was simply pocketed by the few already controlling the land.[20]

This fateful stance by the Kennedy administration had deep historical roots. The United States had no experience redistributing privately-owned lands, only in dividing a frontier from which Native Americans were forcibly removed. The experience of 1960s officials, moreover, had often been with highly capitalized and productive agribusiness. And the one major agricultural complex they had restored, in Western Europe, only had to be restored, not created or fundamentally reformed.

Those who administered Kennedy's Alliance were, in a sense, victims of the European success. Lincoln Gordon served on early Kennedy task forces that drew up the Alliance, then became U.S. ambassador to Brazil and, in 1966, rose to assistant secretary of state for Inter-American Affairs. He and Donald Palmer—after 1966, Gordon's deputy in the Department of State—had been deeply involved in the Marshall Plan. They, not unnaturally, used that experience to argue against such production disincentives as price controls or limited credit in Alliance planning. But such measures, although successful in Europe, merely helped Latin America's largest landowners. Gordon showed little enthusiasm for reforms that might cause political or social problems or that could not instantly boost aggregate production. Under Gordon and Palmer, AID was preoccupied, if not obsessed, with immediate results, not long-term reforms.[21] Not for the last time, the Marshall Plan experience was thoughtlessly applied to Third-World development.

As early as 1969, experts testifying before a Senate Foreign Relations subcommittee warned against viewing the Latin American farm problem "as one of mere shortage of food." It would be unwise, they said, "to increase food production through improved technology" without paying sufficient attention to land distribution. These agricultural specialists noted that the original Alliance Charter stressed institutional reforms in rural Latin America, but "the emphasis has more recently shifted to modernization of agriculture without special concern for structural change."[22]

In truth, the Alliance for Progress was trapped. Latin Americans needed farm productivity to curb rising food imports, provide foreign exchange, finance development programs, stop capital flight, and fight inflation. These were the immediate issues, as was urban food scarcity, which could trigger urban riots. In the end, such vital short-term problems so dominated official attention that the need for institutional and political reform was ignored.

Kennedy and Johnson administration officials repeatedly argued that U.S. funds did not have to be spent on land redistribution because individual Latin American countries could use regular, lawful expropriation and long-term reimbursement in local currency. But this response ignored the reluctance of those nations to pass expropriation measures, and it kept the Kennedy and Johnson administrations from pushing for reform. Then too, U.S. officials and business executives had long worked closely with conservative Latin American elites, and North Americans opposed on principle measures that endangered private property ownership. Washington officials pushed for tax reforms in Alliance programs, but not for fundamental land reform. Tax reforms were a North American tradition, while land reform was an alien, even dangerous, idea.[23]

Kennedy's emphasis on social progress was explicit at Punta del Este, but those who attended that meeting also agreed that the Alliance should aim at a per capita annual growth rate of 2.5 percent (or 5.5 percent annual growth minus the roughly 3 percent population increase in Latin America).[24] Soon, however, the Alliance successes seemed to be measured largely in terms of growth rates—which supposedly would benefit everyone. Between 1961 and 1967, the average annual growth rate of Latin American GNP hovered at or below 2 percent. In 1968, however, it hit the target of 2.5 percent.[25] By that time, few still claimed that aggregate growth rates, no matter how impressive, triggered reform and democracy. During the 1960s, military rulers overthrew seventeen Latin American governments: more uniformed dictatorships existed in 1970 than in 1960, and none but the Peruvian military instituted widespread populist-type reforms. At first, Kennedy refused to recognize the military regimes in Peru (1962) and Honduras (1963), but not long afterwards he came to terms with the Peruvian regime. Lyndon Johnson then began recognizing any conservative government that gained power, regardless of the tactics it used. The United States' emphasis on aggregate growth, obviously, eclipsed its concerns for reforms.

These premises, then, shaped Alliance policy: the use of North American and Latin American models (such as Costa Rica) that were the exception rather than the rule; the U.S. refusal to encourage expropriation of private property on a national scale; the IDB's failure (largely because of U.S. pressures) to be more active in land redistribution; and an emphasis on production rather than reform. Some of these were more implicit than explicit in U.S. policy, but all had historical roots in the North American experience; for guidance, or misguidance, the United States repeatedly turned to its own past.

The Alliance was also sculpted by its early bureaucratic experiences. Initially, either the Organization of American States (OAS) or the United Nations Economic Commission of Latin America (ECLA) was to dispense the aid. But the United States was disenchanted with the slow, cumbersome machinery of the OAS (in which, moreover, North Americans had only one vote), and ECLA was strongly influenced by economist Raul Prebisch, who blamed dependence on larger industrialized nations for much Latin American underdevelopment. Prebisch concluded that

Latin Americans had to find their own solutions (albeit with U.S. cooperation). With Washington rejecting both agencies, Alliance decision-making came from the United States Agency for International Development (AID). Kennedy had established AID in 1961 to unify all foreign aid programs, but its real importance was to give the United States near-total control over Alliance policy. AID funds were channeled through the IDB, which the United States controlled with its veto power. Supplemental funding came from the Export-Import Bank (a U.S. institution funded by Congress), or the World Bank (which North Americans also controlled through their veto power). The United States had the power of the purse.

A group called the Committee of Nine distributed Alliance funds. The 1961 Charter established the Committee (originally comprised of two North Americans, two Central Americans, a Cuban, and four South Americans) to coordinate and evaluate the external aid and national reform elements of the Alliance. But the larger nations, led by the United States, kept any real decision-making power to themselves. The Nine could recommend but never enforce, and it had no independent source of funds. By 1963, the United States so dominated the program that an evaluation team recommended a new Interamerican Committee of the Alliance for Progress (CIAP) to infuse Latin American views into Alliance plans. But the United States fought CIAP until the group possessed mere review powers. By 1966, the Committee of Nine had resigned and CIAP had proved ineffective in making the Alliance more multilateral. The United States tended to give money on terms dictated by its own short-run political and economic needs, not recipients' long-term needs. But the largest Latin American nations, especially Argentina and Brazil, also fought any multilateral agency wishing to oversee the funds; they believed they would fare better dealing with the United States one-on-one. The United States could thus play the game of divide-and-conquer. The Latin Americans had no institutional channel for responding jointly to Washington pressures. Decisions about the allocation of Alliance funds came not from an "Alliance" for Progress—for no such decision-making alliance existed—but from Washington officials after they consulted, usually bilaterally, with Latin American nations.

Meanwhile, the AID administrator for Latin America—
Teodoro Moscoso, a gifted politician who guided the post-1945
industrial development of his native Puerto Rico through "Operation Bootstrap," a program that used tax incentives to bring in
U.S. capital investment—had to work with cautious State Department professionals, who had learned to cooperate with Latin
American elites. To carry out a reform program through the State
Department, one frustrated Kennedy administration official declared in 1961, "is like performing an appendix operation on a
man carrying a piano upstairs."[26] Moscoso fought battles with
other AID and Treasury Department officials who thought reform
could be advanced by a Madison Avenue agency that could "sell"
the Alliance to the Latins. Moscoso killed that idea, but once
complained to Kennedy that "I have no secretaries, I have an
agency spread all over town, and the bureaucracy is getting me
down."[27]

When Lyndon Johnson assumed the presidency in November
1963, he stopped bureaucratic infighting by appointing as head of
AID, Thomas Mann, the State Department's top Latin American
desk officer and the president's White House advisor on the
Western Hemisphere.[28] An old Texas friend of Johnson's, Mann
was tough, politically adept, and experienced in Latin America
and Washington. He had also warned the Eisenhower Cabinet in
1959 that a program such as the Alliance would fail because it
would change few structures and raise many expectations. He
had little faith that U.S.-initiated reforms could either cleanse
Latin American political processes or accelerate resource development equitably. And, within months, Mann had switched the
program's priorities. Business, not government, would take the
lead in U.S.assisted development efforts. To encourage private
investment, the administration would publicly recognize military juntas even if they overthrew democratic governments.[29]
The trend that had vaguely appeared in the first months of
Kennedy's Alliance was now official policy—an all-out emphasis
on stability and aggregate production. Top administration officials expressed no concern about the contradiction between
equitable growth and U.S. economic and political goals. Population growth and resource management, though increasingly
critical to Latin America's future and U.S. security interests,
were ignored.

As Vietnam preoccupied and then obsessed Johnson, the scant attention he gave to Latin America was shaped by what Ralph Dungan, a close White House advisor and later U.S. ambassador to Chile, describes as "a romantic Tex-Mex view of Latin America." According to Dungan, Johnson's idea that he "knew" the Southern Hemisphere because he knew something about Mexico "really distorted his view of Latin American relations."[30] If Dungan's assessment is correct—and others agree with it—Johnson's use of the Mexican prism was like Moscoso's use of Puerto Rico's experience or the early Kennedy advisors projecting Venezuelan development possibilities over the rest of South America. Mexico had already experienced its revolution (one that Lyndon Johnson doubtless would have condemned had he been a public figure in 1914 or 1927), and it had a corrupt, but stable, efficient, one-party system that Johnson did not publicly condone but privately understood. With its historic land-reform program and a nationalized oil industry, Mexico offered an illusion of revolution and reform quite compatible with political stability.

PAYING OFF THE DEBT

Initial results of Alliance decision-making demonstrated how easily development funds could be diverted. More than half the Alliance funds in 1962–1963 were used to service Latin America's growing foreign debt instead of developing resources. Monies were invested in productive enterprises by the mid-1960s, but the dominant syndrome during the so-called "Decade of Development" was out-of-control indebtedness. Unfortunately, debts were not incurred to increase production but to pay off earlier debt or enrich overseas bank accounts. In 1950, the cumulative external public debt of the nineteen Latin American republics was $2.2 billion; in 1960, $6.6 billion; in 1962, $8.9 billion; and by 1970, $19.3 billion. The Alliance was stymied partly because by the end of the decade "about the only thing the Latin American countries had to show" for the Alliance effort "was an enormous foreign debt."[31] Only two nations, Argentina and Venezuela, maintained a surplus.

The debt sucked away domestic resources. The external public debt of the nineteen nations rose from 5.7 percent of their GNP in 1950 to 8.5 percent in 1960 to 10.7 percent in 1965, then doubled to about 20 percent in 1970. The Alliance loans became, as one close observer put it, "addictive" rather than curative drugs.[32] Domestic sources increasingly paid public and private debts: 25 percent of Latin America's export income paid profits and interest to foreign investors and lenders in 1959; in 1968, 36 percent did. By 1970, new lending could no longer cover payments on past lending. Johnson termed the 1960 to 1967 years "the greatest period of forward movement, progress, and fruitful change," but Latin America paid $13 billion to developed nations for debts and profits in those seven years, compared with $14 billion in the previous fourteen years. Had a comparable amount been used to import the technology and services peasants needed to produce staple foodstuffs, import volume could have risen over 20 percent.[33]

U.S. funds also supported other nonproductive endeavors, especially the military, which was central to the second Alliance's goal of maintaining stability. From the start, the Kennedy administration was intensely concerned with the region's security problems. One result was the removal of police training for Latin American forces from the auspices of the Central Intelligence Agency to the direction of AID. With State Department help, AID trained and armed internal security forces. In several nations, especially Colombia and Venezuela, these forces helped destroy guerrillas who threatened legitimate governments. In the other nations, however, "the counterinsurgency business was a great blind spot on the New Frontier." In the words of Kennedy's best-known biographer, "In our concern with protecting the external processes of democracy, we were too far removed from what the thugs were doing behind the screen."[34]

Funds flowed into so-called civic action programs, where native military (whose officers were often U.S.-trained) worked on grass-roots community and infrastructure projects. These public works, agriculture, and health projects aimed, in the words of a standard study, "to improve the standing of the military forces with the population."[35] The results were hardly beneficial. Civil action units filled civilian jobs needed by unemployed *campesinos*; some of their members turned out to be counterinsurgency agents more concerned with ferreting out dissenters than with developing the community. The $3.3 million of

U.S. funds devoted to civic action in fiscal year (FY) 1962 had more than tripled by FY 1964; indigenous input into the program was several times that amount. Meanwhile, even where civic action scored successes (notably in Peru, Colombia, Venezuela, and Nicaragua), the effort was more to preserve institutions by force than to solve national resource problems.[36]

Thus did the Alliance founder first on the rock of "stability," then on the shoals of nonproductive debt repayments. The last hope for real progress appeared to be the private sector.

LYNDON JOHNSON AND THE FAILURE
OF THE MARKETPLACE

During the Alliance's first two years, Kennedy stressed government programs over private enterprise. His erratic recognition policy—recognizing some right-wing takeovers, as in the Dominican Republic, but refusing to accept others, as in Peru and Honduras—made investors wary, so private enterprise was initially a small part of the Alliance. A CIA report to the White House in April 1964 even admitted that the "climate for private enterprise has taken a sharply adverse turn."[37]

Thomas Mann tried to warm the climate both with private assurances and public policies. But his efforts again demonstrated how stability preceded reform in the Johnson administration's view. In 1965, for example, Chile's and Peru's democratically elected presidents pleaded with the United States to create a reserve fund to guarantee Latin American agrarian reform bonds. Johnson and Mann rejected the proposal,[38] deciding instead to jawbone private U.S. investors into taking their development capital south. Led by Chase Manhattan Bank chairman David Rockefeller (whose family long had held large interests in the region), by Rockefeller's Council for Latin America (composed of 224 large U.S. corporations), and by such groups as ADELA (the Atlantic Community Development Group for Latin America, chartered in Luxembourg in 1964 and owned by more than 130 multinational firms), private capital began to flow southward. Brazil's new military regime, which assured tranquility through repression, undoubtedly smoothed the way. Indeed, Mann's announced policy changes and the Brazilian generals' cooperation with that policy helped reroute the Alliance's course. Soon ADELA alone was pumping more than $20 million into such projects as Brazilian pulp and paper, Argentine petrochemicals, and Ecuadorean glass manufacturing—three of some twenty-seven major investments between 1964 and 1966.[39]

Unfortunately, several defects marred the private sector's efforts. First, the investments occurred unevenly. Of the total $16 billion invested in Latin America in 1966, one-third was in Venezuela (almost entirely related to oil). Argentina and Brazil together received one-third, and all other nations divided the remaining third. Second, even though many private ventures eventually profited, by 1968 the annual average return on U.S. investments in Latin America reached 12.4 percent—relatively little was reinvested in the region. Between 1960 and 1968, total earnings of North American direct investments in the region were $9.9 billion, according to the U.S. Department of Commerce, but at least $7.7 billion returned to the United States. Meanwhile, an apparently unrelated—but important— problem was that much indigenous capital left the region. While the net outflow of Latin American capital amounted to about $5 billion between 1946 and 1962, $1 billion left the region in 1961– 1962 alone.[40]

A SHAKY ALLIANCE: MISSING LINKS OF SOCIAL AND POLITICAL REFORM

By 1966, the Alliance was stumbling. The Johnson administration, beset by Vietnam and domestic unrest, searched for inexpensive methods to accelerate Latin American growth. Policies for structural reform (especially in agriculture) aimed at furthering social and political equity had disappeared. The administration finally decided that the Latin American Free Trade Area (LAFTA) and the Central American Common Market (CACM) (which supported larger markets and removed customs barriers) were natural complements to the Johnson-Mann emphasis on private investment. Equally significant, the approach muted the explosive question of redistribution by promising a bigger pie with profits for everyone and arguing that capitalist competition (not political interest groups) could best generate and distribute wealth. The five-member CACM had already generated spectacular growth. The nine-member LAFTA had lower growth rates, but in early 1967 pledged with CACM to remove all tariff barriers within Latin America by 1980.[41]

Committed to attend a Western Hemisphere summit meeting at Punta del Este in early 1967, Johnson's priorities for discussion were, according to one of his briefing papers, "Latin American economic integration and industrial development," then "Multinational action for infrastructure projects," and, third, "Measures to improve international trade conditions in Latin America." Only after discussing those problems did he and his advisors want to consider agricultural and educational-scientific developments.[42] Rostow, now Johnson's national security advisor, told the president that while agriculture and the "distorted" education system required answers, the need for new industrialization could be answered immediately by "the integration of Latin America." Expanding the Latin American marketplace had become a policy goal in its own right, instead of an arena within which a policy might work. And the policy hinged on pushing back tariff and investment frontiers rather than developing human and natural resources.[43]

At Punta del Este, Johnson discovered that the answers were not as simple as Rostow made them sound. Johnson opened a long talk with Carlos Lleras Restrepo of Colombia with kind words about LAFTA only to have Lleras Restrepo respond that LAFTA was less important than Latin American access to U.S. markets. North American tariffs, the Colombian president charged, excluded his nation's cheaper products and so ruined the possibility of "a more rational division of American labor" to exploit efficiently the hemisphere's resources. Rostow and Secretary of State Dean Rusk tried to deflect Lleras Restrepo by returning to the subject of Latin American markets, but Lleras Restrepo demanded to know why the United States insisted on a widening of already competitive markets and then restricting access by establishing North American quotas.[44]

The Colombian president posed a fundamental question. He had been the key writer of his country's 1962 agrarian reform bill, and he now wanted the beneficiaries of that legislation to have access to the U.S. market, not merely to neighboring countries that produced similar products. That access required U.S. political decisions that Johnson preferred not to make in 1967. Lleras Restrepo also implied that he and other Latin American leaders could go no farther in bolstering consumption at home by socio-economic reforms to help the poor. This point was crucial. Now Lleras Restrepo saw the need to export Colombia's problems to the United States rather than handle them at home through redistributing resources and opportunities.

The high hopes for LAFTA and CACM had collapsed by 1970: nationalism poisoned discussions between countries; war, especially the 1969 conflict between Honduras and El Salvador nearly destroyed CACM; and inflation worsened in the western economies. Two other factors also stand out. First, the United States refused, even in the Kennedy Tariff Round, to open its market more widely to Southern Hemisphere goods. More important, the Latin American nations refused to increase significantly the purchasing power of their own poor at the possible expense of the elites.[45] Lifting customs barriers among the five Central American nations would, therefore, help the peasants little since they had little income with which to purchase CACM-generated products anyway.

The Alliance years taught few lessons more interesting than this. Johnson, Mann, and the Latin American leaders had exactly reversed the priorities that would encourage Latin American development. It was equitable resource development (especially among peasant populations) that would allow the common market to work, and not the common market that would lead to equitable resource development. Again, the Marshall Plan and European Common Market experiences were probably responsible for the error. In Western Europe, a political process that could promise (and produce) equitable results preceded the common market concept. In Latin America, Alliance officials and other leaders tried to turn the process upside down. They hoped that common market organizations, firmly controlled by elites who cared little about equitable development, might trigger painless reform. It never occurred.

Even more, LAFTA and CACM caused inequitable development not only within, but between, nations. In CACM, for example, El Salvador's cheap labor, concentrated capital resources, and rigorous work habits allowed the country to prosper within the common market, especially at the expense of less efficient Honduras. Five CACM governments had devised a plan to intervene when such an imbalance became obvious. But the oligarchs' opposition to government intervention proved insurmountable. Honduras consequently began discriminating against Salvadoran exports, both material and human. Political tension built until the brief but bloody war erupted in 1969 and destroyed most of the progress CACM had made during the development decade.[46] The United States might have helped avert that result, but chose not to.

In 1964, Thomas Mann hoped to circumvent tough political decisions by encouraging private enterprise, downplaying government involvement, accepting any government that promised stability (regardless of how that regime came to power or proposed to exploit its resources), and later, by allowing common markets to help allocate resources.[47] By 1969, it was painfully obvious that none of this had worked. The Spanish appellation, Alianza para Progreso, became the butt of jokes. Cynical Latin Americans noted that *para* ("for") is also the third person present of the verb *parar* ("to stop"), so "the Alliance Stops Progress."[48]

THE FRONTIER THESIS AND THE ALLIANCE

In 1969, a U.S. Senate-commissioned survey of the Alliance for Progress made the surprising observation that almost "two-thirds of the increased agricultural product in Latin America has come from pressing more land into production," not from redistributing or reinvigorating settled lands. The Senate report justifiably assumed that "this kind of expansion probably cannot continue for long," especially in hard-pressed Central America, where "in 5 to 10 years, given the current rates of population growth and migration, there will be no remaining frontier." Unused lands, the report concluded, echoing studies of the U.S. frontier's effect on North American life, could not "long provide an economically viable 'safety valve' " for the growing discontent.[49]

The tendency to resolve Alliance problems by finding fresh resources on new frontiers, rather than tackling the implacable political problems in the older areas, permeated policymaking in the 1960s. Many North and South Americans alike seemed obsessed with the idea of developing frontier areas as a solution to social and economic problems. The most influential U.S. journalist of the era, Walter Lippmann, upon taking his first extensive trip to Latin America (at the age of 76) in 1965, had this to say:

> The central task is to stir up and finance the South American equivalent of the opening of the West in North America. It is in the truest sense of the term an engineering problem—to build roads, to connect the great river systems of the Amazon, the Orinoco, and the La Plata, to build landing fields, to make the jungle lands habitable with modern refrigeration and modern science.[50]

Once again, the North American experience was to serve as the model for Latin American resource development; once again, the example misled. The American West belonged to a single nation when it was opened in the nineteenth century. Before then, when the West had more in common with Latin American frontiers, the problem had not been one of "engineering," but of politics and strife. The region first had to be unified and the competing factions disciplined, bought off, or—in the case of the Native Americans—annihilated and conquered before "engineering" began. Nevertheless, Walt Rostow used a similar historical perspective five months after Lippmann's column appeared. Johnson's close advisor proposed the largest power project in the world on the Paraguayan-Brazilian border, as a wedge to open Brazil's entire frontier to agricultural and industrial production. The costs would exceed $10 billion, a figure that gave pause even to the broad-thinking Lincoln Gordon. The United States would provide at least half the money, although domestic pressures had already crippled Alliance funding: "AID [Gordon observed] has been under heavy pressure to limit dollar local cost financing as a means of assisting the U.S. balance of payments effort." Gordon's objections were more fundamental: "One needs only to glance back at 'The Winning of the West' in our country to realize the long time-span which must be considered in assessing adequately the benefits of rolling back the frontier."[51] Gordon apparently was not certain that the pressing problems of Latin America allowed the necessary time.

Harvey Perloff, an economist intimately involved with Alliance planning in 1966–1967, shared Gordon's pessimism, but for slightly different reasons. The project demanded a quick payoff in production, Perloff argued, but also the political planning for resource development sorely needed for Latin American "new lands":

> A focus on agriculture provides an extremely useful base for decisions on the conservation, development, and use of land and water resources. In a poor country, it is difficult, if not impossible, to get adequate support for investment in natural resource surveys, research, education, and related elements unless it can be shown that such investment brings positive returns. Land development and conservation measures, resource surveys, and research are all enormously expensive. The scale, the form, and the timing of all such investments must be related directly to productive possibilities. . . . The problem is particularly great in the case of "new land" development where major capital investment may be needed for forest clearings, flood control, irrigation, drainage or desalination . . . as well as direct assistance for settlement in some cases.[52]

ALLIANCE WITH THE MILITARY IN BRAZIL

The country where "new land," adequate capital, and need for agrarian reform opened the greatest opportunities for the Alliance was *Brazil*. In many respects, Brazil became the test of how Washington officials chose between the Alliance for Progress—whose goal was to meet people's "basic needs" (Kennedy's phrase)—and the shadow Alliance that stressed stability over social change.

During the late 1950s, President Juscelino Kubitschek launched massive industrial and export programs that produced a 7 percent annual growth rate. His poorer countrymen benefitted little, however, because Kubitschek needed political support from the wealthy conservative landowners. Indeed, the poor began moving to the cities, while rural areas went without schools. When Jañio Quadros replaced Kubitschek in 1960, inflation and debt were also mounting. Quadros promised to help the poor, especially in the coffee-growing regions dominated by the large growers. In post-1946 Brazil, however, the president was caught between two competing—and irreconcilable—demands: he rose to power by making populist appeals to a growing electorate, but once in office found that his power to rule depended on negotiating effectively with the economic (especially corporate) elite.[53] After eight months as president, Quadros found these political problems so frustrating that he resigned.

João Goulart, Quadros's successor, continued Quadros's policies despite rampant inflation and a foreign debt that in 1962 absorbed 45 percent of Brazil's export earnings. In 1963, Kennedy injected nearly $400 million to buoy the economy and agreed with Goulart's plan to buy the U.S.-controlled American and Foreign Power Company, a target for anti-Yankee feelings. But Goulart's move to nationalize foreign-owned property and his rural policies won little business support in either the United States or Brazil. The president was trapped between Alliance-type reforms and Brazil's economic crisis that required dropping reform and imposing controls. As the nation's foreign creditors demanded repayment and consequent austerity inside Brazil, Goulart leaned toward his populist support, especially to a left-wing movement comprised of agrarian leaders, Roman Catholic Church officials, and intellectuals. Then, despite promises to Washington to curb inflation, Goulart tried to buy off the military and civil service with wage increases of 30 to 70 percent.

By early 1964, Goulart was obviously diverging from the Johnson-Mann policies. In January, the CIA told the White House that Goulart could not handle the crisis, "and he continues to draw primarily on leftist-nationalists for his political advice."[54] The Johnson administration promptly cut back assistance, and the Brazilian economy spun out of control. By March, Johnson's advisors noted that Brazil's net per capita income had dropped for the first time since the 1930s. The only good news from Washington's perspective was rising coffee prices (which could help Brazil repay debts) and "good" relations with the Brazilian military.[55] During discussions in early 1964 about Alliance spending in Brazil during FY 1965, AID concluded that Goulart was "an inept President, easily influenced by extreme leftist advisors and cronies . . . opportunistically searching to obtain political advantage from the economic and social discontent resulting from a stagnant economy" and decided not to expend further FY 1964 funds. Thus, the agency would "avoid rewarding incompetence and . . . maintain pressures for economic sanity."[56] In response, the Brazilian president held huge rallies and promised massive nationalization, voting rights for millions of rural illiterates, and a new rural social structure.

On March 31, 1964, however, the armed forces, with support from a threatened middle class, overthrew Goulart and inaugurated a twenty-year dictatorship. The United States knew the coup was coming, and Johnson ordered a U.S. naval task force (that included aircraft and helicopter carriers) to drop anchor off the Brazilian coast and await possible orders from U.S. Ambassador Lincoln Gordon. As Gordon later explained, "We feared the possibility of a civil war . . . and one side might need some outside help."[57] Washington officials probably did not consider Goulart that "one side." In May 1964, Gordon publicly compared the civilian government's overthrow to the Marshall Plan, the Berlin Blockade, the Korean War, and the Cuban missile crisis as "major turning points in world history in the middle of the 20th century." Later, analysts agreed that the overthrow had marked a turning point, though for different reasons: the creation of a centralized military-authoritarian state in Brazil simultaneously disciplined labor and opened a vast new frontier in the Amazon Basin for the formerly threatened capitalist classes.[58]

If the coup had proved a turning point, it was to guide the Alliance back toward "traditional" approaches to Latin America. The United States quickly pressured the new government of General Humberto Castelo Branco to reopen the American and Foreign Power Company settlement to give the foreign owners a better deal. (The Brazilian legislature rejected this, even though legislators faced arrest for opposing the army.) Castelo Branco soon bobbed like a Johnson puppet. His regime offered favorable terms to other North American-based power and mineral companies that Goulart had threatened to nationalize. In 1965, the generals imposed tough credit and wage policies that cut the previous year's 85 percent inflation rate in half; then the government issued new laws giving tax breaks to foreign investors. AID quickly relaxed its squeeze on funds and signed new contracts with U.S. corporations that insured them against expropriation, war, or currency incontrovertibility in Brazil. Castelo Branco killed Goulart's plans for a government monopoly over Brazil's minerals and opened the nation's extensive iron ore reserves to foreign investors. The U.S.-controlled Hanna Mining Company became one of the country's leading multinationals by developing not only iron ore but petrochemicals and bauxite as well. North

American and other foreign investment capital flooded the country as Brazilian industrial output shot to an average 10 percent increase for 1966–1969.[59]

The military, meanwhile, ruthlessly suppressed dissent, especially student, labor, and peasant groups. U.S. officials, however, paid more attention to Brazil's growing GNP and export earnings than to human rights violations. Ambassador Gordon even argued that the post-1964 regime in Brazil demonstrated that Latin American militaries existed not only to fight communists but to efficiently build national development projects—an echo of the sentiments expressed by John Kennedy just before he died. (Frustrated with incompetent civilian regimes, Kennedy had come to believe that military regimes might be a little more reactionary, but certainly more efficient.)[60] Theoretically, the uniformed officers could provide stability and sidestep the plague of politics so the technicians could speedily and economically administer their plans.

But the Brazilian example demonstrated once again that development inevitably involves political and ideological choices. The industrial and large agricultural export sectors soon received governmental favors and investment from Alliance sources and prospered at the expense of the rural area. While manufacturing output climbed, annual agricultural growth sank from 4.4 percent in 1961–1965 to 2.7 percent in 1966–1969; by 1969, per capita growth actually declined by 2.4 percent. New frontier lands fell into the hands of big ranchers and agribusiness. *Campesinos* were neglected or repressed. In the Northeast state of Pernambuco, a poor area of sharecroppers, landless peasants, and salaried sugar workers, more than 100 peasant leagues and unions appeared between 1961 and 1964, organized by Roman Catholic priests, communists, and liberal political leaders. After 1964, the military exiled or imprisoned key leaders, and the unions consequently offered only legal and medical aid to the peasants—not political advice.[61] Quadros's and Goulart's social reforms, especially minimum wage laws and agrarian reform, were smashed.

Both material and human resources suffered in the Northeast. A U.S.-financed study in the mid-1960s demonstrated that the region could annually produce its 900,000 tons of sugar at lower costs and on half the land if mechanization, irrigation, and transportation were better. The remaining land could be given to peasants to grow badly needed staple crops to help restore the resource balance. Plantation owners, however, refused to give up land, and U.S. officials would not pressure Castelo Branco to modernize or reform. (The Johnson administration could have exerted such pressure by threatening to reduce Brazil's quota in the North American sugar market or by attaching conditions to Alliance funds.) In the end, Brazil's peasants were hurt more than helped by this new manifestation of the Alliance for Progress.[62]

Brazil didn't lack land to give small farmers. Excluding the area drained by the Amazon River and its tributaries, enough good land existed to deed about ten acres to each family. But 1 percent of the farmers (many of them corporations and absentee landlords) owned about 40 percent of the farmland, and the military would not risk alienating the elite. Instead, the government made a fateful decision to open the southern hemisphere's last great frontier, Amazônia's rich rainforests. The half million Indians living in the region were subjected to eviction, disease, and murder. The U.S. Army Corps of Engineers helped the Brazilian Army Corps of Engineers forge roads through the jungle, and Hanna Mining and U.S. Steel were two of several North American multinationals that the Brazilian regime allowed to rush into the region. Between 1966 and 1975, about 22 million acres of forest were opened for settlement. Migrants flooded the retreating frontier, but few became landowners; most were poorly-paid wage laborers on ranches hacked out of the forest. Wealthy Brazilians bought large chunks of better land at low prices; the peasants shared the rest, which usually had poor soil. Even privileged ranchers saw their land worn out or eroded: it was discovered that Amazonian rain forests were not as amenable to agriculture as the American plains.[63]

By the time Lyndon Johnson left office in early 1969, Castelo Branco had already suspended the Brazilian Congress, but AID— satisfied with the regime's stability if not its social planning— still funneled loans into Brazil with the understanding that the country was soon to open its markets to more foreign goods. As one account of the Alliance concluded, "Monetary stabilization and import liberalization had become key objectives of the AID program in Brazil."[64] The program had thus moved a considerable distance from Kennedy's original ideals. Nearly a decade later, agronomist Lester Brown made a final point about the "new frontiers" in Amazônia. The hopes of the 1960s and 1970s, he concluded, were "often overrated" because the military regime mistakenly thought it could vanquish ecological reality. "The principal constraint here," he wrote, "is the inherent poor fertility of the soil and its limited capacity to sustain cultivation over an extended period of time."[65]

Under the Alliance-Brazilian military partnership, Brazil's economy was increasingly dominated by foreign (especially U.S.) multinational corporations and skewed toward agro-exports at the expense of staple food production. This occurred not through any *ad hoc,* piecemeal approach, but through an integrated, planned program that linked Alliance-military objectives and the plunder of Brazil's material and human resources. "Operation Amazon," announced by Castelo Branco in 1966, was a five-year, $2-billion project aimed at systematically exploiting the Amazon's riches. It was partly financed with $3.5 billion in U.S. aid to Brazil between 1964 and 1971. As a result, Brazil became a major international debtor. In addition, scores of Indian tribes were virtually destroyed, large cattle ranges and agribusinesses drove out peasant populations, and attempts by the Indians and peasants to seek legal help and protection led to violence and repression by Brazilian officials. As Shelton Davis concluded in a landmark study, "a silent war is being waged against marginal peoples, innocent peasants, and the rain forest ecosystem in the Amazon Basin." The objectives of Operation Amazon were not even to help most Brazilians, but to follow a "very specific 'model of development' " that was destroying lives and irrationally depleting resources.[66]

FAILURE IN CENTRAL AMERICA

The Brazilian story was repeated on a greatly reduced scale in another frontier area, *Guatemala,* but the political result there was revolutionary outbreak. A Guatemalan land-reform program previously had made raw, undeveloped tropical jungle land available between 1955 and 1962, but the government refused to build needed access roads and only about 4,000 families settled on the land. Then the military government established the Institute for the Development of the Petén. A vast undeveloped jungle area making up nearly one-third of Guatemala, the Petén became the escape valve for the nation's *campesinos,* especially the impoverished Indians who made up one-half of the country's population. During the decade after the 1954 CIA-supported coup that overthrew the reformist, constitutionally-elected Arbenz government, a major purpose of the colonization was to quiet peasants who had been made politically aware by the pre-1954 reform programs.

The land, however, turned out to be better than officials expected, and the promise of oil development soon appeared. Thus the first coordinated, U.S.-supported colonization and development program in Guatemala's history metamorphosed into an opportunity for the elite to establish large cattle farms and ranches. Scandals over land sales and giveaways plagued the government and peasants were forced off the new lands. In 1966, a new civilian regime tried to make amends (and damp down the growing village unrest) by promising to turn over 375,000 acres of land to about 12,000 families who lived on national state-owned property. The government argued that something had to be done because more than 80,000 families were either without land or lived on farms too small for efficient production. The plan touched no private lands. Yet, both conservatives and the radical left attacked the program for offering too much or too little and Guatemala's reform program was stillborn. Large chunks of the Petén fell into the hands of the military and the oligarchy, while the Indians tried to scratch out a living on considerably less fertile soil and subsist on an average annual income of under $90.

Overall, the pace of land distribution between 1963 and 1970 was slower than it had been before the Alliance was fully in effect, and maldistribution worsened. About half the land distributed after 1955 exceeded the size needed to sustain a family; most went into farms larger than 100 hectares—in a warm climate, with possible year-round production, a very substantial spread.

The Guatemala experience was yet another example of how AID's emphasis on export earnings (in part to pay mounting public debts) and crop diversification rebounded against the Alliance-for-reform's interest. As Guatemalans began to colonize the lowlands and other long-neglected areas, credit went almost entirely to large farms producing export crops. Production of staple crops rose only half as fast as the population increase. Nor did rural wage labor benefit. As the country moved away from dependence on coffee and put more acreage into cotton and then sugar in the newly opened coastal lowlands, transient seasonal workers outnumbered permanent laborers by ratios as high as twenty to one. Seasonal and displaced workers went into urban areas, but labor demands in industry developed so slowly that new applicants there outnumbered available jobs thirty or even forty to one. Neither AID nor the Guatemalan government could resolve these problems, which arose out of the Alliance's emphasis on new frontiers for diversified export crops, and on capital-intensive industry.

Before long, the long quiescent Guatemalan Indian population became more politically active. By the late 1960s an insurgency movement, begun in 1960–1961 by disaffected middle-class army officers, found willing recruits among the Indians. U.S. military advisors and as many as one thousand members of the Special Forces (Green Berets) led counterinsurgency teams that were involved in killing as many as 8,000 guerrillas and peasants between 1966 and 1970. (The insurgents responded by gunning down North American military advisors, then the U.S. ambassador.) Meanwhile, rural living standards continued to fall, until one expert told the United States Senate that the Guatemalan rural and other reform efforts appeared to be "standing still." But, he added, perhaps the civilian president could do little else "if he wishes to remain in office." A land ownership system had developed that created inequalities "more serious than in all the countries in Central America and most other Latin American countries," according to a 1982 AID-sponsored report. Farms of 450 hectares and larger constituted only 1 percent of all farms, but held 34 percent of the farming land. A rampant farm tenancy system, combined with insecure titles to lands, left peasants with the fear that they could be easily evicted. Such were the bitter fruits of the Alliance for Progress—or, more accurately, the Alliance for Stability that overshadowed it.

Two radically different Central American nations, El Salvador and Costa Rica had similar unhappy experiences with the Alliance. *El Salvador* had been ruled by an oligarchy since the nineteenth century, or, after 1931, by military regimes that cooperated with the oligarchy. The oligarchs dominated the coffee-growing lands by the 1880s, then controlled the entire economy under the so-called Fourteen Families—actually forty to two hundred families who reigned supreme. Costa Rica, on the other hand, enjoyed the most open and fair democracy of any Latin American nation throughout most of the twentieth century. Costa Rica had no institutionalized military, though it maintained an efficient five-thousand-man "police" force. Costa Rica's landholdings became more concentrated, particularly after 1950, and the holdings were never as equitably divided as Costa Ricans liked to think, but its property system was certainly the region's most equitable. Despite these differences, the Alliance years affected both nations in much the same way, even if the results, by 1970, were markedly different.

El Salvador's development demonstrated how rising economic growth rates could obscure not only the Alliance's failures but also the environmental devastation they caused. El Salvador, the hemisphere's most densely populated mainland country, had an average population growth rate of 3.5 percent between 1961 and 1971, one of the world's highest, and spurred "the destruction of virtually all the indigenous natural habitats from coastal mangrove swamps to high elevation cloud forests, the extinction of more than twenty mammalian taxa since 1900, among them monkeys and porcupines, and the accelerated erosion of an estimated 77 percent of the land area."[67] Sixty-five of every thousand newborns died and 80 percent of the children under five years of age suffered moderate to severe malnutrition. The crux of these disasters was inequitable land distribution. Approximately 1 percent of the owners controlled 50 percent of the land in production—the same people who dominated the entire economy.[68] The families' wealth long rested on coffee exports, which accounted for nine-tenths of El Salvador's export revenues. No other Latin American nation, not even Venezuela with its oil, was so dependent on a single commodity.

In 1961, a somewhat reform-minded Salvadoran military group deposed a brutal regime, but Kennedy refused to recognize the new government because he suspected a few officers were sympathetic to Fidel Castro. Conservatives overthrew the short-lived government, and from 1962 until 1970 Salvadorans used

Alliance funds to pump their growth rate to an amazing 12 percent. The government did little, however, to encourage tax or land reforms. To Washington, El Salvador's growth became "the model" for the Alliance.[69] However, when brave Salvadoran legislators threatened to pass minimum wage laws (of one dollar per day), the oligarchs and U.S. investors pressured the U.S. embassy in San Salvador to quash the measure.[70] Ambassador Murat Williams refused to cooperate, but the threat of such reforms was soon over anyway. The oligarchs used Alliance funds to increase their export crop acreage, driving more peasants off the land and forcing 10 percent of the country's population of 3 million into neighboring Honduras.

Salvadoran agricultural production changed dramatically. Only sugar and vegetable oil produced from cotton (both key export crops) rose in volume between 1959 and 1965, while production of all food staples declined. Sorghum, a livestock feed, became a staple for poor Salvadorans because it grows on steep eroded hillsides.[71] Shockingly, at the same time about one-third of the oligarch-controlled land lay fallow and almost half the land on the largest farms was seeded to pasture for beef exports.[72] Salvadoran industry expanded in the mid-1960s, as a disciplined labor force and native capital rushed to the Central American Common Market (CACM). But new industrial jobs absorbed fewer than one-sixth of the unemployed. Other job-seekers moved to Honduras until, in 1969, Honduran authorities tried to force the emigrants home, causing the "Soccer War." The conflict ended only after El Salvador invaded Honduras, forcing the Organization of American States to orchestrate a truce. Bitter feelings continue into the 1980s, hindering the Reagan administration's efforts to construct a Central American front to overthrow the Nicaraguan government. Thus, the mistakes of the 1960s still produce political and diplomatic waves two decades later.

Although the Soccer War virtually destroyed the CACM, it did force El Salvador to move rapidly to avert mass starvation and political upheaval, especially as the country's 1969 per capita growth plummeted to zero and Honduran cereal shipments were cut. AID helped El Salvador expand an agricultural extension service, assist small farmers, and increase the country's public investment in staple agriculture. By 1972, production of corn, beans, and sorghum rose by as much as 100 percent over the 1966–1967 levels.[73] However, the increase barely eased the population crunch and the results of the decade's earlier misguided programs. By 1970, El Salvador was home to at least one important revolutionary movement.

Costa Rica endured many similar changes during the Alliance years, but at the decade's end the country had no revolutionary movement. Costa Rica, too, depended overwhelmingly on the export of a few crops. The land that produced coffee and bananas (which accounted for 85 percent of export earnings) had become concentrated in the hands of a few, although not to the extent it had in El Salvador. Costa Rica's population growth topped 4 percent—at one point, the world's highest. Infant mortality also rose, to 85 per thousand births in the 1960s.[74] As landowning concentrated and population rose, production of staple crops declined. Here too, the "decade of development" was again producing more agricultural products but also starvation and misuse of resources.

During the 1960s, Costa Rica's rich grew richer and the poor got poorer. This stemmed from increased export crops, concentrated landholdings, and foreign investors. Peasants migrated into urban areas or neighboring countries and surrendered communal lands. The country slid into an international marketplace over which Costa Ricans had no control, while these changes destroyed staple crop production that made up the national diet. Medium and large-sized farms grew at the expense of both small peasant holdings and huge, underutilized *latifundia*. Between 1963 and 1973 the staple crop sector virtually disappeared. Land use became, in the words of one analyst, "anarchic and irrational," especially in the drastic expansion of pasture for cattle grazing and the exploitation of some 300,000 hectares of potential cropland for other purposes.[75] Costa Rica's experience during the 1960s dramatized the effect the Alliance had on both human and material resources, even in Latin America's most stable democracy.

Despite these problems, Costa Rica did not end the decade in war and revolution. Several factors explain the different outcome. Even though peasants were evicted from Costa Rican land as coffee spread, the government opened virgin land in other parts of the country. This land, plus new banana-growing areas, soaked up labor surpluses and helped keep wages fairly high for those working coffee plantations. Particularly under the Central American Common Market, Costa Rican industry gained capital and diversity, while becoming controlled by a few wealthy families. Although Costa Rican industry made great strides, it also reduced many artisans to poverty and did not provide substitutes for expensive imports. But industry did not have to absorb all the victims of coffee and banana expansion, as it did in El Salvador. Many peasants, moreover, simply invaded or squatted on land claimed by plantations. The government recognized many squatters and helped relocate others to government-owned land.[76]

Costa Rica's handling of the squatters provides a key to why the Alliance's bias toward stability had different results in Costa Rica than in El Salvador or Guatemala. The Costa Rican political system already was more open and pluralistic; no army was employed to gobble resources and forcibly evict or kill squatters. Since the 1940s, the Ticos boasted socialized medicine and a high rate of literacy. By the late 1960s, these programs had become too expensive, but they cushioned shocks that elsewhere sparked revolution. Costa Rica's political system—not the United States or the Alliance—protected those displaced by Alliance-induced changes.

THREE ATTEMPTS AT AGRARIAN REFORM

Unlike El Salvador and Costa Rica, *Colombia* began land reform in the 1930s. The program was reinvigorated in 1961 with a new reform bill (which was needed after rural violence of the 1950s), and further changes were legislated in 1963. The 1961 law followed the Punte del Este Conference that shaped the Alliance, but the results were hardly those Kennedy had envisioned. The new Colombian measures exempted cultivated private land from redistribution, required repayment for land acquired in cash, and forced settlers to pay for past improvements to the land as well as for the territory itself. INCORA, the Colombian land reform institute, worked with a budget of only $25 million, which meant that even if all the money were used at a rate of $150 per hectare with each family receiving ten hectares, fewer than 17,000 families would benefit.

370

Meanwhile rural population increased by 14,000 families a year. The actual annual rate of settlement between 1961 and 1971 was probably only 1,900 families.[77] At no point were the landholdings of the elite affected. Indeed, new credit and technology transformed semifeudal holdings into large commercial farms that produced exports and luxury goods. Thus began the strange but now familiar pattern of food shortages amid rising agricultural output. Between 1960 and 1970 farms over fifty hectares expanded rapidly, while family plots under ten hectares declined. The World Bank concluded at the end of the development decade that the bottom one-third of the rural population was no better off than it had been in the 1930s.[78]

The oligarchs, moreover, evaded the Alliance's tax reform demands through tax loopholes that prevented both rural development and reform. In the department of Antioquia, large landowners influenced tax laws so that they paid practically nothing: only 32 cents per person was available for investing in social and economic infrastructure. Thus, new roads, schoolhouses, and hospitals were not built, even as Antioquia's population rose 3 percent annually. By 1973, as urban unrest and peasant militancy increased, Colombia cancelled its land reform program. The poor had received neither land nor education, and AID had done little to help.[79]

Meanwhile, INCORA and other Colombian agencies had even fewer resources to distribute. The United Nations estimated that erosion robbed the country of 426 million tons of topsoil each year, and Colombia's topsoil was already thin.[80] Another problem arose from well-intentioned members of the U.S. Congress who passed PL-480 to help undernourished peoples and simultaneously relieve North American farmers of their crop gluts. The effect on Colombian wheat growing was nearly catastrophic. Between 1955 and 1962, PL-480 imports were 53 percent of total Colombian wheat imports. After 1963, U.S. credit tightened, but Colombia was by then addicted. Wheat consumption rose 4 percent a year as domestic output declined from an average of 140,000 tons yearly in the 1950s to 49,000 tons in 1971. Imported wheat jumped from 25 percent of consumption in the early 1950s to almost 90 percent by 1971. But a large portion of the 165,000 hectares that no longer produced wheat was not seeded with

371

other food staples, and many workers once employed in growing wheat lost out.[81]

Meanwhile, the development of new crop strains produced the same effect. For example, new coffee varieties requiring costly fertilizers led Colombian credit sources to finance larger, better capitalized growers. Of some 65 growers studied in one sample, 17 adopted the new varieties and did well; of the 48 who did not or could not adopt the new varieties, 14 lost their land and 9 moved to the cities. Land and resources thus became more concentrated.[82]

By the mid-1960s, Colombia's guerrillas were gaining strength and numbers—thanks largely to problems created by the reform program and the dramatic decision by Father Camil Torres Restrepo, a member of the country's elite, to join the insurgents in 1965. Torres, killed several months later, became a charismatic martyr for the left. Insurgency erupted in 1967 and was stifled by Colombia's U.S.-advised counterinsurgency forces. Peace reigned in 1968–1969, but, as a witness told the U.S. Congress in 1969, "the more fundamental sources of peasant unrest remain . . . in the need for rapid implementation of agrarian reform and rural development programs. Without these, communist guerrillas may hang on for many years."[83] The Colombian episode also illustrates how Alliance hopes were undercut by the best of intentions—in this case, PL-480 laws and new crop varieties—as well as by indigenous obstacles that prevented the fair working of land reform legislation.

In *Chile,* the Alliance's policies ended more happily, at least in the short run. With AID help, Eduardo Frei won the 1964 election against leftist candidate Salvador Allende, and over the next six years Chile received the second highest per-capita economic assistance of any Alliance member. Frei passed new minimum farm-wage legislation in 1965 and relaxed antiunion laws. He also enforced a 1962 land reform act, and later claimed that, between 1965 and mid-1969, 2 million hectares were expropriated and 18,859 families received places in cooperative settlements. The president also claimed that, unlike other countries where land reform had hurt production, Chile's agricultural output rose 1.8 percent in 1965 to 3.1 percent four years later, despite drought conditions. Frei used Alliance funds to organize peasants, too. Before 1964, 24 *campesino* unions had fewer than 2,000 members;

372

by 1969, 3,500 leagues had between 100,000 and 200,000 members.[84]

In 1970, Chile was a more equitable and prosperous society because of Frei's rural reforms and new controls on the U.S.-controlled copper industry. But inflation and stagnation continued, and only a third of the 100,000 families scheduled for resettlement were on their land. Some 730 estates still controlled half Chile's agricultural land, while nearly half the rural population owned no land at all. Yet, Frei's programs proved costly and the country's foreign debt shot upward, a spiral of spending that demanded more export crops to pay the debt. Frei did manage to pass some of Latin America's best tax reform laws during the Alliance years, but (despite Johnson's and Mann's efforts) Allende won the presidency in 1970. When Allende fell in 1973 to a U.S.-supported military coup, the reforms of both Frei and Allende fell with him.

Few Latin American nations accomplished as much as Chile between 1964 and 1970. That the accomplishments were not enough, both politically and economically, shows how far even Chile had to come to make its society more equitable, and how the Alliance raised expectations that not even Chilean and U.S. efforts could meet.

The Alliance had more success in *Venezuela,* where a reform-minded party (Acción Democrática, or AD), rich oil resources, and a new land policy combined made rural change possible. The new 1960 land law stemmed from peasant invasions of the 1950s to reclaim land taken from *campesinos* in the late 1940s. By 1963, after reelection of the AD ticket and with strong support from the powerful peasant organization FCV (Federación Campesina de Venezuela), 33,000 families had been settled on expropriated private land and 34,000 more on public plots. Some 78 percent of the applicants, or about 41,000, received land in 1965. The oligarchy tolerated the reform to avoid more uprisings and because former owners were compensated handsomely. The 119,000 Venezuelan families who received land also received the money and support crucial for any effective land reform. Other numerically significant land-reform programs (in Mexico after the revolution and in Bolivia from 1952 to 1969) too often exchanged one form of poverty for another, by not providing needed services and infrastructure along with land.[85]

373

In Venezuela, moreover, somewhat better resources also allowed a more successful, if limited, use of the frontier. However, Venezuelan land use was inefficient, credit and technical aid lacking, and markets limited; as a result, most settlers remained poor. And Venezuelan reform did not stop the exodus from rural to urban areas: Caracas' population doubled during the 1960s to 2 million. Thus, the land reform was not wholly successful but it helped dampen revolutionary tinder, and became one of the few Alliance achievements.[86] In truth, however, the country's oil wealth—not the Alliance—allowed Venezuela to compensate and assist new landowners as no other Latin American nation could. As it had in Western Europe, U.S. aid proved most effective when it could assist existing programs in societies with the political and economic base needed for reform.

THE PROBLEM OF OIL AND PERU

The land use and population distribution problems are endemic in Latin America; the Alliance mostly failed to address them, or made them worse. But what of extractive resources, especially oil? For nations such as Venezuela and Peru, and for certain Washington bureaus, notably the Pentagon and the CIA, oil was more important than agriculture. The results were similar: a two-headed Alliance was unable both to protect U.S. interests in the oil-producing countries and honor the Latin Americans' desire to determine their own oil policy.

The Alliance's most significant failure occurred in *Peru.* For decades, Peru had enjoyed close economic ties with the United States. Peru's largest foreign-owned corporation and biggest employer, was the International Petroleum Company (IPC), a subsidiary of Standard Oil of New Jersey. But IPC's labor practices had long made it a target for anti-North American feelings, and these boiled over in 1958 when IPC fired one thousand workers to force the government to raise gasoline prices.[87]

In 1963, as Peru-IPC relations deteriorated, Fernando Belaunde's elected government replaced the military regime that (much to Kennedy's vigorously expressed displeasure) had seized power the year before. Belaunde knew that with a restless military, his political position would be weak, especially because his party did not control the Peruvian legislature. The United

374

States understood this and pressured Belaunde to meet ɪᴘᴄ demands, especially the oil company's claim to a new oil field. The legislature responded by claiming control of all subsoil rights, then demanded back taxes from ɪᴘᴄ. Belaunde further complicated U.S. decision-making by undertaking agrarian and tax reform in the Alliance spirit.

Johnson now faced a different choice. If he approved Belaunde's actions, he might encourage other countries to challenge U.S. multinationals. If Johnson dissented he could create stronger anti-U.S. feelings in Peru and undercut Belaunde's attempt to advance Alliance goals. In 1963, he sent Latin American ᴀɪᴅ administrator Moscoso to Peru to pressure Belaunde to accept ɪᴘᴄ demands, but the effort was unsuccessful. As a result, ᴀɪᴅ monies ran dry, and in 1964 Johnson and Mann cut funding to Peru entirely. A year later, Senator Robert Kennedy asked a State Department official why assistance had been cut to a pro-Alliance government, while it gushed to Brazil's military dictatorship. His answer prompted Kennedy to observe, "What the Alliance for Progress has come down to, then, is that you can close down newspapers, abolish Congress, jail religious opposition, and deport your political enemies, and you'll get lots of help, but if you fool around with a U.S. oil company, we'll cut you off without a penny. Is that about right?" The State Department official glumly replied, "That's about the size of it."[88]

Johnson and Mann did not ease the pressure until 1966, and even then all new loans for Peru required the president's direct approval. Some ᴀɪᴅ money trickled into Peru in 1966, but the following year Johnson told Belaunde that Peru was prosperous because of "private enterprise," and "we hope it will . . . not take any actions which would destroy private investors' confidence." The president wanted assurances that Peru was financially (and apparently ideologically) responsible before he sent more loans and that Belaunde would not spend millions on long-coveted French jet fighters. As with oil, Johnson also did not accept Peru's claim of a two hundred-mile jurisdiction into the Pacific Ocean, a move to protect Peru's rich anchovy fishery. Johnson wanted continued access to the fishery—even though the United States used anchovies mainly as cattle feed.[89]

Belaunde, however, held firm on the fishing dispute and bought the jet fighters. U.S. credits and loans immediately

stopped. Peru then negotiated with IPC that the corporation surrender subsoil and other rights but retain oil refineries (the most
profitable part of the business), and all past tax claims were cancelled. Outraged Peruvians protested and Belaunde's political
support collapsed. On October 3, 1968, the military seized power,
repudiated the IPC deal, and nationalized the oil industry. After
intense discussions with the United States, the new regime offered IPC $71 million in compensation if the company agreed to
pay a debt of $691 million for alleged illegal profits. Of course,
neither the company nor the U.S. government agreed to that
deal. In 1970, several new laws were passed to further control foreign investments in basic industry and create worker-ownership
plans. The new government also revived agrarian reform laws,
nationalized 247,000 hectares of land belonging to U.S. owners,
and expropriated and settled some sugar plantations with peasant families.[90] By the mid-1970s, Peru's military-populist
experiment would be in deep trouble, but so would U.S. influence in the nation. North America's previously close ties with
Peru were so badly severed that the Soviet Union became Peru's
major source for armaments in the 1970s.[91]

In Lyndon Johnson's hands, then, Kennedy's Alliance had
become a mere tool in U.S.-Peruvian relations. Funds for agrarian reform or modernizing Peru's economy became chits to
protect narrow North American interests. But the strategy back-
fired. By the end of the Alliance decade, these parochial U.S.
interests had suffered badly in Peru, although other U.S. businesses fared well in the country. Peru's new military leaders,
meanwhile, believed that they were realizing the broader objectives of Kennedy's dream.

THE DECADE OF DEVELOPMENT AND AFTER

In 1973, a top AID official, Herman Kleine, summed up the Alliance years for a U.S. Congressional committee. "The daily lives
of the large part of the population [in Latin America] have regrettably not been significantly changed," he admitted. Education
expenditures, for example, rose from 9 percent of central government budgets in 1961 to 13 percent by 1972, and enrollments rose
dramatically, but population growth was so high "that the actual
number of school age children not in school is higher today than

in 1960." The typical small farmer, representing "one-third or more of Latin America's population," Kleine continued, scratched out a livelihood on a small plot "without fertilizer, pesticides, or improved seed, growing corn or beans [the two staples of the family diet] with some of the lowest yields in the world." This family's income was "less than $100 annually" and their only "health facility is a local midwife with no knowledge of preventive or curative medicine or family planning." Because so little good land was available, young adults "migrate to the cities to join the already large number of untrained and unemployed."[92] The Alliance's most significant results were revolutionaries on the left and military regimes on the right.

What had happened? First, an unorganized Washington bureaucracy, whose sense of history was unconnected to Latin American realities initially stifled useful responses to Latin American needs. Then, concern for stability and military security superseded a commitment to reform. Lyndon Johnson and Thomas Mann finally sidestepped the responsibility of choice by turning the Alliance over to the U.S. private sector. They also tried to apply the European Common Market experience to Latin America. But the Johnson-Mann approach only realized the fear expressed earlier by Perloff and others that the Alliance would fail resoundingly unless it devised an overall development program that worked on a multilateral rather than bilateral basis, and thus demonstrated greater sensitivity to Latin American concerns—especially the needs of the multitudes of poor farmers. Such an approach, of course, assumed that the Latin American governments cared about their poor. Where such concern existed, as in Costa Rica and Chile, the Alliance aided development that was already relatively equitable. In countries that lacked this concern, as in Brazil and El Salvador, the Alliance did little to further equitable development. A feasible program required large-scale land reform, well-financed infrastructure, tax changes (to make the wealthy bear some financial burden), and subtle U.S. pressure to ensure implementation. The Alliance simply never offered such a program.

As for resource development, the Alliance's emphasis on stability rather than reform meant that AID funds often landed in the pockets of a controlling regime rather than the coffers of the development project. Sometimes, notably with Peru, AID money never left Washington if letting it go would help governments gain control of their own resources. Then too, an obsession with "quantifiable" progress—i.e., economic growth—encouraged farmers to grow export crops instead of staple foods even as a rapidly growing population demanded more food supplies. The result? Increased imports of foodstuffs combined with technology and capital for rapid industrialization that burdened Latin America with a huge foreign debt by the early 1970s. Colombia, a country once self-sufficient in wheat now had to import, at great expense, large amounts of North American wheat to feed its people. In many nations, the lack of reform meant that peasants left their land to settle in city slums or remained at home or on new frontiers as low-wage laborers. Some, through necessity, farmed their small plots even more intensively leading to exhaustion and erosion of a most fundamental asset: the soil.

Above all, equitable development required new political—not technical—choices. In Amazônia and in El Salvador's small industrial complex, the capital and technology appeared, but only for the classes that had long dominated the two economies. Little new thinking and even less political courage surfaced in offering capital and technology to the peasants. In Costa Rica, some reform resulted through an open, responsive political system. In Venezuela, oil profits eased class friction. In Peru, development became more coherent after a reform-minded military seized power and appropriated foreign holdings. But few other equitable models for development existed in the 1960s. All in all, the legacies of the Alliance—accelerated resource development for the benefit of a few, and revolutionary and/or anti-U.S. sentiment where none existed ten years earlier—were hardly positive accomplishments.

THE BIPARTISAN COMMISSION

In early 1984, President Ronald Reagan's National Bipartisan Commission on Central America, chaired by Henry A. Kissinger, issued a widely-debated report that called the Alliance "a bold and unprecedented effort." The Alliance was indeed both, but would the Kissinger Commission investigate why it had failed? The report noted little from the history of the 1960s and the Alliance's impact on Latin America. Key questions about the

378

Alliance's economic results and social impact were never asked. The commission even ranked the Alliance with the Monroe Doctrine and the Good Neighbor policy as praiseworthy landmarks in hemispheric relations. The Alliance's "most important contribution to Central American growth," in the commission's view, was the Central American Common Market, although it admitted that of the Alliance's original three goals—"economic growth, structural change in societies, and political democratization"—only the first had progressed significantly.[93]

The commission's report was divided into two sections— "security" and "economic aid"—thereby reflecting the distortion that caused the Alliance's failures. Predictably, the report tilted toward military action. The economic development section did urge the United States to spend about $8 billion in the region over five years. Such aid would travel mainly through U.S.-controlled agencies, although the commission created two new agencies. One, the Central American Development Organization (CADO), would include all the Central American nations plus the United States but would be open to any "democracy" willing to give development resources. CADO was to depend heavily on private sector involvement. Besides increasing political liberties and "pluralism" in Latin America, CADO would promote "sound growth policies." The Kissinger report also emphasized "accelerated agricultural development" to occur through "the purchase of land by small farmers" with "long-term credit at positive but moderate real interest rates." Extension and research services would be improved and farm prices protected. Notice was given that agrarian reforms should be initiated "where appropriate"; but the commission did not endorse needed land redistribution, or U.S. funding for such a program. The need, noted by Perloff, for extensive planning and large auxiliary expenditures to assure the success of agrarian reform went unanalyzed. The report touched this problem only incidentally, when it recommended that large numbers of North American teachers and medics be sent to Latin America.[94]

The Reagan administration welcomed much of the report, especially those sections stressing military pressures on Nicaragua and the Salvadoran revolutionaries. But outside the administration, the commission's work met widespread criticism. The

Central America Report, a well-informed Guatemala City week-ly, claimed that the recommendations indicated the commission's desire to tighten the region's dependence on the United States, shape Latin America's culture as well as its economy, and use economic tactics to forward U.S. security interests at the ex-pense of most Central Americans.[95]

Such criticisms had been anticipated fifteen years earlier. Al-liance experts—whose ranks included some disillusioned Alliance veterans—had warned from 1969 onward that a single blueprint for developing such a diverse region inevitably would falter. Nowhere were problems more likely, they declared, than in land reform. Some land redistribution succeeded somewhat and some not at all; but any successful plan needed extensive credit and research (which the commission noted), and each plan had to fit the particular needs of each country (a criterion that the commission missed).[96]

To some experts, it is not obvious that U.S. and Latin Ameri-can interests often diverge, and that North Americans will sometimes use their leverage to protect themselves rather than help Latin Americans. This was not evident to the architects of the Alliance, or, apparently, to the authors of the Bipartisan Commission report. Members of the commission seem to believe that U.S. economic and security needs can be easily reconciled with Latin America's need for economic growth and that growth's equitable distribution.[97]

THE ALLIANCE LEGACY

Policy recommendations spring naturally from study of the Alli-ance years, and they are not necessarily those offered by the Bipartisan Commission. To begin, there can be no large, overarching plan to effectively develop Latin American resourc-es over time. The United States does not have the resources, either political or economic, to carry out such a plan. Also, Wash-ington's attention span on Latin American affairs tends to be short, even when such skilled political communicators as Ronald Reagan or John Kennedy are issuing the calls to action. The am-bitions of U.S. foreign policy, moreover, overwhelm the resources Congress allocates for foreign aid. When cuts must be made, as in the late 1960s, programs designed for Latin

America — which have few political constituents — get dropped.

Second, the nations that did make some progress during the 1960s (Venezuela, Peru, and Costa Rica) advanced because their internal politics allowed them to use their resources—and, in some cases, those of the Alliance—with a concern for the masses. They used their resources with minimal concern for North American wishes. El Salvador and Brazil, on the other hand, received great amounts of attention and money, but hardly heeded U.S. calls for reform. When El Salvador belatedly tried equitable resource distribution after 1969, it did so mainly in response to internal pressures.Clearly, sustainable resource development occurs only when the government involved is concerned about equitable distribution as well as aggregate growth. In some instances, those governments will be democratic (as in Costa Rica); in other cases, they will not (as in post-1968 Peru or post-1979 Nicaragua). Some experts argue that before development can occur, new political alignments must be formed (for example, between the urban proletariat and the *campesinos*) to buttress the reform program.[98] But new political coalitions can only be formed in societies that allow political change. Indeed, even the most ingenious resource development plan can work properly and equitably only when political preconditions are met. Such a conclusion was not obvious to the framers of the Alliance for Progress; and the Kissinger Commission acknowledges the need for political change only by implicitly assuming that U.S. military power can create the necessary political preconditions for reform—an assumption for which there is no evidence in twentieth century U.S.-Latin American relations.

Given political preconditions, the Alliance experience shows that the pivotal development problem is to carry out land-reform programs that stabilize the rural population by slowing urban migration and produce more staple foods instead of export crops. The objective should be national self-sufficiency in food, thus reducing the need for expensive imports and creating producers who can create a large market for domestic products.[99] A 1975 World Bank survey of the Third World's rural development problems concluded that large farmers are generally more efficient than small ones, but that rural development and economic growth do not "necessarily conflict with the objectives of higher food production." The bank had learned that alleviating rural poverty and increasing food production could be reconciled by emphasizing loans to "smallscale farmers—those with holdings of up to five hectares," who then represented 40 percent of land cultivated in developing countries.[100] A subsequent study of Chilean agrarian reform showed that, after receiving their own land, peasants increased income per hectare at twice the rate of increase for the rest of the country's agriculture; moreover, family income rose to twice that earned by laborers receiving minimum wages. Some families climbed the economic scale and others slipped; no guarantee exists that land reform will benefit every recipient. For those who benefitted, however, the national and individual rewards were significant.[101]

"The preeminent problem for Latin America," a U.S. Senate-commissioned study concluded in 1969, "is how to evolve a new set of political institutions which will be capable of dealing with social change."[102] These words rephrased Robert Heilbroner's warning of seven years earlier, when he wrote that development of Latin American resources was preeminently a political—not economic—question. The Alliance proved that warning correct. It also proved that in a two-pronged Alliance, security and stability were always chosen over reform. Unfortunately for the Alliance and U.S. foreign policy, the security and stability were fleeting at best. Contrary to the Bipartisan Commission's recommendations, the Alliance demonstrated that U.S. security interests differ from Latin American economic interests and that the first constantly undermined the other—until, by the 1980s, both were deeply endangered.

NOTES

1. For Kennedy's quote, see U.S. Government Printing Office, *Public Papers of the Presidents of the United States. John F. Kennedy. 1961* (Washington, 1962) 174–175.

2. Arthur Schlesinger, *1,000 Days. John F. Kennedy in the White House* (Boston: Fawcett, 1965) 302–303; and Walt Whitman Rostow, *The Diffusion of Power, 1958–1972* (New York: MacMillan, 1972) 52.

3. *Washington Post,* Sept. 12, 1977, A17.

4. Robert L Heilbroner, "Counterrevolutionary America," *Commentary,* April 1967, 31–32.

5. Arthur Schlesinger, Jr., "The Alliance for Progress: A Retrospective," in *Latin America: The Search for a New International Role,* Ronald G. Hellman and H. Jon Rosenbaum (eds.) (New York: Halsted Press, 1975) 7.

6. See the quote and background in Theodore C. Sorensen, *Kennedy* (New York: Harper & Row, 1965) 533–535; the "iron law of growth" phrase is in Henry Fairlie, *The Kennedy Promise* (Garden City, New York: Doubleday, 1973) 131–132.

7. Schlesinger, "Alliance for Progress," 60–61.

8. *Commission on U.S.-Latin American Relations* (not published, 1975), 22.

9. U.S. Congress, Senate Subcommittee on American Republics Affairs, *Survey of the Alliance for Progress; Compilation of Studies and Hearings,* 91st Congress, 1st Session (Washington, 1969), 174; and Harvey S. Perloff, *Alliance for Progress: A Social Question in the Making* (Baltimore: The John Hopkins University Press, 1969) 69, 157.

10. Perloff, *Alliance for Progress,* 159.

11. The study referred to in these two paragraphs is R. Paul Shaw, "Land Tenure and the Rural Exodus in Latin America," *Economic Development and Cultural Change,* October 1974, vol. 23, 123–132; see also U.S. Congress, *Survey of the Alliance for Progress,* 278.

12. Edward J. Williams and Freemand J. Wright, *Latin American Politics: A Developmental Approach* (Palo Alto, Calif.: Mayfield Publishing Company, 1975) 365–366; and Perloff, *Alliance for Progress,* 160–162.

13. A discussion of this trade-off and how it was handled in the United States is in Walter LaFeber, *The New Empire: An Interpretation of American Expansion, 1865–1898* (Ithaca: Cornell University Press, 1963).

14. The classic accounts of this key development in the United States are Richard Hofstadter, *The Age of Reform* (New York: Knopf, 1955); and William Appleman Williams, *The Roots of the Modern American Empire* (New York: Random House, 1969).

15. U.S. Congress, *Survey of the Alliance for Progress,* 278–279.

16. *New York Times,* Dec. 26, 1965, F3; for background see Jerome Levinson and Juan de Oñis, *The Alliance That Lost Its Way: A Critical Report on the Alliance for Progress* (Chicago: Quadrangle Books, 1970) 220–223, 249; the Johnson speech at the United Nations in 1965 can be found in U.S. Government Printing Office, *Public Papers of the Presidents of the United States. Lyndon B. Johnson. 1965* (Washington, 1966) 951.

17. Bowdler to Rostow, March 28, 1967, Harry McPherson Papers, Box 10, "Latin America," Lyndon B. Johnson Library, Austin, Texas (hereafter cited: LBJ Library).

18. U.S. Congress, *Survey of the Alliance for Progress,* 14–16.

19. Levinson and Oñis, *The Alliance That Lost Its Way,* 222–223.

20. U.S. Department of State, *American Foreign Policy. Current Documents. 1961* (Washington, 1965) 395–409.

21. Levinson and Oñis, *The Alliance That Lost Its Way,* 229–230.

22. U.S. Congress, *Survey of the Alliance for Progress,* 172.

23. U.S. Congress, *Survey of the Alliance for Progress,* 187–188; and Levinson and Oñis, *The Alliance That Lost Its Way,* 228–230.

24. Levinson and Oñis, *The Alliance That Lost Its Way,* 66.

25. A discussion of this sometimes disputed figure is in Schlesinger, "Alliance For Progress," 68.

26. Joseph Kraft, "The Comeback of the State Department," *Harper's Magazine,* November, 1961, 43–50, especially 50; for a discussion of the Committee of Nine and the Interamerican Committee of the Alliance for Progress, see Levinson and Oñis, *The Alliance That Lost Its Way,* 108, 128–130; and Rostow, *Diffusion of Power,* 215–216.

27. *Newsweek,* April 9, 1962, 55.

28. The general problem of bureaucratic government in an ideological political arena is considered, with reference to Kennedy, in Theodore J. Lowi, *The End of Liberalism* (Princeton: W.W. Norton and Company, Inc., 1973), 95–96.

29. "Comments on Interamerican Economic Problems," 27 Feb., 1959, Cabinet Meetings of President Eisenhower, Dwight D. Eisenhower Library, Abilene, Kansas; and Robert Packenham, *Liberal America and the Third World* (Princeton: Princeton University Press, 1973) 95–96.

30. Oral History of Ralph Dungan, LBJ Library, 23–24; and Philip Geyelin, *Lyndon B. Johnson and the World* (New York: Praeger, 1966) 25.

31. Penny Lernoux, *Cry of the People* (New York: Penguin, 1982), 211.

32. A good analysis is in Laurence Whitehead, "Aid to Latin America: Problems and Prospects," *Journal of International Affairs,* 1970, vol. 14, no. 2, 181–200.

33. See the analysis by Whitehead, 1970, "Aid to Latin America"; also E. Bradford Burns, *Latin America,* 2nd ed. (Englewood Cliffs, N.J.: Prentice-Hall, 1977) 261–262.

34. Thomas L. Hughes to Rusk, Nov. 18, 1964, National Security Council Country File, Latin America, LBJ Library; and Schlesinger, 1975, "Alliance for Progress," 74–75 has the quote.

35. Willard F. Barber and C. Neale Ronning, *Internal Security and Military Power: Counterinsurgency and Civic Action in Latin America* (Columbus, Ohio: Ohio State University Press, 1966) 6.

36. Barber and Ronning, 1966, *Internal Security and Military Power,* especially 197–204, 239–240.

37. Ray S. Cline to McGeorge Bundy, April 17, 1964, attaching CIAs "Survey of Latin America," April 1, 1964, NSC Country File, Latin America, LBJ Library; *New York Times,* March 27, 1966, 6.

38. Levinson and Oñis, *The Alliance That Lost Its Way,* 230.

39. *New York Times,* April 30, 1966, 35.

40. Whitehead, "Aid to Latin America," 187, 191–192.

41. *New York Times,* April 2, 1967, E4.

42. "Agenda for OAS Summit Meeting," Feb. 26, 1967, OAS Summit File, George Christian Papers, Box 3, LBJ Library.

43. "Background Briefing," April 6, 1967, Christian Papers, Box 3, LBJ Library.

44. "Notes of conversations at OAS Summit," April 1967, Christian Papers, Box 3, LBJ Library.

45. Gary W. Wynia, "Central American Integration: The Paradox of Success," *International Organization,* Spring 1970; vol. 24: 329.

46. Miguel S. Wionczek, "U.S. Investment and the Development of Middle America," *Studies in Comparative International Development,* 1969–1970; vol. 5: 4–5.

47. Memorandum for the President, from Mann, returned from President, June 27, 1964, NSF Agency File, Boxes 3-4, LBJ Library.

48. Tom Buckley, *Violent Neighbors* (New York: Times Books, 1984) 69.

49. U.S. Congress, *Survey of the Alliance for Progress,* 51.

50. *Washington Post,* Dec. 14, 1965, 15.

51. Lincoln Gordon to Rostow, May 6, 1966, NSC Country File, Latin America, LBJ Library.

52. Perloff, *Alliance for Progress,* 158.

53. Marta Cehelsky, *Land Reform in Brazil: The Management of Social Change* (Boulder, Colo.: Westview Press, 1979) 76–77, 130.

54. Thomas E. Skidmore, "U.S. Policy Toward Brazil: Assumptions and Options," in Hellman and Rosenbaum, *Latin America: The Search for a New International Role,* 198–200; Riordan Roett, *Brazil: Politics in a Patrimonial Society* (Boston: Praeger, 1972) 20–21; the quote is from McCone to Johnson, Jan. 8, 1964, NSC Files, Latin America, Box 1, LBJ Library.

55. Chase to McGeorge Bundy, March 19, 1964, NSC Files, Latin America, LBJ Library.

56. "Aid and Alliance for Progress Programs and Project Data Related . . . FY 1965," NSC Agency File, Boxes 3-4, LBJ Library.

57. Phyllis Parker, *Brazil and the Quiet Intervention, 1964* (Austin, Texas: University of Texas Press, 1979) xi, 58, 63, 68–70, 81, 92–93, 99, 102–103 has the best account of this operation codenamed "Operation Brother Sam."

58. Gordon is quoted in Robert Packenham, *Liberal America and the Third World* (Princeton: Princeton University Press, 1973) 171; the analyst paraphrased is Joe Foweraker, *The Struggle for Land: A Political Economy of the Pioneer Frontier in Brazil From 1930 to the Present Day* (London and New York: Cambridge University Press, 1981) especially 207–234.

59. *New York Times,* Dec. 14, 1965, 62; Levinson and Onis, *The Alliance That Lost Its Way,* 96; also *New York Times,* Dec. 28, 1965, 44.

60. Cynthia Arnson, *El Salvador: A Revolution Confronts the United States* (Washington: Institute for Policy Studies, 1982) 19; Sorensen, *Kennedy,* 535–536; and Levinson and Onis, *The Alliance That Lost Its Way,* 96.

61. Williams and Wright, *Latin American Politics,* 158; Skidmore, "U.S. Policy Toward Brazil," 199–200; and Roett, *Brazil,* 21–23.

62. Levinson and Onís, *The Alliance That Lost Its Way,* 245–247.

63. This paragraph draws from two important analyses: Shelton H. Davis, *Victims of the Miracle: Development and the Indians of Brazil* (London and New York: Cambridge University Press, 1977) 32–43; and Nicholas Guppy, "Tropical Deforestation: A Global View," *Foreign Affairs,* Summer, 1984, vol. 62: 939–941. See also Foweraker, *The Struggle for Land,* 158–159.

64. Levinson and Onís, *The Alliance That Lost Its Way,* 200; also Ernest Feder, *The Rape of the Peasantry: Latin America's Landholding System* (Garden City, N.Y.: Anchor Books, 1971) 242–243.

65. Lester R. Brown, "The Worldwide Loss of Cropland," *World Watch Paper 24,* October 1978, 34.

66. Davis, *Victims of the Miracle,* 32–41, 161–168.

67. William H. Durham, *Scarcity and Survival in Central America* (Stanford: Stanford University Press, 1979) 6–7; and U.S. Congress, Senate Committee on Foreign Relations, 90th Congress, 1st Session, *Latin American Summit Conference,* Washington, 1967, 111.

68. John P. Powelson, *Latin America: Today's Economic and Social Revolution* (New York: McGraw-Hill, 1964) 37.

69. Graham H. Stuart and James L. Tigner, *Latin America and the United States* (Englewood Cliffs, N.J.: Prentice-Hall, 1975) 530–531.

70. Speech of Murat Williams, reprinted in *Congressional Record,* 97th Congress, 1st Session, Nov. 16, 1981.

71. Durham, *Scarcity and Survival in Central America,* 22–24.

72. Durham, *Scarcity and Survival in Central America,* 51–52, 124.

73. Harlan Davis, "Foreign Aid to the Small Farmer: The El Salvador Experence," *Inter-American Economic Affairs,* Summer 1975; vol. 29: 81–92.

74. U.S. Congress, *Latin American Summit Conference,* 111; the best study of land concentration in Costa Rica is Mitchell A. Seligson, *Peasants of Costa Rica and the Development of Agrarian Capitalism* (Madison, Wis.: University of Wisconsin Press, 1980), especially xxxi and Part I; and Powelson, *Latin America,* 36.

75. Marc Edelman, "Recent Literature on Costa Rica's Economic Crisis," *Latin American Research Review,* 1983, vol. 18, no. 2: especially 172–173; and Seligson, *Peasants of Costa Rica,* 153–154.

76. Seligson, *Peasants of Costa Rica,* 125–226, especially 168; Edelman, "Recent Literature on Costa Rica's Economic Crisis," 173; and Dwight Heath, "Costa Rica and Her Neighbors," *Current History,* February 1970; vol. 58: 98–99.

77. The World Bank, *Economic Growth of Colombia* (Baltimore, 1972) 301.

78. Alain de Janvry, *The Agrarian Question and Reformism in Latin America* (Baltimore: The Johns Hopkins University Press, 1981) 132–135; The World Bank, *Economic Growth of Colombia,* 9; Williams and Wright, *Latin American Politics,* 178; and Feder, *Rape of the Peasantry,* 247–249.

79. U.S. Congress, *Survey of the Alliance for Progress,* 292.

80. Brown, "The Worldwide Loss of Cropland," 25.

81. Leonard Dudley and Roger J. Sandilands, "The Side Effects of Foreign Aid: The Case of Public Law 480 Wheat on Colombia," *Economic Development and Cultural Change,* January 1975; vol. 23: 326–327, 331–336.

82. A. Eugene Havens and William Flinn, "Green Revolution Technology and Community Development: The Limits of Action Progress," *Economic Development and Cultural Change,* April 1975; vol. 23: 469–482.

83. U.S. Congress, *Survey of the Alliance for Progress,* 224.

84. Williams and Wright, *Latin American Politics,* 175–176.

85. U.S. Congress, *Survey of the Alliance for Progress,* 195; Feder, *Rape of the Peasantry,* 81–82; and Williams and Wright, *Latin American Politics,* 168–170.

86. Sheldon Liss, *Diplomacy and Dependency: Venezuela, the United States, and the Americas* (Salisbury, N.C.: Documentary Publications, 1978) 222–224; U.S. Congress, House Subcommittee of the Committee on Government Operations, 90th Congress, 2nd Session, *U.S. Aid Operations in Latin America Under the Alliance for Progress* (Washington, 1969) 792–793; and Levinson and Oñis, *The Alliance That Lost Its Way,* 257.

87. Steven Krasner, *Defending the National Interest* (Princeton: Princeton University Press, 1979) 235–237; and David P. Werlich, *Peru: A Short History* (Carbondale, Ill.: Southern Illinois University Press, 1978) 26.

88. Schlesinger, "Alliance for Progress," 80; Cole Blasier, *Hovering Giant,* (Pittsburgh: University of Pittsburgh Press, 1976) 253–254; and Krasner, *Defending the National Interest,* 238–241.

89. "Memorandum for the President," from R. W. Komer, February 21, 1964, White House Central File, Confidential File, Box 11, Peru, LBJ Library; and "Peru—President Fernando Belaunde Terry," President's Appointment File, Backup, April 12, 1967, LBJ Library.

90. Robert H. Swansbrough, "Peru's Diplomatic Offensive: Solidarity for Latin American Independence," in Hellman and Rosenbaum *Latin America: The Search for a New International Role,* 115–127; for the compensation offer, see Jessica Pernitz Einhorn, *Expropriation Politics* (Lexington, Mass.: Lexington Books, 1974) 45–46, 71–74; *Washington Post,* January 3, 1971, B1; Williams and Wright, *Latin American Politics* has a useful survey of the Peruvian developments; "Introduction" in *U.S. Foreign Policy and Peru,* Daniel Sharp, (ed.) (Austin, Texas: University of Texas Press, 1972) 4–5; Charles T. Goodsell, "Diplomatic Protection of U.S. Business in Peru," in *U.S. Foreign Policy and Peru,* Daniel Sharp, (ed.), 244–245, 248–249; and Werlich, *Peru,* 294–296.

91. Abraham Lowenthal, "A Sagging Revolution," *Foreign Policy,* Spring 1980; no. 38: 186–188.

92. U.S. Congress, House Committee on Foreign Affairs, 93rd Congress, 1st Session, *Mutual Development and Cooperation Act of 1973: Hearings,* Washington, 1973, 306–308.

93. *Report of the National Bipartisan Commission on Central America. January 1984,* Manuscript copy, 7, 36–37 especially.

94. *Report of the National Bipartisan Commission,* 53–62.

95. *Report of the National Bipartisan Commission,* 25–26; Policy Alternatives for the Caribbean and Central America, *Changing Course* (Washington, 1984) provides a critical overview.

96. This point is stressed in U.S. Congress, *Survey of the Alliance for Progress,* 180; and in Perloff, *Alliance for Progress,* 157.

97. One mundane but instructive example of the failure to reconcile the two sets of interests appears in the trade tables of the 1960s: the Latin American share of the U.S. import market dropped from 21 to 13 percent. That decline reflected both U.S. political decisions on tariffs and quotas as well as the Latin American failure to compete in certain fields. Meanwhile, Alliance rules required the use of U.S.-committed dollars largely for North American goods, even as the price of those goods rose steeply in the late 1960s.

98. De Janvry, *The Agrarian Question,* 259–268.

99. W. Arthur Lewis, *The Evolution of the International Economic Order* (Princeton: Princeton University Press, 1978) 9–10, 76–77.

100. World Bank, *Rural Development. Sector Policy Paper. February 1975* (Washington, 1975) 62–63. A good short case study of the small farmer credit situation is Graber, *Guatemala. General Working Document #2,* 43–45.

101. William P. Thiesenhusen, "Chile's Experiments in Agrarian Reform: Four Colonization Projects Revisited," *American Journal of Agricultural Economics,* May 1974; vol. 56: 323–330.

102. U.S. Congress, *Survey of the Alliance for Progress,* 18–19. The oberservation is by Pat Holt.

CHAPTER 11

Saying Aye or Nay

JANET WELSH BROWN
AND ANDREW MAGUIRE

MOST North Americans have fragmented knowledge and mixed feelings about Latin America. Since the enunciation of the Monroe Doctrine in 1821, the United States has considered Latin America as our sphere of interest. We still periodically trot out the Doctrine, although we apply it these days to the Soviet Union and Cuba rather than to the nineteenth-century colonial powers of Western Europe. In extensive relations with Latin countries we are often patronizing, possessive, and prescriptive. But little do most of us understand the intimacy of those relations, the predominant power of the United States for over a century, and the resulting ambivalence that today still figures in Latin-U.S. interaction. Our ignorance amounts to arrogance—potentially dangerous arrogance.

While a Fellow at the Kennedy Institute of Politics at Harvard University in the spring of 1983, editor Andrew Maguire met for half a day with a group of visiting Latin American political leaders. Their critiques of U.S. policy differed, but they were unanimous in pleading that North Americans seek to understand better their societies, perspectives, and desires. All sought harmony as friends and neighbors. That otherwise privileged moment was tinged by a saddening recognition: more than twenty years before, at a similar meeting attended by the same editor as a graduate student, the plea had been precisely the same. In the meantime, the Alliance for Progress has come and gone, governments have risen and fallen, and the dynamics of our unbalanced and exploitative relationships within the hemisphere have altered not at all. Today, the public's understanding of the issues remains foggy and U.S. policymakers' neglect of the real problems of Latin America has become a habit.

Latin Americans should not have to plead. It is in both Latin and U.S. interests that we move toward a different and more sophisticated relationship with our neighbors to the south.

Generalizing about Latin American problems or solutions presents certain hazards. But countries as different in history and economic potential as Venezuela and Brazil, Honduras and Jamaica, Panama and Mexico do have common experience with the relationship of human and natural resources management— or mismanagement—to their political and economic problems. In the foregoing chapters, the authors discuss some obvious ones shared to some degree by most Latin American countries: rapid population growth and excessive concentration in one or two huge cities, stagnating food production, environmental degradation, and vulnerable, often inflexible, economic and political systems. These difficulties are exacerbated in turn by the same set of fundamental, unsettling conditions, which U.S. policies and the international lending agencies have too often reinforced: (1) economic inequality, reflecting unequal access to resources and services; (2) political repression, often heavily reliant on the military; and (3) inappropriate economic and social policies.

These are tough problems. And most are getting worse.

All of the Latin American states face severe economic crises that also threaten political stability. Latin and North Americans share a sense of urgency. Shrewd observers of the international scene, including *Foreign Policy's* editor Charles William Maynes, sense that the gathering storm in Latin America and elsewhere in the Third World is on the verge of spawning political upheavals and disasters that can greatly damage America's security and welfare—and gravely endanger the United States in a world more disordered than at any time since the 1930s. No Latin nation is likely, under present conditions, to achieve the sustainable growth necessary to avoid one or more of the disasters brewing. The problems are complex and need to be attacked on many fronts.

Fortunately, the same policies that will protect the environment will also keep people healthy and better fed and curb population growth, allowing sustainable, balanced, and equitable economic development—*if* leaders and institutions, both North and South, can be brought to see, and to embrace, the rightness and the necessity of such policies. Latin America's problems must be solved by Latin Americans, of course, but they will need outside help, especially from the United States.

THE U.S. ROLE REFORMED

Current U.S. policy cannot create the trust and cooperation between the United States and Latin American countries that both sides need. It is much too steeped in the prejudices and oversights of the past—a heavy reliance on military might to create the "right atmosphere" for development and peace (for instance, U.S. policy in El Salvador and Honduras), an unwillingness to wrestle with land tenure and population growth, a tendency to promote solutions with which we have experience (that is, large dams, super highways, modern factories, and corporate farming), whether they are appropriate in each Latin situation or not. And, most serious from the standpoint of sustainable development is the traditional neglect of environmental and resource factors in U.S. development policy formulas. Preoccupation with military adventures in Grenada and Central America will get us about as far as the Bay of Pigs, and it will obscure the truly threatening problems in Latin America.

The first step for the United States is to get a more rational perspective on the genuine, epoch-shaping problems in Latin America and to examine the causative factors that the United States can influence. Of these, the most important is to get the United States' debt, interest rates, deficit, and dollar under control. Our own inability to behave with fiscal prudence and responsibility costs jobs and well-being at home. It also immensely increases the barriers to economic development in the Third World. What is of primary importance to the United States in this respect also turns out to be the single most important step that could be taken toward Latin America's return to economic and political health.

In 1984, the so-called Kissinger Commission (the National Bipartisan Commission on Central America) concluded, surprisingly, that U.S. monetary policy had "spurred" economic collapse in Central America.[1] The Washington-based Institute for International Economics declared that the "basic cause" of excessive interest rates in the early 1980s was the "unusual mismatch between loose fiscal policy and tight monetary policy in the United States, which drove up domestic (and therefore international) interest rates in textbook fashion." Real interest rates (basic rate minus inflation) averaged 1.7 percent during the 1960s and 1970s, but shot up largely as a result of U.S. policies to 7.5 percent in 1981 and to 11 percent in 1982. This added tens of billions of dollars to developing-country debt beyond what "could have been anticipated on the basis of past real interest rates." Moreover, these high interest rates, along with further oil shocks, were largely responsible for the severe international recession of 1980–1982. The developing countries' loss of export volume and value attributable to the recession was two and a half times greater than the direct increase in the debt caused by rising interest rates. Developing-country debt among countries without oil multiplied almost five times between 1973 and 1982, and more than 80 percent of the increase of almost $500 billion stemmed from interest rate increases, export losses, and oil price hikes.[2]

High interest rates, collapsing commodity prices, international recession, and spiraling debts have exacerbated economic hardship, widening the debilitating embrace of poverty, unemployment, and suffering in Latin America and elsewhere in the developing world. An increase of one percentage point in U.S. interest rates, for example, increases what Latin America must pay on its 1985 debt of $360 billion by $3.6 billion. By the same token, the benefits of reducing real interest rates would far outweigh any real or imaginable increases in direct economic aid to Latin America. Clearly, U.S. and Latin interests coincide. What is so readily labeled "the debt crisis of the developing countries" is first of all *our* problem, and cleaning up our own house is the most important move that will help Latins solve their problems.

BEYOND DEBT

Step two is getting the Latin countries through the "debt crisis"— which is more correctly described by Third World countries as a "development crisis." The International Monetary Fund (IMF), the multilateral banks, the United States, and other creditor nations are working on ways to ameliorate the current debt burdens, and some kind of political solution will be found to extend the pay-back period to ease the impact of enormous interest payments on debtor nations.

The possibility of debtor countries defaulting on their loans threatens creditor countries, too. The risk continues that repudiation of outstanding loans would cause a banking crisis in the United States and severely strain other Western economies. The Latin American debt-servicing breakdown that started in Argentina and Mexico in 1981–1982 and quickly spread could well undermine the security of the international financial system itself. To avoid such eventualities in 1982, the United States put together $2 billion in commodity credits and prepayments for oil for Mexico and a large emergency loan for Brazil, taking the lead in these two international debt "rescue operations."[3] President Reagan offered financial assistance to Mexico again in late 1985 and early 1986.

Such emergency actions by the United States, the IMF, and others suggest that the problem of Latin American and Third World debt is taken very seriously by policymakers. Yet, the obvious conclusion—that we must recognize and act on the interdependence of U.S. economic policymaking and economic progress beyond our borders—has not moved from crisis response to planning and prevention.

Most important from the Latins' point of view is getting investment going again, reversing the outflow of capital from many countries in the region, and bringing in the money essential to revitalizing their economies. Most important from both the Latin and donor institutions' points of view is that future investment and lending, both private and public, be used to build rather than exhaust the resource base. Essential here is avoiding the mistakes of the 1970s, a decade of excessive concentration on capital-intensive, large-scale, urban, industrial projects and commercial agriculture, while ignoring equity and other key social issues.

Some loans will be required to repay interest on debt, some to finance the purchase of U.S. goods. But all lending over which the United States has any control—that is, the multilateral banks, the IMF, the Export-Import Bank, and the Overseas Private Investment Corporation (OPIC), as well as American private banks—should be evaluated for its impact on the resource base. It should be the U.S. position that loans to finance large amounts of imported consumer goods, loans that unwisely exploit resources, loans for expensive capital-intensive rather than labor-intensive projects, and loans for environmentally unsound or polluting projects will not be made. As the most influential of the development banks, the World Bank should set appropriate standards for other multinational and private banks in this respect. As the World Bank's largest donor, the United States can and should throw its weight around, insisting on sustainable, conservation-minded development as a prerequisite for future lending.

LIBERALIZED TRADE

Both the United States and the Latin American nations stand to benefit if trade is liberalized. Unfortunately, Congress is gravitating in the opposite direction. In the name of protecting U.S. workers from the competition of less expensive imported goods, certain industries are pressuring Congress to restrict imports. Lost in the debate over national trade policies are the facts that almost 40 percent of the markets for U.S. exports are in the developing countries (a third of them in Latin America and the Caribbean) and that hundreds of thousands of U.S. workers have already lost their jobs because Third World countries have been forced to reduce their imports from the United States.[4]

Some tariffs and quotas have been reduced for Caribbean states through a presidential initiative. But Mexico and Venezuela are excluded from its terms, as are some industries, such as sugar and textiles, that might offer comparative advantage in the Caribbean.[5] The United States has prepaid on oil deliveries when Mexico has edged up to the brink of default.[6] U.S. security interests would certainly be considered threatened if we could not obtain energy supplies from our neighbors as needed, but we are unwilling to enter into long-term supply contracts for oil with Mexico and Venezuela, even though such contracts would allow these nations to plan ahead and would help stabilize their economies.

Of course, the United States has no corner on unwise trade policies. The Latin countries have restricted trade among themselves and with the United States and other industrialized countries. Numerous Latin nations discourage labor-intensive exports—by excessive protection of their own markets and import-substituting industries, unrealistically over-valued currencies, and taxes on both agricultural and industrial exports. These policies tend also to favor urban areas over rural ones, thus working against attempts to manage and slow internal migration.[7] The Latin nations need foreign exchange earnings to pay interest on the debt, to buy food, and to purchase capital goods necessary for development and growth. Their trade depends on the export of labor services, either as migrants who remit payments to their families back home or in the form of labor-intensive processed goods.

If trade were liberalized on both sides, U.S. exports would rise in step with the Latin countries' ability to sell their goods abroad. A general and mutual reduction of trade barriers will benefit trading partners. As economist Robert Repetto explains:

> More than any other measure, the progressive elimination of quantitative restrictions on simple labor-intensive manufactures, textiles and apparel, foot wear, and the like, would benefit low-income countries. Simplification and standardization of border requirements, codification of safeguard procedures, and more recourse to compensation and retraining for workers displaced by imports, rather than trade restrictions, would all encourage Third World exports. Reducing tariff rates on products from Third World countries and eliminating tariff escalation on the various stages of processing would enable these countries to expand employment by exporting processed instead of raw materials. At the same time, consumers in advanced countries would benefit from lower prices, and dynamic export industries in advanced countries would expand as Third World economies grew more quickly.[8]

INVESTING IN PEACE AND PROSPERITY

Appealing to Congress for increased funds for foreign assistance, Robert S. McNamara, former secretary of defense and former president of the World Bank, asserts that, dollar for dollar, at the margin, the United States can buy itself more security by investing in the AID budget than in the Defense Department.[9] Clearly, the economic impact of development assistance on recipient countries is but one side of the coin. These same funds are also investments in political stability and in reducing international tensions. The effects of such investments are cumulative, tending to further reduce the necessity for military spending.

Development assistance from the United States to the poorest of the Latin countries must be increased, especially where disaster seems close at hand. At the same time, U.S. development assistance—loans, materials, commodities, training, and technical assistance—should be available only to support development policies that conserve the resource base and manage natural resources wisely. These will be policies that meet certain criteria, such as improving the prospects of low-income households, or accelerating employment opportunity through labor-intensive economic development strategies that build from the bottom up.[10] It makes sense, for instance, to expand minimum health services to all households before spending any more on high-tech equipment for urban hospitals that serve primarily the middle and upper classes.

The development policies we now need are those that emphasize investment in rural rather than urban areas and that help small farmers increase their ability to grow food for domestic consumption. They include the extension of basic education to all villages and the provision of safe water supplies to all. Basic health services, especially maternal and child welfare and family planning services, are also a necessary part of the package. So is agricultural research directed at the small farmer's needs for hardy drought- and pest-resistant varieties. And so are credit and technical assistance. Without the last two critical inputs, small farmers cannot succeed even when government provides irrigation—witness the case of central Mexico's fertile valleys. A decade after title to irrigated lands was turned over to small farmers, many have been forced to lease their plots to modern agribusinesses and to work as part-time seasonal laborers on their own land.

The right kind of economic development will also provide technical assistance and credit to rural small businesses—including women traders, shopkeepers, and food processors—and provide affordable appropriate energy sources for those businesses. These development strategies encourage appropriate pricing policies, and remove subsidies from resource exploiting and capital-intensive industries. They are strategies that encourage redirection of some government programs and a decentralization of some planning and budget authority. Above all, these strategies will work because they encourage sustainable growth and conservation of the resource base by getting at the underlying problems of land tenure and population pressure.

LAND TENURE

Nothing is more important to regional security in Latin America than assuring farmers secure title to the land that they work. Without it, they have little motivation to stay on the land and take care of it. In *Bordering on Trouble*, frequent mention is made of the pervasive destruction of the land base by poor people who, repeatedly displaced from their land, move inexorably onto more fragile, often steeper areas. In many Latin countries, there are also large amounts of land held in large estates by absentee landlords, usually urban. On these large holdings, farming is often inefficient. Often, it is inappropriate as well—witness the vast hectareage dedicated to raising cattle.

In many Third World countries, concentration of land ownership is extreme. But Latin American nations lead the world in skewed ownership patterns: in 1975, 7 percent of landowners possessed 93 percent of the region's arable land. In Guatemala, 2 percent own 80 percent; in El Salvador as recently as 1980, 2 percent owned virtually all the arable land; in Nicaragua before the 1979 revolution, the Somoza family alone owned one-fourth of the nation's agricultural land; in Honduras 5 percent own 60 percent; and even in Costa Rica, which has a reputation for promoting equity, 3 percent control 54 percent of the land, and land pressure is partially relieved by widespread toleration of farmers who squat on government-owned lands, including biological reserves. In Central America overall, 1 percent of landowners controlled 40 percent of the land in 1970, and by the end of the decade, three-quarters of the rural population—some 7 or 8 million persons—faced extreme poverty and over a million children were malnourished.[11]

Pervasive poverty for millions of Latin American families is one consequence of these land-tenure patterns; devastation of the resource base is another. And the latter assures continued poverty for future generations. Fundamental to correcting the current course of agricultural stagnation, rural poverty, deforestation, and soil loss is correction of land-tenure systems. The few countries that have tried (Costa Rica, Mexico, Peru, Venezuela, Bolivia, El Salvador, and Nicaragua) need encouragement, and the others more pressure.

Of course, the United States cannot force land reform on even the smallest of these countries. Only Latin governments can take the lead. But the United States can make clear our aid and support for land reform—as we did a generation ago in Japan and Korea. Some Latin countries are again trying to move on this issue. In El Salvador, land reform has limped along despite the civil war. Although still far short of announced goals, it is recognized, finally, as a critical issue. Brazil's new government has announced a plan to redistribute idle *latifundia* to 10.6 million landless peasants by 2000. According to Brazil's minister of development, land conflict is endemic in all twenty-three states; in 1984 alone, some 180 people were killed in a thousand violent incidents. Only a thoroughgoing agrarian reform program, he says, can "prevent the country from becoming, within a decade, an immense battlefield."[12]

The United States' failure to encourage land reform over the last generation is probably its most regrettable—and expensive—error of omission. The current system increases inequity between rich and poor, foments political revolutions, and despoils the environment. It defeats the purpose of the millions of dollars that the United States has poured into agricultural research and development in Latin America over the last generation, even exacerbating the problems that now threaten the existence of the states we sought to help.

What was hard to do a generation ago has become more difficult today. What is required now is a very clear statement of U.S. policy on social justice with regard to the land. Based on a clear understanding of the relationships among land-ownership, rural welfare, economic growth, and good resource management practices, our policy must be complemented by legal and technical assistance for title registration and land surveys. There must be loans for compensating some current landowners—perhaps through U.S. contributions to national or regional land banks that would finance the transfer of acreage from larger land-holders to small land-holders by issuing long-term marketable securities.[13] At the same time, the United States should also be prepared to help provide the credit, extension services, transportation, and marketing assistance necessary if land reform is to succeed. The Kissinger Commission acknowledged the need for all of these reforms, as Nations and Leonard point out in Chapter 3, but earmarked none of its proposed $8 billion for the effort. Strong U.S. support, political and financial, for Latin programs of real structural reform could be one of our most important contributions to long-term, ecologically sound development of the region.

A QUICK REVERSAL ON U.S. POPULATION POLICY

Rapid population growth—with all its attendant ills of poverty, poor health, pollution, and heavy pressures on air, land, and water resources—cannot go unchecked much longer. Unmanageable population pressures may also lead to violence and threaten political stability. El Salvador and its pattern of rebellion and repression are familiar enough now to North Americans, but few understand what AID found in 1982: "The fundamental causes of the present conflict are as much environmental as political, stemming from problems of resource distribution in an overcrowded land."[14]

The Reagan administration's *laissez-faire* approach to population will not solve these problems. In fact, every methodologically sound study done over the past twenty-five years has concluded that rapid population growth at levels being exceeded in most of Latin America today retards the growth of per capita income and efforts to raise living standards in poor countries. To be sure, production may be stimulated by increasing demand. But these gains are outstripped by rapid increases in the number of dependents per active worker, by reductions in savings and diversions of investment from raising living standards to providing for the added people, and by reductions in labor productivity as new job seekers flood the market.[15]

There is no denying the meaning of demographers' projections. Latin countries do not have the world's highest birth rates, but the size and youth of their population base promise that if population continues to grow at current rates, resources will be stripped and consumed faster than they can be replaced. In Central America, for instance, the population will double in twenty-five years—a *very* fast rate of growth exceeded today only in some parts of Africa.[16] In many of these countries, the labor force doubled between 1960 and 1980, and it will double again in twenty-five years, adding nearly 100 million new Latin American workers from the births that have taken place in the past decade.

For a large portion of these 100 million people, the only alternative to unemployment and poverty appears to be migration—from the countryside to the cities, across borders to neighboring countries, and north to the United States. Latin cities are growing more rapidly and to far greater size than any others in the world, now or at any time in human history. Mexico City is three times the size of New York City now—nearly a thousand square miles. In another ten or twelve years, it will quadruple New York's population. By 2000, Mexico City will be twice as populous as the legendary Tokyo-Yokohama urban complex. Ciudad Nezahualcoyotl, recently a rustic squatters' suburb, is already twice the size of Los Angeles. Each day more than 1,000 rural migrants arrive, and each year the city will add 800,000 to 1 million new people (more than the entire population of San Francisco and most other large American cities) swelling to a fantastic 30 million or more before another fifteen years have passed. Similarly, São Paulo will reach a population of 25 million and four other Latin American megalopolises— Rio de Janeiro, Buenos Aires, Bogotá, and Lima—will be beyond 10 million persons each.[17]

Even if such gargantuan cities can somehow be managed—a big *if* even considering the enormous government subsidies they receive—their uncontrolled expansion creates one of the most "costly pile-ups in world history," according to former president of Mexico, José Lopez Portillo. It poses a potential nightmare for the United States, as U.S. ambassador to Mexico, John Gavin told the author of Chapter 2, David DeVoss. If millions go hungry in Mexico City or basic services break down—as they almost certainly will one day—this concentrated center of government, industry, and distorted demographics could collapse in disorder, unhinging the entire country.

The social, economic, political, and international consequences of breakdowns in Mexico City or other major cities in the hemisphere—most of them capitals—threaten U.S. security just as surely as breakdowns caused by civil wars or other military confrontations do. These cities will continue to grow despite the most heroic of efforts, but their growth must be slowed sufficiently to offer some hope that basic services and necessities can be provided.

Migration of landless, unemployed poor families may also spread across national boundaries—from one Latin country to another and to the United States. Latin Americans and Asians, not Europeans, now dominate U.S. immigration. Latin American legal immigrants enter at ten times the pre-1950 rate, mostly from the Caribbean region, one-third from Mexico. One million Cubans, and perhaps half a million Colombians, most of the latter undocumented, have come to the United States since 1959. Half a million or more Latin Americans continue to migrate— legally or illegally—to the United States annually.

Even more troubling to the political peace of the hemisphere are the substantial migrant flows *within* Latin America—from Brazil to Paraguay, from Colombia to Venezuela, from Haiti to the Dominican Republic and other Caribbean isles, from El Salvador to Honduras, from Guatemala to Mexico. Political violence in Latin America, especially in the countryside, has often involved economic refugees crossing a border. In the famous "Soccer War" of 1969, neighboring countries El Salvador and Honduras went to war over migration. A CIA report leaked to the press in early 1985 listed continuing tension between those two countries and similar situations as potential "hot spots" of concern to the United States in the next decade.[18] Fair immigration laws and evenhanded enforcement along borders may reduce some of the tension associated with migration in the short run, but only moderating Latin America's explosive population growth and attaining sustainable economic growth can provide lasting tranquility.

Most countries in Latin America, fortunately, have some leeway in which to deal with their population crises. Most—the exceptions are El Salvador and some of the island states—have some underused lands that, if redistributed and developed as recommended in *Bordering on Trouble*, could support many families. Most countries know that the problem is serious and most have national population policies in place. Some—Cuba and Barbados, for example—have already drastically reduced birth rates. But most countries need to deal more resolutely with the issue, and they will need outside help if they are to make the enormous investment required to come to grips with this problem, before there are still another 100 million looking for work.

If the United States is to help the hemisphere keep its population at supportable levels, the first order of business is to restore the population and family planning assistance programs that the Reagan administration abandoned in 1984. Voluntary programs offering information, services, proven technologies, and a full choice of ways for men and women to limit fertility are the only surefire solution, and these programs deserve strong U.S. support. U.S. assistance programs and such multinational programs as the United Nations Fund for Population Activities (UNFPA) can make a tremendous difference. Not long ago, the United States led the way in progressive population programs. The current unthinking reversal of that proud bipartisan tradition must be reversed again by Congress with help from all who value social justice, economic growth, and environmental protection.

Family planning programs must be coupled with Latin American commitment to the other social programs known to reduce rates of population growth, namely basic health services and opportunities for women. As the *World Development Report 1984* spelled out so clearly, fertility decreases more rapidly when mortality is also reduced and when the social and economic status of women is improved.[19] On these tasks also, U.S. assistance programs should concentrate their efforts.

In every society, women have fewer babies when they have greater opportunities for education and employment. Latin American women have the primary responsibility for safeguarding the family's health and survival and in regulating fertility. But they also play major, if unsung, roles in development, resource management, and environmental protection. Especially among the poor, family survival depends on women's economic contribution.

Fertility won't decline until the meaning of "sex education" changes. Entrenched attitudes and habits have to be rooted out and transformed. Elementary and secondary schooling for girls, literacy training for women, and training opportunities for women in jobs opening up in the modern sector are also needed. Opportunities are needed even more in the rural, traditional, and labor-intensive parts of the economy, where the poorest women work. Equally important is removing legal barriers to women so that they can own and control property, get credit for their businesses, and have access to technical assistance. In this respect, it's the rest of the society and the courts that need to be educated.

Decline in mortality can also accelerate fertility decline. Such relatively inexpensive preventive health measures as vaccination, adequate nutrition for babies and children, improved water supplies, and sanitation reduce mortality, mostly by saving children's lives. Additional basic health services—like pre- and postnatal care and oral rehydration therapy—make an enormous difference, and the cost is low: China provides these basic health services for $4 per person per year.

As an investment to shield Latin countries and the United States from future population and resource problems, these programs are well worth the cost. But most Latin countries cannot organize them on a large enough scale soon enough without U.S. and other foreign assistance. Even a U.S. administration whose leaders personally oppose fertility control should be able and willing to invest significantly in measures to reduce mortality—a "pro-life" move by any standard.

POLLUTION CONTROL AND RESOURCE PROTECTION

How many inhabit the planet is half the story. How is just as important. Here the scope for U.S. assistance to its Latin neighbors is tremendous. The United States can help them research, monitor, and control pollution, and restore and sustain the resource base that must support future generations. Yankee know-how clearly has its political and humanitarian purposes, especially in monitoring and assessing the hemisphere's resource and environmental conditions, trends, and needs. Using what we already know and already have on the shelf, the United States could work with Latin countries to identify their information needs and develop information systems that fit each country's requirements. The United States could also provide technical and financial support to Latin states that want better baseline data on environmental conditions and resources, carrying out the surveys and providing the monitoring systems that good resource management requires.

In most Latin countries national environmental profiles fall far short of being the statistical, detailed, comprehensive blueprints government officials need to plan programs, budgets, and schedules. With U.S. financial support and technical assistance, these profiles could be upgraded to truly useful tools, with goals against which progress can be measured.

If there is one area in which Latin admiration of U.S. power is unequivocal, it is in scientific research and technological innovation, so our help with both will be welcome. North America's research laboratories churn out information and materials of enormous help in solving Latin resource, environmental, and population problems—from biotechnology applications to agricultural and integrated pest management, to research on tropical disease and immunization strategies. For the small farmer and rural business in Latin America, collaborative research and demonstration projects undertaken jointly by the United States and Latin countries could mean a new lease on land and life. So too, the United States should increase its support of Latin research institutions. It is in the U.S. interest, for instance, to help Brazilian, Peruvian, and other scholars of the Amazon Basin unlock the secrets of how modern human intrusions affect the Amazon. While some of the rich primordial landscapes still remain intact, we need to speed up the collection of species taxonomies, the study of newly discovered species, and the contributions to germplasm-storage facilities. We need research to deepen our understanding of this unique ecosystem and to manage it more intelligently. The whole world stands to gain from the pharmaceuticals still unknown, from the role of vast forests in climate regulation, from the potential food and energy crops still undiscovered.

Some of the research and development of greatest interest to Latin America has already been done. The United States has pollution-control technology to sell, to adapt, to teach. It also has considerable experience to share in the organization of services, emergency preparedness, rehabilitation, and recovery techniques. As Lawrence Mosher points out in Chapter 7, U.S.

oil-spill recovery techniques are already employed in Caribbean cooperative efforts. Similar assistance could make a big difference in some of Latin America's troubled cities. Those subject to peculiar climatic inversions, like Mexico City, especially need effective air pollution abatement programs, vehicular controls to limit exhaust and precipitators, baghouses and other conventional technologies to limit air pollution from industrial sources—technologies that are commonplace in the United States. These same large cities need help with water pollution control—not only for sewage treatment and drinking water supplies, but also for industrial waste treatment.

U.S. regulatory experience may also prove helpful in Latin America. Neither technology nor regulations can be transferred wholesale without adaptation to suit local circumstances, but U.S. experience can certainly show the way.[20]

While Latin America has more trained personnel than most of the developing world, the need for training at all levels remains. For industrial planning and factory management in Venezuela, for coastal pollution control for the Caribbean isles, for integrated pest management in Nicaragua and Mexico, for reforestation, health workers, nutrition education, and sanitation virtually everywhere, the need is great. In education, especially the education of educators, the United States has much to offer. The United States has the wherewithal and the incentive to help each Latin nation develop its own indigenous conservation capability and improve resource management. This kind of U.S. contribution will find political favor both here and in Latin America, providing North American instructors learn to respect differences in culture and natural surroundings and to adapt our knowledge and technology to Latin needs.

Besides monitoring, planning, research, pollution control, restoration, and training, some specific programs deserve U.S. political and financial support. Joining with the Carribean nations in the Regional Seas Program and contributing to its Trust Fund, as proposed by Lawrence Mosher in Chapter 7, is clearly advisable. The program won't get far off the ground without U.S. participation. Moreover, a multilateral approach gets partially around the problem of the giant United States trying to deal equitably with tiny island states.

U.S. help to halt tropical forest loss also affords a double dividend. Forest clearing—one of Latin America's most serious environmental problems—takes place at rates of 3.5 percent per year in states like El Salvador, Costa Rica, and Paraguay. Even Brazil, where the rate is only 0.4 percent, still loses nearly 4 million acres of forest annually, more than any other nation on earth.[21] Deforestation threatens the livelihood of poor farmers and indigenous tribes, and it leads to extensive soil erosion and the siltation of rivers, lakes, and seas. It contributes to flooding, to climatic perturbations, and, as habitat disappears, to extensive species loss. Silt from denuded hillsides has halved the lifespan of the Peligre dam in Haiti. Silt from the surrounding hills is filling in the Panama Canal, where continuous, costly dredging operations are required. Land reform and reforestation, including agroforestry, would be cheaper.

In 1985, the administrator of AID supported a tropical forestry action agenda that calls for a concentrated international effort to stop forest loss, restore watersheds, and expand agroforestry and sound management practices to areas at risk.[22] So far, that commitment remains vague, containing no promise of new dollars, although the United States will be expecting the Latin countries and other donors to invest millions. Some U.S.-sponsored projects are under way, and others are planned, but the total effort is still too small and proceeding too slowly to address the deforestation crisis. Two bills introduced in Congress, one on tropical forests and another on biodiversity (40 to 50 percent of the world's remaining biota are in tropical forests), would redirect and increase funding, especially in AID. Both bills have strong support in the House and have been introduced in the Senate, although mandated budget cuts will exert downward pressure on the AID forestry budget in the absence at countervailing Congressional action.

As evidence of its commitment to tropical forests and biological conservation, the United States should take the lead in establishing a global system of protected areas. Ten times the current effort is needed! The United States should mobilize funding and provide technical assistance from the ranks of our own National Park Service and Fish and Wildlife Service to help train

developing-country professionals and to enhance national conservation capabilities—a key to stemming forest and species
losses over the long term.

Fortunately, some creative thinking is going on in Washington on helping developing countries to help themselves. A 1985
report by the Congressional Environmental and Energy Study
Institute (EESI) proposes a variety of imaginative, practical, and
low-cost initiatives to help less developed countries maximize resource use and solve environmental problems.[23] Some important
proposals, such as long-term assistance to Sub-Saharan Africa to
increase agricultural productivity and reduce long-term food aid
requirements through better resource management, involve an
authorization of new funds. Others include some institutional
changes, such as the creation within AID of a new Bureau of Environment, Forestry, Energy and Natural Resources. According to
the task force that produced the report, it makes sense to
strengthen and expand the Peace Corps' environmental and forestry efforts. The EESI also suggests expanding the PL-480 "Food
for Peace" program to include conservation of biological diversity and urged strong U.S. support and encouragement for private
voluntary organizations at work in the developing countries—
such groups as Ecuador's Fundación Natural, a development
organization run by two women who have organized projects to
reduce forest destruction.

PROMOTING U.S. VALUES

Bordering on Trouble reminds us that the United States has at
times intervened militarily or clandestinely to topple an elected
government or bolster a "friendly" military regime. This book
proposes that elected responsive civilian governments committed to equity and human rights have a better chance of solving the
economic and ecological problems facing Latin America. Can
any doubt remain that it is in the U.S. national interest to foster
these basic tenets of western democracy? Surely, the United
States has no reason to be bashful about championing democracy
and human rights in Latin America, as President Reagan did in
his 1985 speech before the United Nations General Assembly.

In some other areas of the world, the prospects for elected civilian government and the guarantee of basic human rights are

dim. But in Latin American countries, democracy is viable. Indeed, the persistent desire for responsive and responsible government throughout the hemisphere—even in countries that have known more years of repressive dictatorships than of elected government—is astonishing. Just look at the ecstatic popular enthusiasm at the inauguration of Guatemala's new president in early 1986—the first elected civilian president since 1970. With great tenacity, Latin Americans adhere to the ideal of elected governments. Their continuing desire is for self-determination, both within their separate countries and internationally. Even Cuba's leaders must be itching to be free of the Soviet yoke.

The United States needs in practical ways to recognize and encourage democratic institutions. The United States should support processes that are open, choices that are free, civilians who command the military. Certainly, our support should be consistent, even when we do not approve of every policy of every government, and we must not confuse ideology with process. In some cases, as in Venezuela and Brazil, this may mean continuing U.S. aid and loans to nations that do not number among the poorest of the poor. In some other countries, it will mean that aid and loans will be contingent on making those processes more open. Such a path will make some policy choices as difficult as Solomon's. In Haiti, for instance, suspending development assistance to apply pressure for human rights in the last months of Duvalier regime risked a delay in the AID reforestation project.

The role of the military in Latin America has grown over the last generation, especially during the 1970s and often with U.S. encouragement. And, although Latin America has not seen as rapid a build-up of arms during this period as elsewhere in the Third World, especially the Middle East, arms budgets represent a major drain on most countries' budgets. In the strife-torn Central American states, these costs are crippling: $60 million in Honduras in 1982, $93 million in Guatemala, $145 million in El Salvador, and $200 million in Nicaragua. Even noncombatant countries foot big military bills: Mexico spent over $1 billion in 1982, Brazil $2.5 billion, Colombia $0.5 billion, and even the small island state, the Dominican Republic, paid out $106 million in military expenses.[24] Although dwarfed by the military budgets of the industrialized countries (whose largest markets for arms lie also in the Third World), these sums represent other commodities foregone. And the price of weapons has increased much faster (by 100-fold) than those of other commodities since World War II.

The Third World arms buildup only widens the gap between rich and poor countries, and no end is in sight. As Princeton University's Richard H. Ullman points out: ". . . the real Third World . . . will continue to be one composed of governments made fragile and insecure [and therefore reliant on military force] because of their inability to meet the needs (let alone the expectations) of their citizens."[25] Many Latin countries are caught in a vicious circle: governments will be weaned from reliance on force only as they are able to meet their people's development needs. Whatever the past U.S. contribution to Latin militarization, it is time now for the United States to throw its full support behind civilian control, open political systems, and equitable economic growth.

CONCLUSIONS

In its relations with Latin America, the United States is bordering on trouble. A generation of rapid growth and change in Latin American countries—a period in which the United States has had a constant role and an occasionally heavy hand—has produced severe fiscal and monetary dislocations, inequitable distribution of benefits, political repression and instability, population pressure in both city and countryside, and widespread resource degradation. With Latin America's future growth and stability hanging in the balance, the United States cannot look upon this situation with equanimity.

To protect our own economic and security interests, the United States must focus on Latin America's real problems and acknowledge clearly what we can and cannot endure in the region. The U.S. economy can endure competition from imported labor-intensive goods, even the dislocation and hardship that it causes in parts of our own workforce. We can afford to soften the impact of such dislocation with increased adjustment assistance for affected workers and industries. But we cannot afford a continued steep decline in Brazil's real standard of living, nor risk the collapse of the newly elected civilian government there. Neither can the United States afford the continued decline of our markets in Latin America and the job losses that this decline precipitates in the United States. We in the United States can absorb some Mexican workers; indeed, many U.S. employers want and need them. But can we withstand the collapse of Mexico City and chaos among the 22 percent of Mexican citizens who live there? The U.S. taxpayer can ease U.S. and multinational banks by stretching out overdue loans, but cannot endure an epidemic of defaults and the collapse of the international monetary system.

The United States can endure independent and proud Latin neighbors that aggressively pursue dynamic social change. We can even stand Marxist rhetoric or some state-owned enterprises, especially when their direction and judgments are debated in an open society and endorsed in popular elections, as in Venezuela. What the United States *cannot* endure is the prospect that the current situation will get worse and that irresponsible demagogues will topple beleaguered governments. No matter how powerful, the United States cannot find lasting security in a hemisphere of impoverished, hostile states whose citizens all have automatic anti-American reflexes.

The United States has contributed its share to Latin American problems—partly, as *Bordering on Trouble* shows, because we have defined "security" too narrowly and based aid and investment policies on inappropriate models, experience, and technologies. But we erred also because we did not, until recently, understand any better than anyone else the connections between environmental degradation and the continuing capacity of the resource base to sustain economic growth.

We should not blame ourselves, or anyone else, too strongly for this failure. When the U.S. government prodded and encouraged U.S. involvement in Latin America in Lyndon Johnson's day, no policymaker anywhere was thinking of environmental costs. Even in the United States, the environmental movement was newborn and just beginning to find its way. Few imagined in the 1960s and early 1970s the extent to which population pressures and environmental degradation would deepen the divisions between rich and poor. In the heady optimism of the expansive 1970s, pervasive landlessness and poverty were assumed to be on their way out.

Today, our understanding is deeper and our optimism tempered. Nor has that insight been limited to the industrialized nations. Since the 1972 United Nations conference on the environment at Stockholm, there has been in Latin America and throughout the developing world a dramatic shift in the awareness of environmental problems and their relationship to development goals. In some countries, that awareness translates into changes in development policies. Some are de-emphasizing monumental showcase dams and highways and plants in favor of smaller scale, labor-intensive, decentralized projects from which smaller population centers and rural communities benefit. In 1985, Mexico initiated a major new rural development program. Peru's new democratic government puts top priority on helping farmers. Venezuela and Brazil—both industrial success stories—are now putting more emphasis on agriculture. Even the difficult issue of land reform is again on the agenda in El Salvador and Brazil.[26]

Development assistance institutions are changing, too. AID, Western European governments, and the United Nations Environment Programme (UNEP) are exploring ways to involve private voluntary organizations in small-scale decentralized assistance projects. AID now helps countries that foster agriculture and emphasizes more small-scale, community-based, and private initiatives. The World Bank and the International Monetary Fund are providing more incentives for countries to nurture agriculture and free markets. As concern grows at these lending institutions about persistent poverty and its impact on sustainable development, local health care, fuelwood, agroforestry, technical assistance to small farmers, and other low-cost, high-impact initiatives are receiving more support.

Reversing major ecological and population trends, altering styles of development, and distributing its benefits are difficult by any measure. Sustainable development, even when the resources and political will are there, requires great skill and enormous effort, and persistence. But the time does now seem right to make an extra effort.

Indeed, in George F. Kennan's words: "the environmental and nuclear crises will brook no delay." Should we not face up to these "two apocalyptic dangers" we will, in Ambassador Kennan's judgment, be pursuing immoral ends:

Of all the multitudinous celestial bodies of which we have knowledge, our own earth seems to be the only one even remotely so richly endowed with the resources that make possible human life—not only make it possible, but surround it with so much natural beauty and healthfulness and magnificence. Is there not, whatever the nature of one's particular God, an element of sacrilege involved in the placing of all this at stake for the sake of the comforts, the fears and the national rivalries of a single generation? Is there not a moral obligation to recognize in this very uniqueness of the habitat and nature of man the greatest of our moral responsibilities, and to make of ourselves, in our national personification, its guardians and protectors rather than its destroyers?[27]

The United States has every reason to care and to act, and it has a principal role to play in solving the vast transnational problems explored in this book. Indeed, there are some contributions that only the United States can make in this hemisphere. But our efforts will come to naught without a comparable effort by the Latin nations. They, of course, must initiate and expand the fertility-control, mortality-reduction, and pro-women policies necessary to stabilize population growth. Only they can alter pricing policies and trade practices that work against sustainable development. They must protect their own fragile resources. Only they can set priorities to correct institutional inadequacies. Only they can provide the leadership these efforts require.

But the Latin countries will not succeed without the consistent, firm backing of the United States. The United States is so rich, so powerful, and so dominant in this hemisphere that no large enterprise can move forward effectively without its support. When the United States drags its heels, even the next largest and most powerful countries can accomplish little without the greatest extra energy. The colossus of the North can say aye or nay. If it merely acquiesces, history will register a no vote, and the United States will be bordering on generations of trouble.

NOTES

1. The National Bipartisan Commission on Central America, *Report of the National Bipartisan Commission on Central America* (Washington, D.C., January 1984) 10.

2. William R. Cline, *International Debt and the Stability of the World Economy* (Washington, D.C.: Institute for International Economics, 1983) 23–25.

3. Cline, *International Debt,* 30–31, 40–41.

4. Robert Repetto, "Population, Resource Pressures and Poverty," in Robert Repetto (ed.), *The Global Possible* (New Haven: Yale University Press, 1985) 161.

5. Michael S. Teitelbaum, *Latin Migration North* (New York: Council on Foreign Relations, 1985) 55, 74.

6. Cline, *International Debt,* 40.

7. Repetto, "Population, Resource Pressures and Poverty," 161.

8. Repetto, "Population, Resource Pressures and Poverty," 161–162.

9. Personal communication from Robert McNamara, January 19, 1986.

10. See Repetto, "Population, Resource Pressures and Poverty," 146–164 for a discussion of development policies that will curb population increases, encourage economic growth, and maintain the resource base.

11. United Nations Economic Commission for Latin America, "La Pobreza y la Satisfacción de Necesidades Básicas en el Istmo Centroamericano (Avances de una investigación regional)," Mexico City, March 1981, 23; also see Charles Teller, Mauricio Culagovski, Juan del Canto y José Aranda Pastor, "Desnutrición, Población y Desarrollo Social y Economico: Hacia un Marco de Referencia," in Charles Teller, Mauricio Culagovski and José Aranda Pastor (eds.), *Interrelación, Desnutrición, Poblacion y Desarrollo Social y Economico* (Guatemala, Instituto de Nutrición de Centro América y Panamá, 1980) 37.

12. Mae Morgolis, "Land Disputes Trigger Wave of Violence in Brazil," *Washington Post,* August 29, 1985.

13. See Robert Repetto and Andrew Maguire, "The Kissinger Commission: A Critique," *Interaction,* Spring/Summer 1984 for a more detailed proposal on regional land banks.

14. United States Agency for International Development, *Perfil ambiental de El Salvador,* draft version, 1981.

15. Robert Repetto, "Why Doesn't Julian Simon Believe His Own Research?" *The Washington Post,* November 2, 1985.

16. United Nations, Department of International Economic and Social Affairs, *World Population Prospects as Assessed in 1980* (New York: UN Population Studies, no. 78, 1981) 16–21.

17. Jonathan Kandell, "Nation in Jeopardy," *Wall Street Journal,* October 4, 1985.

18. Hobart Rowan, "Global Overpopulation," *Washington Post,* February 17, 1985.

19. The World Bank, *World Development Report 1984* (Washington, D.C.: The World Bank, 1984) 51–188.

20. Jorge E. Hardoy and David E. Satterthwaite, "Third World Cities and the Environment of Poverty," in Repetto, *The Global Possible,* 171–210.

21. J.P. Lanley, "Tropical Forest Resources," FAO Forestry Paper no. 30, Rome, 1983.

22. *Tropical Forests: A Call for Action,* Report of an International Task Force convened by the World Resources Institute, The World Bank, and the United Nations Development Programme (Washington, D.C.: World Resources Institute, 1985) 28.

23. Environmental and Energy Study Institute, *A Congressional Agenda for Improved Resource and Environmental Management in the Third World: Helping Developing Countries Help Themselves* (Washington, D.C.: Environmental and Energy Study Institute, October 1985) 11–13, 29, 35, 48–49.

24. Ruth Leger Sivard, *World Military and Social Expenditures 1985* (Washington, D.C.: World Priorities, 1985) 35.

25. Richard H. Ullman, "Arresting the Militarization of the Third World," in Jagat S. Mehta (ed.), *Third World Militarization, A Challenge to Third World Diplomacy* (Austin, Texas: University of Texas, 1985) 203.

26. Ellen B. Geld, "Brazilian Reform Cuts off the Hands that Fed the Nation," *Wall Street Journal,* September 6, 1985.

27. George F. Kennan, "Morality and Foreign Policy," *Foreign Affairs,* Winter 1985–86, 216.

CONTRIBUTORS

Gene E. Bigler

Dr. Bigler is Research Analyst for Latin America at the U.S. Information Agency and Professorial Lecturer at The School of Advanced International Studies, the John Hopkins University. He has held positions at the Instituto de Estudios Superiores de Caracas, Venezuela, and is co-author of *Modelo Demo-Económico De Venezuela* and *La Política y el Capitalisimo de Estado en Venezuela.* (The opinions expressed in Dr. Bigler's chapter are his own and do not reflect those of the U.S. Information Agency.)

Janet Welsh Brown

Dr. Brown is a Senior Associate at the World Resources Institute, specializing in U.S. policy. Dr. Brown was the Executive Director of the Environmental Defense Fund, a senior program officer on science policy at the American Association for the Advancement of Science, and a professor of political science and international relations.

David DeVoss

Mr. DeVoss was a correspondent with *Time* magazine for sixteen years, the last two of which (1983–1984) were spent in Mexico City as Mexico Bureau Chief. Mr. DeVoss contributed to *Time*'s 1984 cover story on Mexico City's growth and population problems. He now writes for the *Los Angeles Times Magazine.*

Sergio Diaz-Briquets

Dr. Diaz-Briquets is Director of Research at the Institute for World Concerns, Duquesne University. He was associated with the Population Reference Bureau in Washington, D.C., and the International Development Research Centre in Ottawa, Canada, and served as Associate Director of the University of Maryland's research project on migration and development in the Caribbean. He is the author of articles on population and development, and of *The Health Revolution in Cuba.*

Elizabeth de G.R. Hansen

Dr. Hansen, an anthropologist, recently spent two years on a post-Doctoral Rockefeller Fellowship at the Centro Internacional de

Agricultura Tropical in Colombia. There she conducted surveys and evaluations of land and fertilizer use in a frontier area. She has authoured journal articles on rural agriculture and translated works on Latin America. Presently she serves as Assistant to the President for International Education and Special Programs at the City College of New York.

Walter LaFeber

Dr. LaFeber is Professor of History on the Marie Underhill Knoll Fellowship at Cornell University. He is an expert on United States' diplomatic history. His most recent book, *Inevitable Revolutions: The United States in Central America,* won the Gustavus Myer Award for the best study on the history of American political intolerance.

Jeffrey Leonard

Dr. Leonard is Senior Associate with the Conservation Foundation, where he is responsible for the foundation's programs in Latin America and other developing countries. Dr. Leonard is author of the forthcoming *Natural Resources and Economic Development in Central America: A Regional Environmental Profile* and editor of *Divesting Nature's Capital: The Political Economy of Environmental Abuse in the Third World.*

Andrew Maguire

Dr. Maguire is Vice President for Policy Affairs at the World Resources Institute. He was Advisor on Political and Security Affairs with the U.S. State Department, a member of five U.S. Delegations to the United Nations General Assembly, a consultant to the Ford Foundation, and a U.S. Congressman from New Jersey. He is the author of *Toward "Uhuru" in Tanzania: The Politics of Participation.*

Ronald H. McDonald

Dr. McDonald is Professor of Political Science at Syracuse University and serves on the Editorial Boards of *Third World Review* and *Polity.* His extensive field research on Latin American politics has resulted in *Party Systems and Elections in Latin America,* together with numerous contributions to books, journals, and newspapers.

Lawrence Mosher

Mr. Mosher is an environmental writer based in Washington, D.C. He is Editor of *The Water Reporter,* a semimonthly report for water resources professionals, and a contributing editor of *National Journal.* Mr. Mosher is also the North American Correspondent for *Ambio,* a bimonthly journal published by the Royal Swedish Academy of Sciences in cooperation with the World Resources Institute.

416

Contributors

James D. Nations

Dr. Nations has devoted twelve years to field research on rainforests and among the rainforest peoples of Latin America, in particular the Lacandon Maya of Chiapas, Mexico. His research has led to the publication of numerous articles on these and related Latin American subjects. Dr. Nations is Senior Researcher at the Center for Human Ecology in Austin, Texas.

Robert Pastor

Dr. Pastor is Professor of Political Science at Emory University in Atlanta and Director of the Latin American and Caribbean Program at the Carter Center. He has been Fulbright Professor of U.S. Foreign Policy at El Colegio de México in Mexico City, and Senior Staff Member for Latin American and Caribbean Affairs for the National Security Council. He recently edited *Migration and Development in the Caribbean: The Unexplored Connection.*

Marc P. Reisner

Mr. Reisner writes extensively on natural resources. His articles have appeared in the *New York Times,* the *Washington Post, GEO,* and numerous other magazines and newspapers. He was staff writer for the Natural Resources Defense Council. His recent book on water and the growth of the American West is titled *Cadillac Desert.*

Tad Szulc

Mr. Szulc is a foreign policy specialist who concentrates on Latin America and Brazil, where he was educated and later spent six years as the *New York Times* Latin American correspondent. A freelance writer, he has written fourteen books on various aspects of Latin American politics. His latest book is titled *Fidel Castro: A Critical Portrait.*

Franklin Tugwell

Dr. Tugwell is an expert on energy policy and Latin America and has a particular interest in Venezuela. He has published widely on these subjects, including his recent book, *The Politics of Oil in Venezuela.* Dr. Tugwell is Professor of Government at Pomona College and Claremont Graduate School and a consultant to U.S. AID for the development of renewable energy resources in Latin America.

APPENDIX

Appendix

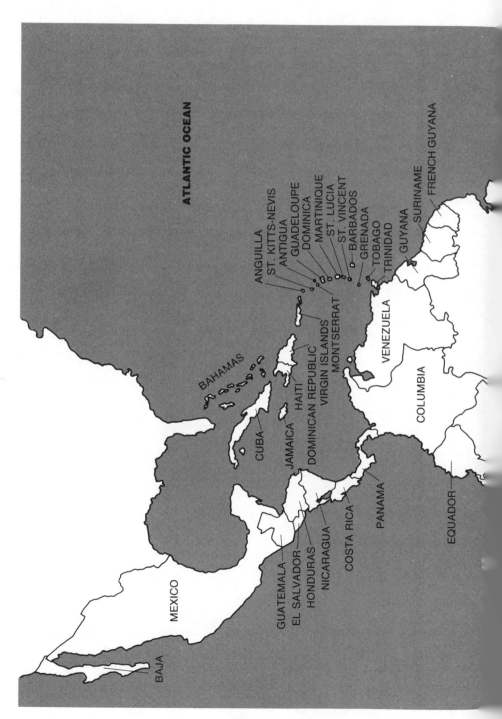

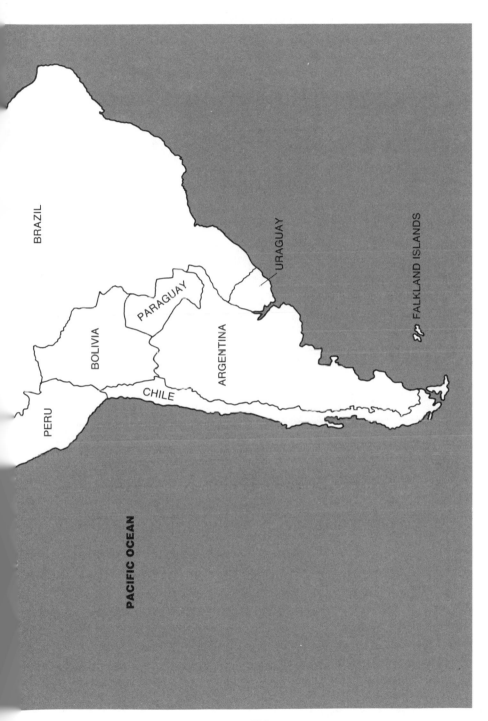

Appendix

Trade with United States

	1980		1984		External Debt (1983)[1]		
	Exports to U.S. ($ millions)	Imports from U.S. ($ millions)	Exports to U.S. ($ millions)	Imports from U.S. ($ millions)	$ millions	% of GNP	% exports
Antigua & Barbuda	—	—	—	—	—	—	—
Argentina	792	2,630	1,042	900	24,593	32.1	24
Bahamas	1,524	396	1,218	555	—	—	—
Barbados	99	137	257	242	—	—	—
Belize	63	58	48	53	—	—	—
Bolivia	189	172	160	106	2,969	77.7	30.5
Brazil	4,000	4,352	8,273	2,640	58,068	29.3	28.7
Chile	559	1,354	871	800	6,827	39.2	18.3
Colombia	1,327	1,736	1,253	1,450	6,899	18.3	21.3
Costa Rica	405	498	544	423	3,315	126.3	50.6
Cuba	—	—	—	—	—	—	—
Dominica	—	—	—	—	—	—	—
Dominican Republic	828	795	1,068	646	2,202	26.7	22.7
Ecuador	953	864	1,804	655	6,239	63	32.5
El Salvador	444	273	406	426	1,065	29.2	6.4
Grenada	—	—	—	—	—	—	—
Guatemala	465	553	475	377	1,405	15.8	11.7
Guyana	135	96	88	51	—	—	—
Haiti	264	311	395	419	433	26.8	5
Honduras	475	379	450	322	1,570	56.3	14.9
Jamaica	419	305	415	495	1,950	65.2	15.4
Mexico	12,835	15,146	18,267	11,992	66,732	49.1	35.9
Nicaragua	227	250	69	112	3,417	133	18.3
Panama	353	699	365	757	2,986	73.6	6.8
Paraguay	85	109	44	64	1,161	28.6	14.9
Peru	1,443	1,172	1,402	751	7,932	48.1	19.6
St. Kitts & Nevis	—	—	—	—	—	—	—
St. Lucia	—	—	—	—	—	—	—
St. Vincent & Grenadines	—	—	—	—	—	—	—
Suriname	126	136	112	100	—	—	—
Trinidad & Tobago	2,454	680	1,411	601	—	—	—
Uruguay	103	183	576	80	2,523	48.4	19.8
Venezuela	5,571	4,577	6,820	3,377	12,911	19.8	15
USA							

Source: *(International Monetary Fund,) Direction of Trade Statistics,*, 1985
Internationlal Monetary Fund, Washington, D.C.
[1]The World Bank *World Development Report 1985,* Oxford University Press, 1985, pp. 204-205.

Appendix

Immigration to United States

	Total Immigration to U.S. (through 1980)	Year of Immigration (% of Total Immigration)				Median Household Income of U.S. Immigrant, 1979 ($)
		up to 1959	1960-69	1970-74	1975-80	
Antigua & Barbuda	3,920	19.3	28.5	24.2	28.0	12,241
Argentina	68,887	16.5	40.3	17.9	25.3	18,892
Bahamas	13,993	40	15.9	15.5	28.7	12,235
Barbados	26,847	19.8	24.3	26.3	29.6	14,290
Belize	14,436	9.7	35.2	27	28.1	14,067
Bolivia	14,468	11.8	33.7	24.1	30.4	18,247
Brazil	40,919	20.6	31.3	16	32.1	16,067
Chile	35,127	11.3	26.8	26	35.9	17,259
Colombia	143,508	7.9	37.1	25.4	29.6	15,883
Costa Rica	29,639	14.3	38.9	22	24.8	14,397
Cuba	607,814	12.8	60.4	20.5	6.3	16,326
Dominica	3,296	8.4	31.4	20.6	39.6	11,531
Dominican Republic	169,147	6.1	37.2	25.8	31	10,130
Ecuador	86,128	7.6	39.2	27.7	25.5	15,402
El Salvador	94,447	6.1	16.8	25.9	51.3	12,261
Grenada	7,101	10.3	26	29.8	33.9	15,786
Guatemala	63,073	6.4	24.3	29.2	40.1	13,385
Guyana	48,608	7	20.6	26.3	46.1	15,913
Haiti	92,395	4.6	30.8	31	33.6	13,377
Honduras	39,154	15.6	32.2	24.5	27.7	13,435
Jamaica	196,811	11.6	29.8	28	30.6	15,290
Mexico	2,199,221	20.3	21.9	24.7	33	12,747
Nicaragua	44,166	18.5	20.5	15.6	45.3	13,295
Panama	60,740	29	31.5	15.8	23.8	15,255
Paraguay	2,858	11.1	38.3	21.3	29.3	17,859
Peru	55,496	9.7	30.9	27.7	31.7	16,513
St. Kitts & Nevis	1,903	20.9	33.3	15.4	30.4	14,284
St. Lucia	1,901	15.9	26.1	26.4	31.6	14,331
St. Vincent & Grenadines	4,044	10.9	26.5	28.3	34.2	16,019
Suriname	1,433	32.2	30.1	15.7	22	20,547
Trinidad & Tobago	65,907	7.4	30.7	34.2	27.6	14,733
Uruguay	13,278	5.7	28.8	30.5	34.9	18,755
Venezuela	33,281	10.6	16.1	11	62.2	10,493
USA	—	—	—	—	—	—

Source: U.S. Bureau of the Census, "Statistical Profile of the Foreign-Born Population: 1980 Census of Population," U.S. Bureau of the Census, October 1984.

423

Population Statistics

	Area (sq. km.)[1]	Population[2] 1970 thousands	Population[2] 1985 thousands	Urbanization[2] 1970 (% of Pop.)	Urbanization[2] 1985 (% of Pop.)
Antigua & Barbuda	280	—	—	—	—
Argentina	2,771,300	23,962	30,564	78.4	84.6
Bahamas	11,396	—	—	—	—
Barbados	430	239	265	37.1	42.4
Belize	22,973	—	—	—	—
Bolivia	1,098,160	4,325	6,371	40.8	43.7
Brazil	8,521,100	95,847	135,564	55.8	72.7
Chile	756,626	9,368	12,074	75.2	83.4
Colombia	1,139,600	20,803	28,714	57.2	67.4
Costa Rica	51,000	1,732	2,600	39.7	45.9
Cuba	114,478	8,572	10,038	60.2	71.8
Dominica	790	—	—	—	—
Dominican Republic	48,692	4,289	6,243	40.3	55.7
Ecuador	274,540	5,958	9,380	39.5	47.7
El Salvador	21,400	3,582	5,552	39.4	43
Grenada	344	—	—	—	—
Guatemala	108,888	5,353	8,403	35.7	41.4
Guyana	214,970	709	953	29.4	32.2
Haiti	27,713	4,605	6,585	19.8	28
Honduras	112,150	2,639	4,372	28.9	39.9
Jamaica	11,422	1,869	2,323	41.6	53.8
Mexico	1,978,800	51,176	78,996	59	70
Nicaragua	147,900	2,053	3,272	47	59.4
Panama	75,650	1,531	2,180	47.6	51.9
Paraguay	406,630	2,290	3,681	37.1	41.5
Peru	1,284,640	13,193	19,698	57.4	67.4
St. Kitts & Nevis	261	—	—	—	—
St. Lucia	616	—	—	—	—
St. Vincent & Grenadines	389	—	—	—	—
Suriname	142,709	372	353	45.9	45.7
Trinidad & Tobago	5,128	1,027	1,118	21.5	22.6
Uruguay	186,998	2,808	3,012	82.1	85
Venezuela	911,680	10,962	18,386	76.2	85.7
USA	9,372,614	205,051	237,660	73.6	74.2

Population under 15 yrs.[2] (% of Pop.)[2]			1985 Population Density[2] (per sq. km.)
1970 (% of pop.)	1985 (% of pop.)	2000 (% of pop.)	
—	—	—	—
29.4	31	28.5	11
—	—	—	—
37.4	27.6	24.7	616.3
—	—	—	—
43.0	43.8	43.5	5.8
42.2	36.4	31.8	15.9
38.1	31.2	28	16
45.4	37.2	32.7	25.2
46.1	36.7	32.5	51
37.2	26.4	24.1	87.7
—	—	—	—
48.3	40.7	33.6	128.2
45.3	44.2	41.3	34.2
46.1	44.6	40.7	259.4
—	—	—	—
45.7	43.1	39.5	77.2
47.6	37	28.2	4.4
42.9	43.6	43.4	237.6
47.5	46.9	42.3	40
47	36.8	29.9	203.4
46.7	42.2	36.5	39.9
48.3	46.7	42.7	22.1
44.2	37.5	31.5	28.8
45.7	41.7	31.7	9.1
44	40.5	35.6	15.3
—	—	—	—
—	—	—	—
—	—	—	—
48.3	42.6	36.3	2.5
41.2	31.6	27.6	218
27.9	26.9	25	16.1
46	41	35.7	20.2
28.3	21.9	21.7	25.4

[1]*1985 World Almanac & Book of Facts 1985*. The Newspaper Enterprises Association, Inc., New York, 1984.

[2]United Nations, *World Population Prospects (Estimates and Projections as Assessed in 1982)*, United Nations, New York, 1985.

Appendix

Quality of Life Indicators

	Life Expectancy at birth 1980-85[1]	Annual Pop. Growth 1980-85[1]	% Gov. Expend. on Educ. 1980[2]
Antigua & Barbuda	—	—	(1975) 14.4
Argentina	69.7	1.6	15.1
Bahamas	—	—	(1978) 22.9
Barbados	71.6	.8	(1981) 19.6
Belize	—	—	—
Bolivia	50.7	2.7	25.3
Brazil	63.4	2.2	(1970) 10.6
Chile	67	1.7	11.9
Colombia	63.6	2.2	14.3
Costa Rica	73	2.6	22.2
Cuba	73.4	.6	(1975) 30.1
Dominica	—	—	—
Dominican Republic	62.6	2.3	16
Ecuador	62.6	3.2	33.3
El Salvador	64.8	2.9	17.1
Grenada	—	—	(1975) 12.5
Guatemala	60.7	3.0	(1981) 10.7
Guyana	68.2	2.0	(1979) 14.0
Haiti	52.7	2.5	10.7
Honduras	59.9	3.4	15.0
Jamaica	70.3	1.4	13.1
Mexico	65.7	2.6	16.7
Nicaragua	59.8	3.3	10.4
Panama	71	2.2	19.0
Paraguay	65.1	3.0	(1979) 12.4
Peru	58.6	2.6	15.2
St. Kitts & Nevis	—	—	10.2
St. Lucia	—	—	(1975) 16.8
St. Vincent & Grenadines	—	—	—
Suriname	69.4	.1	25.0
Trinidad & Tobago	70.1	.9	9.5
Uruguay	70.3	.7	10.0
Venezuela	67.8	3.3	14.7
USA	74.0	.9	(1975) 18.1

GNP per Capita (1983 $)[3]	% Access to Drinking Water (1983)[4]	Combined Primary/ Secondary School Enrollment Ratio (1980)[5]	
		Females	Males
—	—	—	—
2,070	67	95	91
—	59	—	—
—	52	99	98
—	67	—	—
510	43	64	76
1,880	75	77	76
1,870	85	96	95
1,430	91	86	81
1,020	88	81	79
—	—	90	91
—	—	—	—
1,370	62	—	—
1,420	59	76	77
710	55	63	63
—	—	—	—
1,120	51	41	48
—	80	—	—
300	33	40	47
670	69	69	69
1,300	93	79	75
2,240	74	86	89
880	56	80	74
2,120	62	91	90
1,410	25	64	69
1,040	52	84	93
—	—	—	—
—	—	—	—
—	—	—	—
—	89	77	79
6,850	87	80	77
2,490	83	83	81
3,840	83	73	75
14,110	—	99	99

[1]United Nations, *World Population Prsopects (Estimates and Projections as Assessed in 1982)*, New York, 1985.

[2]UNESCO 1984 Statistical Yearbook.

[3]The World Bank, *World Development Report 1985*, Oxford University Press, 1985, pp. 204-205.

[4]Pan-American Health Organization, "Progress in International Drinking Water Supply and Sanitation Decade in the Americas (1981-1983)," 1984.

[5]United Nations, *Selected Statistics and Indicators on the Status of Women*, May 1985.

Note: The Primary/ Secondary enrollment ratio is the ratio of total primary and secondary enrollment (regardless of age) to the number of persons in the primary and secondary age groups.)

INDEX

A

Acid rain, in Mexico, 22
Acción Democrática, 155, 162, 170–71,
    177, 188, 373
ADELA, 353–54
Agency for International
    Development, 411
Alliance for Progress funding, 358
approach to Caribbean Action Plan,
    253–55
assistance related to population
    problems, 345
Bureau of Environment, Forestry,
    Energy and Natural Resources, 407
contribution to Caribbean
    development, 265–66
control over Alliance for Progress
    policy, 349–50
lending for water development, 301
loans to Brazil, 360–64
and Marshall Plan experience, 347
terms for loans, environmental
    protection in, 302
training and arming of internal
    security forces, 352
tropical forestry action agenda, 406
Agent Orange, used in Brazil, 221, 297
Agrarian Bank (Colombia), 110, 112–13
Agricultural development. See also
    specific nation
international funding for, 71
Agricultural labor, and export-crop
    system, 68–69
Agricultural productivity, and tropical
    forest destruction, 81
Agricultural research
for Amazon Basin, 142
and economic growth, 104
Agricultural Trade Development Act.
    See Public Law 480
Agriculture. See also Food production
in Caribbean, 321
in Central America, 64
initiatives for, 85–87
commercial
    growth of, 70
    vs. peasant farming, 105
estate system, 67

growth, in Central America, 77–78
vs. industry, trade-off between, 344
small-scale. See also Small farmers
    initiatives for improving, 86–87
and switch to export crops, 69
Agroecosystems, sustainable, obstacles
    to developing, 87
Agronomists, Colombian, 135
Agropecuarian Finance Fund, 112, 124,
    134
Agrovilas, 226
Aguilar, Luis Sánchez, 42
Aguirre, Ramón, 31, 36
AID. See Agency for International
    Development
The Alamo, 48
Alatorre García, Horacio, 34
ALCASA, 166
Alemán, Miguel, 25
Alencar, Marcel Nuñez de, 304–5
Alfonzo, Juan Pablo Pérez, 156, 165
Allende, Salvador, 372–73
Alliance for Progress
approach to land reform, 345–51
and Brazilian military regime,
    359–64
emphasis on stability and aggregate
    production, 345–51
failure of, 364–70, 376–78
and frontier thesis, 357–59
funding of counterinsurgency agents,
    352–53
funding of debt repayments, 351–53
and private enterprise, 350, 353–54
and social and political reform,
    354–57
weaknesses, 338–39
Alumina
mining in Caribbean, 325
Venezuelan, 168
Aluminio del Caroní. See ALCASA
Amazon Basin, 191
agricultural research for, 142
deforestation, 194, 198, 223
development of, 193–94
environmental implications, 191–92,
    198, 221–24

429

Index

Index

Index

434

Index

Electrificacíon del Caroni. *See*
 EDELCA
Electronorte, 297
El Salvador, 56, 58, 239, 271, 298–99,
 311. *See also* Soccer War
 agricultural initiative in, 89
 agricultural problems, 368–69
 beef production, 61
 and CACM, 356–57
 coffee exports, 367
 deforestation, 78
 environmental devastation, 367
 erosion in, 81, 320
 export crops, 67, 69–70
 failure of Alliance for Progress in,
  366–69
 forest, 319
 geothermal energy use, 324
 illegal immigrants from, 329
 inequitable land distribution, 367
 irrigation in, 321
 land ownership in, 65, 397
  and instability, 328
 land reform, 89, 322, 398, 411
 land use in, 68, 319
 legacies of Alliance for Progress in,
  377, 378
 main export, 250
 mangrove depletion, 82
 military aid to, 63
 military expenses, 408
 political violence, environmental and
  political causes, 84–85, 399
 population characteristics, 242–43,
  250, 314–16, 367
 reform programs, effect of political
  structure, 381
 revolutionary movements, 62
 rural population growth, and
  resource degradation, 75
 rural poverty in, 83
 school attendance in, 317
 United States foreign aid for, 262–63
 United States policy in, 391
Emigration. *See also* Illegal aliens;
 Immigration
 from Caribbean, 318
Employment initiatives, 331
 for Central America, 90–91
Energy conservation, and lending
 policies, 304
Environmental and Energy Study
 Institute, initiatives to maximize
 resource use and solve
 environmental problems, 407
Environmental problems, relationship
 to development goals, 410–11

Erosion. *See* Soil erosion
Eximbank, 189
Export-Import Bank, 349, 394
 lending for water development, 301
 loans to Colombia, 115

F

Falcón, Pablo Tellez, 21
Falklands crisis, 183
Family planning. *See also* Population
 control
 assistance programs, 402
 in Central America, 90
 in Chile, 344
 in Honduras, 345
 in Mexico, 25, 52
 in Peru, 345
 in Venezuela, 345
FCV, 373
Federacíon Campesina de Venezuela.
 See FCV
Federacíon de Colonias Proletarias, 41
Fertility rates
 in Caribbean, 316
 in Central America, 316
Fertilizer practices, 133–34, 136, 149
 Latin American, 342
FFAP. *See* Agropecuarian Finance
 Fund
Figueres, Jose, 341
Figuls, Jorge, 283–86
Filho, Henrique Bergamin, 223
Fishing industry, Central American,
 and resource exploitation, 82–83
Flooding, and deforestation, 80–81
Fondo Financiero Agropecuario. *See*
 Agropecuarian Finance Fund
Food for Peace, 140, 150
Food production
 in Central America
  growth, 74
  initiatives for, 86
 Colombian, 114
 subsistence, and export crops, 68–70
Food security, 139
Food shortage, in Latin America, 103
Ford, Henry, Brazilian rubber
 plantations, 211–13
Ford Foundation, 117
Fordlândia, 211–13, 220
Forest, loss. *See also* Deforestation
 in Mexico City, 31
Forest colonization
 Central American, 66–67
 by landless and refugees, 76
Forest destruction. *See* Deforestation

ABOUT THE MAKING OF THIS BOOK

The text of *Bordering on Trouble* was set in Times Roman by Compositors, Inc., of Cedar Rapids, Iowa. The book was printed by Edwards Brothers, Inc., of Ann Arbor, Michigan. The typography and binding were designed by Tom Suzuki of Falls Church, Virginia.